P9-DFB-066

Arnulfo L. Oliveira Memorial Library

UTB
TSC

"War Stories"

Related Titles from Potomac Books, Inc.

Legacy of Discord: Voices of the Vietnam Era
—Gil Dorland

Open Doors: Vietnam POWs Thirty Years Later
—Taylor Baldwin Kiland and Jamie Howren

Bernard Fall: Memories of a Soldier-Scholar
—Dorothy Fall

*Getting Away with Torture: Secret Government,
War Crimes, and the Rule of Law*
—Christopher H. Pyle

"War Stories"

False Atrocity Tales, Swift Boaters, and Winter Soldiers—
What Really Happened in Vietnam

GARY KULIK

Potomac Books, Inc.
Washington, D.C.

Library of Congress Cataloging-in-Publication Data

Kulik, Gary.
  "War stories" : false atrocity tales, swift boaters, and winter soldiers—what really happened in Vietnam / Gary Kulik. — 1st ed.
      p. cm.
  Includes bibliographical references and index.
  ISBN 978-1-59797-304-5 (hardcover : alk. paper)
  1. Vietnam War, 1961–1975—Veterans—United States—Anecdotes. 2. Veterans—United States—Biography—Anecdotes. 3. Veterans—United States—Social conditions—Anecdotes. 4. Vietnam War, 1961–1975—Anecdotes. 5. Vietnam War, 1961–1975—Atrocities—Anecdotes. 6. Vietnam War, 1961–1975—Political aspects—United States. I. Title.
  DS559.73.U6K856 2009
  959.704'3—dc22

                                                2009023888

Printed in the United States of America on acid-free paper that meets the American National Standards Institute Z39-48 Standard.

Potomac Books, Inc.
22841 Quicksilver Drive
Dulles, Virginia 20166

First Edition

10 9 8 7 6 5 4 3 2 1

——————————— *To Barbara and Mike* ———————————

Contents

Acknowledgments

I could not have written this book without the loving support and encouragement of Barbara Melosh, my wife. She was the one who first urged me to write about the war in Vietnam. She sustained me as I struggled through the writing and read every word of every draft, even as she faced her new and formidable task, as a newly ordained Lutheran pastor, of writing a weekly sermon rooted in gospel truth and personal authenticity. Those who have never done it have no idea how hard it is.

Zofia Burr offered her insight and encouragement as she read substantial portions of early drafts. Linda Miller invited me to her class at Penn State, Abington, to talk about Phillip Caputo's *A Rumor of War.* She and her husband Randy warmly encouraged me, and Randy invited me to his campus, St. Joseph's University, to critique a film that allowed me to voice my skepticism about just how pervasive and debilitating was PTSD. I would never have met the Millers without George Vogt, then the director of the Hagley Museum & Library, and his extraordinary gift for friendship.

My deep thanks to the staff of Potomac Books, to Hilary Claggett, who believed in this book, to Bud Knecht who edited it, and to John Church, Kate Hallenbeck, and Claire Noble for their supportive and diligent work; and a special thanks to Sam Dorrance who took the financial risk at a time when no one knows the future of book publishing.

My thanks also to David Moltke-Hansen, then president of the Historical Society of Pennsylvania, who appointed me an honorary fellow and invited me to present a portion of my work. John Baky, a fellow Vietnam veteran, and the Director of the Connelly Library, LaSalle University, was unfailingly generous in opening his extraordinary collection, "Imaginative Representations of the Vietnam War," to me.

A number of old friends and colleagues listened to my thoughts on the Vietnam War, and offered encouragement and skeptical questioning. My deep thanks to the late Roy Rosenzweig, to Judith Smith, to the late Sue Benson and to Ed Benson, and to two former Marine officers who became professors—Pat Malone and Peter Rollins.

I deliberately omitted my former wife, Andrea Sarokin, from the narrative of my years in VISTA, Brown University, and Vietnam, as I believe she would have wished. I thank her here for the support she gave me during those years and for her gracious return of my letters to her from Vietnam.

My deep thanks to Michael Nunno, my best friend from college, who accompanied me as I presented my case as a conscientious objector to Draft Board 83, Springfield, Massachusetts.

My thanks to all those who were the recipients of my "cold" calls and e-mails, and who shared with me their memories of having served in the First Marine Division in 1967–1968: John C. Bailey, Gordon Batcheller, Rick Bazaco, Albert Belbusti, Robert Black, Ken Campbell, Scott Camil, Russell Corey, James Ehlers, Michael S. Frazer, Ronald D. Kincade, Robert Labicki, Robert Menard, Fred Nienke, Paul Olimpieri, Edward Stollenwerk, Ronald Toon, and Al Zehner. And a special thanks to Herbert Ing, Eldon Luffman, and Rudy Diener for allowing me to join them for a lunch deeply special to them.

Olaf Skibsrud deserves a deeper thanks, for his witness in Quang Tri in the fall of 1967, and for all that he endured.

My thanks to Anita Coley, U.S. Judge Advocate General's Office, Rebecca Knight, Morris Library, University of Delaware, Susan Dillon and Patricia Mullen, U.S. Marine Corps Archives, and Amy Hooker and Kelly Crager, Vietnam Archive, Texas Tech University, for their research assistance. Thanks also to Sarah Malino, Fred Graboskie, and Jim Banner for their encouragement and assistance.

Steve Streeper assisted me with his memory and the records of his service as a medic in the 67th Evacuation Hospital, Pleiku.

This book would have had a wholly different tenor were it not for the Kulik family of Manchester, New Hampshire. The brothers were Stanley, Adam, and Fred. I loved and honored them all, even as I turned away from the choices they made. I served for twenty-two months as a conscientious objector medic in the Army. Stanley, my father, served four years in the Marine Corps prior to WWII, then volunteered for the Army Air Corps. Assigned as a bombardier during WWII, he remained in the Air Corps Reserve as it became the Air Force Reserve, retiring as a lieutenant colonel. Adam graduated from the Naval Academy in 1946, served in three wars, commanded submarines, and retired from the Navy as a captain. Fred graduated from West Point in 1958, served in Vietnam with the 1st Infantry Division, and retired as a colonel.

Holding the family together was an extraordinary woman, Gen. She grew up in a cold-water flat in Manchester, New Hampshire, with aspirations to become an artist. When her father, Karol, died young in 1939, she gave up a job in a department store that paid poorly but offered the promise of upward mobility to toil in the knitting mills of Manchester to support her mother and her three brothers. Her deeply accomplished paintings and needlework grace our house.

And then there is Teddy Sas, my childhood friend whose memory deeply lingers. If you cut through backyards and one side street, he lived only four houses away, this on the outskirts of Springfield, Massachusetts, in an area known as Sixteen Acres. I can't remember when I met him—sometime in the early 1950s. We didn't visit much. I think I had lunch in his house only once—I don't even remember him in mine.

We were in the same class in fifth and sixth grades. I had no interest then, and certainly no memory now, of which of us got better grades. But I clearly remember our relative athletic skills. What we did was play sports together—baseball, softball at school, football, basketball, and later, hockey.

I recall one rare and honest discussion. We agreed that Teddy was a better baseball player, and that I was better in football and hockey—we must have been eight or nine. I don't remember who brought it up, but I remember it to this day as an extraordinary kind of honesty for pre-adolescent boys—and it was true for the moment.

In my memory, we had one great time together. It was a hockey game in Claremont, New Hampshire. Late in the third period, with the score tied, Teddy gathered the puck at the blue line and fired a hard rising slap shot that hit the goalie in the mask. It stunned him, and the puck dropped at his feet. I was there to chip it into the net. It was a garbage goal. Teddy had done all the work. I still have the hockey stick. It sits above my desk at home—a Northland Pro, Lie Number 6, made by Northland Ski Manufacturing Company, Laconia, New Hampshire.

At fourteen Teddy had grown into his heft. I remained spindly. My football career was over, my hockey career would soon be. We drifted apart—Teddy went to Technical High School, I to Cathedral. Teddy played all three sports, surpassing me in each.

We met up again as teammates briefly on a Parks Department basketball team in the spring of 1963. In New England, basketball was what some of us played between the time the ice melted and the mud hardened on the baseball fields. Neither of us was particularly good at basketball, but Teddy was now the leader, a strong, muscular young man, sending me out and encouraging me to defend the best and tallest player on the other team. We could drive then, and the earthy smells of those spring nights were delicious intimations of adulthood, of leaving Springfield behind.

I went to college in the fall of 1963—I assume Teddy did too, but by then we had drifted far apart. For some years I believed that Teddy had gone to Vietnam while I was still in college. But, I was wrong. My mother sent me the newspaper clipping when I too was in the Army, serving at Walter Reed Medical Center in Washington, D.C., in early 1970.

I remember my deep-voiced first sergeant at Walter Reed that spring, a tall and muscular man, comfortable in his body, who blustered that in Vietnam only the strong survived. I thought then, and continue to believe, that he was a fool.

Lieutenant Theodore S. Sas, a strong young man, a platoon leader in the 9th Infantry Division, died in Kien Hoa, in the Mekong Delta, from an enemy mine, on February 15, 1970. He had turned twenty-four just eight days earlier.

GARY KULIK
WILMINGTON, DELAWARE

Introduction

Where do you think they need medics—on the Jersey Turnpike?
—A clerk at Fort Dix, responding to my comment that
I wasn't going to Vietnam

On June 18, 1969, in Springfield, Massachusetts, I raised my right hand and was inducted into the U.S. Army. I had not come easily to that moment. In late November 1968 I had appeared before Springfield's Draft Board—No. 83. I had taken the bus from Providence, Rhode Island, where I was a first-year graduate student at Brown University. After long and troubled thought, I had typed out my application as a conscientious objector (CO) on October 4, 1968, two days before my twenty-third birthday, and this was to be my hearing.

I have no memory of what I expected the outcome of the hearing to be. In retrospect, however, the outcome was foreordained. My application as a CO professed my willingness to serve in a noncombatant role in the military, that is, as an army medic. I was asking to be placed in the 1-Y-O draft classification, as opposed to the 1-0, those for whom religious conviction precluded any service in the military, so I would "count" in whatever quota Board 83 had to meet. My claim was also religious. I was a Catholic.

My family wore its Catholicism faithfully but lightly. We went to Mass each Sunday and on the holy days of obligation. We ate fish on Friday. But we were not deeply devotional—we observed no first Fridays, no Holy Week vigils, nor did we pray the Rosary. In truth, we did the minimum necessary.

1

There was nothing in what I learned in preparation for First Communion and Confirmation that would explain how I became a Catholic CO.

There was a testy moment in my hearing when a draft board member, I presume Catholic, grew defensive and accused me of judging his service during World War II. I was quite sure I hadn't, and I believe I said so. But in retrospective fairness to him, a Catholic CO might have seemed to him an oxymoron. There was then no tradition of Catholics embracing such an all-encompassing reverence for life.[1]

But the Church was in a state of creative ferment in those years and I found my way, with the help of friends, to Dorothy Day, Thomas Merton, and the Berrigan Brothers. The Church was capacious enough to offer the intellectual and theological resources I needed. I had gone to a Catholic high school, after eight prior years of public school, and then to a Catholic college, St. Michael's, in northern Vermont, where twelve credits of theology and twelve credits of philosophy—neo-Thomist philosophy—were required of all students. I suppose it was that preparation that allowed me to address the critical question I knew members of my draft board would ask. Would I have served in World War II? Deep in my heart, I knew that the answer was yes. But the question was hypothetical and anachronistic. How could I be morally sure of what I would have done in 1941? And so, I came to believe that I could not answer the question with moral certainty, an argument of which any Jesuit, or Edmundite (never affirm, rarely deny, always distinguish) would have been proud.

I drew on resources outside the Church as well. I was self-schooled in the literature of authenticity and nonconformity. In the summer of 1963, between high school and college, I was drawn to popular writers like Vance Packard. *The Status Seekers* confirmed me in my contrarian ways. I also read David Riesman's *The Lonely Crowd,* romanticizing his depiction of the "inner-directed," led only by a stern, internal moral compass, and failing to grasp that there were virtues in being "other-directed." William Whyte's *The Organization Man,* with its sweeping indictment of the stifling conformity of upper-level management, closed off a whole set of careers for me. I dipped into Erich Fromm's pop-Freudianism and read more seriously Walter Kaufmann's anthology, *Existentialism from Dostoevsky to Sartre,* in the tan, orange, and black paperback. Then I found my way to the Lutheran pastor executed by the Nazis, Dietrich Bonhoeffer, and his *Letters and Papers from Prison.* None of this, of course, added up to a coherent whole in my mind, but reinforced my sense of difference from my peers, and placed before me the necessity of faithful, authentic choice and of the risk such choice entailed.[2]

I had brooded over this application for many months, invested in the intense moralism of those years. I had also acted on that moralism. I had spent parts of two summers in Elizabeth City, North Carolina, inspired by the moral grandeur of the civil rights movement, teaching English to promising black high school students under the auspices of St. Michael's. After graduation, I joined Volunteers in Service to America (VISTA)—the domestic Peace Corps—serving as a community organizer in East Nashville, Tennessee.[3]

My fellow VISTAs were from Brandeis, Queens, Penn, Harvard, and Brooklyn College, among other such colleges. Many had read Herbert Marcuse and the Port Huron Statement while I was reading Henry Adams's *Mont-Saint-Michel and Chartres*, Pierre Teilhard de Chardin, Thomas Merton, and the poetry of Daniel Berrigan. I had no highly developed sense of politics in those years, just a bundle of left-liberal and moralistic sensibilities. But it wasn't really about politics, narrowly defined. I was a moralist, then and now.

I had come to be deeply opposed to the American war in Vietnam. I believed it wrong, for all the reasons young and earnest men and women of the left then believed—we were propping up a corrupt government in the face of civil war, conducting the war in a reckless, inhumane way, and so what if the communists won? Ho Chi Minh didn't seem like such a bad sort, and, after all, didn't he invoke our Declaration of Independence when he and his army took control in Hanoi in 1945?[4]

So why did I agree to serve? Why not claim opposition to all military service? I suppose the pragmatic answer was that such a sweeping claim, rooted in my then Catholic faith, would have been unpersuasive to a draft board likely made up of Catholic veterans. Springfield in those years was run by a tough-minded group of Irish-American Democrats. But pragmatic answers are never the whole story. I had grown up in a family closely tied to military service, and I had spent many years, and would spend many more, deeply proud of that, and of them.

My father, Stanley Ignatius Kulik, the child of Polish immigrants, had enlisted in the Marines after graduating from Central High School, Manchester, New Hampshire, in June 1937. He left the Corps—the "Old Breed"—in June 1941 as a corporal. He subsequently volunteered for the U.S. Army Air Corps (USAAC), earned a commission as a lieutenant and emerged a bombardier just as the war was ending. He remained in the reserves as the USAAC became the U.S. Air Force, and was a major at the time of Vietnam—his duty to recruit high school students for the Air Force Academy. As a child with my first camera, I had insisted that he pose for me in his 1940s' army uniform, "the pinks and greens," the last truly stylish army uniform, with his bombardier wings and his campaign ribbons. He retired from the Air Force Reserve as a lieutenant colonel.

He had grown up in a cold-water flat in Manchester, with an older sister and two younger brothers. His father, Karol, the grandfather I never knew, died young while running a small corner grocery. His mother, Anna—Babcia, as I knew her—had only halting English. His sister, Gen, held the family together after her father's death, abandoning ambitions to be an artist and giving up a job in a local department store that paid poorly but offered prospects of something better. She went to work in the knitting mills of Manchester and never earned more than $7,000 a year. But it was enough, and she continued to paint and knit. Her northern New England landscapes and her afghans remain important presences in our house. She died some years ago and was buried alongside her father and mother in a cemetery outside of Manchester.

The two younger brothers, Adam and Fred, supported by their sister, went on to remarkable careers. Adam earned an appointment to the Naval Academy, graduating early in 1946. Fred's appointment was to the U.S. Military Academy at West Point. He graduated in 1958. Our tours in Vietnam would overlap. Adam, a navy captain, who died in 2002, commanded an oiler, the USS *Tolavana,* supplying the gun line off the coast of I Corps. He had previously served as a submarine officer, commanding officer of the *Trigger,* executive officer (XO) of the sub-tender *Hunley.* He would cap his career as the commanding officer of the navy's communications base in Iceland, monitoring the secrets of the Soviets' submarine fleet. Fred, an army major then, served as an air-artillery staffer in the 1st Infantry Division, later moving to a staff position at Military Assistance Command, Vietnam, in Saigon, retiring some years ago as a colonel.

But that isn't the whole story either. Were it not for a prickly and contrarian moral conscience, however formed, I could have chosen easier options. I was in Air Force ROTC for one academic year, 1963–1964, but opted not to stay, a decision then of no great moral moment. I just didn't want to spend four years in the air force. In those years, the draft did not threaten. Up until 1966, graduate students were routinely deferred for the duration of their graduate education, and I had decided by then that I would continue my education, either in law school or in pursuit of a Ph.D. Only later did I decide that I could not serve as an officer in a war I opposed.

Then there was the option of the National Guard. My high school American history teacher, Fr. Peter Laughran, a special mentor, was the chaplain of our local Air National Guard unit. I was still in high school at the time. I mentioned that I had just registered for the draft, and he immediately offered his assistance. I didn't think deeply about it at the time. Several years went by and it became increasingly obvious to me that the true function of the National Guard in those years was to offer a haven for those with connections seeking to avoid service in Vietnam. Recall the photo of former Vice President Daniel Quayle, a National Guard clerk, one hand on his hip, his garrison cap askew, staring out at his photographer as if he were the coolest person in the world. By the end of 1968, the Army National Guard reported a waiting list of 100,000. Two and a half years later, not only had the waiting list vanished, but the Guard was 45,000 men under strength. I have no memory of even considering asking Father Laughran for his assistance. By then, I had come to believe that using influence to rise to the top of a National Guard list was deeply inauthentic, something I could not do. I would get a chance to revisit my moral absolutism on the use of such influence.[5]

Then there was also the physical exam. I was spindly in build. A few days fasting would have put me below the weight limit for my height. But I believed then that such an act was wholly dishonest and inauthentic—a belief later reinforced by a chance viewing of the film version of Thomas Mann's *The Confessions of Felix Krull, Confidence Man*, which contained a scene, repulsive to me, of Krull's fakery during his induction physical. I would subsequently learn how common such fakery would become among my middle-class generational peers.[6]

I wasn't going to Canada, Sweden, or jail, though I admired those who chose jail, so I raised my right hand that June day, though not before penning some words on my induction form indicating that I knew the difference between legal and illegal orders—this was after the My Lai massacre—and indicating I would disobey any illegal orders. I recall the induction sergeant showing what could only have been my induction form to another staffer with the comment: "We'll let the UCMJ [Uniform Code of Military Justice] deal with him." But I had written nothing that challenged the UCMJ. Soldiers have a duty to disobey patently illegal orders, though that was not a principle widely taught at the time.

Off I went that day to Fort Dix, New Jersey, on a bus. A few days later I had my orders to Fort Sam Houston, San Antonio, Texas, where COs received an abbreviated six-week basic training. I joined Echo Company, 4th

Battalion, Class 1-B. My athletic days had long been over, and Basic was physically hard at first, but that passed and I rose to the physical challenge. I actually came to like my drill instructors. They were tough but fair. The loss of privacy and routine freedoms, however, wore on me. So, too, did the specter of Vietnam.

Fear, anxiety, and self-pity overwhelmed me that sweltering summer and broke through my moral resolve. Should I apply for 1-O status? Should I consider deserting, or just quitting, accepting whatever punishment the army had to offer? Should I seek reclassification as a clerk? Could I get a job in Washington as a military historian? Even raising the questions qualified the initial integrity of my first decision—to serve as a medic. I knew that my training as a medic could lead to Vietnam, but I never truly faced the reality. I had waved aside a clerk at Fort Dix who knew I was bound for medical training. "Well, you're going to Vietnam," he said. I said, "I don't think so." His response: "Where do you think they need medics—on the Jersey Turnpike?"

One night I made a panicked call to my parents. We had connections in Congress. I wanted out. I had written to the Chief of Military History requesting an assignment in that office, and I would wait nervously while our political connections worked their special magic. I was painfully aware of the lack of authenticity of my actions, but my fears and anxieties led me to rationalize them away.

In the meantime, a surprise inspection yielded copies of *Ramparts; The Village Voice;* and *The Old Mole,* a Students for a Democratic Society pub-lication, in my footlocker. I was called before the company commander, a short artillery officer, no older than me—a veteran of Vietnam—now overseeing the training of COs, hardly a career-enhancing assignment. I reported in proper form, saluting while at attention. I deliberately chose to call him "captain." He demanded I call him "sir." I did. He told me that my reading matter wasn't on the army's "approved list," and that it was "anti-establishment and anti-military." He had prefaced his comments, I recall, by acknowledging the First Amendment, that is, I could read what I wanted. He threatened me, however, with court-martial should I share my reading matter with others—of course, I already had, but he didn't know that—and then read me the statutes on sedition and mutiny. It was a bootless threat. We both knew there was nothing he could do to me. He chose, however, to "cover his ass" and referred my "case" to military intelligence. I had forgotten that. It took a recent reading of my letters home to confirm it.

And it would take some time before that referral, and its subsequent tale, unspooled. I thought him small and petty. I'm sure he thought me arrogant, but one of his comments stuck with me: "You know, the Viet Cong aren't the Concord Minutemen."

I graduated from Basic and stayed at Fort Sam for medical training, moving across post to newer, air-conditioned barracks as a member of Class 65, Delta Company, 3rd Battalion (Delta "Free" as our speech-challenged platoon sergeant knew us). New freedoms—weekend passes to San Antonio, and its new River Walk—made life far more bearable, and medical training had its integrity. I learned how to clear an airway, apply a splint and a tourniquet, how to use the plastic packaging on a field dressing to treat a sucking chest wound, how to perform a cricothyroidotomy—and why that was safer than a tracheotomy, and why I would need a ballpoint pen for the procedure. I learned how to draw blood and give shots, how to recognize typhus and the symptoms of malaria, and the many conditions in which the administration of morphine was contraindicated. I was well trained on medical procedure.

But then there was our final field training at Camp Bullis in the foothills north of San Antonio. In a three-day exercise I learned how to evacuate wounded soldiers on stretchers from a set-piece battlefield and to carry them to an aid station set up just behind the front lines. I recall being deeply, unthinkingly, "into it," in the same way I had been "into it" as I crawled under barbed wire through the infiltration course at Basic as .50-caliber machine-gun rounds ripped ten feet over my head. It made my training seem real. But it had nothing to do with Vietnam.

In Vietnam there were no set-piece battlefields, no front lines, no stretchers in the field, and no aid stations in walking distance of a fire fight. I had been trained for WWII. Thinking only of myself, I wasn't at all angry about being so trained at the time, though I've since come to believe such training was inexcusable. We were then four years into an intense jungle war. Army medics deserved better.

But, I wasn't going to Vietnam. As my fellow medics received their orders for Vietnam—yes, a few went to Germany—I had mine for the Historical Unit, Office of the Surgeon General, in Washington, D.C. The company XO distributed the orders. "You must know somebody," he said, with more admiration than rancor. My family's contacts had done their work.

The Historical Unit was part of Walter Reed Army Medical Center, then a proud and honorable command. I was a private first-class (E-3) authorized to wear on my epaulets the maroon and silver crest (sanguine and argent in the language of heraldry) of Walter Reed—a caduceus flanked by an open book and a flaming torch, symbols of knowledge, topped by the helmet of Minerva, goddess of wisdom, and bearing the motto *Scientiae Inter Arma Spirtus*, "In the Spirit of Science and Arms." I was also officially a "military historian," with a small stamp proclaiming my name, rank, and title—the only enlisted man in an office headed by a colonel, with majors, captains, long-serving civilians, and a few lowly lieutenants in retinue.

The Historical Unit occupied an office at Forest Glen, Maryland, just north of the District of Columbia, in an ornate Queen Anne building—all turrets and porches—originally built as a hotel in 1887. It later became the National Park Seminary, a finishing school for girls, and a series of sorority houses were added, modeled on Swiss chalets, Japanese pagodas, California missions, and Greek temples. The school was foundering by the late 1930s, and the army bought it as a convalescent center for wounded veterans and made it an annex of Walter Reed in 1942. While I served there, it housed—in addition to the Historical Unit—dental, radiology, and psychiatry offices, as well as a carefully isolated ward filled by psychiatric casualties from Vietnam. I have no memory of ever thinking deeply about those young men. I ran into them in their blue hospital smocks only rarely, and of course they exhibited no outward signs of their maladies, unlike the veterans I saw at Walter Reed proper with their physical wounds—absent limbs, damaged faces—all too visible.[7]

I couldn't have wished for a better assignment. I was treated well, and outwardly I kept my part of the bargain, keeping my uniform pressed, my shoes polished, my bearing military, fully committed to the standards of military courtesy—saluting, "siring," learning to walk with superior officers on the proper side of the sidewalk. I was given an assignment researching the history of aeromedical evacuation, later changed to writing the last two chapters of the history of the Medical Corps in the European Theater of Operations in WWII. The former required a security clearance that I thought I might not get after my encounter in Basic, and I did not want to embarrass my command, so I admitted my doubts about obtaining a security clearance and drew an alternative project. I fully expected to serve out my enlistment in this job, and in the midst of this bizarre architectural landscape.

But I remained opposed to the war. I had published an article, not under my name, in San Antonio's underground GI-Press, *Left Face*, while in medical training. Once in Washington, I volunteered at the Student Mobilization Committee to End the War in Vietnam. I took the bus from Walter Reed to the "Mobe's" offices at 1029 Vermont Ave., NW, and eventually authored two articles—this time in my name—in *Open Sights,* Washington's GI-Press. I foolishly wrote a letter, using my rank and title stamp, to the then-secretary of the navy, Rhode Island's John Chaffee, protesting the treatment of a sailor named Roger Priest, I believe. I have a memory that the letter was returned through my command, but I don't recall anyone admonishing me, though they had every right to. Then I was arrested in a demonstration. I was in civilian clothes, and my hair was not short enough to give me away. While being hauled off to the New York Avenue police station, I hid my military ID in my sock. Interviewed prior to release, I could answer honestly—No, I did not have my draft card. I had surrendered it at induction, but if my police interviewers preferred to believe, as they appeared to, that I had burned it, I wasn't going to argue.

But my Forest Glen idyll was about to end. In March 1970 my name appeared on the May "levy" for assignment to Vietnam. My superiors knew about my security clearance concerns and about my letter to John Chaffee, and I presume someone at Walter Reed knew about the articles I had written.

The arrest, I'm sure, remained a secret. Despite what they knew, or might have known, they came to my defense. I never saw the memo written in support of my retention at Walter Reed until after I made a request for my military records in 2002, but I knew in 1970 that the memo had gone forward. It was well and persuasively written under the signature of the Historical Unit's XO, writing for the Director. Moreover, it was endorsed at the highest levels of Walter Reed, a fact I did not know in 1970.[8]

The Surgeon General's Office denied the request. I don't have a copy of the command response, but I recall it being brief. The continuing need for medics in Vietnam overrode Walter Reed's request. Newly promoted to Specialist Four (E-4), I was to report in early June to Fort Lewis, Washington, for transshipment to Vietnam.

At the time, and for many years after, I suspected that my orders to Vietnam were punitive. I also believed that my "indiscretions" reflected my guilt for using influence to avoid Vietnam. The latter is likely right, but the former has become harder to maintain given what I now know. Walter Reed officials had to know more about my activity than the personnel bureaucrats in the Surgeon General's Office.

I can't now recall if I ever thought seriously of calling my political "protector," or my parents. In any case I never did. I accepted my orders, whatever their origins—that acceptance a form of redemption for acting basely on my fears and anxieties the previous summer.

I arrived in Vietnam June 6, 1970, at Cam Ranh Bay after a twenty-hour flight from McCord AFB in Washington, stopping in Anchorage and at Yokota AFB, Japan. I was soon assigned to the 4th Infantry Division, then located at Camp Radcliff, near An Khe in Dien Bien Province in the Central Highlands. When I was queuing for my orders, a kindly and elderly sergeant—he must have been all of thirty-five—said to me in words I roughly remember: "Watch out son, they're shooting themselves up there." I don't recall my response. But he was right. During my first "red-alert" in An Khe on June 25, I learned that a guard had killed a fellow soldier whom he could not identify.

The 4th Division had a long and distinguished history. It had held the right flank at the Marne in the Great War, earning the sobriquet "Right of the Marne." In WWII the 4th was the most bloodied division in Europe, suffering a casualty rate of 252 percent over the ten months between D-Day and victory. I knew none of this at the time. The 4th's reputation in Vietnam, however, was not good, as that honest sergeant knew. The 4th had not distinguished itself in the Cambodian invasion in the spring of 1970, and a sapper attack a few months later breached the perimeter at Camp Radcliff, resulting in serious casualties in a maintenance company.[9]

But the 4th Division was not without honor, though again I knew nothing about it at the time. Thomas W. Bennett, a medic in Bravo Company, 1st Battalion, 14th Infantry, 4th Infantry Division (ID) was awarded the Congressional Medal of Honor, posthumously, for his repeated efforts over three days to tend to wounded soldiers while under attack from a well-entrenched and numerically superior North Vietnamese Army (NVA) unit in the Chu Pa region of Pleiku Province. On the third day, February 11, 1969, Bennett was killed as he braved enemy fire to retrieve a wounded soldier who had fallen in advance of his company's position. Bennett was a CO, one of only two COs to be awarded the Medal of Honor in Vietnam, and now, with the draft's demise, likely one of the last. There is a building named for him on the campus of West Virginia University.[10]

After four days of training, I was assigned to Headquarters and A Company (Head and A), 4th Medical Battalion, Clearing Platoon. We operated a full-service aid station, with lab techs for blood and x-ray work, an optometry unit; a small ward, largely for malaria patients; and a pysch unit— "mental hygiene" in the army's oblique terminology. We provided medics for day-and-a-half perimeter patrols—as a "newbie," I was so assigned—and we managed through the occasional rocket attacks, always thinking of the risk of sappers. I went out on "med-caps"—sick call for Vietnamese villagers. There was a field hospital near by, for serious cases, but we performed minor surgery and suturing. I learned how to do both.

A few weeks after my arrival, on July 13, two military intelligence officers appeared in the company asking questions about me. What did I read? How much mail did I get? Where did it come from? Did I belong to any organizations? Was I loyal to the government? My platoon sergeant and section chief, with nothing else to go on, thought I was being considered for some "secret" assignment. My peers, however, thought I was a Criminal Investigation Command (CID) plant, intent on exposing them for their marijuana use. But, of course, that wasn't it at all.

I met with three officers subsequently. One was a graduate of Queens College and of Yale Law School—a "fellow Ivy Leaguer," he noted. He also said he was on my side. It may well have been true. He would tell me only that they had been given my name and had to investigate. I recall speaking freely, answering their questions. I felt I had nothing to hide. They said they'd be back with a written report. I told them I would not sign it. They never returned. At the time it fed my suspicions of punitive orders to Vietnam, but more than likely the army had finally followed up on my visit to Military Intelligence in San Antonio, the summer before. I became a minor celebrity in the company, but the visit had no effect on how I was treated.

By the end of my time in the 4th, I had been promoted to Specialist Five (E-5)—a sergeant's pay grade, given charge of the aid station, and awarded the Army Commendation Medal for "meritorious service." I had treated one wounded soldier—answering the call "medic." The 4th was on its way home—to Fort Carson, Colorado—five months after I arrived. Years later I learned that GEN Creighton Abrams, our commander, wanted whole units to go home together, but he was overruled in Washington by GEN William Westmoreland—those of us whose tours were just beginning would stay and be reassigned. I am grateful now for Westmoreland's decision. I would have hated garrison duty at Fort Carson. I loved being a medic in a war zone, though I never would have admitted it then.[11]

My new unit was Headquarters and Headquarters Detachment, 61st Medical Battalion (dustoff), in Qui Nhon, some 40 miles east of An Khe on the coast. The 61st had responsibility for all non-divisional medical evacuation in I Corps and the northern half of II Corps. It had command of an air ambulance company (the 498th), six air ambulance detachments, two ground ambulance detachments, and a bus ambulance detachment. Prior to February 1970, it had been a full-service medical company operating at Cam

Ranh Bay. It had been formed in 1942 at Camp Breckinridge, Kentucky, as the 61st Medical Battalion, Motorized, and supported the invasion of France.[12]

It had a unit crest and a motto that still brings tears to my eyes. The crest displayed a maroon unicorn rampant on a green hill, flanked by two oak trees whose trunks have been entwined by two snakes facing each other. Maroon and white are the colors of the Army Medical Corps, the unicorn's horn was a symbol of healing, the entwined snakes evoked the Staff of Aesculapius, the Greeks' god of medicine, and the green represented the grass of Kentucky, where the 61st was first formed. The motto, *Inest Clementia Forti*, was arranged in black letters in a half circle below the imagery. *Inest Clementia Forti*—Mercy is Inherent in the Brave. It is the noblest of mottos—so different from the sanguinary or quotidian mottos of other army units—but one that is utterly false. The army is full of brave and merciless men. But subsequently I would learn that at least one of our number would fully live up to the motto.

I originally thought I would be sent to one of the 61st detachments with the opportunity of joining a flight crew. It wasn't to be. The battalion at that time was run by an insufferable lieutenant colonel who made life miserable for the junior staff officers. He required typed drafts of all correspondence, pristine and perfect notes for his talking points, and a previous clerk had been assigned to flawlessly type a six-carbon, multipage report on the unit's history while under his command. But the clerk had not succeeded. Without knowing any of this at the time, I answered truthfully to the question could I type. I had a year of graduate school and I'm sure I scored highly on the army's battery of tests—that was the reason that once assigned to a battalion, I would remain with the headquarters company. A medic with less education and lower test scores ran a greater risk—such was the unfairness of life. I was to become the clerk to the battalion adjutant.

I protested, carrying my case to the executive officer, an irenic major. I was a medic, I recall saying, it can't be right to assign me to do a clerk's job, though there was substantial bravado in that claim. After all, I had relinquished any right to my Military Occupational Specialty (MOS) while I happily accepted the privilege of serving as a historian at Forest Glen.

But I wanted out. I wanted to fly. The major was the soul of reasonableness. He would try to help, he said. And eventually, he kept his word, but only after his boss, the insufferable lieutenant colonel, rotated home. I finished all of his reports flawlessly, after numerous tries. Then I began the army's battery of flight physical tests. All went well until the vision test at An Son. I didn't pass, and I couldn't persuade anyone to give me a waiver. My vision, correctable to 20/20, was perfectly adequate for having my ass shot off in the infantry, but not as a member of an aircrew. I served out my time in Qui Nhon.

I was treated well, and I did my job. The adjutant always referred to me by my rank—"Specialist Kulik." I'm sure I garnered respect for volunteering to fly. I traveled into Qui Nhon as often as I could, volunteering to teach English at the Baptist English Language Center at 204 Vo Tanh Street. I had four or five students whose names I did not preserve. One was an especially intelligent Army of the Republic of Vietnam (ARVN) captain. I've often wondered what happened to him and to them.

It was in Qui Nhon when the army's investigation of me finally unwound. I did not save the document, but its message was that I was not eligible for a security clearance or for reenlistment, but I was to be retained in the army—this after I'd already served three quarters of my tour. I did not take it well. I did not like the idea of a public record questioning my loyalty. In the end, however, I opted not to challenge it. My letter home at the time stated that the document was contradictory—a regulation had been cited incorrectly, this deduced simply from the document itself. Moreover, it was my understanding that COs were already barred from reenlistment and had no four-year reserve obligation, unlike other draftees. Army intelligence would prove to be less than thorough. No record of the investigation survives in my permanent file. I reveal it here for the first time. And when I mustered out on May Day 1971, my discharge paper, DD-214, made clear I was to be assigned to an Army Reserve Training Unit and that I was fully eligible for reenlistment. The investigation of my loyalty was an absurd waste of the army's time, initiated by a young and petty artillery officer, whose name I have long since forgotten.

There was much else happening, only some of which I knew about at the time. The 61st was called to support Operation Lam Son 719, the invasion of Laos by South Vietnamese infantry that began February 5. The 61st received no advance notice of the operation, thus there was no medical planning. During the first three weeks, aircrews complained of the absence of gunship support, of incorrect coordinates, of false reports of secure landing zones (LZs), and of intense anti-aircraft fire. Healthy soldiers, seeking only to escape the fighting, swarmed the medevacs.

On February 18, one of our crews flew to evacuate wounded from the 39th Ranger Battalion, ARVN, nine kilometers inside Laos. They encountered NVA fire as soon as they appeared in the airspace. After landing, and as the crew was loading the wounded, healthy Rangers, trying to escape, rushed the ship, making it harder to lift off. A mortar round shattered the cockpit, wounding the pilot. A second round wounded a medic and the crew chief, Specialist 4 Dennis M. Fujii. They found safety in a bunker. There were two efforts to evacuate them—the first was driven off by enemy fire. The second succeeded in evacuating all but Fujii—mortar fire had pinned him in his bunker. A third attempt, this to get Fujii alone, also failed. Fujii asked that no more attempts be made that night. He would stay the night, the only American on an ARVN LZ, surrounded by two NVA regiments, tending the wounded and calling in American air support, neither of which he had been trained to do. Twice that night NVA troops breached the perimeter, forcing Fujii to become a rifleman. Eagle Dust-Off of the 101st Airborne finally mounted a large rescue mission the next afternoon. Fujii requested that 150 wounded Rangers be evacuated before he was. The mission commander, a lieutenant colonel, ordered him to board the first ship that landed. He did, bringing fourteen wounded Rangers with him. Fujii had helped to save the lives of 122 Rangers while calling in and coordinating more than twenty air strikes. He finally had his own wounds—shrapnel to the back and left shoulder—treated at the 85th Evac in Phu Bai, and was awarded the Silver Star. The army later upgraded the award to the Distinguished Service Cross, the army's second highest award for valor. *Inest Clementia Forti.* I never met Fujii, but I am proud to have served with him. By the operation's end, six crewmembers were dead, nine had been wounded, eight helicopters were lost.[13]

My war was soon to be over. I left Qui Nhon in late April for Cam Ranh Bay. I had enrolled in a summer French course at NYU, in preparation for my doctoral language requirements, and qualified for an early-out. I flew from Vietnam on April 29 to McCord AFB and processed out of the army from Fort Lewis three days later.

I returned home, picked up the pieces of my graduate education, and thought little about Vietnam. Over time, however, my interest returned. I read an occasional novel, James Webb's *Fields of Fire,* John Del Vecchio's *The 13th Valley,* saw the obligatory films, *The Deer Hunter* (1978), *Coming Home* (1978), *Apocalypse Now* (1979), *Platoon* (1986), *Full Metal Jacket* (1987)— all of which grossly caricatured the war and the Americans who fought it; and dipped into the reportage more randomly than selectively; Michael Herr, C. D. B. Bryan, Neil Sheehan, among the better known; S. L. A. Marshall, Richard Gabriel, and Paul Savage's analysis of army leadership, as well as a defense of the war by Guenter Lewy and the turgid work of Robert Jay Lifton. Some books I read simply because their authors were nearby: the late Lewis "Chesty" Puller taught with my wife, Barbara Melosh, at George Mason University; John Wheeler occupied an office in the National Museum of American History, where I worked.[14]

All of this reading came to have a distinctly academic purpose—after all, that was my training. I began to imagine a book as a Vietnam memoir. At the time, there were several such books or chapters written by English professors, only one of which struck me as having any gravitas—Samuel Hynes's *The Soldiers' Tale*. Hynes was himself a WWII veteran, and the author of a memoir of war, *Flights of Passage: Recollections of a World War II Aviator*.[15]

Hynes offered a brief and brilliant dissection of Michael Herr's *Dispatches*, a book whose "war story" was what the American reading public wanted in 1977, a war entirely different from any previous one, "emptied," in Hynes's words, "of meaning, values, coherence, reasons." Hynes was especially good at capturing the contrasts between Vietnam memoir and memoir from previous wars: the honest reporting of vulgar language and sexual encounters, the "double betrayal" some writers felt—not just a betrayal by the politicians and generals, as in World War I, but "by the war protestors of their own generation," the "guilt" that seeped into some memoir, and the therapeutic character of the homecoming epilogue—or the "Psychiatrists' Tale," as he wryly put it.[16]

And yet Hynes was still too much the English professor, attentive to stories known to be "mythic," but it wasn't his job to dig deeper, to try to find the hard, small fact. The most popular of the memoirs were of course the early disillusioned ones—Kovic and Caputo and O'Brien and Mason— feeding "the anti-war myth of national dishonor," in Hynes's words, as well as those memoirs that offered the "after-myth" of veterans numb, broken and suicidal, when they weren't dangerously violent. To his credit, Hynes poked below the latter myth to quote a study indicating that 71 percent of Vietnam veterans were glad they served, and 66 percent would serve again. Too frequently, Hynes would question a story—"Did Ketwig really see that melted little boy?" only to claim it really didn't matter, or to baldly report the story of a "tunnel rat" who claimed to have killed a "classroom full of kids." "Dead children are everywhere in Vietnam narratives," Hynes tells us, "they become a convention, like Homeric metaphors . . . dead children are what Vietnam *meant* to the men who tell its story." Perhaps, but it's the small hard fact beneath the story that drives me. Ketwig is one of the least reliable of

Vietnam memoirists, and Hynes's "tunnel rat" was a mentally ill fraud who never served in Vietnam.[17]

Not wanting simply to write a book about men in battle, I began with the nurses. My wife had written her first book on the history of American nurses, and I had been in the same business in Vietnam. There were several memoirs and collections of oral histories. Army nurses working in field and evacuation hospitals were the vast majority. Their work was similar, but their experience of it was strikingly different, despite the efforts of editors and reviewers to suggest a common sensibility, always one of disillusionment and painful homecomings. Indeed, what was most striking was the tone deafness of some editors and reviewers whose desired antiwar "narrative" ignored the contrary nursing voices they had themselves collected or reviewed. So, one Internet reviewer could stunningly claim that "all of the women," in Ron Steinman's *Women in Vietnam: The Oral History* "suffer severely from delayed stress reactions of PTSD . . . and each paid a terrible price for her sacrifices." Each "kept silent for many years until something triggered the overwhelming grief and anger," when even a casual reading refuted such blindness. An air force flight nurse: "if I had it to do over again . . . I would"; an army nurse who served at the 85th Evac recalled her tour as "the best year of my life. I felt like I was needed, that I was doing something useful, that what I was doing I knew how to do"; and another, a "donut dolly": "With all the horror of Vietnam . . . I would still go. . . . It changed me forever and I gained strength from that time I would never have had, if I had not gone." Hynes's "after-myth"—better yet the "homecoming myth"—trumped the evidence before a reviewer's own eyes.[18]

One book stood out: Lynda Van Devanter's *Home Before Morning*. It was by far the most popular, the most widely read, the most frequently assigned. It had informed the war stories of other nurses, though by no means most. Its popularity rested on its conversion narrative, and by the growing sense that the principal victims of the war, as one reviewer put it, were those Americans who fought it. It had even managed to make a high school reading list in the company of Jane Austen, Alexander Solzhenitsyn, and Elie Wiesel. It had been reviewed in glowing and stunningly credulous ways.[19]

The book was a clumsy rewrite of those WWI antiwar narratives of innocence lost and betrayed, given a special Vietnam twist—innocence lost, betrayed, healed by therapy. It was also a deeply unreliable book, a pastiche of stories that flitted between exaggeration and implausibility, its humor, even some of its stories, informed by the widespread cultural influence of

MASH. But like *Dispatches*, it told a war story that American readers and their teachers wanted to hear. It also contained the longest, ugliest "I was spit upon" story in the entire literature of Vietnam memoir and oral history.

The "I was spit upon" stories became a key part of the "homecoming myth" of Vietnam. They served as a powerful metaphor for the ways in which Vietnam veterans felt themselves ignored, dishonored, made to feel like naïve fools. I recall telling my CO story during a graduate student lunch after returning from Vietnam to Brown. An especially smarmy American history graduate student, who later made his fortune in the law, seemed dismissive. There were lots of ways to "avoid" service, he said, suggesting that I hadn't been imaginative enough. I later learned that he had pulled a "Felix Krull" at his medical exam. I decided then that I would be more discriminating in telling my story in future. That was my only "I was spit upon" story, but it rankled enough to leave a memory.

Such stories were not "false" in any probative sense—maybe, somewhere a returning veteran had been literally spit upon—but they were stories that had emerged only well after the "spitting" itself, inspired in part by Rambo's rant in *First Blood* (1982); they were formulaic, the ur-spitter was a solitary female hippie in an airport, and witnesses were rare—though as I write this I know I'm offering license to some veteran with a new story—yes, I wasn't spit upon, but my buddy was. So be it.[20] The "I was spit on" stories were linked to the ugliest of insults—"baby-killer"—and were thus fed by veterans' perceptions of how some of their fellow countrymen viewed them. And those perceptions weren't wrong.

After the massacre at My Lai became widely known, after *Life*'s publication of the gruesome photographs, 52 percent of Americans believed that such massacres were common, that is, a majority of Americans believed that their fellow Americans routinely gathered up women and children and killed them. Only 24 percent thought that such massacres were isolated, and 81 percent believed that similar war crimes were being hidden. Such beliefs persist today. In the spring of 2001, when former senator Robert Kerrey was accused of the deliberate murder of women and children, one columnist refused to be shocked—"that's how we fought the war." Susan Faludi's *Stiffed: The Betrayal of the American Man* (1999) employed My Lai as the lens through which to portray "the dangerous prescriptions of manhood" into which Vietnam veterans had been "drafted." She appears never to have doubted that the massacre of as many as 500 women and children at My Lai was typical of the way we fought the war.[21]

It remains impossible to write about Vietnam without addressing the prevalence of war crimes. A war crime was at the center of the most widely read and extravagantly praised memoir of the war, Philip Caputo's *A Rumor of War*. Caputo, a Marine lieutenant, had knowingly given an ambiguous order to his men, an order that led to the deaths of two Vietnamese villagers. By any measure of officer accountability, Caputo was responsible for those deaths. Marine command thought so as well, recommending courts-martial for Caputo and his men. The moral crux of the book turned on Caputo's dismissal of moral responsibility—"this was what the war had done to us," he wrote, "they had taught us to kill . . . and now they were going to court-martial us for killing." No, the charge was murder. Reviewers in all the leading newspapers lavished praise on Caputo, wholly accepting his moral reckoning. The massacre at My Lai, of course, loomed in the background as a defining moment. Critics and supporters of the war had found a rare common ground in their respective refusals to hold individuals accountable— supporters of the war, because civilian death was inevitable—it was the nature of war. Critics, because civilian death in Vietnam was also inevitable—it was the peculiar nature of that war alone or as Robert Jay Lifton put it, the war in Vietnam was uniquely "atrocity producing." "A People's War," as the far left understood Vietnam, meant that the oppressor must kill the "people."[22]

In 1971 a hundred or so Vietnam veterans gathered in Detroit for the Winter Soldier Investigation (WSI), an inquiry into American war crimes. The WSI was sponsored by Vietnam Veterans Against the War (VVAW) and funded, in part, by Jane Fonda. There they would testify to war crimes that they committed, or witnessed, or sometimes just heard about. The testimony was searing, as some Americans admitted to grotesque war crimes. A documentary, *Winter Soldier*, soon followed. The veterans' testimony was inserted in the *Congressional Record* and Beacon Press would also publish portions. But it would take more than thirty years for *Winter Soldier*'s impact to be truly felt. John Kerry's opponents in the presidential election of 2004 would use snippets of the film. Kerry had attended the WSI and uncritically reported its conclusions in his testimony before Congress—the speech that made him a rising political star. In the midst of an unjustified war in Iraq the 2004 campaign would come to turn upon thirty-year-old "war stories," as former "Winter Soldiers" would confront the "Swift Boat" veterans. Kerry's own war record would rise to center stage, but "war crimes" remained the gory backdrop. That same snippet, two former Marines talking of a "ville wiped out in Quang Tri," would lead me to a year-long search for the truth about that ville.[23]

When *Winter Soldier* was re-released in the aftermath of the 2004 election, it was met by resounding and largely unqualified praise in the major media outlets. For some, *Winter Soldier* helped to explain Abu Ghraib. Some commentators have made the connection between the command "environment" in both Vietnam and Iraq as a principal cause of war crime. It is not an argument readily dismissed. There can be little doubt that the Bush White House's dismissal of the Geneva Conventions as "quaint" validated the torture and abuse of prisoners. Nor can there be any doubt that Westmoreland's strategy of waging a battalion-level war in the countryside of Vietnam, heavily reliant on firepower and demanding the displacement of Vietnamese villagers, produced far more civilian deaths than were justified. But American armies have never needed White House "permission" to torture or kill prisoners, nor did Westmoreland's strategy lead directly to American soldiers and Marines shooting unresisting women and children. The serious problem of war crime deserves serious answers.

As I read more deeply those memoirs, oral histories, and testimonies offering up to the American public stories of hideous atrocities said to be performed or witnessed by the authors, I grew more skeptical about such war stories. As I read the uses that scholars and others have made of such stories, I grew incredulous. And as I read reviews of such works, I grew outraged. I began collecting "war crime stories," intent on revealing the utter improbability of some, hoping to find evidence to contradict others.

In doing so, I had come to believe that Vietnam was the first war in which men had lied about committing war crimes that they had not committed, utterly reversing the usual lie—no, I didn't do it. They told such lies—misremembering is not a word that stands up to the moral gravity of such falsehood—for reasons many and various. We'll explore them. False war crime stories lie at the moral heart of this book.

But this book is not a defense, *tout court*, of American behavior in Vietnam. Soldiers and Marines committed war crimes, officers covered them up. We still do not know the full extent of American war crimes. So, why a book centered on the exposé of false war crime stories? If we cannot discriminate between what is true and what is false, then it's all noise. Of course, the pundits say—that's how we fought the war. In the concluding chapters of this book, I will tell the story of the murder of a single nameless Vietnamese woman. That story is the underlying truth countering a false tale of 300 villagers killed, of children rounded up separately and later killed. If we believe all of the false tales, then we lose our ability to mourn for that particular woman, as well as our sense of outrage over her death.

So where do I stand on the Vietnam War now? Unlike writers such as Mark Moyar, Lewis Sorley, and the late Harry Summers, I have no brief that we could have won the war, if only we had adopted different tactics, or different strategies. Granted, the way we fought the war was doomed to fail. Committing ground troops to a war of attrition in the countryside while failing to stem the continued influx of troops and supplies from the North led where it must. Those of us who served in Vietnam were betrayed by politicians who had no clear strategy either for victory or stalemate, betrayed by generals who sought to refight WWII, on the ground and in the air, and who failed to demand clear strategies from those same politicians.

For some years, I thought the North had deserved to win, even as it became increasingly impossible to believe what many of us on the left believed at the time—that the Viet Cong (VC) and the Vietnam National Liberation Front (NLF) were independent forces, that the communism of the North Vietnamese was substantially leavened by nationalism, that the North Vietnamese would prove to be gracious and humane winners, that there would be no widespread retaliation, and that communist regimes would gradually soften and reform over time.

None of this was true, with one exception. Some measure of economic reform was possible, though only because it was necessary. Command economies did not work. I recall an argument on the left from many years ago. Fascism could not be reformed. It had to be overthrown. But communism could reform itself from within. Such was the hope. It was a half-truth at best. The collapse of Western communism after 1989 bore the unmistakable marks of revolt from below, not reform from above. So now, the pathetic remnants of the Soviet ideal in Vietnam, China, Cuba, North Korea, and Laos remind us of the repressive costs of ideology. Yes, there has been a freeing of markets, but not of conscience. In the spring of 2007, after a five-minute trial, the Socialist Republic of Vietnam imprisoned Fr. Ly Van Nguyen for eight years for "carrying out propaganda against the Socialist Republic." It was the fourth time in the last twenty years he had been jailed as a prisoner of conscience. As Fr. Ly attempted to recite his own poetry in response to his sentence, a court policeman muzzled his mouth.[24]

I wish that we had been able to save South Vietnam, though I cannot retrospectively imagine how we could have. So here I stand, on the narrowest of moral ledges, condemning the way we fought the war, but wishing that the South Vietnamese had prevailed; claiming that I and others were betrayed by politicians and generals, but proud of my reluctant, conscience-driven service, outraged by war crimes like the one at My Lai, but intent on exposing false war crime stories. So be it.

What follows examines the damage done by "war stories" that are facile, exaggerated, and sometimes just false. Chapter 1 offers an overview of the "framing" of the Vietnam War as "meaningless," guilt producing, and atrocity driven. Chapter 2 offers a skeptical reading of the most widely read nurse's memoir, a work that reinforced strongly held beliefs about the pervasiveness of PTSD and contained the longest, and ugliest, "I was spit upon" story in the literature. Chapter 3 examines those stories and concludes that they are remarkably formulaic, largely were not witnessed, and are difficult to believe. Chapter 4 moves on to the attacks of the Swift Boat Veterans for Truth (SBVT) on John Kerry's military record and on the identities of those anti-war veterans who testified at the WSI, concluding that both attacks were dishonest and dishonorable. Chapter 5 examines the testimony of the Winter Soldier veterans with a skeptical eye. They were not "frauds," as the Swift Boaters painted them, but their testimony in many instances was deeply unreliable. Chapter 6 is an essay on individual moral accountability in a time of war and offers a critical reading of the war's most widely read memoir, Philip Caputo's *A Rumor of War*. Chapter 7 makes the case that "false atrocity" stories, credulously believed, were among the most disturbing and unusual legacies of the war. Chapter 8 takes up one of the worst of those false stories and disproves it while revealing what actually happened on a Marine patrol in Quang Tri in 1967.

one

Framing the War

The least we owe the dead is the obligation to be honest.
—Charles A. Krohn

In the spring of 2001, Gregory Vistica, in an article in the *New York Times Magazine*, led his readers to believe that former senator Robert Kerrey was guilty of the deliberate killing of at least fourteen unarmed women and children while serving as a navy SEAL in the Mekong Delta on February 24–25, 1969. Kerrey, then a navy lieutenant, had led his SEAL team on a night mission to capture a Viet Cong (VC) official in the village of Thanh Phong. The mission went badly. By the time it was over more than twenty villagers were dead, and no VC official had been captured.[1]

What happened that night was ugly—an elderly man, his wife, and three of their grandchildren were knifed to death by Kerrey's SEALs. Kerrey recalled years later that they were "sentries," and their hootch an "enemy outpost." They had to be killed if the mission was to continue. It did continue, as the SEALs made their way to the main village. What happened then remains in dispute. Kerrey's memory is that his team was fired upon, and fourteen villagers—women and children—died in the crossfire. One member of the team, Gerhard Klann, claimed, also years later, that the second killings were ordered and deliberate. The mission had been compromised. The villagers had assembled in front of their hootches. They were effectively prisoners. But, according to Klann, their presence put the SEALs' exit at risk. There were too many to tie up, and it would take too long.[2]

23

All the other SEALs—five—came to support Kerrey's account. And, in 1969, so too had the navy. LT Roy Hoffman, who, as a retired admiral, would lead the Swift Boat attack in 2004 questioning the legitimacy of the medals of presidential candidate John Kerry—medals that he had authorized—awarded Robert Kerrey, the leader of a thoroughly botched mission, the Bronze Star for Valor, the citation justifying the award was egregiously inaccurate.[3]

The question of whether Kerrey and his men committed a war crime hung in the air. As ugly and brutal as the killings at the first hootch were, they were preceded by a commander's retrospective belief that he had encountered "sentries." Kerrey recalled that he had been trained to "kill the people we make contact with or we have to abort the mission." No military or naval court would construe the killings as murder. If Klann told the truth, however, the killings in the village were murder. U.S. policy on land warfare makes clear that a "commander," even in a "commando" operation, "may not put his prisoners to death because their presence retards his movement or diminishes his power of resistance."[4]

One commentator, Nat Hentoff, said he believed Klann because "he was voluntarily incriminating himself as a participant in an atrocity that may well have been a war crime." There is a principle in the law that gives greater weight to the testimony of someone incriminating himself. But Hentoff gave no evidence that he was aware that the war in Vietnam produced a strange and troubling legacy. As we shall see, some men returned to lie, not about war crimes they committed, but about war crimes they never committed, and that never happened.[5]

The response to the story was mostly predictable. So much so, that the responses stand as a pure case of "confirmation bias"—the tendency to interpret new information in a way that merely confirms one's preconceptions. On the left, Alexander Cockburn expressed surprise that anyone was shocked— this was "how we fought the war." America's leaders were intent on terror. He was "pretty sure" this was a part of the notorious Phoenix program— CIA led assassination teams—"as was My Lai," the latter a baseless claim. Antiwar liberals, such as Robert Mann, were quick to shift the blame upward, a response common in the time of Vietnam. "More than a quarter-century after the war ended, it seems more apparent than ever that our political leaders were culpable in the senseless deaths of Americans and Vietnamese— perhaps more so that Mr. Kerrey and the hundreds of thousands who took up arms." Others, including some veterans, remained skeptical of Kerrey's story.

Vistica's account seemed to make better sense of the facts, and Klann had no obvious motive to lie. Kerrey's supporters came from across the political spectrum. They accepted his account, though at times with the seemingly contradictory admonition that terrible things happen in war. Tobias Wolff, the author of a memoir of Vietnam service, argued that both Klann and Kerrey were in a sense right. They both believed their own memories, one "shaped by a sense of innate decency," the other by "self condemnation." But is it really plausible that Kerrey, or any of us, would forget whether we killed innocents accidentally or deliberately?[6]

The editorial writers of the *New York Times* more than matched Wolff's unconvincing venture into memory's fog. Expressing "compassion" for Kerrey and for Klann, the *Times* asserted that the war in Vietnam left Americans "with a greater burden of guilt and remorse than any other conflict in American history," a plausible and comforting claim for those who opposed the war, but one unsupported by the vast majority of Vietnam veterans. The *Times* offered its own effort at closure. The Kerrey story "with its conflicting evidence, undeniable carnage, and tragic aftermath—sums up the American experience in Vietnam and the madness of a war that then, as now, seemed to lack any rationale except the wrecking of as many lives as possible on both sides," the "sums up," a harsh synecdoche making one terrible part of the war stand for the whole. More disturbing is the stunning assertion that the war seemed to have no rationale. For James Bowman, this was nothing less than "a statement of astonishing historical ignorance." American soldiers went to Vietnam, however wrongly, however mistakenly, to stop the takeover of South Vietnam by communists. That was a clear, unambiguous rationale. The failure to remember that is not only a measure of how deeply divided we remain but an impediment to any historical understanding.[7]

The *Times* had deftly summarized the meaning that the war in Vietnam had for many. First, it "seemed to lack any rationale"—a meaningless war. Second, it left Americans guilty and remorseful. Third, it was defined by "carnage" and "tragedy," and summed up by a purported but unproven war crime. These three assertions have had a long history, and as the *Times*' invocation of them suggested, a continuing resonance.

To focus on the way the war in Vietnam was initially "framed" reverses the thrust of most academic writing on the war in recent years, writing that has chosen to emphasize the ways in which, as Robert Buzzanco has put it, the war "was politically and intellectually rebuilt" in the years since 1980, when Ronald Reagan called it a "noble cause." There is a measure of accuracy to this, though often purchased at the cost of "naturalizing" the antiwar perspective of the majority of scholars as a "truth" now distorted by right-wing memory makers—politicians, film-makers, and the media. In fairness, some of this work is thoughtful and intellectually sophisticated. But what has been lost is an understanding of how the war was initially framed as senseless, guilt inducing, and atrocity producing by its very nature. Recovering that history is intended as a challenge to all those readers who have their own "confirmation biases" about the war in Vietnam.[8]

"War on a Cracker Jack Box"

The idea that the war had no meaning owes something to the nature of the war itself. No front lines, no ground taken and held, no strategy for victory, and no victory. "There it is!"—a phrase frequently invoked by American soldiers who served in Vietnam as ironic resignation, what else could we expect? No doubt the televised snippets on the evening news, rarely communicating anything other than episodic violence and body counts, contributed to the growing sense of the senselessness of the war.

But this was far from a majority position. There was a powerful minority sensibility, held by most of the articulate left, that the war was not merely senseless, but morally wrong. Americans had no business intervening in an internal war. And within the left was another minority, those caught up in the hope that the future lay in popular, indigenous opposition to American imperialism. Those who were honest about such beliefs were the ones waving VC flags in demonstrations. But all the era's polls suggested that the majority of Americans supported the war, that is, supported the effort to keep South Vietnam from a communist takeover—until Tet, 1968, and President Lyndon B. Johnson's response to it. According to one scholar, it was Johnson's withdrawal from the 1968 election, and his reversal of course on the war, that swelled the ranks of those favoring withdrawal from Vietnam. We now know that one result of Tet was a decisive military defeat for the VC. After Tet, the VC no longer had the ability to put battalions in the field and thus wage an effective war. I was the beneficiary of that, assigned as I was to Binh Dinh Province, once the center of VC strength. But Tet also, of course, put the lie to American optimism and moved many former supporters of the war into the growing camp of skeptics, though this was a skepticism less concerned with the morality or even the goals of American intervention than with their efficacy. And then into this heady mix of argument and sentiment came Michael Herr.[9]

Herr's *Dispatches* was published in 1978, though portions of it had appeared as early as 1968, to extravagant, embarrassing, over-the-top praise. Ward Just located Herr in a line stretching back to Stephen Crane, George Orwell, and Ernest Hemingway. John Leonard compared Herr to Dante: "It is as if Dante had gone to hell with a cassette recording of Jimi Hendrix and a pocketful of pills: our first rock and roll war." John le Carré went even further calling it the "the best book I have ever read on men and war in our time."[10]

Dispatches is now part of the new canon of American literature, anthologized in the *Heath Anthology of American Literature*, and has been the subject of much scholarly writing. A more modest appraisal, however, would be that Herr had plucked a minor chord, first played in full by Joseph Heller in *Catch-22* (1961), a book of comic brilliance and absurdist sensibility whose ostensible subject was WWII, but whose popularity derived largely from the connections readers drew to Vietnam. The 1970 movie of the same title reinforced those connections, as did the movie *MASH*.[11]

Herr did more than any other writer to frame the war as senseless, a war with a sound track, fought by stoned soldiers, and led by officers whose principal gift was self-deception. Herr's Vietnam was a surreal nightmare, meaningless but for its effects, themes that Herr would elaborate on as a screenwriter for the acclaimed *Apocalypse Now* and the popular *Full Metal Jacket*, the most surrealistic and least realistic of Vietnam war films. Herr's framing was so powerful that to question it now will seem to some like questioning a received truth. But, as we've seen, there was nothing inherent in the war that would inevitably lead to the idea of its senselessness as a defining characteristic.

Dispatches, however, successfully captured a moment. It was an artfully contrived book, deliberately constructed, beneath a veneer of the let-it-all-hang-out machismo of the "new journalism." The title, however, was deceptive, as Herr would later acknowledge in a 1990 interview with the *Los Angeles Times*. The book was not a series of dispatches from the war. He wrote only one portion while he was there, the rest was patched together from his notes and his memory and it took eight to nine years to write.[12]

Nor was it truly reportage. The lively exchanges between "Day Tripper," a black Marine at Khe Sanh, and "Mayhew," a naïve white Marine, were "totally fictional." Herr admitted: "A lot of *Dispatches* is fictional." Apparently only the French got it right, publishing it as a novel. "I have told people over the years," Herr said, "that there are fictional aspects to *Dispatches*, and they look betrayed. They look heartbroken, as if it isn't true anymore. I never thought of *Dispatches* as journalism." Herr went on: "A lot of the lines I put in the mouths of composite characters. Sometimes I tell a story as if I was present when I wasn't. . . . A lot of the journalistic stuff I got wrong." Herr was not alone in employing composites or blurring the distinction between a story heard and a story witnessed, but the vast majority of Vietnam memoir writers said so in a preface or introduction. Herr never did.[13]

Herr has been notably reclusive. He refused to do interviews after the book came out. Nor would he appear on television. He turned down an opportunity to do a network special, *Michael Herr's Vietnam*, in 1985. Whether principled or not, his reclusiveness meant that few readers or scholars would know of the fictional character of the book. But it's unlikely it would have mattered.[14]

After all, Tim O'Brien, the most writerly of the war's novelists, would memorably capture the writer's justification for blurring truth and fiction. Do soldiers fall on grenades to save their buddies? O'Brien asked. "You'd feel cheated if it never happened. Without the grounding reality, it's just a trite bit of puffery, pure Hollywood, untrue in the way all such stories are untrue. Yet even if it did happen—and maybe it did, anything's possible—even then you know it can't be true, because a true war story does not depend upon that kind of truth. Absolute occurrence is irrelevant. A thing may happen and be a total lie; another thing may not happen and be truer than the truth."[15]

Beneath O'Brien's cleverness, and Herr's, is this—a soldier falling on a grenade to save his buddies— a moral story of self-sacrifice ("greater love hath no man") was once the frame in which such a story would have been told, and post-Vietnam, will continue to be told. But O'Brien chose not to tell it that way; it no longer fit his frame or that of many of his readers. And so we heard no stories in the 1970s of wartime heroism or of self-sacrifice. Highly literate Americans rewarded those who told us the war was absurd, or worse, and know nothing of those who served with heroism and honor.[16]

Dispatches is full of stories told, rumor, second-hand reporting, the war seen through the briefing room, honest reporters confronting dishonest officers, the stoned revelry of soldiers and reporters, and always Herr's intrusive subjectivity stitching together a story of futility and insanity, the war as "psychotic vaudeville." Samuel Hynes, one of the few scholars to take a skeptical view of Herr, wrote of the "ironic incoherence" of *Dispatches*. A veteran of WWII and an English professor at Princeton, Hynes identified three themes holding the book together: the experience of the war was like being stoned, like being crazy, and like a movie. These were of course all '60s clichés—"crazy" was borrowed from Heller, but "stoned" and "like a movie" underlines Herr's influence. As Hynes first noted, very few Vietnam memoirs have much to say about drugs. Drug use increased among soldiers only well after Herr's departure. Herr framed the popular notion of stoned soldiers, just as he certainly framed and reinforced the idea of the war as a surreal movie.[17]

Hynes's "ironic incoherence" gets it exactly right. None of it made sense to Herr. The VC tactic of "Find and Kill," he said was the American equivalent of "Search and Destroy": "Either way it was us looking for him looking for us looking for him, war on a Cracker Jack box, repeated to diminishing returns." "War on a Cracker Jack box?" *Dispatches* is full of such efforts at cleverness that do not yield their meaning even after several readings. You learned about fear, he wrote, "it was hard to know what you learned about courage. How many times did someone have to run in front of a machine gun before it became an act of cowardice?" Maybe what he meant was that there was a fine line between courage and foolishness, a fact many soldiers recognized. But that's not what he said. It's as if adopting an incoherent style was the only appropriate way to tell the story of a war he believed to be incoherent.[18]

In re-reading *Dispatches* after many years, what is surprising is how little it conveys of the actual war. It is a pastiche of sardonic vignettes, capturing the timeless cynicism of front-line soldiers. If you edit out the '60s language, the sexual frankness, the vulgar exclamatories, capturing the way soldiers actually talk (recall Norman Mailer's, or his editor's, invention of the word "fug" in *The Naked and the Dead*), you could be hearing a report from any American foxhole or bunker for the last 100 years.[19]

Front-line soldiers have long gone about their work with a cynical fatalism, an abiding distrust of senior officers and of all those who did not share their risks, or worse, put their lives at risk, and a humor so dark that it cannot help but offend the sensitive. What was different about Vietnam was simply how all this was expressed and reported, and Herr had a great ear and captured that language brilliantly.

"There it is!" and "don't mean nothin," were the signature phrases of the war for those who served. "What does it all mean?" written across the cover of an intelligence report. And then the bravado: "Yea, though I walk through the valley of the shadow of death, I shall fear no evil, for I'm the meanest mother-fucker in the valley," a vulgar use of Psalm 23 that quickly became a cliché scrawled across countless flak jackets. A black soldier claimed

he was called the "Entertainer," because, he said, "I rock and I roll" as he
flipped the selector switch from semi to full on his M-16. "I've gotta get out
of this place," and "There's something happening here," played over and
over.[20]

And the dark humor. The C-47s rigged with Vulcan guns capable of
300 rounds a second—one in every square inch of a football field in less
than a minute—were a fearsome and welcome weapon at night as its tracers
illuminated the sky and killed anything within range. Soldiers, with a richly
inventive irony, called it "Puff: the Magic Dragon." The Marines, according
to Herr, called it "Spooky," yelling, "get some" as it did its work. "Spooky
understands," a Marine said after the firing stopped. A joke went: "What
you do is you load all the Friendlies onto ships and take them out into the
South China Sea. Then you bomb the country flat. Then you sink the ships."
Another: "How can you kill women and children?" Answer: "You don't lead
them as much."[21]

"What's the difference between the Marine Corps and the Boy Scouts?"
Answer: "The Boy Scouts have adult leadership." Herr seemed to get this
one. He acknowledged that it was only a joke that could be told by Marines
to Marines, softening its meaning, suggesting the dark humor of a fragile but
often real esprit de corps. But it would be hard to find an officer in *Dispatches*
presented positively. Briefing officers were founts of "mindless optimism."
"Excellent," "real fine," "outstanding," "first-rate": talk like that poured over
you until it was all you could do to keep from seizing one gray-haired crew-
cut head or another and jamming it deep into the nearest tactical map." Staff
officers on the roof of the Rex Bachelor Officers' Quarters (BOQ) in Saigon
were "nailed to the bar . . . shiny irradiant faces, talking war . . . drinking like
they were going to the front." Officers in the field wanted to search out a
little action merely for the journalist's sake, or who only reluctantly agreed to
medevac a heat casualty.[22]

Hostility between officers and men is a staple of all wars, but it is a half-
truth at best. Soldiers and Marines understood what it took to be a good
officer and readily recognized it. Officers willing to share the risk, to lead,
to tell the truth, and not to put men at risk recklessly are nowhere to be
found in *Dispatches*. The hostility between front-line troops, "grunts" and
"REMFs"—rear echelon mother-fuckers—is again a staple of all wars, though
the language of grunts and REMFs was an invention of the war in Vietnam.
Herr's belated acknowledgment that much of *Dispatches* was made up calls
into question one of the darkest moments of his book. Ground troops could

be hard and harsh, for example, toward those flying air support. Helicopter pilots flying combat assaults often didn't want to land, preferring to hover a few feet or more off the ground so they could exit more quickly, expecting heavily burdened soldiers to jump several feet. Not all medevac pilots were heroes—not all would risk landing in a hot landing zone (LZ). So when Herr reports he heard a story, that out of anger, frustration, and contempt, Marines at Khe Sanh cheered the death of a door gunner, a fellow Marine, can we believe it? It's another of Herr's stories told, but not witnessed.[23]

William Broyles Jr., a Marine lieutenant and the author of a memoir of the war that deserves to be better known, got the essence of the story right. It was far more humorous than macabre. One night on a hill outside of Danang, Broyles received a message that the North Vietnamese Army (NVA) were rocketing Danang and an order to move out to intercept the rocket team. He took it seriously. When his radioman woke and learned what was happening, the radioman responded: "All fucking right!" And when the radioman yelled out the news to the sleeping platoon, Broyles heard an unexpected response—"All around the perimeter my fellow marines, the descendants of the heroes of Guadalcanal and Iwo Jima, were shouting with joy. 'Get those REMFs!' was the gist of what they said." Broyles' platoon recognized that the "enemy" was "everyone who wasn't out there with us." And this was little different from the WWII GIs' wish that the bullets be distributed as the pay.[24]

And then a story that Herr said it took him a year to understand, but which deftly summarizes *Dispatches*. A soldier tells him, "Patrol went up the mountain. One man came back. He died before he could tell us what happened." "I waited for the rest," Herr writes, "but it seemed not to be that kind of story; when I asked him what had happened he just looked like he felt sorry for me, fucked if he'd waste his time telling stories to anyone dumb as I was." O'Brien offered his own gloss on Herr's story, in remarkably similar terms. A six-man listening post goes out for a week and hears the noise of a cocktail party and glee clubs and opera and "weird chanting" and finally loses it and calls in a massive air/artillery strike. When they return, a colonel wants to know what they heard. They just look at him—"and the whole war is right there in that stare . . . [t]hen they salute the fucker and walk away, because certain stories you don't ever tell." The story makes no military sense. Here is Broyles again reflecting on Herr's story: "It is a great story, a combat haiku, all negative space and darkness humming with portent. It seems rich, unique to Vietnam. But listen, now, to this: 'We all went up to Gettysburg, the summer of '63: and some of us came back from there: and that's all, except the details.'"[25]

Then there was the war as movie. "I keep thinking about all the kids who got wiped out by seventeen years of war movies before coming to Vietnam," Herr wrote, "and getting wiped out for good." It was a powerful conceit. One academic would later write that images of John Wayne in the heads of young soldiers would lead them to their deaths. "You don't know what a media freak is until you've seen the way a few of those grunts would run around during a fight when they knew there was a television crew nearby; they were actually making war movies in their heads," Herr wrote. No doubt. But the presence of journalists was like Heisenberg's metaphorical thermometer in water—it changed what was measured or seen. Herr again: " The first few times that I was fired at or saw combat deaths, nothing really happened. . . . It was the same familiar violence, only moved over to another medium; some kind of jungle play with giant helicopters and fantastic special effects, actors lying out there in body bags waiting for the scene to end."[26]

There is no question that men and women went to Vietnam with movies of the last wars in their heads. But it defies common sense and the experience of too many soldiers to suggest that it would take more then a nanosecond to realize how quickly the movie ended and reality imposed its hideous presence. I heard John Wayne invoked several times while I served in the army, always, however, as a warning and an admonition, as in "Don't pull a John Wayne, this ain't a fuckin' movie."[27]

Herr will remain an important writer for all those who believed the war was senseless, that it was fought by crazed and drugged young men, and barely competent officers. The book will retain its power because like all clichés there is an element of truth lurking somewhere beneath it. Most soldiers and most journalists after all have only one war to attempt to understand, and far too many have gone to war with stories and images of glory in their heads. War, as Paul Fussell has suggested, is the ultimate irony. But distinctions matter.[28]

The direct experience of war is an experience of utter senselessness and likely has always been. Herr got that right. We make sense of war only after the fact, but even then, there are articulate soldiers who resist the easy and simplistic moral closure associated for example with phrases like the "good war," and the "greatest generation." Paul Fussell writes of WWII: "it was a savage, insensate affair, barely conceivable . . . and hardly approachable without some . . . theory of human mass insanity and inbuilt, inherited corruption." But his was a contrarian voice, and after all, we won.[29]

We could not make sense of Vietnam in the same way, and so the great public memorial to the war in Washington, with its stark and funereal list of the dead, conveys only one meaning—loss. But loss is not the same thing as senselessness. There is an inscription on the nearby Korean War Memorial that says this: "Our nation honors our sons and daughters who answered a call to defend a country they never knew and a people they never met." The same could be said for those who served in Vietnam. Contrary to the *Times'* cant about senselessness and guilt, the vast majority of veterans, perhaps even knowing that they were betrayed by politicians and generals, were proud to have served, would serve again, and have exorcised whatever demons of senselessness and guilt that highly literate Americans had framed for them.

The "Guilt" of Soldiers

In 1996 Kim Phuc came to a Veterans Day ceremony at the Vietnam Veterans Memorial in Washington, D.C. She was the nine-year-old who had been an innocent victim of a napalm attack in 1972 at Trang Bang, her picture captured by Nick Ut, a Vietnamese photographer, as she ran naked toward him, her mouth open in a silent scream. It would become an iconic photograph, summing up for many the war's evil.[30]

Kim Phuc had come a long way to Washington that day. She was in critical condition for more than a month, and lived with acute pain for years. But she graduated from high school in 1981, and sought a career as a doctor. She was, however, rediscovered by Western journalists and by the Vietnamese communist government. She was told she was "an important victim of the war," and against her wishes assigned to a propaganda office as a secretary. A trip to Moscow would follow. Tiring of the attention she received, she desired only to finish her education, and was allowed to enroll in the University of Havana in 1986. Before then, she had left the Cao Dai faith to become a Christian, and in 1992, newly married and disillusioned with life under communism, she defected to Canada.[31]

Jan Scruggs, a veteran and antiwar activist, introduced Kim Phuc that fall day, telling the assembled that Phuc was burned and that two brothers of hers were killed as the result of an American ordered air strike on a pagoda. The only truth in that statement was that Phuc had been badly burned. In her brief comments she said, ironically: "Even if I could talk face to face with the pilot who dropped the bombs I would tell him that we cannot change history but we should try to do good things for the present and for the future to promote peace." A man in the audience wrote a brief note—"I am THAT man"—and passed the note up to her. They embraced, the man sobbing as Phuc said: "I forgive you."[32]

The man was John Plummer, a former helicopter pilot who had a troubled return from Vietnam. He was twice divorced and had been a heavy drinker—the incident at Trang Bang "ruined my life," he said—but he recovered, married again, and had recently been ordained as a Methodist minister. Newspapers and television picked up the story. The event appeared spontaneous, and perhaps some part of it was. But Plummer had previously communicated his guilt to a poet, who happened to know Nick Ut, who knew the Canadian filmmakers who were filming what would become "Kim's Story: The Road from Vietnam." Phuc was aware that an American soldier had confessed his guilt.[33]

Plummer appeared on ABC's *Nightline*, in a documentary on A&E, and, according to his own account, made more than 30 public appearances over the next year. His story of forgiveness became a centerpiece of his ministry in Purcellville, Virginia, and he looked forward to writing a book on forgiveness. Contrary to his written note, however, he had quickly admitted that he was not the pilot but the officer who ordered the attack. In an article he wrote for *Guideposts*, a religious magazine, he claimed that the air attack was one "I had called."[34]

But this wasn't true either. At the time, he was a low-level staff officer in Bien Hoa with no authority, according to his former commander, then-COL Niles J. Fulwyler, to order planes in the air—never mind South Vietnamese planes. The pilot that day was a South Vietnamese officer responding to a call for air support from South Vietnamese troops under attack by both the VC and the NVA and that was how the story was first reported in 1972.[35]

In December 1997 Tom Bowman, an investigative reporter for the *Baltimore Sun*, broke the story of Plummer's deceptions: "Veteran's admission to napalm victim a lie." Plummer admitted to Bowman that he had not ordered the attack but continued to insist that he was involved in some way and felt deeply responsible. He seemed to dismiss his use of the word "ordered" as a mere matter of "semantics," and said that his *Guideposts* article contained words he had not written. "I think I could have been misinterpreted," he told Bowman, "but I did not intentionally misrepresent my role." Asked why he wrote "I am that man," he responded: "Maybe I attached myself to the events that day. Maybe I was saying that even though I wasn't the pilot that dropped the bombs, I am responsible for the bombs being there." According to Bowman, Plummer said he only wanted to apologize to Phuc and was "not interested in publicizing it." Asked why he had in fact done so, he said he came to realize "the power of that story" as a result of the Internet and a Virginia ministers' meeting. He believed his story changed lives and promoted forgiveness.[36]

But more recent research casts doubt on Plummer's entire story. According to the late Ronald Timberlake, a helicopter pilot incensed by what he believed was Plummer's phony claim of guilt, Plummer's command, the Third Regional Assistance Command, had, according to its declassified logs, no involvement in the tragedy at Trang Bang. There were no American advisers on the ground, as Plummer once claimed. The entire operation came under the command and control of the 25th Army of the Republic of Vietnam (ARVN) Division. There was no American involvement. In the wake of Bowman's expose, Plummer's story appeared only to be falsely embellished, but it now appears to have been wholly manufactured. Plummer's initial confession, his troubled post-war life, and his embrace of guilt made for a dramatic and compelling story, one that was credulously believed for over a year, so accustomed had many Americans become to the idea that guilt gnawed at the souls of Vietnam veterans.[37]

The idea that those who served carried a special burden of guilt was first advanced by a group of antiwar psychiatrists, notably Robert Jay Lifton and the late Chaim F. Shatan. Lifton, a prominent psychiatrist and writer, a student of Erik Erikson, a professor at Yale, the winner of the National Book Award for *Death in Life: Survivors of Hiroshima* (1968), was deeply opposed to the war in Vietnam. In December 1970, at the behest of Jan Barry, then the head of a little-known organization, Vietnam Veterans Against the War (VVAW), Lifton began conducting weekly "rap" sessions with antiwar veterans. He asked Shatan to join them. Shatan was a Freudian psychotherapist, educated at McGill University, a faculty member at New York University, and also a deeply committed antiwar activist.[38]

The "rap" sessions, an unorthodox form of therapy in which therapists yielded some of their authority to the group, lasted for several years and formed the basis for an extraordinarily influential piece of writing. In May 1972 Shatan published an op-ed piece in the *New York Times* under the title "Post-Vietnam Syndrome." It opened with the heart-rending story of Dwight Johnson, a young African American from Detroit, awarded the Congressional Medal of Honor, the nation's highest award for military valor, for his heroism at Dak To while a member of the 4th Infantry Division, and who returned home to die on the floor of a Detroit grocery store he was attempting to rob with a pistol in his hand. A reporter from the *New York Times* framed the story around the Veterans Administration (VA) failure to treat successfully a deeply troubled veteran who had been diagnosed with "depression caused by post-Vietnam adjustment problems." The psychiatrist's report indicated that Johnson suffered from "survivor guilt," a concept that Lifton had done much to make visible. Why had he survived and not others? Survivor guilt is certainly real, but the link between it and armed robbery is by no means clear.[39]

It was, Shatan said, a galvanizing moment for him as he threw himself into his work with Vietnam veterans. As a result of his rap group involvement, he identified six themes shared by the veterans with whom he had worked. First, was guilt for those who had been killed and maimed. Some vets sought "atonement." Joining the antiwar movement was high on the list of effective strategies for atonement. Others engaged in destructive self-punishment leading to "high proportions of one-car accidents"—suicides in other words. It was a comment that would help to feed the idea that Vietnam veterans were killing themselves at alarming rates. Second, veterans had a feeling of being scapegoated, "deceived, abused, and betrayed." Third, they felt rage. Fourth, they were the victims of "combat brutalization," a "dehumanization" so profound that it had "no clear-cut boundaries, leading to a generalized hatred for "Orientals," and eventually for "civilians." Fifth, they were alienated and experienced a "systematic numbing" of human responses. Sixth, they had "agonizing doubt" about their ability to love. Closing with an invocation to Freud's belief that grief was the path to letting go "of a messy part of life," he asserted that post–Vietnam syndrome prevented the work of grief, that the grief of veterans he knew was "unconsummated . . . impacted." Shatan never mentioned that the veterans he had known were members of VVAW, a tiny minority of Vietnam veterans.[40]

Shatan's op-ed piece drew, by one account, an "overwhelming response." More than 1,200 rap groups contacted him, a number that seems implausibly high, as well as "student health and financial aid offices on many campuses, and even veterans in prison." Shatan spoke and published widely within his professional community. He reinforced the growing sense that there was something truly terrible and soul-destroying about combat service in Vietnam and that veterans were coming back badly damaged.[41]

Lifton expanded on all this in his *Home from the War* (1973), his report on his meetings with members of VVAW. He described them as "survivors who cannot justify what they have seen and done—and are caught in a vicious circle of death and guilt." Though he acknowledged in his "Prologue" that his subjects were unrepresentative, that did not keep him from sweeping generalizations. "The resulting death guilt," he wrote, "at whatever level of consciousness, is the fundamental psychological legacy of this particular war."[42]

But it would appear that he had already come to these conclusions almost two years before he began meeting with the VVAW vets. In the spring of 1969, the *Washington Post* quoted Lifton's view that the unpopularity of the war would make it difficult for returning veterans to justify their participation in the war with a "minimum of inner guilt," and that this "may intensify the violence in his [*sic*] collective behavior. It creates a jingoistic attitude . . . a hatred of all Vietnamese . . . an unstable equilibrium that could express itself in any direction [including] against any minority group."[43]

Lifton elaborated on these themes in testimony before a Senate sub-committee in January 1970, as reported in the *Washington Post*. The war in Vietnam, he said, was "producing a very large pool of young, embittered veterans" who would, he predicted, have more severe mental problems than the veterans of other wars. The "inability to find significance or meaning in their extreme experience leaves many Vietnam veterans," he said, "with a terrible burden of survivor guilt." He went on: "Vietnam veterans I have talked to were not really surprised by the recent disclosures of atrocities committed by American troops at My Lai and elsewhere. . . . Virtually all of them had . . . witnessed or heard of similar incidents, if on a somewhat smaller scale." The result of all this led to "a psychic numbing—the loss of the capacity to feel—and of general brutalization." Lifton went on to predict that veterans would display psychiatric problems, according to the *Post*, "ranging from withdrawal to depression to severe disabling psychosis"—and that these disturbances "could lie dormant for as much [*sic*] as ten years." "We sent the GI as an intruder in a revolution taking place in a small Asian society," Lifton said, "and he returns as a tainted intruder in our own society."[44]

Without benefit of sustained research, Lifton had framed a view of Vietnam veterans that would be widely believed and find its most "persuasive" expression in films such as *Taxi Driver, Coming Home,* and *Apocalypse Now,* as well as many others. Veterans were returning home as psychological cripples, guilt ridden, having witnessed or heard about the routine murder of unarmed women and children, which was what happened at My Lai. They would have far more mental trouble than the veterans of other wars, and there was no telling how they might act this out, perhaps even directing violence against other minorities. They were for Lifton wholly other: "tainted intruders in *our own* society" (emphasis added).

Lifton and Shatan were not alone in the efforts to bring recognition to the travail of Vietnam veterans. In fairness, several veterans of the war played leading roles. Charles Figley was a Marine veteran of Vietnam who returned home, completed a doctorate at Penn State in human development and family studies, and as a young professor at Purdue began building a series of case studies of Vietnam veterans that eventually yielded his edited volume, *Stress Disorders Among Vietnam Veterans* (1978). Jack Smith was also a Marine veteran, a member of VVAW, and an early participant in Lifton's rap sessions who became the director of the National Veterans Resource Project and helped to initiate the "Vietnam Generation Study." William Mahedy had been a Catholic chaplain in Vietnam and joined the staff of the Brentwood VA in 1973 as a social worker. He would later write *Out of the Night: The Spiritual Journey of Vietnam Vets* (1986), a book that argued, on the basis of his experience alone, that young soldiers lost their belief in God in Vietnam.[45]

And then there was Shad Meshad. Floyd Meshad was of Lebanese descent and grew up in the South. He earned a Masters in Social Work and served as a Medical Service Corps officer in Vietnam, assigned to the army's "Mental Hygiene" units. After the war, he went to work for the Brentwood VA Hospital. He embraced "rap" group therapy and brought emotional energy, a flair for publicity, and true zealotry to the cause. "I was a madman, a maverick. Had long hair, a beard, wore a field jacket. But they referred vets from all over the country to me," he claimed. He championed a method of intensive therapy called "walking through Vietnam." The prominent nurse-writer, Lynda Van Devanter, described the experience. Van Devanter had Meshad's full attention every day for a week. "We spent the bulk of every day talking intensively about my year in 'Nam," she wrote, "and about what I had gone through when I came home." The idea that you had to work through your trauma with a therapist or with a rap group, recall it, identify it, confront it, became the key to overcoming it for many therapists. All else was simply repression.[46]

Meshad, while in Vietnam, refused a direct order to trim his mustache, and demanded a general court-martial, rather than accept nonjudicial punishment. The army, in its own wisdom, simply reassigned him. He claimed to have been wounded—the helicopter he had been in was shot down, the pilot and co-pilot killed. His account of his wounding was unique in its use of metaphor. "I split my head. I was scalped. I could feel my whole face slipping. Like an old basset hound, my face just kinda fell down. I tied a bandanna around it to hold it up." Meshad's military record, according to B. G. Burkett, does not include the award of a Purple Heart, awarded to all those wounded as a result of enemy fire.[47]

There was one other key figure. This was the late Sarah Haley. She had just received her Masters in Social Work and began work at the Boston VA Hospital in September 1969. She would tell an interviewer that on her first day on the job she met an agitated and troubled veteran just back from Vietnam who claimed to have witnessed the killing of women and children at a place called My Lai. His account was confused and his memory muddled. But he recalled that he refused to fire his weapon and that his fellow soldiers had threatened him. They would kill him if he told, even if they had to search him down in the United States. Haley said she had not yet heard of My Lai. The story had only started to break that month. Later that day she found out that her patient had been diagnosed as a paranoid schizophrenic, and that her new colleagues thought he was "delusional." But Haley believed him. Her father, a WWII veteran, had told her stories of American war crimes as he drank to forget them. She also believed that the reason her patient could not remember clearly was that he repressed that memory. Her arguments failed to persuade her colleagues, though she did succeed in convincing them to allow her to offer weekly counseling to the young man. She would later introduce his case to Lifton who would write about him in *Home From the War*.[48]

Haley had found a mission, and over the next few years she would expand her caseload of veterans and reach out to more, participating in rap groups at the VVAW office in Cambridge. The litany of atrocity stories continued, and would lead to the writing of "When the Patient Reports Atrocities" in the *Archives of General Psychiatry* in 1974, a "widely read . . . landmark paper," according to one practitioner, for what would become the growing field of trauma study.[49]

Haley wrote that she had treated 130 Vietnam vets, forty of whom had confessed responsibility for "atrocious acts." To her credit, she argued that these numbers could not be used to quantify atrocities in Vietnam. Her patients were not representative of all those who served. In her abstract, she made clear her thoughts that Vietnam was a different kind of war and that previous methods of treating troubled veterans too quickly assumed that persistent guilt or depression was "neurotic," that men who could not get over the trauma of war must have deeper symptoms. For Haley, a child of the '60s, the key was empathy. The therapist should not judge, but should rather imagine that he or she could be capable of the same thing—there but for the grace of God. Forming a "therapeutic alliance" with the patient "is" the therapy, Haley argued. It followed that the therapist "should not deny the reality of the patient's perceptions." She closed with the following: "Combat veterans may play down or embellish their 'war stories,' but initially their reports should be taken at face value." The only reports that should not be accepted at face value were the "patient's report that combat in Vietnam had no effect on him."[50]

One of her patients was a Marine named "John." "John" told her that he went to Vietnam believing that his enemy was not truly human, and for some time acted on that premise. But then he got to know a group of "high-ranking VC" prisoners. He interacted with them for a week and came to understand the common humanity he shared with them. When he claimed his commanding officer, a Marine officer, ordered him to kill the prisoners—that is to murder them—he refused, though, according to his "war story" other Marines did not. It is a story that defies plausibility. "High-ranking VC" had great intelligence value, and even greater value if they chose to defect, as many VC did. If they had been held for a week, they were almost certainly being held by intelligence officers who fully understood their value, not by hair-trigger infantrymen in battle seeking pay back for the death of buddies. Marines in Vietnam were court-martialed for the abuse and murder of prisoners under circumstances far less egregious than those recounted by "John." Protecting her patient's confidence, Haley never identified when, where, or with what unit he served, so there can be no independent confirmation of "John's" reported war crime.[51]

Haley was, no doubt, a kind and helpful therapist, and I believe that many of the veterans she counseled were better for it. But her methods, and the methods of Lifton and Shatan, never considered the possibility that veterans with atrocity stories to tell were not telling the truth, or that their self-reports of later trauma might not be wholly accurate. Haley, Shatan, and Lifton offered no evidence that they attempted to validate the stories of their patients. For Haley, it was all empathy. And she went one step further, so convinced was she of the trauma of combat service in Vietnam. The only people we should disbelieve, she argued, were those combat veterans who claimed to be normal. It was a stunningly circular argument flying in the face of reason and of empirical evidence. Combat veterans of Vietnam who claimed to be unaffected were in denial.[52]

Shatan, Lifton, Figley, Meshad, Haley, and others would lead the fight to make Post Traumatic Stress Disorder (PTSD) a disorder recognized by the American Psychiatric Association's *Diagnostic and Statistical Manual (DSM)*. They would succeed by 1978, though *DSM-III* would not be published until 1980. To enter a new disorder into the *DSM* was far more than an academic exercise. It not only provided a form of scientific validation, it was the necessary step to justify treatment and reimbursement for the VA as well as for insurance companies. The best student of the process, Wilbur J. Scott, a sociologist and an infantry platoon leader in Vietnam, argued that the advocates for PTSD succeeded for reasons that were as much political as scientific. "PTSD is in *DSM-III*," he wrote, "because a core of psychiatrists and Vietnam veterans worked consciously and deliberately for years to put it there." This did not mean for Scott that PTSD was "merely a social construction," but it was recognition that PTSD's proponents were well connected professionally, "better organized, more politically active," and ultimately able to prevail over skeptics who believed the evidence was lacking.[53]

PTSD was a diagnosis that filled a vacuum left by the absence of any explicit reference to war-related neuroses in the *DSM-II*, published in 1968. It became the newest designation for what had been known as "soldier's heart," in the Civil War, "shell shock," during World War I, and "combat fatigue" in World War II. PTSD wholly reversed the logic that had previously structured cases of combat stress. Army psychiatrists in World War II advanced two conflicting, but not contradictory, explanations. Some men were more susceptible, given their histories, but all men had their breaking point. But now war alone was the stressor and trauma was its pervasive, delayed, and long-term byproduct. As Scott put it, PTSD's advocates were now arguing that it was "normal to be traumatized by the abnormal events of war," leading inescapably to the reverse, that not to be traumatized was abnormal, or as Haley and others would have it, to be in denial.[54]

PTSD's symptoms, according to Richard J. McNally, a leading scholar, were "recurrent intrusive recollections" manifested through dreams and "flashbacks," psychic numbing leading to "feelings of estrangement" and "loss of interest in formerly enjoyable activities," and a cluster of other symptoms, among them, "hypervigilance for threat," "sleep disturbance," and "memory and concentration impairment" . . . and "excessive autonomic arousal." In a more emotional register, Shatan asserted that the disorder "confronts us with the unconsummated grief of soldiers . . . in which [a] . . . never-ending past deprives the present of meaning."[55]

But these are symptoms, as other scholars have recognized, that do not necessarily have a clear connection to each other. PTSD was not something that was discovered, as a medical disease might be discovered. It was "invented," as Allan Young would write, "glued together by the practices, technologies, and narratives with which it is diagnosed, studied, treated and represented and by the various interests, institutions, and moral arguments that mobilized those efforts and resources." None of this is meant to suggest that PTSD isn't "real" or is merely a social construction, but that its "reality," as Scott and Young argue, came to be affirmed through the antiwar activism of a small but well connected group of psychiatrists, through its ability to help explain the antisocial behavior of some Vietnam vets paraded through the media, and through the growing narratives of troubled vets offered by writers, psychiatrists, and vets themselves. And if any are now to doubt the objective reality of PTSD, they must confront the legions of believers who have extended the range of PTSD's explanatory power to explain an ever growing number of cases of traumatic memory. There is now talk of something called "secondary PTSD."[56]

The belief that Vietnam veterans suffered from a form of PTSD that was latent, chronic, and severe was undergirded by the related belief that the war in Vietnam was much worse than previous wars in the effects it had on those who fought it. According to Lifton, the absence of a "clear enemy," or of sharply defined battle lines, the emphasis on "body count" as the only measure of success, made the war, in his well-known phrase, an "atrocity producing situation." Lifton, in earlier testimony, offered, like the *Times,* his own ugly synecdoche. The well-known atrocity at My Lai, Lifton wrote, "illuminates, as nothing else has, the essential nature of America's war in Vietnam." The massacre of innocents was, thus, the "essential" truth of the war.[57]

The belief that the war in Vietnam was somehow worse than previous American wars in its effects on its veterans became a widely held belief, but a moment's reflection on the carnage of previous wars should have at least prompted skepticism. In the eleven months between D-Day and Germany's surrender, eighteen American infantry divisions out of forty-six suffered a casualty rate of 100 percent or higher. Five divisions, the 1st, the 3rd, the

4th, the 9th, and the 29th, suffered a casualty rate of more than 200 percent. The 4th Division had the distinction of being the most bloodied, with a casualty rate of 252 percent. The Marines' victories in the Pacific, especially on Pelelui and Iwo Jima, came at the cost of similar numbers. No division in Vietnam remotely approached such casualty rates.[58]

The advocates for PTSD and its effects on Vietnam veterans had to account for or dismiss one prominent and embarrassing fact. Psychological casualties in Vietnam were far fewer than they had been in previous American wars. The military had finally learned the lessons that Thomas Salmon had articulated during WWI. Salmon, the senior psychiatrist with American troops in France, had devised a program of treating psychological casualties quickly, as close to the front as possible, and with the firm expectation that after a few days of rest the afflicted soldiers would return to their units.[59]

This may well seem to many good-hearted people as wrong. Why would you send traumatized soldiers back into combat? Most of the young infantrymen who served in WWII, Korea, and Vietnam did not come from environments where mental illness, even temporary mental illness, was well understood. Notions of character, courage, and cowardice were far more pervasive. Sending a man back into battle certainly risked his life. Sending him home risked that he might live the rest of his days believing that he was a coward.

When the first American troops landed in Vietnam, they did so with a psychiatrist and staff attached to every combat division and with a version of the Salmon program in place. The rate of psychological breakdown from 1965 through 1968 averaged about 11 per 1,000 troops, with the numbers actually increasing as the war wound down. In Korea the initial rate was 50 per 1,000, accounting for nearly one-quarter of all battlefield evacuations. After the Salmon procedures were reinstituted the rate fell to 30 per 1,000. For the period from July 1950 to December 1952, the rate was 37 per 1,000. During WWII, and despite a screening program designed to weed out potential psychological casualties, the First Army in Europe reported a rate of 102 per 1000, though other units reported lower numbers—the lowest, 9th Army's 28 per 1,000. But the lowest measured rate in the European theater was almost three times the rate in Vietnam.[60]

Sarah Haley accepted the factual basis of a low rate of psychological casualties in Vietnam but called it misleading. It failed to account, she argued, for the delayed onset of stress. Lifton offered a more sweeping argument, that the military's numbers were a form of "psychiatric technicism," no different from "body count." They may have emptied the psych ward beds, but there was no follow-up, no long-term treatment, no ethical concern other than getting soldiers back into battle. It was all evidence for Lifton, of military psychiatrists corrupting the profession. Others argued that the military's numbers were false because cases of breakdown were treated as discipline problems and were thus unreported. But the military reported all this. By 1972, 61 percent of all medical evacuations out of country were for psychological causes, the vast majority for heroin addiction. The rate of psychological casualties actually increased as the war for Americans wound down and became far more prevalent among men serving in support rather than in the field.[61]

But Vietnam's low rate of psychological casualties would soon be forgotten as the first national studies of PTSD appeared. The most often cited was the National Vietnam Veteran Readjustment Study (NVVRS) undertaken by the Research Triangle Institute and issued in 1988. The study found that 15.2 percent of male veterans suffered from PTSD, with higher rates for black and Hispanic vets, 20.6 percent and 27.9 percent, respectively. Another 11 percent of veterans suffered from partial PTSD. A quarter of Vietnam vets suffered full or partial PTSD. The study went on to estimate that another 30.9 percent of men and 26.9 percent of women had post-war PTSD at some time. So during the course of their post–war lives a majority of men (53.4 percent) and a near majority of women (48.1 percent) had symptoms of PTSD. The numbers are staggering—over 1.7 million veterans with PTSD, and the problems of divorce, violent behavior, drug and alcohol use, even homelessness that seemed to follow in its wake. Hidden in the numbers, however, were extraordinary rates of co-morbidity. Those who had symptoms of PTSD also exhibited high rates of alcohol and substance abuse, as well as depression.[62]

There were other voices at the time. The Centers for Disease Control (CDC) released its own study in 1988 as well. The CDC reported that only 15 percent of Vietnam vets experienced some form of PTSD at some time during or after service. Vietnam vets did face adjustment problems: 14 percent battled alcohol dependence, compared to 9 percent of veterans who did not serve in Vietnam. Anxiety and depression were also higher, 5 percent for both, compared to 3 percent and 2 percent for non-Vietnam vets. But drug abuse was equally low for both groups, and few men from either group were in jail or otherwise institutionalized. The CDC did find that those who enlisted prior to turning nineteen and those who scored low on army tests were more likely to exhibit psychological difficulty (as defined by the MMPI—the Minnesota Multiphasic Personality Inventory). Soldiers with less than a high-school education were also at far greater risk for becoming psychological casualties in Vietnam. In the experience of one army psychiatrist, a staggering 62 percent of the psychological casualties he treated were not high-school graduates, and 17 percent never advanced beyond 8th grade.[63]

The CDC's findings about the psychological problems encountered by poorly educated, teen-age enlistees were true regardless of service in Vietnam, and regardless of Military Occupational Specialty (MOS)—that is, those who served in the combat arms were no more likely to experience psychological difficulty (again, as defined by the MMPI) than those who served in support roles. This did not, however, hold for those who suffered from full-blown PTSD. Those who served in combat, or as the CDC defined it, those with "tactical MOS's" were twice as likely to develop PTSD. "Military service in Vietnam was, undoubtedly, an emotionally and psychologically difficult experience for many U.S. servicemen," the CDC reported. "Vietnam veterans have more psychological and emotional problems compared with veterans who did not serve in Vietnam," the CDC concluded, "but, they are not of a magnitude that has resulted in Vietnam veterans having, as a group, lower social and economic attainment." The CDC's report also indicated that 90 percent of Vietnam veterans were employed, 90 percent of those who were married were satisfied with their marriages, and that there was no evidence that the children of Vietnam veterans were at greater risk for birth defects. The only pronounced physical difference between Vietnam veterans and non-Vietnam veterans was that the former exhibited higher levels of hearing loss—a fact that will surprise no one who was close to the sound of the guns.[64]

There were other contrary voices. Dr. Jonathan F. Borus authored a study published in 1973 based on sixty-four interviews he conducted with Vietnam veterans still in the service. For draftees or enlistees who had served in Vietnam, it was common that they would have additional time to serve once their tour in Vietnam was over. He had access to military records indicating both legal and emotional problems among these soldiers, and he weighted his sample in a way that would exaggerate maladjustment, so that roughly one-third were men with legal difficulties, one-third with emotional problems, and one-third who were reasonably adjusted. What he found would surprise no one with military experience. Men returning from a war zone who had faced life and death decisions, who often had been invested with extraordinary responsibility at a young age, returned to the tedium and the whitewashed rock "chickenshit" of peace-time garrison duty. Almost all praised their officers in Vietnam, even though roughly a third were sympathetic to the antiwar movement. Only 20 percent considered their garrison leadership excellent. One quarter reported emotional disturbances, 40 percent reported that they were irritable upon return, but that it was temporary. One-quarter reported getting in fights, but such incidents they said were less frequent than they had been prior to their military service. Most reported an increase in drug use while in Vietnam, but a decline after. Ninety percent were not sorry they served, and many of those remarked on the positive effects of their service.[65]

In 2006 a third study using the data of the NVVRS, but crosschecking it against available military records, produced yet another set of numbers. The authors of the new study, Bruce Dohrenwend and others, found that 18.7 percent of veterans suffered from PTSD in their lifetime, a decline of 40 percent from the NVVRS, and 9.1 percent were suffering 11 to 12 years after the war, a decline of one-third from the NVVRS. Although the Dohrenwend group was critical of the CDC study for using only half the items in a preferred diagnostic interview module, its numbers for lifetime PTSD were far closer to the CDC's than those of the NVVRS. Further, according to Richard J. McNally, if the Dohrenwend team had required a finding of a "clinically significant functional impairment" then the decline in PTSD rates from the NVVRS study would have been 65 percent, not 40 percent, resulting in a current (late 1980s) rate of 5.4 percent.[66]

The Dohrenwend group also came up with one finding that was widely reported, and several others that were not as widely reported. The group found that there was little evidence of veterans falsifying their combat records. Crosschecking against the veterans' military records, they were able to devise a military history measure that took account of medals and badges received and casualty rates in the units in which they served. More than 96 percent of those who were rated low on combat exposure self-reported low or moderate exposure. Such a finding was taken as refuting those critics who believed that veterans' own accounts of combat trauma were not always reliable.[67]

But the Dohrenwend study made no mention of contradictory findings in another recent study. In 2005, B. C. Frueh et al. published a paper in the *British Journal of Psychiatry*. Frueh, who had previously argued that there was systematic bias in the psychological assessment of Vietnam veterans because of the overreporting of trauma, gained access to the military records of 100 men who had claimed combat service in Vietnam and were being treated by the VA for PTSD. Only 41 percent of the veterans had confirmed combat exposure. Another 20 percent had served in Vietnam but their records offered no evidence of combat exposure. And the remaining 39 percent fell into the category of highly unlikely to have seen combat. 32 percent of the total served in roles far removed from battle, 3 percent never served in Vietnam, 2 percent never served in the military. So one-third likely exaggerated, and 5 percent lied. The question of the reliability of veterans' testimony on their combat exposure remains open.[68]

The Dohrenwend group also revised the conventional wisdom on the percentage of Vietnam veterans in combat roles. For some years, the figure 15 percent has been taken as accurate, and so too the related numbers that for every soldier in combat in Vietnam there were seven in support. The war in Vietnam had the most lopsided "tooth to tail" ratio in the history of twentieth century warfare. Some critics used the 15 percent number to question the high rates of PTSD found in the NVVRS. How could 30 percent have PTSD when only 15 percent saw combat? In fairness, I've long thought that 15 percent was too low. Helicopter pilots, engineers, and medical personnel would all be classified as support, but all would have likely either seen combat, been shot at on a regular basis, or had to deal with the terrible effects of combat. To their credit, the Dohrenwend group revised the numbers. They argued that 10.5 percent served in infantry units, and another 14 percent served in artillery, engineers, or other units in direct combat support. But, unfortunately, rather than accept their own findings that roughly a quarter of Vietnam veterans were likely to have served under fire, or to have treated those who were, they took the estimate of Gabriel Kolko, a historian with no expertise in military history, to claim that fully 50 percent so served. The argument from authority, and a questionable authority at that, trumped their own useful research.[69]

But three other findings cast doubt on long and fiercely held beliefs about PTSD. One, the majority of combat veterans never suffered PTSD. War itself did not create traumatized veterans, contrary to Haley and other early proponents. As the World War II psychiatrists understood, men in battle respond differently because they bring widely different personal resources to those battles. Second, the trajectory for those suffering with PTSD was toward amelioration or complete remission. The functioning of veterans who once had PTSD was little different than that of veterans who never had it. So much for the chronic and long-term nature of PTSD as the early advocates would have it. And third, of those who once had PTSD, only 44.9 percent received treatment, suggesting that there were other factors that "may contribute to initial resistance and psychological adjustment." So therapy of any kind—never mind the intensive therapy of rap groups and regimens like Meshad's "walking through Vietnam"—was not always necessary.[70]

More than 30 years after the initial claims of pervasive, severe, and chronic PTSD, a breath of common sense has begun to reach a wider audience. Not that you couldn't find it earlier, if you looked hard enough or asked the right questions. Many of those who believed that PTSD would likely recede as time went on, a wholly common sense view, have been vindicated—so too, those who believed that men and women brought different resources to the face of trauma. It is an embarrassing and perhaps painful truth for the deeply empathic among us, that limited education and lower general intelligence levels are risk factors for PTSD. This will have the sound for many of "blaming the victim," and will be rejected because of that. It should better be seen as the lifting of the shroud of victimhood from the vast majority of the men and women who served in Vietnam. But the evidence of differing capacities in the face of trauma is there and could have been noted and widely publicized. The American men who suffered the most severe trauma during the war were our POWs. Who could argue with that? Yet only three of seventy navy pilots captured and imprisoned in North Vietnam developed PTSD.[71]

Common sense has also returned in assessments of Vietnam veterans committing suicide. Recall Shatan's off-hand comment about the prevalence of one-car accidents among vets, though he never said how he learned that. Stories of remarkably high suicide rates among Vietnam vets began appearing in the mid-1970s. The most influential was a piece by Tom Wicker in the *New York Times* in 1975. Addressing the pervasiveness of Post–Vietnam Syndrome, Wicker cited *Penthouse* as his source that 500,000 veterans had attempted suicide. But *Penthouse*'s claim could not be traced. The *Times* printed a retraction, but the damage had been done. The numbers would fluctuate, but the numbers remained large. In 1988 Dan Rather asserted in a television special, "The Wall Within," that somewhere between 26,000 and 100,000 had killed themselves "depending on what reputable source you believe." And as recently as 1998, Kristin Ann Hass, a professor at the University of Michigan, wrote that "in the first five years after . . . the war, more than fifty-eight thousand Vietnam veterans committed suicide," more than were killed in combat. So pervasive had the belief become that the editors at the University of California Press did not demand a source; and Professor Hass provided none, because she had none.[72]

A modest familiarity with social statistics should have at the least prompted skepticism. Suicide is far more common among the elderly. A simple fact check would have revealed that the claimed suicide rates of Vietnam veterans were more than six times the rate of their civilian peers. But most of these stories were accompanied by heart-rending anecdotes, some of them true. But over the years, there were other stories. B. J. Burkett has written of the suicide of Robert Fife in 1989. Fife had claimed to his wife that he had been a navy navigator shot down in North Vietnam and held as a POW before he managed to escape. He left a 449-page manuscript of his service in Vietnam. His wife, with the help of his therapist, argued that his name should be included on the wall of the Utah Vietnam War Memorial. The stewards of the Memorial agreed. The story attracted an Associated Press reporter who found that Fife had never served in Vietnam. He had enlisted in the navy in September 1965 and was discharged for medical reasons eight months later. Fife had his demons from whatever source, and he and his wife deserve deep sympathy, but he had latched on to an all too convenient and believable excuse that it was Vietnam that killed him. Then there was John Kolosowski, who died in a vacant field in Houston with a card of the Brotherhood of Vietnam Veterans, a group that ran a homeless shelter, in his pocket. The *Houston Chronicle* ran a series of stories, later followed by the Associated Press. The *Chronicle* reporter actually found men who claimed to have served with him—he was a "tunnel rat," a small, wiry man able to descend into VC tunnels. We called him "Ski," claimed a veteran. There were many "Ski's" in Vietnam, and some of them were no doubt "tunnel rats," but Kolosowski was not one. He never served in Vietnam, having been discharged from the Marines after two months for "mental ineptitude."[73]

Once again, there were other voices at the time. A CDC study from 1987 argued that the slight increase in suicides of Vietnam veterans compared to non-Vietnam veterans was "statistically insignificant." In 1988 the Department of Veterans Affairs studied the causes of death for over 50,000 veterans, roughly half veterans of Vietnam, the other half veterans who did not serve in Vietnam. The study found the Vietnam vets had a 7 percent lower risk of suicide. In 1990 Daniel Pollock and others, working with the CDC data and with additional data from the Wisconsin Division of Heath, estimated that fewer than 9,000 suicides occurred among Vietnam veterans from the time of discharge through the early 1980s. Studies of whether Vietnam veterans are at higher risk of suicide have largely been inconclusive—some estimating higher risk, others not. Because suicide tends to be underreported, the authors cautioned, the numbers could be slightly higher, but the authors "found no evidence to substantiate" the claim of 50,000 suicides.[74]

Coda

The power of PTSD as "frame" has become stunningly evident in the first reports on the veterans of Iraq and Afghanistan. The readers of the *New York Times*, for example, have read of an expected "surge" in the numbers of homeless veterans, of PTSD rates of 25 percent, of growing numbers of suicides, and, in a widely critiqued article, of growing numbers of veterans returning to commit murder. The *Times* found, through a search of local newspapers, 121 homicides committed by veterans over a period of six years. By comparing a six-year period prior to the wars, the article asserted an 89 percent increase in murders committed by veterans. It is a tale of human tragedy, but it is also a tale with an eerie and troubling similarity to the demonizing tales of Vietnam veterans common in the early 1970s. The article asserted the "links" between combat trauma and social dysfunction, but cited only the 1988 study, not the 2006 revision, and offered readers quotes from Robert Jay Lifton and Jonathan Shay, both with long commitments to one side of the argument. At no point did the *Times* tell its readers what the comparable homicide rate is in the general population. Conservative blogs answered immediately with outrage, and gradually the mainstream media picked up the story. Although the numbers cited used differing bases, there was no question that returning veterans were committing far fewer homicides than their civilian peers. By one estimate, returning vets would have to have killed more than 700 over six years to match the civilian rate. A later, well-researched article discovered that almost one-third of the 121 had yet to go to trial, and one-fifth of the total were cases of vehicular manslaughter or homicide. The article did say that some of the veterans awaited trial and carried a quote by a military spokesman questioning the lumping of manslaughter and murder cases, but the authors offered no percentages and no admission that many of these cases were vehicular ones.[75]

It is of course too early to tell where all this suicide, PTSD, and murder talk will lead, but over time we should expect more rigor, precision, and balance. There are two comparative statistics to note. The war in Vietnam was, at least to date, far bloodier than the war in Iraq. Mortality in Vietnam was 22 per 1,000 per year. In Iraq, according to a study published in the fall of 2007, it is 4 per 1,000 per year, one-fifth of the Vietnam rate. Whether that will lead to lower rates of PTSD is unclear. Soldiers who have been wounded are at higher risk for PTSD, for all the obvious reasons. Dramatic advances in military medicine, along with the prevalence of lightweight body armor, have increased the percentages of soldiers surviving battlefield wounds. Where 76 percent of Vietnam and Persian Gulf troops survived their wounds (in World War II, 70 percent survived), a full 90 percent of those serving in Iraq and Afghanistan are surviving their wounds. Would that Americans will come to support those survivors, and all those who have served, with compassion, but also with a clear-headed honesty and truthfulness, resisting the frame of a demonized victimhood.[76]

two
A Nurse's Tale

There is so much of that year in Vietnam and the long years after that
that I cannot remember. I needed to forget during those early years,
and now that I want it back I have to struggle to regain it.
—Lynda Van Devanter and Christopher Morgan

American women have nursed the broken, diseased, and eviscerated bodies of soldiers since at least the time of Clara Barton and Louisa May Alcott. Yet they have left only the shallowest of literary footprints. If we think of prominent American writers engaged in wartime medical care, the names of Walt Whitman and Ernest Hemingway would come to mind more quickly than any others. No American woman writer compares to Vera Brittain, whose *Testament of Youth* (1933) was popular at the time and remains in print. None of the American nurse/writers of the World Wars or of Korea, however competent, can now be recalled by anyone other than a specialist. None are associated with the grand theme of twentieth century war memoir—Brittain's theme—innocence lost and betrayed.[1]

In 1975, when the last American helicopters left Vietnam, no one would have predicted that the writings and oral histories of American nurses would reach the broad audience they did. The most popular by far was the late Lynda Van Devanter's *Home Before Morning: The Story of an Army Nurse in Vietnam* (1983). Though no one would compare her to Brittain—and Van Devanter gave no evidence of having read her—the reviews were uniformly positive, and her reputation has grown. Her theme was an extension of Brittain's—not just innocence lost and betrayed, but innocence lost, betrayed, and healed by therapy. Van Devanter's framing was so powerful that subsequent writers and reviewers could see little else. Yet *Home Before Morning* was neither representative nor reliable.[2]

Lynda Van Devanter Buckley died on November 15, 2002, at the age of fifty-five of a systemic collagen vascular disease. She had attributed her disease to Agent Orange, a defoliant containing the carcinogen dioxin. The Veterans Administration (VA) did not acknowledge the claim, but her family intended to pursue it. Her story was heartrending and implicitly implicated a callous government. Yet the VA had gone to great lengths, under intense political pressure, to greatly expand its coverage of Agent Orange-related diseases. If any Vietnam veteran contracted a disease linked in any way to dioxin, the VA assumed it was the result of Vietnam service. Veterans were under no obligation to prove that they had even been exposed to Agent Orange. Van Devanter's disease had not been so linked.[3]

Home Before Morning was the single most important book in shaping the popular perception of Vietnam nurses and for evoking the plight and pain of all women who served in Vietnam. This was, in part, the result of Van Devanter's public visibility. She was the first head of the Women Veterans Project of the Vietnam Veterans of America, the first mainstream Vietnam veterans' organization. A theatrical speaker and impassioned antiwar writer, she brought a clear and resounding woman's voice to the travail of Vietnam veterans and to the ignored nurses and other woman who served—a voice that effectively caught the pervasive disquiet and despair that the war elicited. Her memoir would help to shape the popular TV series *China Beach,* and Colin Powell would quote her poetry at the dedication of the Vietnam Women's Memorial.[4]

In 1981 she was the centerpiece of a *Washington Post* article on the then still emerging understanding of the impact of the Vietnam War on women veterans. The story she told to the *Post* reporter, through tears and trembling hands, was horrific. A young soldier, his face blown away, white teeth visible above a jaw dangling loose, was her patient in the neurosurgical Operating Room, 71st Evacuation (Evac) Hospital, Pleiku. At one point during the eight hours she and the doctors worked over him, she accidentally dislodged a photograph from his fatigues on the floor. It was a prom picture—he was "gazing sweetly" at his high school girl. The photograph made him painfully real. "He was a person who could love and think and plan and dream," she said, "and now he is nothing, there is nothing left." She stood with him while he died.[5]

She would tell the story frequently, and "with the flair of an actress," according to a sympathetic reporter—for "those who have heard it often, there is a staginess to the tremble, the tears, the melodramatic catch in her voice." Those who served with her noted this theatricality as well. The story would become the pivotal moment of her best-selling book. In the aftermath of that death, Van Devanter wrote, "I knew a profound change had already come over me. . . . I had lost an important part of myself. The Lynda I had known before the war was gone forever."[6]

Home Before Morning sold more than 100,000 copies. It came out near the time of the dedication of the Vietnam Veterans Memorial, a moment of belated acknowledgment of the service and travail of Vietnam vets. Passionately written as a form of therapy, and with the help of a professional writer, Christopher Morgan, *Home Before Morning* touched a chord.[7]

With Morgan's help, Van Devanter presented herself as the "all-American girl," raised in Arlington, Virginia, the oldest of four sisters. Her father was a college graduate, civil servant, and devout Catholic, who had been rejected for service in World War II. Her mother was a clerk-typist and was frequently ill. She dreamed of becoming an actress and singer. Encouraged by her father, she began performing at the age of two. At five, dressed as a "pint-sized vamp," she sang, "I'm the Last of the Red-Hot Mamas" at the Lyons Village Community House. Her mother's illnesses led her to a more practical dream of nursing. After high school, she enrolled at the Mercy Hospital School of Nursing, a Catholic school in Baltimore. A visit by an army recruiting sergeant in January 1968 would decisively shape her life.[8]

She signed up for the Army Nurse Corps—"it didn't take much convincing," she wrote. She had heard the words of President John Kennedy's inaugural address on TV, with her family around her—"we will bear any burden, pay any price." She had also seen the seven o'clock news with wounded soldiers in Vietnam She believed that "we were saving [Vietnam] from communism." She volunteered. "I want to go to Vietnam," she said to a skeptical friend. "The sergeant told us nurses don't get killed. . . . They're all in rear areas. The hospitals are perfectly safe."[9]

On June 8, 1969, she arrived in country, within hours of the death of 1LT Sharon Lane in Chu Lai, the first and only nurse killed by hostile fire in Vietnam. *Home Before Morning* is dedicated to Lane and to "all of the unknown women who served forgotten in their wars," and her death is invoked as a direct challenge to that blithe recruiting sergeant. She would tell another version of this story to a reporter, claiming falsely that the nurse killed that day was a member of her unit.[10]

Her descent into Tan Son Nhut airport in Saigon was met, she wrote, by apparent Viet Cong (VC) fire: "there was a burning in my stomach and an overpowering fear that paralyzed me as I observed the bombs and red tracer rounds. We went into a steep climb. . . . In a single moment every idealistic thought I had ever had was gone. To hell with 'Ask not' . . . I wanted to go home right now." The pilot would divert to Long Binh. At Long Binh she would await her first assignment and grow more disillusioned. A female army major mocked her recruiter's promise of safety—"there might not be many nurses dying, but there are enough being wounded to discourage anyone with half a brain from being here"—an assertion hard to credit. So she "learned" the doubtful "truths" that nurses and doctors were at serious risk, that VC sappers (demolition specialists) targeted hospitals, that hootch maids were likely VC, and that some hospitals were far more dangerous than others. In my experience, none of this was true. One of the most dangerous, she was told, was the 71st Evac, "a MASH-type facility," in her words, in Pleiku Province, an area of heavy combat near the Cambodian border.[11]

The army so assigned her. The 71st Evac, however, was not a "MASH-type facility," that is, a "Mobile Army Surgical Hospital" (MASH) designed for the Korean War to follow the lines of battle. The 71st was a hospital fixed in place, within a much larger and well-protected compound of army facilities. It bore no resemblance to the well-known opening image of the TV show *MASH*, suggesting a small, isolated hospital with no obvious perimeter defense. Despite her efforts to suggest danger, service at the 71st posed minimal risks.[12]

On her very first day, she wrote that she encountered fifteen wounded soldiers ready for surgery—traumatic amputations, stomach wounds with intestines visible, "ordinary" AK-47 wounds—and another twenty-five delayed primary closures. This would not be the worst. Mass casualities (Mascals), when they came, would keep her up twenty-four to thirty-six hours. She learned to face the horror and the smell of napalm victims "covered with a sickly blue-green slime, called pseudomonas." She could not hold her food. The daily routine was numbing—"the casualties kept coming in a seemingly endless torrent of human flesh." She was instructed to be hard—"it's easier if you tell yourself they're not people," one surgeon, "Carl Adams," told her, "but merely bodies. We're not in a hospital, Van. This is a factory."[13]

The Pleiku operating room in *Home* is a Gothic horror—a constant stream of badly wounded men, blood-covered walls, dismembered legs, endless nights of surgery conducted under rocket attack, and mud-filled floors. She would write:

> The mud that poured down the hills would ooze through the cracks in ways that were reminiscent of a fifties horror film. . . . Once we found ourselves operating in an inch or more of mud. It was worse during the rocket attacks, when we had to lower the table and kneel in the muck.

A former medic who served with her recalled none of this, not the frequent attacks, the torrent of wounded, operating in mud, or lowering the operating tables. Substantial revetments protected the 71st's surgical ward. The only fear was a direct hit, in which case lowering the tables wouldn't matter. It was such a direct hit that killed Sharon Lane. "Reading her version," the former medic wrote, "I wondered where I was when all this was going on."[14]

Upon returning from her second R&R, she descended into Pleiku only to see "a line of body bags that seemed as long as a football field, some stacked two and three deep." The wounded could not all fit into the ER, at least fifty were on litters outside. These were the casualties of the assault into Cambodia in the spring of 1970. She would work in the OR for the next forty-eight hours. An earlier version of this story, told to a writer for the *Boston Review*, presented the scene even more dramatically. Three Chinooks unloaded body bags at the rate of forty to fifty per chopper. "They came in all day and all week, in an unending stream. They just dumped the wounded at the door of the hospital and took off again to pick up more casualties. We knew that we would be there for days"—120 to 150 dead, a casualty stream lasting "all week," though she claimed to be there just two days, the wounded "just dumped." Her interviewer would report that the 71st's surgery stints were extended to seventy-two hours, "treating 300 to 400 to 500 casualties in a day," mind numbing and false numbers. The death reports for the 71st for April and May 1970 record a total of twenty-five deaths—six Americans, seventeen Montagnards, and two others. "Montagnards" is the name given to the Degars of the Central Highlands by the French colonists.[15]

Holding her up in the face of all this was the extraordinary professionalism of her colleagues—"Adams" was one, the other was another surgeon, "Jack Olsen," who, she claimed, devised an ingenious solution to "a liver wound problem that had been plaguing doctors since before [she] arrived in country."

Livers bleed profusely, but if you could clamp the aorta and tube the blood flow to the kidneys and lower limbs, you could create a bloodless field that would allow a longer time to repair the liver. Clamping the aorta by itself, however, would "in about ten minutes . . . create dead kidneys and lower limbs." "Olsen" worked out his solution only after extended experiments, first on dogs, then on the cadavers of American soldiers. The after-hours work in the morgue repulsed Van Devanter. It was a world of "hideously contorted faces," and the stench of death. "Once, while walking to the table," she wrote, "I tripped over an arm and fell in between two cadavers that were already starting to decompose." She drew the line. Remaining experiments would be done only on soldiers who had just died in the OR. It was all worth it. At the end of November 1969, they saved a soldier who would have previously died. Such success, she wrote, "would mean that hundreds of lives could eventually be saved."[16]

Home Before Morning is a paean to the skills of the 71st's doctors and nurses. But the surgical procedure she described, according to doctors at the Borden Institute, Walter Reed Army Medical Center (WRAMC), is "without foundation." Cross-clamping the aorta was standard procedure faced with "uncontrollable truncal bleeding." And the specter of army surgeons experimenting on cadavers struck the same WRAMC doctors as "unusual to the point of bizarre." Moreover, "casualties killed in action are not taken to a hospital; they are removed and prepared for shipment by designated units of the Quartermaster Corps. . . . No surgeon would have access to rooms filled with bodies of American soldiers." And it stretches plausibility to imagine an army morgue in such grotesque disarray. Bodies and body parts would have been in body bags, the stench of death eliminated by the intensive use of air conditioning. "Olsen's" heroic surgical interventions are not believable.[17]

The long hours of professionalism in the OR were matched "by equally long hours" of partying. "We partied as hard as we worked and when we slept, it was frequently because we had passed out from too much alcohol or too much exhaustion." Marijuana, packaged as cigarettes, was available for $1.00 a pack—"we learned to blot out the bad memories with the right amount of booze or grass." Parties led to more elaborate efforts to counter the horrors of the OR. The 71st had an unofficial social director, "Bubba Kominski," who organized the madcap "First Annual Seventy-Worst Ejaculation Hospital Olympic Games," included running, three-legged races, volleyball, and swimming in the hospital's pool. Coincidentally, year six (1977–1978) of the TV series *MASH* included an episode, "The Mash Olympics," featuring similar odd races.[18]

Intimacy helped. *Home Before Morning* may well be the first sexually frank memoir by a military nurse. She had three sequential affairs, with the two surgeons previously mentioned and, against regulations, with a young infantry sergeant. The affairs were important and consoling to her. She was discreet about her nursing peers, but not about "Major Mary Ellen Swanson," a Medical Service Corps administrator.

"Swanson," as "Morals and Ethics Officer," was upset that too many women were entertaining men in their billets after hours while others were "involved in illicit entertainment elsewhere." It was widely known, however, that Swanson had a lover, a "petite blond" nurse, junior to her. "Swanson's" nickname, the "Orgasmic Banshee," suggests why it was so widely known. The nurses devised a plan to blackmail her with the use of a microphone and a tape recorder. This exact mix of extraordinary competence in the OR with hard partying, sexual suggestiveness, and the flouting of military authority was the formula that made the TV series *MASH* so popular. Two reviewers grasped the connection. The *Harper's* reviewer, for example, heard in *Home*, "the merry chuckles that echo from the *MASH* laughtrack."[19]

The connections were even closer than the *Harper's* reviewer imagined. The original 1970 Robert Altman movie featured this exact scene, though not with two women. A hidden microphone connected to the hospital's public address system captured the guttural passions of the chief nurse, "Major Houlihan," in the embrace of "Major Frank Burns." "Houlihan" was the same stick figure as "Swanson," an uptight, hypocritical "lifer." It is hard to write this off as mere coincidence.[20]

Professionalism, intimacy, and dark humor all had their limits. In the aftermath of that horrible night in the late fall of 1969 when she uncovered the prom picture, Van Devanter's belief in the war had been shaken. She had initially worn a rhinestone flag on the lapel of her uniform and stridently defended the war. Her parents' letters and tapes, interspersed like a contrapuntal Greek chorus proclaiming the justice of the American cause, were foils to her own growing disillusionment. On the evening of December 7, the beginning of America's "moral war," she wrote, and after drinks at the Air Force Officers' Club, she said she "lost control and became hysterical." Sobbing and shaking, she screamed, "I want my mother. I want my father. . . . I want to go home! Vietnam sucks! We don't belong here! This is wrong!. . . . The whole thing is wrong!"[21]

Christmas tapes from family and friends would preface the clearest statement of her opposition to the war. The tapes revealed her change of heart. Her mother told her that she had published one of her first letters in the *Arlington Sun* (Thanksgiving Day 1969) "asking us to fly the flag everyday" to counter antiwar demonstrators; her father confirmed that the flag was still flying. Her words followed directly. "Maybe there were people in Vietnam who spent their entire tours motivated by blind patriotism and an unquestioning belief in the American way of doing things." Maybe there were those who failed to see "the corruption of the South Vietnamese officials and their rigged elections . . . their senseless brutalities against their own people . . . their soldiers' lack of commitment to the South Vietnamese government. And the total disregard for the value of human life in war." She went on: "Maybe there were American soldiers who could forget about the inane regulations . . . the petty harassment and make-work details . . . and who could avert their eyes from their buddies who were dying . . . from the young children without limbs . . . from the Vietnamese women . . . forced to prostitute themselves to stay alive . . . and [m]aybe there were . . . normal, healthy all-American men and women who could spend 365 days in that crazy environment and never once ask why. If there were, I never met them."[22]

It is a strident, strange, and hyperbolic indictment. The anger of American soldiers at the South Vietnamese government and army is now widely known, but it is only glancingly evidenced in the prior pages of the book. Indeed, by Van Devanter's account, it was the VC who committed "senseless brutalities"—cutting off the head of a Catholic priest and impaling it on a stake, cutting off the penises of dead American soldiers and stuffing them into their mouths. "Inane regulations" and "petty harassment" are the constant bane of all enlisted men, but most recognized there was less of that in Vietnam, and much less the closer to the field one was. Averting one's eyes from death and maiming to the extent possible was how soldiers and nurses survive. Many Vietnamese women were dependent on Americans, but not solely as prostitutes. Surely some soldiers never asked why, but many did, and many would have affirmed what they believed to be the rightness of the American cause.[23]

Consider her most disturbing and difficult-to-believe story: "One day," she wrote, "I saw some dead American soldiers lying outside the morgue . . . the [North Vietnamese Army (NVA)] butchers had cut off our soldiers' penises and stuffed them into the GIs' mouths." This horrific scene is buried toward the end of a long paragraph that begins with Van Devanter claiming a growing personal toughness that would be poorly reinforced by alcohol and marijuana, and would lead to a gradual disillusionment with the whole war. Americans and Vietnamese were dying of diseases that she thought had been "eliminated from the face of the earth." And then directly following, she wrote of those American dead. It "outraged" her, but then she was quick to say, not as much as when she saw a similar scene of dead VC: "It was the first time I realized that our clean-cut, wholesome American boys could be as brutal as the 'godless communists.'" These horrific sights are mentioned only in passing, and then quickly passed over.[24]

Compare this to the heartrending account of the late E. B. Sledge, a Marine veteran of some of the worst fighting of WWII. On Pelelui, while passing a narrow defilade, he saw three dead Marines not yet moved to the rear. His buddy groaned "Jesus!" Then he looked "and recoiled in revulsion and pity." "In disbelief," he wrote, "I stared at the face as I realized that the Japanese had cut off the dead Marine's penis and stuffed it into his mouth." Sledge, a modest and decent Baptist, would write, a full thirty years after, that his "emotions solidified into rage and hatred for the Japanese beyond anything I have ever experienced."[25]

Surely this comparison is unfair. It was a different war. Sledge's understated memoir is a classic, one of the best war memoirs ever written. Yet the differences with Van Devanter are not just in the nature of the two wars, or in the quality of writing, but in moral register. And more than that, there is a critical question of credibility.

Van Devanter tells us she saw the exposed bodies of these American soldiers laying outside the Pleiku morgue—Graves Registration, in the army's oblique euphemism. There they were, as the NVA had left them, lying grotesquely in the hot Central Highlands sun. If they had been dead for a day or more, which seems likely under the circumstances, their bodies would have been horribly bloated, crawling with maggots, and emitting a vile, gagging odor. In the earlier *Boston Review* interview, she offered a more elaborate story. It was a whole squad—ten men or so—"who had been hung up by their ankles," their genitals in their mouths. Van Devanter's quoted response was lamentably prissy and narcissistic: "Not a pretty sight. Not the sort of thing a young women of twenty-one or twenty-two expects to see."[26]

In order to believe Van Devanter's story, we must also believe the following: that not one American soldier—not one of the infantrymen who found their grotesquely dishonored comrades, not one member of the helicopter crew who evacuated their bodies, not one member of Graves Registration who moved their bodies to the morgue, had the decency to remove those severed penises, or to cover their faces, or to place their remains in a zippered body bag—protecting them from the flies and vermin of Vietnam. Not one. I served with men who could be callous and cruel, but this was far beneath them. We covered the faces of our dead.

Van Devanter would return to the United States in June 1970 to Travis AFB, uneasy, guilty, sad, bitter. There were no brass bands or ticker tape parades. "In the eyes of most Americans," she wrote, vets were "babykillers, misfits, and fools." Bused from Travis, she arrived at the Oakland Army Terminal at 5:00 AM, when she would discover that the army's direct responsibility for her had surprisingly ended. My own memory of my return is that buses were available to take us to the airport, though it's likely that we had to pay for the trip. Wearing her green Class A's, Van Devanter would try to hitch a ride to San Francisco International, twenty plus miles away.[27]

Her account of that trip is the single ugliest homecoming tale in the literature. She began her effort at rush hour, let's say 6:00 to 7:00 AM. She would not be picked up until 10:30 AM. In the interim, a "few drivers" gave her the finger. "Some" slowed to yell obscenities. One "threw a carton of trash," another a "half-empty can of soda." A red and yellow VW bus stopped, a young man—long hair, bearded, wire-rimmed glasses—led her on, only to slam the passenger door, spit on her and yell, "we don't take Army pigs." A "big gob of brownish-colored saliva" ran down her nametag to be absorbed into her uniform. She had no energy to brush it away—the bus pulled away as the driver yelled, "Fuck you, Nazi bitch." "The drivers of other passing cars . . . laughed." She claimed she was not angry, just confused, and so she continued this painful quest for a "few more hours." Some drivers "hurled insults," others looked through her with surprise—she was a women—and hatred—for what she represented. And then a passing driver's yell would sum up her return—"Welcome home, asshole." If there were women drivers or women passengers who passed her during this awful morning, she did not mention it. Finally, an "old black man in a beat up '58 Chevy," who she claimed had already passed her four times, stopped and ended her ordeal.[28]

Again, what are we to make of this? It needs to be repeated. There is nothing remotely equal to this "I was spit upon story"—three to four hours of extraordinary abuse. There she is—a women in an army uniform—at the side of the road, facing obscene gestures, obscene insults, the spit of a long-haired hippie, the hurled trash of angry drivers. No one—no one—stops to help her, not for hours! She is not angry, only confused. The war deeply divided America, but to this extent?

Van Devanter's victimhood had only begun. Her effort to pick up the pieces of her life went badly. Her relationship with "Jack," the second surgeon, dissolved at his initiative, to be replaced by a depressing succession of one-night stands. She had nightmares about Vietnam. She drank heavily. She went back to nursing in California, but she was unhappy at work. Civilian nursing could never match the challenge and intensity of Vietnam. Nurses were not treated with the respect she had once known, a complaint both accurate and common for many returning nurses. But it was worse for Van Devanter. Her nursing supervisor found her work "totally unacceptable," and offered her the opportunity to resign. Her depressions were so serious that she thought about suicide, even imagining how she would do it. She began seeing a psychiatrist, but she wasn't yet ready to talk about the war.[29]

By the middle 1970s, there were glimmerings of hope. She had acquired the semblance of a normal life. A relationship with "Bill Blackton," a radio news reporter, blossomed and led to marriage. Her experience as a dialysis nurse, gained in her previous job, led to a nursing niche that offered her respect and challenge. Though she mentions it only obliquely, her new specialty was a risky choice for someone fighting depression—dialysis patients do not get better. Her pain and sense of emptiness lurked just beneath the surface.[30]

It finally burst through. Her marriage grew troubled. But it was a series of burn patients who required dialysis to prevent renal failure that would finally drive her from nursing. Dutifully, she helped with dressing changes and debridements, awful jobs causing acute pain to her patients. The oppressive stench of pseudomonas returned, but now mixed in her mind with the petroleum-based smell of napalm. She smelled it everywhere, on her clothes, in her food, on the ocean breeze, on her husband's lips.[31]

Needing time away, she began writing. Sometime earlier, she had been encouraged by an editor to write a text on dialysis nursing, but she found herself writing instead about Vietnam. She saw Jane Fonda's *Coming Home* seventeen times. Then, by a quirk of fate, she met Bobby Muller, the founder and director of Vietnam Veterans of America. Muller was a former Marine officer, a charismatic, tough-minded New Yorker, whose wounds had made him a paraplegic. Upon meeting Van Devanter, Muller immediately recognized that he needed to find a place for women vets. "Bill Blackton" was doing a radio documentary on the group. Muller, embarrassed that he had never thought about women vets, wanted her in the documentary. A new career for Van Devanter loomed.[32]

She began reading about the plight of Vietnam vets—suicide rates said to be 25 percent higher than non-vet peers, higher rates of divorce and unemployment. Some of these numbers, especially those on suicide, were repeated frequently, but would prove wildly exaggerated. She learned of Agent Orange and the possible link with rashes she had had. She learned of PTSD, with its range of symptoms—depression, rage, recurring nightmares and flashbacks, difficulties maintaining intimacy—that "sounded like [she] was reading [her] own psychological profile."[33]

Van Devanter, once a true believer in the Vietnam War, became a true believer in PTSD. At the urging of Shad Meshad, whom we met in the previous chapter, she underwent a week of intensive therapy. Van Devanter had Meshad's full attention every day for a week. "We spent the bulk of every day talking intensively about my year in 'Nam," she wrote, "and about what I had gone through when I came home." This extraordinarily intense therapy has now become increasingly controversial, though it wasn't then. Recent scholarship has suggested that it can make some patients worse, not better. In addition, it stands to reason that a process challenging patients to dredge out the worst of their memories has the very real potential to yield exaggeration and false memory.[34]

Van Devanter believed that Meshad provided her a process for under-standing her experience, the confidence to talk, the permission to hurt, and, most importantly, reminded her of what she had somehow forgotten, that the work of nurses was positive, that it "saved the lives of people who might otherwise have died." Armed with a new confidence and a strong sense of secular mission, she would write, speak, and lobby on behalf of women vets— "thousands" of whom "Vietnam had robbed" of their futures.[35]

Home Before Morning was widely reviewed, and in glowing and wholly uncritical ways. *Ms* thought it "powerful" and "healing." The *Washington Post*'s reviewer wrote that it was "an awesome, painfully honest look at war through a woman's eyes." The *Voice of Youth* echoed the *Post*: "a superb portrait of a nurse working in a combat zone." *Library Journal* found it "well written and compelling" and gave it its best rating: "Highly recommended." Every reviewer took the book at face value. Helen Rogan of *Harper's* wrote that it "reads like a diary, unguarded, heartfelt." Rogan simply repeated the book's core messages, the "nightmare and despair," the "operating rooms that ran with blood," Van Devanter's toiling "under fire for days and nights without a pause." *The Atlantic*'s reviewer also saw it as Van Devanter intended. Her recruiter had lied—"enemy sniping and shelling were commonplace," she saw a "stream of mangled casualties," and she and her comrades fell "asleep in blood-stiffened uniforms only to scramble up and start again." "Between the bouts of action," the reviewer went on, "alcoholic gaiety was relieved by fits of screaming hysterics and at least one suicide." There was no confirmed suicide. *Kirkus Reviews* went further to spell out the larger political meaning: "the personal danger, the fatigue, the heat, rain, and mud . . . and above all the meaninglessness of American involvement rapidly put an end to Van Devanter's blind patriotism, her innocence and her youth." None of these reviewers evidenced any military or nursing experience.[36]

The book had its critics. In a TV interview, Nora Kinzer, a VA special assistant, claimed that Van Devanter's frankness about sex confirmed the image of the army nurse as either "lesbian or whore," using Van Devanter's own language. Two of Van Devanter's superiors went further. COL Edith Knox, former head nurse of the 67th Evac, was distressed by "Lynda's exaggerations and negativism." COL Mary Grace, nursing supervisor at the 71st Evac, responded to a reporter that she "certainly did not recognize" Van Devanter's depiction of long shifts, a "never-ending flow of casualties," and the "50s horror film" character of her work—"I'd say she's been watching too much *MASH*." Jo Ann Webb, a former army nurse, claimed Van Devanter "fictionalized" the workload—that official army figures showed that the hospital was only half full. Webb, then the wife of the Marine veteran and writer James Webb, went further: "I'm incensed that she's become a professional veteran and now she's making money off it." But the criticism of Van Devanter's sexual honesty could be easily dismissed as prissy, and the *Washington Post* story that carried these quotes gave Van Devanter the last word. Her book was not about sex, not about numbers, and not about making money. She intended to donate half her earnings to Vietnam Veterans of America. She dismissed the criticisms as politically motivated.[37]

Webb wasn't through. She cited records showing a "steady, but manageable workload." The army actually eliminated 105 of 305 beds at the 71st Evacuation Hospital from June 1969 to March 1970, the months that Van Devanter worked. June was the worst month—346 surgical cases, 12 per day spread over several surgical teams. Van Devanter was there for two weeks of that. By the fall, the patient count had declined—there were a total of 401 wounded in action between November and January. Make no mistake, the numbers do not reflect the depth of trauma, or the intensity of it. Yet they are not easily dismissed. They simply do not confirm the thrust of Van Devanter's testimony, of an "endless torrent" of casualties. None of these claims came even close to confirming the number imparted to the *Boston Review* —200 to 400 per day. At a certain point, quantitative exaggeration compromises belief. Webb saw Van Devanter as "a shattered woman, telling a histrionic untruth."[38]

Another harsh critic was Patricia L. Walsh, a civilian nurse who served in Vietnam and wrote *Forever Sad the Hearts* (1981), a novel based on her experience. Walsh was so angry with Van Devanter's book that she formed Nurses Against Misrepresentation (NAM) to counter Van Devanter's depiction of medical care. "She portrayed medical teams in an utterly disgusting fashion"—writing "about a neurosurgeon who abused drugs and alcohol and about euthanasia and about GI bodies decomposing in a morgue. And about a nurse and a surgeon who fell into bed together—covered with blood from the operating room. Well, those things didn't happen."[39]

The *Los Angeles Times* story, however, was framed as one of professional jealousy. Walsh's book was "in development" at Paramount as a feature film for Cher at the same time *Home Before Morning* was under consideration as a Sally Field film, and then as a possible CBS miniseries. Walsh and NAM campaigned against it. "We know the power of Hollywood [and] we didn't want what was in Van Devanter's book to be put on the screen." Walsh said she took her book off the market while she attacked Van Devanter. Neither film would be produced. Walsh would make her own film, *The Other Angels*, in 1997, but she has yet to achieve the visibility of Van Devanter.[40]

Over the years criticism would continue. B. G. Burkett and Glenna Whitley, on a mission to expose "Vietnam wannabes" and outright fraud among vets, took Van Devanter on. The most serious charges they uncovered came from Robb and Lynne Morgan Ruyle, who both served at the 71st with Van Devanter, and who shared their memories with her prior to publication. Robb Ruyle thought the book "a trashy form of fiction." "A lot of what she describes as fact in her book simply did not happen, and those episodes that did happen were distorted to make Lynda the central character in them." In a letter to the editor of *Vietnam Magazine* Ruyle offered specifics. Van Devanter had written that a nurse friend, "Coretta Jones," had risked her life to save the crewmembers of a burning medevac only moments before it exploded. Van Devanter wrote that Jones was recommended for a Bronze Star for Valor. But it came back only as a Bronze Star for service, "because they didn't award things like that to nurses," Van Devanter was told. Ruyle wrote that Van Devanter wasn't there—she had been transferred. The heroic nurse was Lynne Morgan Ruyle. It was a dangerous situation, but the helicopter never exploded. Her husband believed that she should have been awarded the Soldier's Medal, but it didn't happen. An award of the Bronze Star for Valor was never possible. That required heroic action under enemy fire. But such criticism had little impact.[41]

More than any other book, *Home Before Morning* brought the experience of women in Vietnam to a broad public. Written with passion, its formulaic— innocence lost and betrayed—character, its *MASH*-like moments of humor helped to ensure a wide readership. As a form of conversion narrative, it clearly had a special appeal to liberal reviewers in liberal newspapers and journals. Its depiction of the war and its devastating impact on one woman could not help but reinforce liberal pieties—the war was horribly wrong and those who opposed and avoided it were right. No such attention would be lavished on the contrary memoirs of other nurses. Although it never became a Hollywood film, it informed the popular television show *China Beach*.

The University of Massachusetts Press reprinted it in 2001 in a paperback edition, ensuring that it will continue to be taught and read. Barry Kroll, an English professor at Indiana University, used the book in a course on the literature of Vietnam and asked his students to comment on it. The response was effusive. No other book elicited such potent responses. One student wrote: "I have never loved a book so much." Another: "I don't think I've ever been as affected by a piece of writing." A third student, apparently reacting to a critical classroom discussion, sought to put such talk off limits: "[It's] OK to question the stories a little but not put them down . . . [she] went through hell and for us to constantly put her down because of the way she writes is wrong." At least one student caught the "Harlequin" character of the book. But that was an isolated voice. The depth of feeling in the book ensured its reliability. As another student put it: "She seems to be very truthful, mostly because of the emotion she uses in writing."[42]

Professors and teachers continue to use it. It was, as of a few years ago, the most widely assigned book on women in Vietnam in American college classes. And *Home Before Morning* is now taught in high schools both public and private. At Westridge in Pasadena, California, it is said to be "a favorite of juniors year after year." It is on a recommended list at the Hotchkiss School. In Honors English in Union City, New Jersey, it is included on a world-literature reading list that also includes Austen, Bronte, Solzhenitsen, Wiesel, and Wright.[43]

Yet at too many critical points *Home Before Morning* is not believable, and the evidence for that has mounted over the years. It is as if the unembellished story wasn't enough for Van Devanter. Her war had to be worse—the never-ending casualties, the risk of death, the specter of grotesquely dishonored American soldiers, faces visible, stacked outside the morgue, the longest and ugliest "I was spit upon story" in the homecoming literature. Her sad and early death, linked now to a posthumous Agent Orange claim, will continue to frame her victimhood. Vietnam veterans no longer even have to prove that they were exposed to Agent Orange. That makes possible her family's claim. She served where I did, near Pleiku and in Qui Nhon, in areas that never experienced the airborne release of Agent Orange.[44]

Home Before Morning framed the discourse, and several subsequent writings echoed Van Devanter. Keith Walker's edited collection, *A Piece of my Heart,* published in 1985 and widely reviewed, presented the oral histories of twenty-six women who served in Vietnam. Walker acknowledged Van Devanter as a "pioneer" whose contributions were "extraordinary" in raising the profile of women vets.[45]

Walker was a painter, filmmaker, and teacher in the San Francisco area who had been drafted in the 1950s and served in Korea. He was "strongly" opposed to American involvement in Vietnam, but not willing to abandon those who served. While working on a photo essay about Vietnam vets, he met Rose Sandecki, a former army nurse and director of the Veterans' Outreach Center in Concord, California. She opened his eyes to the numbers of women who served in Vietnam, to their work and their proximity to danger—"in Vietnam there were no safe areas," he wrote—and their difficulties in readjusting. Sandecki told him "all" the women veterans with whom she was in touch "had difficulty in readjusting to life." Walker took up their "cause," by which he seemed to mean the pain of their return to an indifferent citizenry. He had, he wrote, "seen the scars on wrists carefully concealed beneath watchbands."[46]

Walker's reliance on Sandecki clearly biased the sample. But even given that, a fair reading of the twenty-six interviews makes clear that women who served in Vietnam had no single "cause," while roughly half exhibited no evidence of a troubled homecoming. Of the fifteen military nurses he interviewed, only one mentioned suffering from PTSD, though three others joined support groups. None shared Van Devanter's deep antiwar beliefs.

Walker's introduction glossed over the interviews that did not fit his frame. Donna Cull Peck, a nurse at the 24th Evacuation Hospital in Long Binh, directly challenged her peers who seemed to be "almost glorying" in their problems. She had no regrets and required no therapy. Her friend Kay Johnson Burnette, who also served at the 24th and was interviewed with her, responded directly: "I think that's typical of a lot of women vets that we don't hear about—they've adjusted and had support and they just got on with their life." Grace Barolet O'Brien, who served twenty months at the 85th Evacuation Hospital and the 67th Evacuation Hospital, both in Qui Nhon, was "glad" she served: "Vietnam was for me, then and now, a powerful growth experience." Charlotte Capozoli Miller, who served at the 95th Evacuation Hospital in Danang, thought of her year in Vietnam as "one of the more positive experiences in my life. The only other experience that equates . . . was having my two children." Two nurses wanted to go back. Christine McGinley Schneider, who served at the 95th Evacuation Hospital, "missed the intensity"—a common experience for nurses and other veterans who became, in Rose Sandecki's words, "adrenaline junkies." Cheryl M. Nicol, who served at the 91st Evacuation Hospital, Tuy Hoa, and at the 8th Field Hospital, Nha Trang, "would have loved to go back." Despite the death of her fiancé, a Marine pilot, Maureen Walsh, who served at the Naval Hospital in Danang, was remarkably able to understand one of the war's unintended consequences—that the advances in helicopter rescue and shock/trauma treatment pioneered in Vietnam would save "more lives . . . in peacetime than were lost in that war." An exaggeration? Perhaps. But it is also a deeply generous acknowledgment of one of the lesser-known "lessons" of Vietnam. These were clearly not the women whose watchbands hid scars.[47]

Two years later, Kathryn Marshall published a second collection of oral histories of American women in Vietnam, *In The Combat Zone*, freely crediting Van Devanter for her leadership. Unlike Walker, however, Marshall explicitly recognized that female veterans had no "cause" or any common "position" on the war. Believing, however, that the war was "unjustifiable," she "felt closer" to those who shared her beliefs. Most of these were women who worked for religious organizations and were critical of U.S. policy prior to their service. The nurses and other military women were not so critical.

They had, Marshall wrote, "shakier belief systems" and a "debilitating ambivalence."[48]

The nurses had clearly disappointed her. Of the eight she interviewed, two had been included in the Walker collection—Lily (Lee) Adams and Jill Mishkel. Three were career military—"Lifers," she called then derisively. Of the eight, three or four had returns that could be fairly described as troubled. None of the eight used the term PTSD. One whose return was troubled could also say: "I'm really proud to have served in Vietnam." Others were more positive: "the year I spent in Vietnam was the most satisfying year of nursing I've ever had. . . . I've never regretted going." Ann Powlas, in responding to the VC flags she knew were being waved at antiwar demonstrations, said, "I thought the American flag flying over the compound was a beautiful sight." Her thoughts on Jane Fonda immediately followed: "If it had been any other war, Jane Fonda would have been placed on trial as a traitor." There is nothing "ambivalent" about that. Like Walker, Marshall glossed over what her nurse interviewees actually said. And her reviewers, like Walker's, saw only what fit the frame. The *Nation's* reviewer claimed that both books depicted women who "again and again . . . saw corruption, racism, civilian casualties, soldiers killed by drugs, friendly fire and fragging . . . war's insanity and purposelessness." *Library Journal* claimed that Marshall's interviews offered "familiar stories of alienation, danger, violence, loneliness." Some did, but such hyperbolic language distorts the sentiment and belief these books actually contained.[49]

Van Devanter, Walker, and Marshall were all widely reviewed. The *New York Times Book Review* paid attention. Only one other nursing account could claim that: Winnie Smith's *American Daughter Gone To War: On the Front Lines with an Army Nurse in Vietnam* (1992). Smith served at the 3rd Field Hospital in Saigon, later transferring to the 24th Evacuation Hospital in Long Binh in 1966–1967. Smith thanked Van Devanter for her book "that opened the door for me." She had read *Home Before Morning* at a moment in her life when she was so depressed she was considering suicide. Van Devanter offered an extravagant blurb: "If you never understood the soul-searching, bone-wearying waste and futility of war, you will after reading [this book]. God, what a book!" Smith also had help. Doris Ober, a freelance editor from Bolinas in Marin County, California, worked closely with Smith. Smith would acknowledge, "in the end, we had a publishable manuscript."[50]

The comparisons between Van Devanter and Smith are clearly visible. Both employ the same narrative structure and similar narrative devices while expressing the great theme of twentieth century war writing—innocence lost and betrayed. The lives of both women followed a similar trajectory as each confronted their peculiar demons. While in Vietnam, Smith lost herself in alcohol and in three sequential affairs that were more troubling—less consoling—than Van Devanter's. Both came to oppose the war, Van Devanter more quickly and perhaps more self-confidently, and certainly more publicly. Both had troubled lives after returning from war, troubled relationships with men, considered and rejected suicide, and eventually came to believe that they suffered from PTSD and found help in therapy. Smith found her way to Rose Sandecki and to the Concord Vet Center. Both found civilian nursing unchallenging. Read superficially and uncritically, they might even appear interchangeable.

Yet the differences are important. There are no false notes or exaggerations in *American Daughter Gone to War*, nothing that strains belief. But it isn't just a more reliable book. It offers a more nuanced and less predictable narrative, a life story more modest and uncertain than Van Devanter's boisterous Manichean tale. More than that, Smith gives voice to two dimensions of the experience of nurses in Vietnam that Van Devanter slights in one case and wholly obscures in the second.

The first is the experience of women as women. This ranged from the army's simple neglect of providing sufficient toilet facilities for women to pervasive forms of sexual insult. Smith can't even exit the plane that flew her to Vietnam without "scores of men . . . whistling, cheering . . . and looking up my skirt." A chivalrous pilot comes to her aid. A hapless PFC at Tan Son Nhut can't direct her to a latrine she can use. Sent to Vietnam in her wool greens, she swelters, unwilling to take off her jacket for the attention it would attract while she sits with her skirt tucked "tightly around my knees and my legs under the bench." In Saigon, she must wear nursing whites, not the cooler jungle fatigues of the men. Her visibility as an American woman wears on her. She hates the "gaping," the o-club (officers' club) hustle. She avoids the swimming pool at Long Binh. Her full contempt is reserved for the field-grade officers—majors and above—whose invitations to parties are really commands. Their "insinuating brushes to our breasts and pats to our bottoms" cannot compensate for the lavish villas and excellent food. "I pretend not to notice disapproving frowns," she recalls, "over my refusal to perform."[51]

Second, Smith's story, unlike Van Devanter's, is not one of flawless professionalism. She is brutally honest about her own failings and those of other doctors and nurses. On her first days in recovery, she struggles through one mistake after another. There is so much she doesn't know or has forgotten. Her corpsman helps her, but a nurse and a doctor are harsh and sarcastic. She lets an IV drip run open on a soldier with emphysema. The resulting pulmonary edema threatens his life. She runs for help. "You don't know how to do a CVP?" (central venous pressure monitoring) a nurse "cries incredulously." His pressure is too low, he needs a respirator. There is only one and it's in use by a badly wounded soldier, "a head with fixed and dilated pupils we can put behind the curtains," in the words of the senior nurse. That cruel shorthand—"head"—denotes a soldier with a head wound; while "behind the curtains" is the place for "expectants," a word crueler yet, reversing the common-sense meaning. These are the men expected to die who will receive no further treatment. Her mistake, in her words, has "sentenced a head injury to sure death."[52]

Nor was Smith a model of nursely patience and succor. She loses her temper with a badly injured soldier who had been run over by a tank. One of his legs is "squash meat." She responds to his pained and fearful questions: "stop worrying about your bad leg and be grateful you've got a good one." She treats the Vietnamese parents of a dying four-year-old rudely, shamefully, but she is able to push the shame "back down where I won't have to look at it." She acknowledges what some other nurses could not, that soldiers in hospitals die alone, behind the screens isolating the "expectants." There are no *MASH* scripts here. None of this is discrediting. In extremis, empathy is grace. In contrast, Van Devanter never wavered in her story. She and her colleagues might well party long into the night and flout the lifers, but they were always ready, like the madcap doctors of *MASH*, to serve and to save.[53]

The book closes, as other memoirs do, at the "Wall." Smith traveled with the Concord women vets to Washington for the dedication of the three soldiers statue on Veterans Day 1984. It was her first visit to the Wall. She was deeply moved, feeling despair for the loss, gratitude for the recognition. The next day, Veterans Day, the generals and politicians arrived. "Even though I knew the speakers had lied before and will again, I embraced their words." She cheered Westmoreland when he spoke of a job well done and for serving when so many would not. She rose to her feet in a standing ovation when Casper Weinberger announced that the entire week was dedicated to the women who served. But then there was President Reagan, badly served by his speechwriters, expressing his gratitude to the men who served. "*What about the women? . . . the women!*" Smith's memory is that she spoke first, others in her group followed forcefully. They were close enough for Reagan and his glowering Secret Service officers to hear. They learned only later that their protests were heard over the loudspeaker.[54]

Cheering Westmoreland, shouting over Reagan in anger, Smith's response to the weekend was yet more complicated. Watching ten helicopters in formation overflying the Mall, dipping to honor the dead as they passed the Wall, she and a friend cried "unabashedly." "Sometimes," she said, "I wish I could bring back that year." Is this a case of "debilitating ambivalence," in Kathryn Marshall's term? There is nothing false or incompatible about holding these contradictory thoughts in tension. Thoughtful male veterans have long recognized the enduring allure of war, its life and death intensity, its challenge to character, its impetus to bonding. Now women too will increasingly share that. Smith caught much of this in the following summation: "Part of me longs to be back . . . to have purpose in my life as I did then, to regain the sense of belonging and share the camaraderie that was so unlike anything I have found since."[55]

Van Devanter and Smith, along with the two oral history collections of Walker and Marshall, have been the most prominently reviewed nursing accounts. But they are not alone. Three other nurses have composed memoirs. Lynn Hampton's *The Fighting Strength* (1992) is a singular account from an evangelical Christian and conservative perspective. Bobbi Hovis's *Station Hospital Saigon* (1990) is the only memoir by a career nurse, a large and largely overlooked or dismissed group. Mary Reynolds Powell's *A World of Hurt* (2000) is a forceful antiwar indictment but without a deeply troubled homecoming. There are several additional volumes of oral histories, including Ron Steinman's *Women in Vietnam* (2000), which emerged from an ABC/TLC documentary; Olga Gruhzit-Hoyt's *A Time Remembered: American Women in the Vietnam War* (1999); Dan Freedman's and Jacqueline Rhoads's (editors) *Nurses in Vietnam: The Forgotten Veterans* (1987); and a scattering of other interviews, social science articles, theses, and one scholarly monograph, Elizabeth Norman's *Women at War* (1990), based on interviews with fifty nurses. None of these works received the attention of the former accounts. Part of that was timing. Publication in the mid to late 1980s corresponded with the dedication of the Wall capturing a moment of intense interest in the Vietnam War. Later works didn't evoke that attention. But the later works more importantly did not consistently conform to what had become the expected narrative—a noble and innocent nurse betrayed by her country and its leaders, traumatized by her experience, saved by therapy.[56]

The trauma of return was the thematic frame that almost all reviewers adopted; some explicitly made the link to PTSD, others evoked it implicitly. *Library Journal's* review of Smith focused on "war's cruel effects on its healers," and claimed that the "remarkable thing about PTSD is the similarity of its effects on its victims." Linda Bird Francke, writing in the *New York Times Book Review*: "The Wall honors the dead. . . . Winnie Smith's book honors the war's crushing costs to the living." Marcia Froelke Coburn, reviewing the Marshall oral history collection: "Like male veterans, the women's non-heroic status on returning home was shattering . . . life at a normal pace was unlivable." *Library Journal* read the Walker collection as showing that "even the most casual contact with war has a devastating effect," an absurdly hyperbolic claim. The *Nation's* reviewer went further: "The few post-traumatic stress disorder studies done of Vietnam nurses all found that political or ideological confusion and cynicism about the justification for the war was a major source of stress." So if you didn't agree with those opposed to the war, stress and PTSD would surely follow.[57]

The most widely read article in this vein was Laura Palmer's *New York Times Magazine* piece in November 1993, "How to Bandage a War." Palmer, a journalist, had edited *Shrapnel in the Heart* (1987), a heartrending collection of letters from soldiers who would later die in Vietnam. Deeply sympathetic to the troubled Vietnam nurses she interviewed, she claimed that they experienced "a level of trauma in Vietnam that nurses had never confronted before in wartime." It's hard to know what to do with such a claim. Was the experience of Vietnam nurses really more traumatic than that of the nurses captured on Bataan in WWII? Palmer argues that, even though the death rate in hospitals was far lower than in earlier wars, the incidence of traumatic injury was higher. There were more amputations in Vietnam, she claimed, than in Korea and WWII combined, an astonishing, unattributed, and wholly false assertion. As if to reinforce the point, nurse Jean Roth claimed that her colleagues at the 2nd Surgical Hospital in Chu Lai amputated 500 legs in one month of the Tet Offensive—"That's not arms or anything else. Just legs." That's seventeen per day, operating on anywhere from seventeen to thirty-four soldiers or civilians per day. It's not believable. All this trauma wore heavily—and no doubt it did for the eight nurses she interviewed—Van Devanter and the ubiquitous Lily Adams among them. "Vietnam veterans," Palmer wrote, "taught the therapeutic community about post-traumatic stress disorder." Yes—some of them did.[58]

Women, however, experienced PTSD differently, according to Palmer. They internalized more, they self medicated, and they were remarkably high functioning. Even those who appeared sound could yet be symptomatic. According to one nurse quoted by Palmer: "Nurses hide their pain partly out of fear that admitting to psychiatric problems will cost them their licenses." Another interviewee inadvertently confirmed the reality of such fears: "If you heard the level of symptom and impairment you would be alarmed that they were still practicing." So not only was PTSD a diagnosis, as Sarah Haley had suggested, circular and self-fulfilling, those who suffered from it could be suicidal or high functioning. If you chose not to be treated, it was partly from fear of losing your job. So if few nurses chose to be treated, that was no evidence that they did not suffer from PTSD. The most fervent advocates had every argument covered, so powerful was the frame.[59]

Consider how that frame continues to shape response, even in the face of evidence that can't be assimilated to it. A recent internet review of the Steinman collection put it this way: "All of the women [in the collection] suffer severely from delayed stress reactions of PTSD . . . each woman had her own way of trying to survive, and each paid a terrible price for her sacrifices." Each "kept silent for many years, until something triggered the overwhelming grief and anger. The lucky ones got therapy. By then, it was too late to reconstruct a full, normal life." In fairness, the last assertion was qualified, but at the cost of incoherence, by "but all the women in this book have managed to create a meaningful life." "All the women suffer severely"—"overwhelming grief and anger"—"too late to reconstruct a full, normal life"? A fair reading of the Steinman interviews fails to confirm this. Yes, the interviews reveal some of it—nurses in therapy, a Red Cross "donut dolly" claiming "full-blown PTSD," another nurse claiming that empty Agent Orange barrels found a use in the women's latrine. But then there is an air force flight nurse, Jackie Knoll: "if I had it to do over again . . . I would"; an army nurse who served at the 85th Evacuation Hospital, Joan Garvert, recalled her tour as "the best year of my life. I felt like I was needed, that I was doing something useful, that what I was doing I knew how to do." And another, a "donut dolly," Emily Strange: "With all the horror of Vietnam . . . I would still go. . . . It changed me forever and I gained strength from that time I would never have had, if I had not gone." It's difficult to believe that such words come from people burdened with "overwhelming grief," unable to reconstruct a normal life, or who suffer severely from PTSD. It's not that their response is more truthful or authentic, it's that it has been wholly ignored.[60]

The suicidal thoughts and agonized returns of Van Devanter and Smith advanced and reinforced the frame, but they were not typical. The NVVRS study estimated that 26.9 percent of women veterans had PTSD at some time in their lives, but only 8.5 percent had it currently. The Dohrenwend study of 2006 reduced the overall numbers by 40 percent, though it did not isolate women veterans as a distinct category. But assuming that a 40 percent overall reduction applied to women as well, this would have pushed the lifetime number down to 16 percent. However, if the criterion for PTSD was "significant functional impairment," as Richard McNally has argued, then the numbers could have declined by 65 percent, bringing us to a total lifetime number of 9 percent for women veterans. This is far closer to the 3.3 percent incidence of PTSD found by one study confined to nurses who had remained in the military, whose lower rates might well be explained by higher levels of peer support.[61]

On a more impressionistic level, Elizabeth Norman's book, *Women at War*, combined the results of interviews with fifty nurses and unfortunately clouded the issue. She claimed that forty-four of her fifty experienced symptoms of PTSD as revealed through M. J. Horowitz's "Impact of Event Scale." But these symptoms included such common and understandable emotions as anger—anger at "politicians who lost the war," anger at "draft dodgers," anger at the treatment of male vets. Other symptoms included involuntary thoughts of war triggered, for example, by the sound of helicopters, the smell of fatigues, the playing of the "Star Spangled Banner." "Nurses who visited the Vietnam Veterans Memorial," we're told, "found themselves returning to the war." By such reasoning, any thoughts of the war stirring emotion are symptoms. We all have such symptoms. I'm still angry at those who sought refuge in the National Guard and at the Guard for allowing it. I am still angry that a squad of badly trained and incompetently led National Guardsmen opened fire on demonstrators at Kent State throwing rocks. A better test is that only four of Norman's nurses (8 percent) were so depressed and alien-ated that they sought counseling. Hampton, Powell, and Hovis did not suffer from PTSD, nor did the majority of those interviewed by Walker, Marshall, and Steinman.[62]

While recognizing the reality of PTSD, Lynn Hampton also offered a direct challenge to any therapeutic regimen. That challenge falls wholly outside the conventional frame. Hampton writes that she turned to God after the fall of Saigon, an event that horrified but did not surprise her. She thought the United States had lost its honor. Yet her fellow church members seemed unable to understand the hold the war still had on her. So she turned briefly to a veteran-center rap group in Orlando. Her counselor claimed that hers was a classic case of PTSD. She recognized her unresolved anger, and what she calls "the psychic numbing" that the war induced, but she was also deeply skeptical. She sensed that PTSD was being sold as the "latest package"—"it has become such a 'bandwagon' that in all the hoopla about it, the public has lost sight . . . that the majority of us did not return as 'emotional wrecks' but better, stronger people for our experiences—even *with* PTSD." She found little comfort at the vet center. There seemed no place for faith. The answer to guilt, she wrote—things done and left undone—was not to be found with psychiatrists but with God. In a similar way Donna Cull Peck concluded her interview with Walker: "My prayer for all of the veterans that were in Vietnam is that they can face everything that happened and if they feel they've done something that deserves forgiveness, ask for it, be cleansed altogether from it . . . don't waste twenty years moaning and groaning about Vietnam. It's over."[63]

Van Devanter established the frame that would be embraced widely by critics and teachers, but it couldn't contain the depth and complexity of the actual experience of nurses. In the end there is nothing surprising about that. What is surprising is that the frame would prove so rigid that contrary evidence and stories that didn't fit were simply ignored. If memoirs offered one form of distortion, another form took physical shape on the Mall.

Glenna Goodacre's 1993 sculpture, honoring the service of nurses, depicts three nurses—one holds a wounded soldier in full uniform, evoking the Pieta, another looks skyward in anxiety, a third is hunched over with a look of stark depression on her face, distraught and dysfunctional. They are outside, sandbags at their feet. The nurses' uniforms are poorly rendered, their fatigues resemble state-side issue, not the jungle fatigues of Vietnam. One nurse even appears to be wearing two shirts, a wholly false touch. The grouping lacks the exquisite detail of Frederick Hart's earlier The Three Soldiers—a dog tag laced in a boot, insect repellent under a helmet strap—touches of verisimilitude immediately recognizable to veterans. Nurses deserved better, and the public deserved the truth of what nurses actually did. The scene depicted almost certainly never happened. Nurses did not provide primary or field medical care. That was the job of medics and corpsmen. The statue grouping depicts a false heroism and dishonors the true heroism of nurses. Their job was harder and more painful than ours. GEN Colin Powell, then the army's chief of staff, captured this at the dedication ceremony. For men, he said, "the war came in intermittent flashes of terror, occasional death, moments of pain"; but the sacrifice of nurses "equaled and even exceeded that of the men." For them, "terror, death and pain" were, in a deft reference to Tim O'Brien's *The Things They Carried*, "a constant terrible weight that had to be stoically carried." Each day—every day—in the ER, in the OR, in recovery, on the medical wards—they dealt with the pain of war. The "Nurses' Prayer" of the Army Nurse Corps captured the hope: "Hear my prayer in silence before Thee/ as I ask for courage each day." The nurses such as Winnie Smith and others who so struggled with the memory of war, who opposed it, and who told their stories as honestly as they could, fully deserve our attention. And so too do the nurses whose prayers may have been answered, and who came home stronger for it.[64]

three
Spit-Upon Veterans

It wasn't my war. . . . I did what I had to do to win. But somebody didn't
let us win. Then I come back to the world and I see all those maggots at
the airport. Protesting me. Spitting. Calling me baby killer, and
all kinds of vile crap. Who are they to protest me? Huh?
—"John Rambo" in *First Blood* (1982)

One of the best-known "war stories" from the Vietnam war is that of the
homecoming veteran spit upon by antiwar protestors. The stock story is that
of a uniformed veteran walking through a West Coast airport confronted by
a hippie, often a young woman acting alone. Lynda Van Devanter's variant of
the story remains the most elaborate, most detailed—most implausible—of
all the published "I was spit upon 'war stories.'" No other nurse reported
such abuse. It wasn't just that Van Devanter had been spit upon by a long-
haired male "hippie" in a VW bus while she attempted to hitch a ride to the
San Francisco airport, it was the extraordinary extent of the abuse she faced
that morning—a women in an army officer's uniform—looking at upturned
middle fingers, dodging thrown soda cans, hearing the insults, for hours. Did
it happen? There is no way I can prove it didn't. No one can prove a negative.
All I can do, and will do, is to underline the implausibility of it all, to explain
the context in which such stories came to be told, and to undermine those
stories that are palpably false.

But let me begin by acknowledging the metaphorical "truth" of such
stories. Those of us who served in Vietnam came home to family, friends,

and neighbors, many of whom had already concluded what the war meant to them. It was, at the least, a morally ambiguous war. No one asked about stories of American "heroism," nor wrote about it. It wasn't that kind of war, as Tim O'Brien has told us. But others asked and wrote about "our" war crimes. Most Americans, however—even friends, in my experience—did not want to know about what we saw or did, or in my case, why I served as a conscientious objector. There were so many "ways" to avoid service I was once told. I mustn't have been imaginative enough, or maybe I was just a fool. That's how I heard the comment—as metaphorical spit. The specter of our failed war, and the images of the dead and broken bodies at My Lai, hung over all of us. And for some veterans, especially for those who served early in the war, there was a deep anger and contempt for antiwar protestors. That contempt was still there, later, during my years of service, though partially counter-balanced by increased antiwar and antimilitary attitudes among both junior officers and junior enlisted. After Nixon and Vietnamization, we all knew the American war was over. No one wanted to be the last man or woman to die for a mistake. That attitude was at the heart of the army's corrosive descent into a decline of both morale and discipline.[1]

Still, many soldiers retained their contempt for the antiwar movement. It was just a cover, an excuse, one of my medical trainers told me, for the selfish, self-interest of college students—a comment unfair as a characterization of the most deeply principled antiwar students, but then, the student antiwar movement did lose much of its focused ferocity as the draft faded as an issue. It was probably over-determined that some veterans would come to see the anti warriors as their enemies—men and women who believed Vietnam veterans to be fools or worse, called them "murderers" and "baby-killers." There was evidence of that, but was that contempt and anger so deep that it would lead them to spit upon uniformed veterans?[2]

The earliest such stories began to circulate in the early 1970s. Robert Jay Lifton's *Home From the War* (1973) conveys the account of one veteran in his encounter group who told of being spat upon at an airport, "an experience referred to so often by veterans as to become a kind of mythic representation of a feeling shared by the American people and the veterans themselves," Lifton wrote. Lifton's comment, on which he neither footnoted nor elaborated, suggests such stories were widespread. But his use of language is tellingly ambiguous. Is it a factual "experience" or a "mythic representation of a feeling"? Oddly, however, none of the most popular early memoirs and reportage—Tim O'Brien's *If I Die in a Combat Zone* (1973),

Ron Kovic's *Born on the Fourth of July* (1983), Robert Mason's *Chickenhawk* (1983), John Sack's *M* (1967), and Michael Herr's *Dispatches* (1977)—make any mention of returning veterans being spit upon, though Mason recalls being called "murderer" by a women in an airport gift shop. Nor are there any spitting stories in the earliest and most popular oral histories, Al Santoli's *Everything We Had* (1981), Wallace Terry's *Bloods* (1984), or Mark Baker's *Nam* (1981), though two of Baker's interviewees recalled insulting questions from two women, again in airports—"How do you feel about killing all those innocent people?" a woman asked in a bar in the Philadelphia airport.[3]

There were, however, documented stories of antiwar demonstrators spitting on National Guardsmen and other men in military uniforms. James Reston reported that protesters spat upon the National Guardsmen protecting the Pentagon in October 1967. And the Walker Report, on the police response to the demonstrations at the Democratic National Convention in Chicago in 1968, documented that demonstrators spit upon National Guardsmen as they established a perimeter around the Convention Center. These and other spitting stories—the head of ROTC at Claremont College was reportedly spat upon, so, too, according to uncorroborated newspaper reports was a World War I veteran, Medal of Honor winners, Marine recruiters on campuses, and a midshipman—have come to light through the research of James Lindgren. Lindgren, a professor of law, played a critical role in exposing the faulty and fraudulent scholarship of Michael Bellesiles. Lindgren has recently turned his attention to the sociologist and Vietnam veteran Jerry Lembcke, whose *The Spitting Image* argued that there was no contemporaneous evidence of Vietnam veterans being spit upon as they returned home.[4]

Lindgren's evidence certainly undermines a portion of Lembcke's argument that antiwar protestors opposed the war but supported the troops. But Lindgren's evidence includes only one single first-person ("I was spit upon") account—the stories that are at the heart of Lembcke's book—and it appears that none of the accounts he cites were actually witnessed by a reporter. Moreover, Lindgren does not cite a single case of a Vietnam veteran spit upon as he returned home, and that was the story that would ultimately be repeated and believed. Lindgren has done useful work in documenting the relative frequency of antiwar spitting stories in the late 1960s and 1970s, though he greatly exaggerates when he claims that by the fall of 1971 "the story of spat-upon servicemen was both well-known and much written about." His evidence of this consists of the Walker Report plus nine newspaper articles that cite actual spitting, five of which appeared in such small-town papers as the *Odessa American,* the *Panama News,* and the *Bucks County Courier Times.*[5]

Because of the revived interest in the issue—the result of a series of skeptical articles written by Jack Shafer of *Slate*—two contemporaneous accounts have surfaced, one of them from a *CBS Evening News* segment of December 1971. In the piece, Delmar Pickett Jr. recounted being spit upon in the Seattle-Tacoma airport—"Man, I got into the airport and these two dudes walked up—one of them spit at me," Pickett said. Contacted in 2007, he confirmed that he had been spat on, though there were now four young men, and he was walking with four other soldiers in uniform, none of whom he identified. The spitter, a young man with long hair and a shabby T-shirt, missed his target. Pickett says he chased him, but the four ran off through the terminal. He recalled the date, May 23, 1971—only days after my own uneventful walk through the same airport.[6]

The second story was reported in the *Washington Post* in 1971. In it, Jim Minarik claimed that he was spit upon while in uniform on an Oakland street. Minarik would later turn up as a founding member of the pro-Nixon group Vietnam Veterans for a Just Peace. This, of course, does not invalidate his claim, but it was a claim like so many we shall see that was not witnessed. Nor was it the classic "airport" story, though it further undermines Lembcke's assertion that there were no contemporaneous reports of veterans being spit upon.[7]

It was the movie *First Blood* in 1982 that gave such stories their first pervasive visibility. In the movie's final scene, after having laid waste to the small town where he had been harassed, jailed, and abused, and now surrounded by police and National Guardsmen, "John Rambo" responds to his former Green Beret commander, who asserts that Rambo's mission is over: "Nothing is over. Nothing," Rambo responds. "You just don't turn it off. It wasn't my war. . . . I did what I had to do to win. But somebody didn't let us win. Then I come back to the world and I see all those maggots at the airport. Protesting me. Spitting. Calling me baby killer, and all kinds of vile crap. Who are they to protest me? Huh?" Most of the key elements of a story that rooted itself deep in popular consciousness are here—an airport scene, spitting protestors, the awful epithet "baby-killer."[8]

One critical piece of the story, that antiwar protestors confronted returning veterans with demonstrations as they exited military bases, had actually served as the opening scene of *Coming Home* (1978). There is no credible evidence that antiwar protesters staged demonstrations outside the gates of military bases as returning veterans were exiting those bases. But such stories would circulate after 1978, and find their way into one episode of the TV drama *China Beach*. It would be hard to imagine two "political" films whose intent varied so starkly. *First Blood* imagined a veteran's perverse vengeance and fed right-wing fantasy; *Coming Home* longed for reconciliation on left-liberal terms. Yet both added to the gross and troubling image of the deranged Vietnam veteran and will forever be linked in their indictment of antiwar demonstrators.[9]

First Blood was followed by the first spitting story to appear in an important and widely read memoir. This was Lynda Van Devanter's *Home Before Morning*. In the next few years, a few stories circulated in print. Charlotte Capozoli Miller, a nurse who served at the 95th Evacuation Hospital in 1970–1971, stated that after arriving at Fort Lewis, Washington, and going through the airport that there were "a lot of antiwar protestors in there throwing fruit at us and screaming obscenities and calling us all kinds of names." W. D. Ehrhart had picked up on parts of the story, writing that he had expectations of "placard-carrying flower people" surrounding him at the airport and "drowning me in flowers and chants of 'Baby Killer.'" William Taylor, who appears in Klein's *Payback,* claims "hippies" on a street in Anaheim spit upon him. Then a single soldier, Bob Bowers, interviewed for a special issue of *Newsweek,* focused in substantial part on the homecoming experience of veterans, claimed that in the San Francisco airport he "saw a welcoming party of his countrymen spit on a couple of his fellow returnees and call them baby-killers." That special issue became a much-enlarged book, *Charlie Company: What Vietnam Did to Us,* containing the homecoming memories of fifty-nine members of Charlie Company, 2nd Battalion, 28th Infantry, 1st Infantry Division. The "Black Lions," as they were known, fought in some of the bloodiest battles of the war. Only Bowers mentioned being spit upon.[10]

Then, in July 1987, the *Chicago Tribune's* then popular syndicated columnist, Bob Greene, posed a question to his readers. It was not a question that would qualify as good oral-history technique, but it had the virtue of directness: "If you're a veteran, were you spat upon?" It was oddly framed. Invoking the contested statistics of children abducted by strangers and of marriages ending in divorce, he suggested skepticism. But he then went on to evoke such incidents in a way that could only elicit predictable responses. He simply repeated what was then circulating as the stock story—a returning soldier in uniform "fresh from Vietnam . . . gets off the plane at an American airport . . . where he is spat upon by hippies." And then back to skepticism.

Would a "hippie" confront "a burly member of the Green Berets"? Would the soldier "just stand there and take it"? He wrote that he received over 1,000 detailed, intense, and emotional replies.[11]

Despite what he admitted was the mixed and contradictory nature of the replies, he reported to his readers he now had "no doubt that many returning veterans truly were spat upon . . . [t]here were simply too many letters, going into too fine a detail." He arrogantly dismissed the "surprising number" of veterans who "refuse to believe" the spitting stories. These were men, Greene believed, who were successful after returning from Vietnam and who disparaged the so-called professional veterans they assumed to be at the root of the spitting stories. Greene framed it as class prejudice, with the successful looking down on the "professional" veterans as "losers" clinging to the spitting stories as excuses for their own failures.[12]

Greene's next three columns would offer a sampling of eleven letters: the first from those who were spat upon, the next from those who were received only in kindness, the last from those who may not have been spat upon but were "hounded and hurt" by their fellow countrymen and women in ways that were equally painful. Greene did not publish any of the letters from those veterans he presumed to be successful and who "refused to believe."[13]

He offered the final word to a veteran who requested anonymity: "Now I think you [Greene] should issue another challenge. For every veteran who was spat upon, there was an American civilian who did the spitting. Why don't you ask those people to write you and explain why they did it—and how they feel about it now? I wonder if they will have the guts to answer."[14]

Greene would gather a larger sampling of 234 letters into his book *Homecoming: When the Soldiers Returned from Vietnam* (1989), divided into five sections: sixty letter writers claimed they were spat upon (four others affirmed that it happened to their son, husband, or friend), sixty-eight asserted that it did not happen to them, and an additional nineteen remembered only acts of kindness, sixty-nine letters fit the category that Greene had created for his column—that there were worse things than being spat upon, and fourteen others fit none of the above. Greene published no letters responding to the anonymous challenge to those who had been among the spitters.[15]

There were two major differences between his preface and his columns. First, Greene's preface dropped any effort to characterize those veterans who had refused to believe the spitting stories. They were no longer framed as successful businessmen looking down on those who claimed victimhood. And their letters—sixty-eight of them—now comprised a separate section, distinct from those who only remembered acts of kindness. Greene or his editors had completely reconsidered the inclusion of those letter writers whose motives had been summarily disparaged in the earlier column. Second, his preface was replete with numerous hedges. He sought explicit permissions for every letter published, giving each writer a way out if he or she had lied. Any letters that "raised a red flag" of suspicion did not make the cut, though he never stated his criteria. He vetted others through a source in the Veterans Administration (VA) to determine whether the writers had indeed served, though he was troubled that this might seem "disrespectful"—Greene was not a veteran, he had won the birth-date lottery. After all that, he admitted that a "ringer or two" might have made it in, but "even if several should prove to be not what they appear to be . . . it would not detract from the overall story that is being told." It is a strange and illogical claim—how could false letters not detract from the "overall story"? But poor logic was the least of Greene's problems.[16]

As Greene had suggested, many of the spitting stories took a common form. They took place typically in airport terminals—San Francisco and Los Angeles were the usual sites and the spitters were usually "hippies." But the letters were also shaped in ways that Greene had not helped to explicitly elicit. The spitting was aggressive and wholly unprovoked, almost always accompanied by insults—"baby-killer" the most common. The spitters were a mix of men and women only rarely organized in formal demonstrations. The acts more often seemed random. Surprisingly, the aggressor was frequently a woman acting alone.[17]

John W. Waid, an air force veteran from Westminster, Colorado, recalled that around 10:00 PM on a date in March 1969 that he could not remember, a young women at Los Angeles International Airport "approached me and, in a low voice, called me a 'baby killer' and spat on my ribbons." Waid reported that he was "stunned and unable to respond," and that he had "never talked to anyone about this incident." Clyde J. King of Gallipolis, Ohio, claimed to have served three tours in Vietnam and recalled a lady coming up to him in San Francisco and saying: "Welcome home, you fucking baby killer," and then spitting in his face. "I tried to explain," he wrote, "that I was sorry that she felt that way." But she walked away and "I stood there and watched little kids laughing at what she had done." Chester J. Leblanc, a navy veteran from Lake Charles, Louisiana, remembered that while walking along a concourse in Los Angeles International Airport he was: "stopped by a young lady wearing typical flower child attire—a long maxi-dress with granny-type glasses. She stopped me and, seeing my campaign ribbons, asked if I had been in Vietnam. When I told her I was just coming from there, she spat upon my uniform and ran off." Leblanc ran after her, but then stopped, said "a couple of choice curse words, and thought: Welcome home." Kenneth M. Ball, a twenty-four-year-old senior at the University of New Mexico and a veteran, wrote that in the spring of 1970, following the killings at Kent State, while simply walking on campus he was spat upon by a women "age perhaps nineteen or twenty, braless, overweight, unwashed." He continued: "I believe the words used were, 'Goddamed fascist baby-killer.'"[18]

Older women also appear as spitters. Michael Proctor of Colorado Springs, returning from his first tour in Vietnam, the date unspecified, wrote that he "was jeered and spit upon" in the San Francisco airport: "I was a major then," in uniform, when a woman "came out of nowhere, called me a baby killer, spit in my face and tried to hit me with her purse." She "wasn't a 'hippie,' but a well-groomed little old lady in white slacks and a burgundy jacket" who "looked like someone's grandmother." "The police moved her away," Proctor wrote, "and suggested I not press charges and delay my return home."[19]

Guy Morgan of Ft. Collins, Colorado, said he was a retired Catholic chaplain who served two tours in Vietnam with the air force. He wrote that while he was leaving JFK International in November 1968 "a lady (around 43 years old) told me that 'I napalm babies' and she spit on me. I didn't take her for a 'hippie' though."[20]

Frederick H. Giese of Arlington Heights, Illinois, claimed that he was wounded and sent to a naval hospital in Japan in November 1969. While in Japan, he wrote that he "married a Japanese lady and adopted her son. She became pregnant." And "in early 1970" he and his new family returned to the United States, landing in San Francisco after a long, direct flight from Japan. They walked into a cafeteria. He was in uniform with his awards, "including the Purple Heart and the Gold Star." They were standing in line "when out of the blue, this middle-aged lady walked up to me with a bowl of potato salad in her hand. She threw the potato salad smack in the middle of my chest and spat what salad she had in her mouth in my face. Then she proceeded to call me a 'baby killer,' 'war monger' and a lot of other vile names." Giese was angry, but two other servicemen restrained him. He and all the others spat upon by women, in these stories, did not retaliate; indeed, it is rare that they retaliated even against men. Most reported sadness and perplexity more than anger.[21]

To believe these stories we must first overcome a deep, common-sense skepticism. What is the likelihood that women of this era, however deep their antiwar beliefs, would act in such an ugly, aggressive, and solitary manner? And if they did so act, what is the likelihood that veterans, many of whom were contemptuous of the antiwar movement, would not at least respond in kind? At a deeper level, how many of us can recall even seeing a woman spit in public, for any reason, in this period? I can still remember how odd it was to see an elderly woman, in a desperately poor southern neighborhood, spit from her front porch in Nashville in the summer of 1967.

There are additional reasons to be skeptical. Consider Giese's story. If we take his chronology seriously and assume that a reasonable meaning for "early 1970" is the first three months of that year, then we must believe that he courted, married, and impregnated his new wife, arranged to adopt her son, and to bring them both back to the United States, all in five months and while recovering from wounds. They then flew back as a family on a rare and extraordinarily long nonstop flight from Japan to San Francisco. We have to assume that this was a civilian flight which, against all odds and policies, he had booked. Military flights would not have taken dependents or landed at civilian airports. If we can believe all this, perhaps we can also believe that in claiming the award of the "Gold Star" that he made an innocent mistake. There is no such military award.

James W. Wagenbach, whose letter Greene included in the "Some Things Are Worse" section, wrote that he returned from Vietnam in 1968 without his right arm. On two occasions while he was in uniform, once at the University of Denver, once at the University of Colorado, he claimed he was approached by "student-type individuals" who asked, "Where did you lose your arm? Vietnam?" When he replied yes, he heard the response "Good. Serves you right." Remarkably, Greene's fourth and final newspaper column contained the story of Steve Weeks of Monument, Colorado: "I came back from Vietnam in February of 1968," he wrote, "I returned to college. Although no one spat on me, various people asked me what happened to my missing arm. When I told them, the response was, 'Good, it served you right.' Not particularly nice." Weeks's story did not appear in the book. We can only conclude that Greene, faced with such an unbelievable coincidence, chose to believe one of the stories, or alternatively only Wagenbach gave permission to publish. There was another, more reasonable option—to disbelieve both. A cursory search of Vietnam memoirs would have revealed that Frederick Downs's highly regarded 1978 memoir, *The Killing Zone*, contained the identical story. In the fall of 1968, while walking across the University of Denver campus, Downs was stopped by a man who "pointed to the hook sticking out of my left sleeve." "Get that in Vietnam?" he asked. Hearing Downs answer yes, he said, "Serves you right." Downs's book predated Wagenbach's story by approximately seven years, Weeks's by ten. Greene was not just credulous, but negligently irresponsible.[22]

Several of the other stories Greene published rank somewhere between the impossible and the improbable. Enlisted men did not issue Purple Hearts to wounded soldiers. The award of a Purple Heart was a serious, solemn occasion, always presided over by a senior officer, frequently by a general. No soldier could begin his career as an enlisted man, advance to "senior staff NCO" and then to officer in the space of two years and prior to turning twenty. Soldiers, rotating home from Vietnam, did not return directly to civilian airports, nor were they likely to return wearing bloodied, or even clean, jungle fatigues. And it is impossible to believe that one soldier would return from Vietnam with fifty-seven combat decorations.[23]

That last claim was Lou Rochat's. He wrote from Universal City, Texas. According to his account, he joined the army in January 1969 and became a helicopter pilot. His travails began on his way to Vietnam in April 1970. He wrote that in the Dallas airport he encountered the "Bible flippers," who wouldn't approach him because of his uniform: "Mother fuckin' baby killer was the favorite line we heard," this provocatively ugly insult in America's evangelical—"support our boys"—heartland. Then, in San Francisco, he encountered the archetypal spitter—a "female hippie type who smelled as bad as she looked." Another spitter was a man, "a well dressed young business type who would be called a 'yuppie' today. Him I flattened." The "average American" in the airport—male, female, young and old—did not threaten violence; they simply called him "Murderer," "Baby killer," "Mercenary asshole," "Rapist," and "Fucking Bastard War Monger." These were the Americans that Rochat claimed that he and his fellow officers "were getting ready to die for."[24]

Rochat did not die. He wrote that he came back on a stretcher with "seven bullet holes" and fifty-seven combat decorations, including two Silver Stars. It is an extraordinary record. It is possible, even likely, that a helicopter pilot could return with eight non-valor decorations, including the Purple Heart. There are three medals awarded only for valor of which he claimed only the Silver Star (twice). We're up to ten. There are four other medals that could be awarded either for service or for valor. I've already given him credit for receiving all four. We must now conclude that he was awarded forty-seven oak leaf clusters or V devices for valor, each designating an additional award, an average of roughly one per week. Mr. Rochat was the forgotten "Audie Murphy" of Vietnam.[25]

Not every story that Greene published can be dismissed as easily. Yet it is clear that Greene's "red flag" did not go up nearly as often as it should have. Even the stories that are not obviously false contain clear warning signs. The vast majority of them cannot be corroborated. There are no named witnesses, none. You would think that at least one of these stories would involve two or more veterans who were friends and who could be remembered and named. Only two of the letters recount spitting incidents witnessed by family members, but one is ambiguous—the spitter spits at the ground—the other is at least plausible. Further, the vast majority of the "I was spat on" letters tell a singular story. Only two make any mention that they knew of other soldiers spat upon, or that other soldiers had told them directly that it happened to them. This is in stark contrast to the "it didn't happen to me" letter writers—most of whom claim that they never heard of it happening, and they know no one to whom it happened. And finally, there is not a single letter that claims to have witnessed a spitting—it didn't happen to me but I saw it happen to others. When I left the army at Fort Lewis to book a flight from the Seattle-Tacoma airport, other soldiers and Marines attempting to do the same surrounded me. Processing out of Vietnam was a form of mass production, not a one at a time activity. No soldier or Marine would have walked alone through the airports of Los Angeles, San Francisco, or Seattle-Tacoma at the mercy of vicious "flower children" or spitting waitresses and grandmothers.[26]

Veterans who suffered from Post Traumatic Stress Disorder (PTSD), and especially those who were treated for it, seem to have been especially prone to tell stories of ugly homecomings. In 1990 Shirley Dicks published an obscure collection of interviews with veterans who claimed to be suffering from PTSD. The book contained twenty-two interviews with returning veterans, five of whom refused to give their full names. Many of them had been treated, not be the VA or by mainstream secular agencies, but by counseling groups set up by fellow veterans—Base Camp, Inc., of Nashville, Fort Steer of Charlotte, Arizona, and Point Man Ministries of Washington, the latter an evangelical Christian organization. Like many of those such as Van Devanter, who received more "professional" counseling, these veterans "learned" and repeated extraordinary tales of the plight of returning vets: severe unemployment, drug and alcohol abuse, "100,000" in prison, "200,000" on parole, "80,000" homeless, and "90%" divorced. Also reported were staggering numbers of suicides: 98,000, according to one veteran, 30,000 by another, while a third claimed there were somewhere between 26,000 and 100,000, not including an additional 14,000 killed in single-car accidents—presumed suicides. These are numbers and percentages that were widely believed at the time, even finding their way into scholarly studies published by university presses, but they have subsequently been proven not just wrong, but grossly wrong. For veterans who genuinely suffered from PTSD and whose lives had been broken by divorce, drug and alcohol dependency, and unemployment, there had to be something comforting about knowing that their troubles were not theirs alone and could be at least partially explained by a diagnosis of PTSD. The troubled veterans whom Dicks interviewed frequently introduced their plight by recalling hostile and ugly homecomings.[27]

Upon returning home Jerry Barnet felt "slighted," he said, and "used by my government." He said he encountered an antiwar protest as he returned to Nashville. Women called him a "baby-killer." "I was in a seething rage inside," he recalled, but he chose to ignore it. "It may not have been the best thing in the world for me," he lamented. And then immediately following, he told of his alcoholism and the loss of his wife and children. "Nelson," who did not offer his surname, claimed he was a Marine, had witnessed the grotesque sexual torture of children by the Viet Cong (VC) and claimed that the VC used women and children as suicide bombers, a baseless claim. "I thought I would be a hero when I came home," he recalled. Instead, he was called "baby killer." Unlike the veterans of the Korean War who, he claimed, were greeted with parades and bands and free meals, "no one cheered, no bands played . . . and no one wanted to talk about Vietnam." He began drinking all of the time, missing work, alienating his family. "I felt my life was drifting away, and I had no control." Robert Davis also recalled being called "murderer, rapist, son of a bitch and a lot worse." He had flashbacks, a nervous breakdown, and after fifteen years, his wife left him.[28]

And then there were those who claimed to have been spit upon. Larry Hiller said he joined the Marines in 1967 and was sent to Vietnam. He claimed that "most of the time" he served as point man for my "battalion," and that one night, he and a squad of Marines with only one machine gun were sent to find a "whole battalion." Perhaps he misspoke. Point men led platoons or companies, and a Marine commander who sent a squad, with one machine gun, to contest a battalion—ten to twelve men to confront more than 500—would have been foolishly derelict. "When I came back to the States," Hiller said, "people called us baby killers, spit at us, mocked us and told us we were stupid and foolish." He too suffered from PTSD. John Lohman said he was an army veteran, but offered neither dates of service nor a unit designation. He claimed that after landing in Vietnam, he and others were ordered into formation. Shots rang out. His seatmate from the plane was killed. It is a wildly improbable story. Upon homecoming: "I was surprised that the American public didn't hail us as heroes," he said: "There were people at the airport who yelled obscene things at us as we walked from the plane. . . . They continually threw things at us. We were called baby killers and worse. I was spit at, cursed and called names."[29]

Dale Barnes told a unique story. He claimed that he enlisted in the air force but transferred to the army's Special Forces and took part in what he called "Hatchet and Snatch" teams that recovered two American POWs and five French prisoners, a ridiculous and easily falsified claim. He also claimed he witnessed the effects of hideous sexual torture practiced by the VC and was wounded five times. Upon arriving home, he wasn't spit upon but "hippies" carrying antiwar signs in an airport confronted him. One came at him "as a blur . . . I reacted instinctively," he said, "I struck out and hit his neck and killed him instantly." This killing of a hippie is a singular story. Barnes claimed he was never charged. He had just written a book, *The Warrior Within*, he informed Dicks. There is no such book in the Library of Congress catalogue, nor is there an author named Dale Barnes, nor is there a Dale Barnes with a Special Forces Military Occupational Specialty (MOS).[30]

In 1998 H. W. Chalsma wrote a book based on video interviews of veterans suffering from PTSD. Chalsma worked at the National Center for PTSD in West Haven, Connecticut. Founded in the late 1980s by a former drama student who employed what Chalsma called "drama therapy," the center had veterans enact one-act plays based on their experiences. Chalsma had no interest in the truth claims of veterans, naively accepting all their stories at face value, including stories of being spit upon. In such an environment, where veterans were encouraged to frame their experience as "drama" and where their most outrageous stories were therapeutically embraced and never challenged, is it any wonder that they came to believe events that likely never happened but usefully functioned as "mythic representations of feeling" in Lifton's words.[31]

So, can we prove the negative—that it never happened? No. All we can do is to refute the unbelievable stories, cast doubt on the most egregiously improbable ones, and offer attempts to understand why some veterans embraced such stories. Two of the stories Greene published, however, offer distinct clues to what may have happened and why.

Rose Marie McDonough of Green Bay, Wisconsin, said she was an air force veteran, 1967–1970. She did not serve in Vietnam. In the fall of 1971 she said she enrolled in the University of Wisconsin, Madison, and joined an antiwar group, "Vets for Peace." She recalled joining protest marches in Chicago, Milwaukee, and Madison, usually in company with a "group of veterans from Chicago called Vietnam Veterans Against the War." On Veterans Day 1971, she was walking alone from the college campus to the Wisconsin Capitol wearing an air force overcoat and a "Vets for Peace" hat. She wasn't clear but the context suggests she was either walking to or returning from a demonstration. A "normal looking" young man nineteen to twenty, "looked me in the face and spit right into my face. . . . I will never forget what he did to me."[32]

The story has the ring of truth, but not one that Greene recognized. Consider the context. The wearing of military clothing—field jackets, pea jackets, overcoats—was common among antiwar protestors and counter-culture types. The "young man" likely saw a woman in the uniform of the left protesting the war. How likely was it that he would have recognized her as a veteran? There was no public acknowledgment of women's service in Vietnam until a decade later. It is far more likely that he spat upon her thinking she was a protestor, not a veteran.

And we know that antiwar protestors faced extraordinary levels of abuse. At Kent State, a badly trained and incompetently led National Guard unit opened fire on students throwing rocks, killing four. Ron Kovic, a wounded Marine veteran and paraplegic, reported that while representing Vietnam Veterans Against the War (VVAW), he was spat upon while protesting the 1972 Republican National Convention.[33]

Jerry Lembcke, a sociology professor and a Vietnam veteran, made similar claims in *The Spitting Image*—that "the spit almost always flew from pro-war right-wingers onto anti-war activists." He argued that he could find no compelling evidence that Vietnam veterans had been spat upon by protestors. He did not do a close reading of veterans' accounts, but he did argue that he could find no evidence in newspaper accounts, police reports, or studies of demonstrations.[34]

Lembcke has done original and useful work on the spitting issue, but his book is so marred by poor logic, lack of evidence, and political tendentiousness that its value is sharply compromised. His work is both deeply felt and wholly a part of a 1960s debate that remains remarkably alive to him. He would have us believe that if he can demonstrate that relations between veterans and the antiwar movement were "empathetic and mutually supported," then it must follow "that the image of spat-upon vets must be false." He then goes on to "prove" the premise, and thus the corollary. Even if we stipulate the premise is true, his corollary cannot possibly follow. The antiwar movement was a loose confederation of groups and individuals with differing agendas. It defies reason to believe that every antiwar activist acted on message, with empathy always trumping contempt. Through Lembcke usefully reminds us of the existence of an antiwar movement among soldiers, he exaggerates its extent, ignores those soldiers who deeply despised the antiwarriors, and romantically and illogically accepts the argument that the increase in cases of desertion, of AWOL, of drug and alcohol abuse, and of general indiscipline, which marked and tarnished the army's final years in Vietnam, is evidence of increased antiwar sentiment among soldiers. In the last months of my tour, in a well-protected enclave in Qui Nhon, I shared a barracks room with a heroin addict who would be arrested for losing it one night and firing directly into a Vietnamese settlement immediately outside our perimeter. On another night, a tall and burly enlisted man, convinced that only he would control the passage of Vietnamese prostitutes through our perimeter, beat up our motor pool sergeant who had dared to contract directly with his lady friend. At the forceful insistence of my commanding officer, our erstwhile camp pimp was arrested that night. By what conceivable logic were these antiwar acts?[35]

Lembcke and I, coming to similar conclusions in very different ways, now have a similar problem. If the spat-upon veteran stories are false, or largely false, why have they become so widely believed? Lembcke's solution is to blame Richard Nixon—"the idea that anti-war people spat on Vietnam veterans," he writes, "has its origins in Nixon's haranguing of anti-war protestors for their disloyalty to the troops." Did Nixon and his colleagues attempt to divide the antiwar movement? Yes. Did this mean that they manipulated the image of the spat-upon veteran to their advantage—that they propagated such an image as "a propaganda ploy to discredit the anti-war movement," as Lembcke claims? There simply is no evidence. Lembcke also speculates, again without evidence, that acts of spitting at veterans were the acts of agent provocateurs, or that somehow these stories were simply inverted—the story of spitting at veterans was really the false memory of pro-war protestors spitting at antiwar demonstrators. Or, if none of this is persuasive, that films like *Coming Home* "created a mind-set receptive to suggestions that vets were actually spat upon"—never mind that there is no spitting scene in that film.[36]

There is a more coherent explanation. Greene published the account of Dr. Thomas K. Haverstock of Geneva, Illinois, a dentist who flew from Travis AFB to Vietnam on April 29, 1969. "While being bussed from the San Francisco airport to Travis AFB," he wrote, "I saw that a number of war protesters had gathered along the fence where the bus ran. The busload of personnel was jeered and spit at as it ran the gauntlet." There is no question that some form of what Haverstock recalled happened. Lembcke himself published a photo of antiwar demonstrators blocking a bus carrying inductees to the "Boston Army Base" on May 22, 1970. I have no doubt that such protestors acted out of noble motives. I also have no doubt that these young recruits could not possibly interpret such demonstrations as unambiguously supportive as Lembcke would have us believe. Consider it—Harvard-MIT protestors blocking the route of blue-collar young men, not all of whom were draftees. This could not be perceived as just a protest against the war. It also had to be perceived as a protest against these young men and their decisions. How could it be otherwise? Jonathan Polansky, who served with the 101st Airborne Division, told a similar story in Al Santoli's *Everything We Had*. Walking from the induction station on Whitehall Street in New York, he and his fellow draftees were met, he said, by "all these young kids with long hair . . . screaming and yelling at us." If we seek the origins of the spitting stories, it is likely here.[37]

Let us concede for the sake of argument that somewhere, sometime, someone spit upon a uniformed Vietnam veteran as she or he returned from the war. Let's also assume that some of the earliest stories, Pickett's perhaps, were true. Those stories, however, had no "legs," in the jargon of journalism. They had no impact at the time; most have been uncovered only recently. Rambo gave the story its first national visibility—Lembcke got that right—and Bob Greene gave us dozens of them—"war stories," the "homecoming tale," in Samuel Hynes's words. Such stories in their totality are largely formulaic and largely unbelievable. But they served a purpose for those who wanted to blame the antiwar movement for its betrayal of the troops. Such a stance unfairly characterizes the antiwar movement, though Lembcke's illogical defense of the movement, *tout court*, fails to convince. The image of "hippie" men and women hawking up gobs of phlegm to hurl at the ribbons of veterans, as a pervasive and commonplace act, is surely false.

But, the antiwar movement, especially if we credit stories such as those of Thomas Haverstock and Jonathan Polansky, contributed to the felt belief of many veterans that their fellow citizens had betrayed them.

Coda

The right made great use of that sense of betrayal, even when the context sug-gested a more complex, even a wholly different, story. Steve Pitkin, who served with Charlie Company, 2nd Battalion, 239th Infantry, 9th Infantry Division in 1969–1970, took the stage at the "Kerry Lied" rally in Washington, D.C., on September 12, 2004. He had only recently been identified as a participant in the Winter Soldier Investigation (WSI) of 1971, and had appeared in the documentary *Winter Soldier*. With his long hair tied off in a bandanna, his muttonchops, and his Vietnam fatigues, he fit the image of an antiwar veteran. His first appearance in the film was a cameo with the young John Kerry asking him why he was there. The anti-Kerry film, *Stolen Honor*, used the scene to suggest that Kerry and others were actively soliciting war crime stories. "Is there something that you could— that you'd really kind of want to say in terms of the [war] crimes and why they happened? What brings you here? What makes you say you want to testify, to want to say something?" Kerry asked. Pitkin was not one of the more coherent Winter Soldiers. In response to Kerry, he paused, and in that spaced-out '60s way, said "I'd almost need a book to answer that, man." Kerry, in his own stumbling way, had asked leading questions. But by editing out Pitkin's spaced-out pause, *Stolen Honor* made Pitkin appear direct and forthcoming.[38]

A few days before the release of *Stolen Honor*, Pitkin filed his first affidavit claiming that Kerry and others "pressured me to testify about American war crimes, despite my repeated statements that I could not honestly do so. One event leader strongly implied that I would not be provided transportation back to my home in Baltimore, if I failed to comply." Pitkin went on to claim that Kerry and others instructed him in what to say: "that I had witnessed incidents of rape, brutality, atrocities and racism, knowing that such statements would necessarily be untrue." Fox News and dozens of conservative blogs and websites embraced Pitkin's claims. He later issued a second affidavit after he learned that he had falsely implicated Scott Camil, the only WSI participant other than Kerry that he had named. Pitkin had recently retired after a career in the Coast Guard and repeated his claims at the "Kerry Lied" rally. "They knew I was one of the real combat veterans in the room," he said, reinforcing the right's widespread assertions that those who testified at the WSI were frauds.[39]

Few of those who heard Pitkin, read him, or heard about him denouncing Kerry and repudiating his testimony, would have had the patience to discover that in the proceedings of the WSI, Pitkin never testified to a single incidence of rape, brutality, racism, or atrocity. He did invoke the term "atrocity" so loosely and imprecisely that it had to embarrass the organizers of the WSI. The war "hurt a whole generation of Americans and Vietnamese, and that's the biggest atrocity," Pitkin said. He also used the word to describe newspaper coverage of the war, how he was badly trained at Fort Dix, and how he had to fight back tears when he was mocked and "laughed at" by "four long-haired people" in the San Francisco Airport.[40]

This is one of the earliest accounts of the harassment of a homecoming soldier. Some of its features would, of course, become widely familiar a decade later. Pitkin is alone in an airport, confronted by "four long-haired people" who insult him. He claimed he did nothing or said nothing in response, a common element of the "I was spit upon" stories. But what is more striking is what is missing. They didn't spit on him, they didn't call him "baby-killer," but the more common "pig." "I feel that if people knew more about the human part of the American soldier in Vietnam and about the enormous underground and how well organized it is over there, they might have some second thoughts before they called me a pig or . . . a tin soldier, laughed at me."[41]

But in 2004 he offered a different story. He hadn't just been "laughed at" and insulted. He had, he wrote in his affidavit, "encountered anti-war protestors who," in addition, and "at various times, threw feces, spit, and screamed obscenities." Thirty-four years after his WSI testimony, he now "recalled" that he had not only been insulted, but also spit upon. It could be true. It might have happened. But just as surely, his "new" memory testified to the power of the "mythic" story, and, more pointedly, to the political uses of such stories.[42]

four

The Swift Boat Veterans and the "Truth"

*So-called Vietnam Veterans Against the War . . . would later be
discovered as frauds, men who had never set foot on the battlefield, or
left the comforts of home, or even served in uniform except in mock
contempt of the military. Their lurid fantasies of butchery in Vietnam
were seized upon by John Kerry to help him organize the so-called
Winter Soldier's Investigation.*

*A lot of those stories [told at the Winter Soldier Investigation]
have been discredited.*
—Tim Russert

Actually, a lot of them have been documented.
—John Kerry

Steve Pitkin's "new" memory served the interests of Carlton Sherwood and
the Swift Boat Veterans for the Truth (SBVT). Sherwood's film, *Stolen Honor,*
used the Kerry-Pitkin clip from *Winter Soldier* to underline the argument
that Kerry and others were soliciting war crime stories. Of course they were—
that was the whole purpose of the Winter Soldier Investigation (WSI), to
have American soldiers and Marines lay bare what they had witnessed and
done in their country's name. Kerry's stumbling question, however, was not
an invitation to lie. We have only Pitkin's word that he was so coerced, thirty-
three years after the fact. And then he never did testify to a single war crime.

97

Steve Pitkin, the only Winter Soldier to repudiate his testimony, was a weak link in the case against the WSI.

The WSI was held in Detroit January 31 to February 2, 1971, under the auspices of Vietnam Veterans Against the War (VVAW). The term Winter Soldier derived indirectly from Thomas Paine's first *Crisis* pamphlet of December 1776, the second line of which read: "The summer soldier and the sunshine patriot will, in this crisis, shrink from the service of their country, but he that stands it *now* deserves the love and thanks of man and woman." In effect, the Winter Soldiers were drawing a comparison between resistance to British "tyranny" in the American colonies and resistance to American "tyranny" in Vietnam. Sen. Mark Hatfield inserted the full transcript of the WSI into the *Congressional Record* in April 1971. Beacon Press published an edited version of the testimony and *Winter Soldier*, a documentary first aired in 1972. But the WSI had little impact at the time.[1]

All that would change in 2004, as conservatives trained their guns on John Kerry's past. Kerry was not only a presence at the WSI, he was a leader of VVAW, and he fully supported the WSI's allegations of widespread and systematic atrocities in his testimony before the Senate Foreign Relations Committee—testimony that launched his political career. Kerry was vulnerable. He had risen to national prominence as an articulate anti war veteran, a man who had boldly thrown his medals away in 1971, and who had embraced the "truth" of the WSI. Now, in 2004, he chose to run on his war record—"reporting for service," he said, as he saluted the delegates of the Democratic National Convention, surrounding himself with the men who had served under his command. His service to VVAW was far longer than his actual service in Vietnam, his memory of the former was inaccurate in ways that served his apparent intent of pushing his radical days far into the distant past. No other major party candidate for president in American history had ever emerged from an organization further to the left than VVAW.

The conservative attacks on Kerry began with ads run by the SBVT—comprised of many of the officers with whom he served in Vietnam—and culminated in Carlton Sherwood's *Stolen Honor*. Sherwood was himself a Marine veteran of Vietnam, a former journalist for the *Washington Times*, a contributor to the right-wing *Human Events*, and the author of *Inquisition: the Prosecution and Persecution of the Reverend Sun Myung Moon*, a vigorous defense of the Reverend Moon, whom many regarded as a right-wing cult leader. Moon was part of a group that owned the *Washington Times*.[2]

Sherwood used a second clip from *Winter Soldier*. It is a clip that serves as an extraordinary window into the WSI, into *Stolen Honor* and the Swift Boat assault on John Kerry, and ultimately into the truth of what young Marines of Bravo Company, 1st Battalion, 1st Marine Regiment did—or did not do—in Quang Tri in the fall of 1967. But we are ahead of the story—first, the clip.

Winter Soldier captured a backstage moment meant to suggest the vetting of veterans' bona fides. Ken Campbell, a young man with long blond hair and a tasteful, hounds-tooth sport jacket, recognized the bearded Scott Camil, with unkempt hair and a wary smile. "Sergeant Camino," Campbell called him. Camil displayed no look of recognition. Campbell recalled that they had served at Camp Lejeune together after returning from Vietnam, and they had both been enlisted forward observers, trained in artillery, and assigned to 1st Battalion, 1st Marine Regiment, 1st Marine Division, though their tours did not overlap. Campbell asked: "You might be able to come up—I was trying—trying—to find somebody who knew something about a ville wiped out in Quang Tri." Campbell had heard such a "war story" circulating in Bravo Company after he had joined it in February 1968. "Right, I was there," Camil responded immediately: "We went into the area. It was to set the example to show that we weren't fucking around. The first thing we do was to burn down the village and kill everybody."[3]

Camil went on to say "I forgot that, I didn't even remember that." Then: "whenever they're questioning me, they'll have to get me to elaborate on that," and then—a second time—"I forgot all about that one." "How could you forget that?" Campbell asked, "I remember it and I wasn't even in on it." Camil responded: "Well, that was one of the last ones we did." It was a wholly unpersuasive performance. Camil, who would later claim a Post Traumatic Stress Disorder (PTSD) disability, had twice indicated he had forgotten about having killed "everybody" in that ville, and then seemed to justify his memory lapse illogically by saying it was "one of the last ones we did."[4]

Sherwood's *Stolen Honor* used a piece of the clip—bleeping out Camil's use of "fucking" and capturing only one of his "I forgot" claims—to suggest that atrocity stories were being made up on the spot. The clip didn't "prove" that point, but Camil's unpersuasive descent into the fog of memory served Sherwood's purposes well. Sherwood sought to thoroughly discredit the WSI, because in doing so, he would also discredit Kerry's appearance at the WSI and his use of the testimony he heard. Was the testimony falsely given?

Many on the right believed it was. But the right had seized on an even more powerful argument. Those who testified were not only lying, they were frauds. *Stolen Honor* claimed that "many" of the "so-called Vietnam Veterans Against the War . . . would later be discovered as frauds, men who had never set foot on the battlefield, or left the comforts of home, or even served in uniform except in mock contempt of the military. Their lurid fantasies of butchery in Vietnam were seized upon by John Kerry to help him organize the so-called Winter Soldier's Investigation." It was an extravagant claim, but one widely believed on the right. "The entire Winter Soldier investigation was a lie," wrote Vietnam veteran and conservative columnist Mackubin Thomas Owens. Another website referred to those testifying as "150 pseudo-soldiers," and another asserted that *Winter Soldier* was a "docu-fraud," and had been "thoroughly debunked."[5]

At a showing of *Winter Soldier* in Newark, Delaware, in 2005, one protestor held up a sign in the parking lot claiming that the film was a lie, another brandished a copy of *Stolen Honor* during the question and answer period as if in refutation of the evening's speaker. That speaker was Ken Campbell, a professor of political science at the University of Delaware. Although his hair was thinner and his face older, he was still recognizable as the young veteran with flowing blond hair asking Camil about that atrocity in Quang Tri. Sherwood's editing of that scene, preceded by the claim that "many" VVAW members were frauds, infuriated Campbell. He filed suit against Sherwood for libel.

Though libel is notoriously difficult to prove, Sherwood took the suit seriously, raising money for his defense on the website of the SBVT who were his allies in the 2004 attacks on John Kerry. The suit, initially scheduled for trial in Philadelphia's Court of Common Pleas in the fall of 2006, was post-poned until September 2007. But in July 2006, Campbell withdrew his suit, under circumstances that led to substantial gloating on the part of Sher-wood and his supporters. We'll return to that. But first, the question before us is this: Were "many" VVAW members frauds? Were those who testified to "lurid fantasies of butchery in Vietnam" men who never served in Vietnam? That is the simple and narrow question we will take up first, bracketing for the moment the question of the "truth" of the Winter Soldiers' testimony.[6]

There was at least one fraud. This was Al Hubbard. Hubbard, an African American from Brooklyn, joined VVAW in 1969 and rose to a position of leadership. He was a popular, charismatic, and effective leader. He organized

"Operation Raw," a bizarre, rag-tag march of veterans with plastic M-16s, acting out American "war crimes," on a route, paralleling George Washington's retreat in 1776 from Morristown, New Jersey, to Valley Forge, Pennsylvania. The march ended on Labor Day 1970 in Valley Forge. The speakers that day were Jane Fonda; Donald Sutherland (Fonda's co-star in *Klute*), Mark Lane, the conspiracy theorist and Fonda's new confidant; and a then unknown navy veteran named John Kerry, who according to one observer that day, "looks like Lincoln, and sounds like . . . Kennedy. . . . Get him on the road!"[7]

Kerry and Hubbard became the face of the VVAW. "Operation Raw" had captured press attention, and "Dewey Canyon III" in April 1971—the VVAW's Washington protest marked by the powerful symbolism of hundreds of veterans throwing the medals they earned in Vietnam onto the west lawn of the Capitol—would capture the nation's attention. It would establish the political career of John Kerry, and tarnish the reputation of Al Hubbard.[8]

Hubbard and Kerry had been invited on Lawrence Spivak's *Meet the Press* on April 21, 1971 (see cover image). Spivak introduced Hubbard as an air force captain who had spent two years in Vietnam, was decorated and injured. He had told a reporter a week earlier that he "had caught some shrapnel in the spine" on a flight into Danang in 1966. He would tell another writer that he had flown on American planes bringing supplies to the "beleaguered French" in Vietnam in the 1950s. His moment of fame lasted barely a day. Hubbard had never been an officer, only a staff sergeant (E-5). Two weeks later, the air force revealed the outline of his service record. He had served from October 1952 to October 1966. He had reenlisted twice and was honorably discharged. He had received seven service or achievement medals. He added two other ribbons for his appearance on *Meet the Press*. But there was no record of his service in Vietnam. He had never been awarded the Vietnam Service Medal, for which he would have been eligible, even if his "service" in Vietnam consisted only of occasional flights in and out. There was no record of a Purple Heart or of a hospital stay in Danang. Hubbard did have an extensive medical record and a confirmed 60 percent disability. The air force rightly maintained that the details of his medical records were confidential. Hubbard refused a reporter's request to explain his disability.[9]

Despite his lies, Hubbard remained highly visible in VVAW. He had his defenders within the organization. He traveled to Hanoi with Pete Seeger, championed direct actions like the takeover of the Statue of Liberty in December 1971 and a botched attempt to scale the UN Secretariat Building.

He wrote the "Preface" to Beacon Press's *The Winter Soldier Investigation*, explaining how it was that American war crimes in Vietnam were the "inevitable" result of American policy, but wisely chose to offer no first-hand accounts. He also offered an overwrought poem, reflecting the testimony he had heard at the WSI—"daughters spread-eagled/and/mothers on the run./Reflect./See what you've become,/Amerika." However, he never testified at the WSI. Whatever his lies, he never offered his own testimony to witnessed butchery.[10]

The claim that "many" of those who did testify were frauds had its origins in Guenter Lewy's *America in Vietnam*, a reasoned defense of the war that at times reads like a legal brief, but cannot be dismissed as mere polemic. It was Lewy who first revealed that the Naval Investigative Service (NIS) discovered that "several veterans" who testified at the WSI issued "sworn statements . . . corroborated by witnesses that they had in fact not attended the hearing in Detroit." Lewy went on: "One of them had never been to Detroit in all his life. He did not know, he said, who might have used his name." Lewy made his case in three sentences and did not elaborate. The endnote reference reads simply "Office of the Director, Judge Advocate Division, Headquarters USMC, Winter Soldier Investigation files." Lewy did not mention the names of those who claimed not to be there, and to the best of my knowledge, none have ever been publicly identified. When right-wing blogs refer to those who testified at the WSI as "pseudo-soldiers," this is their sole evidence. The navy had authority, however, only over those members of the navy or Marines who testified. Of the 118 veterans who testified at the WSI, 38 fell under the authority of the navy.[11]

To my knowledge, Lewy's evidence has never been used by another scholar, and now, further complicating matters, the Naval Criminal Investigative Service (NCIS), successor to the NIS, has publicly said that they no longer can find the file. Lewy made matters worse by telling a reporter from the *Baltimore Sun* that he did not recall whether he had actually seen a report or whether someone had told him of the report. In a more recent phone conversation, Lewy was emphatic that he had seen such a report and dismissed the *Sun*'s claim with a comment to the effect, well, you know how reporters are. He then read to me from his notes on the NIS investigation and told me that there were eight men that the navy had determined were represented by fake witnesses. He had his notes close at hand, in preparation for a lawsuit on which he understandably chose not to elaborate. He told me their names.[12]

Two of those Lewy named, however, never testified at the WSI, one of whom was an army officer active in the antiwar movement but in no way subject to navy oversight. Of the six names remaining, I have uncovered decisive evidence about three. One of the men on Lewy's list was a Marine pilot named Randy Floyd. Randy Floyd testified at the WSI, and also testified along with Ken Campbell at the Dellums Committee Hearings in Washington. He accompanied Campbell to testify at the International War Crimes Tribunal in Oslo, and made an impressively articulate appearance in the film *Hearts and Minds*. Ken Campbell sent me a copy of a photograph of him and Floyd sitting on the front porch of Campbell's Philadelphia house in the early 1970s, looking identical to the man who appeared in *Hearts and Minds*. Campbell had no doubt that the real Randy Floyd participated in the WSI, nor should we.[13]

Another veteran on Lewy's list was Paul Olimpieri. I've spoken to Olimpieri, who now lives in Las Vegas. He served as a corporal in Delta Company, 1st Battalion, 5th Marines in 1967–1968. He confirmed to me that he testified at the WSI—"it was the best thing I ever did in my life," he said. A member of his squad, Sergeant Fred Nienke, who also testified at the WSI, witnessed his presence. Nienke told me he was surprised to see him. Recently retired from the Fish and Wildlife Service, Nienke lives in Ellinwood, Kansas, and confirmed to me that the "real" Paul Olimpieri testified in Detroit.[14]

A third Marine on Lewy's list was LCpl Thomas J. Heidtman who served with the 3rd Battalion, 5th Marines from October 1966 to November 1967. Heidtman now lives in Chelsea, Michigan. He was a student at Wayne State when he learned of the WSI. He told me he arrived too late for the first panel, but testified on a subsequent one and later appeared, with Mark Lane, on a local television show hosted by Lou Gordon. He was there in Detroit.[15]

Had the navy thoroughly botched the investigation? Had Lewy misinterpreted what he had either read or heard? Or did Winter Soldiers, intimidated by the presence of military investigators, decide to lie about their presence in Detroit? Three antiwar veterans I've spoken to recalled the intimidating presence of investigators. But when I asked Olimpieri and Heidtman directly if they told the investigators that they had not testified in Detroit, they told me no. They admitted to being there, and Floyd, whom I've not found, had become a public figure. So we are left with no coherent explanation of how the navy, or Lewy, at least in five of the eight "cases," got it wrong, but we know enough to shine a harsh light on the right's irresponsible claims of fraud.[16]

Floyd, Olimpieri, and Heidtman testified at the WSI. But to complicate the matter further, navy investigators, who had authority over Marine criminal investigations, may have had reason to doubt Olimpieri's sincerity. After returning from Vietnam, Olimpieri was assigned to the Quonset Point Naval Air Station in Rhode Island. At the end of August 1968, he went AWOL, and on September 22, under the auspices of the New England Resistance, he took "sanctuary" in the Andover Hall Chapel at the Harvard Divinity School. A twice-wounded veteran of the war, he was a special prize of the left, claiming he had been "brainwashed" by the Marines.[17]

The medieval notion of "sanctuary" did not prevent the navy from removing him from Harvard two days later, before he would have been officially listed as a deserter. Within twelve hours of his removal, however, he held a press conference at the Charlestown Navy Yard to claim they he had made a "mistake" and had been "used" by the left. He told reporters that the press conference was his idea, not the Marines', and that he wrote his own statement. His rapid reconversion led one antiwar veteran to claim that he, along with a fellow Marine who made a similar reconversion, had been Marine "plants."[18]

It was Olimpieri who told me of his bid for "sanctuary." But he did not tell me of the press conference and he did not know of the allegations that he was a "plant." In a troubled tone, he told me that despite the Marines' efforts to get him to do so, he never repudiated the New England Resistance. His "mistake," he explained, was to be drawn in by groups like Students for a Democratic Society "who's [sic] agenda was not just to end the war." "I was not a plant or anti-American," he wrote to me, "just a confused kid who witnessed the horrors of war." He later joined VVAW, coordinated its Connecticut-Rhode Island chapter, and testified at the WSI.[19]

Stolen Honor's extravagant assault on those who testified—recall the words: "many" of the "so-called Vietnam Veterans Against the War . . . would later be discovered to be frauds, men who never set foot on the battlefield, or left the comforts of home"—rests on a document that cannot now be found, that may not have existed, but if it existed, implicated only eight men, only six of whom were subject to the navy's authority—and three of those six were not frauds.

The case that "many" of those who testified at the WSI were frauds was itself a fraud, though there was a case that many of those who later joined

VVAW were neither veterans nor were they truly against the war. By the fall of 1971, VVAW was being infiltrated by members of the Progressive Labor Party, the Socialist Workers Party, the Student Mobilization Committee, and FBI informants. The most insidious of the far-left groups was the Maoist Progressive Labor, soon to become the Revolutionary Union and later the Revolutionary Communist Party (RCP), all under the leadership of Bob Avakian. When Saigon fell in 1975, it was hard for some of the non-veteran leadership of VVAW to understand why some of the dwindling numbers of actual veterans still in their ranks were not in a celebratory mood. It wasn't until the late 1970s that the RCP was finally driven from the organization and forced, after a lawsuit, to identify themselves as VVAW-AI (the AI standing for Anti-Imperialist). But the VVAW's flirtation with the far left was a more complicated story than that of phony veterans.[20]

The SBVT and their allies who vehemently opposed John Kerry in 2004 had all the evidence they needed in Kerry's public remarks, in his visit with Viet Cong (VC) representatives in Paris, in his confusing comments about whether he had thrown his own medals away—and why they had later appeared on the wall of his Senate office—in his conflicting statements about whether he still believed the atrocity tales of the WSI, and in his own political use of his Vietnam service and his war memories. But, not content with those stories, and against the advice of a prominent Republican PR specialist, they elected to attack his military service, claiming that his medals were as fraudulent as the "phony" veterans of the WSI. It was a decision that would make the term "swift-boating" a synonym, for many, of ugly, unprincipled slander.[21]

Who was John Kerry?

Kerry was a child of privilege, though no one since the late J. P. Marquand could precisely calibrate his family's place in New England society. His grandfather was a Jewish immigrant who converted to Catholicism and killed himself in Boston's Copley Plaza Hotel in 1921; his father graduated from Yale and Harvard Law and married into the pedigreed Forbes family. His father found a career in the State Department, and though the family was never rich, young John was schooled in Switzerland, later at St. Paul's and Yale. Kerry emerged as a leader at Yale, president of the Yale Political Union and a serious ice hockey and soccer player. Graduating in 1966, he could have avoided military service altogether by enrolling in graduate school and he considered it. Learning from his draft board that he was likely to be called, he signed up for Navy Officer Candidate School. Despite his growing misgivings about the Vietnam War, articulated in his commencement speech, "an excess of interventionism," he carefully called it, he would honor his decision. In a sense it was foreordained. Never a radical, Kerry had basked in the brief attentions of John Kennedy; listened attentively as William Bundy, sitting in his Yale rooms, urged him to serve; and joined three of his best friends, among them Dick Pershing (grandson of the WWI general, "Black Jack") in service to his country.[22]

Commissioned an ensign in Newport, Rhode Island, in late 1966, Kerry served as an officer of the line for a year on the USS *Gridley*, a guided missile frigate assigned to the Tonkin Gulf. On the *Gridley* he would learn of the death of Dick Pershing, a platoon leader in the 101st Airborne. Toward the end of his sea tour in early 1968, Kerry volunteered for Swift boat (Shallow Water Inshore Fast Tactical Craft) duty. The Swifts were small, fast, and lightly armored boats that had been newly developed and initially deployed for coastal patrolling. Though Kerry's campaign biographer, Douglas Brinkley, attempted to present this as high risk duty—"You had to be a bit of a cowboy to want a Swift," Brinkley quoted one of Kerry's peers, "It meant that you were willing to get shot up all the time," Kerry saw it differently. He understood the Swifts' mission as coastal patrolling—"Although I wanted to see for myself what was going on, I didn't really want to get involved in the war." It wasn't to be. After training in San Diego, he arrived in Vietnam in mid-November 1968. The Swifts' mission had changed. They now were to be deployed in the far more dangerous work of patrolling the brown waters of Vietnam's rivers.[23]

The decision to send the Swifts up the rivers was Elmo R. Zumwalt's. Pro-moted to vice admiral, Zumwalt took command of all navy forces in country in 1968 and sought to increase the navy's tactical responsibilities. There would be a cost. Zumwalt later wrote that the monthly casualty rate for river patrol crews was 6 percent. Sailors serving for a year in the brown-water navy thus faced a considerable risk of being killed or wounded.[24]

Lieutenant (junior grade) Kerry arrived in Vietnam in November 1968 and was assigned to Coastal Division 14 on the southern end of the vast American base at Cam Ranh Bay. On December 2 Kerry went on his first patrol in a small boat, a skimmer—the military equivalent of a Boston whaler—on a river near Cam Ranh Bay. He observed a number of sampans crossing the river at a point known to be used by the VC. Firing a flare, he saw a number of men running for cover. He opened fire. According to the account he offered Douglas Brinkley: "My M-16 jammed, and as I bent down . . . to grab another gun, a stinging piece of heat socked into my arm." He would be awarded his first Purple Heart.[25]

He was accompanied that night by two sailors, William Zaladonis and Patrick Runyon, both of whom have consistently confirmed the essential outlines of the story, but neither of whom could say for certain whether they had been fired upon. They did not doubt that Kerry had been wounded. They saw his wound, but they were too busy—Runyon on the engine, Zaladonis on the M-60—to be sure of enemy fire.[26]

His commanding officer (CO) at the time, George Hibbard, interviewed for the *Boston Globe* book, recalls being initially skeptical—Kerry's wound was slight and Hibbard wasn't convinced his boat had come under attack. The first objection is irrelevant—a wound is a wound, as long as it requires medical treatment. The second is critical—accidents and "friendly fire" wounds do not qualify for the award of a Purple Heart. On May 4, 2004, Hibbard, in a report carried on NewsMax, had now become certain that there had been "no enemy fire," that Kerry had probably been wounded by his own M-79 ricochet (the first mention of an M-79), and that he received "no medical treatment." The latter is false. Kerry reported to the infirmary and was treated, and that record survives. The first attack ad from the SBVT contains the following quote from Dr. Louis Letson: "I know John Kerry is lying about his first Purple Heart, because I treated him for that injury." Letson explained that "Some of his crew confided that they did not receive any fire from the shore, but that Kerry had fired a mortar round at close range to some rocks on shore" and believed that was the cause of Kerry's injury. Small boats are not platforms for mortars, and Letson's memory and the memory of Kerry's crewmen are at odds. Letson's name, moreover, was not on Kerry's treatment record, that of J. C. Carreon was. Hibbard recalls that he washed his hands of it: "if that's what happened . . . do whatever you want. After that I don't know what happened. Obviously, he got it. I don't know how." But you can't nominate yourself for a medal. The normal path for such a nomination proceeds through the CO. In fairness Hibbard was Kerry's CO for only two weeks, long enough however to do a brief fitness report giving Kerry the highest ranking for initiative, cooperation, and bearing. Hibbard was a member of SBVT. Wesley Clark cut to the heart of this—Hibbard's standard of judgment was now political and not military. Hibbard's politics appear to have trumped his memory. So did Kerry legitimately earn a Purple Heart that evening? Short of new evidence, we can't be sure, but Letson's harsh claim that Kerry lied is contradicted by the memories of Kerry's crew. The navy stood by its award.[27]

But the story would not die. In late August it gained new life when retired ADM William Schachte told Lisa Myers of NBC News that he was on the boat that night with Kerry and a sailor whose name he no longer recalled. Schachte offered detailed evidence. The skimmer missions were his idea; two officers and an enlisted engineman were the standard crew; he would never have assigned an inexperienced officer, which Kerry was, to lead such a mission; he had personally led nine such missions—and they received no enemy fire that night; there was no written after-action report that would have been required had they been fired upon. Kerry's wound was accidentally self-inflicted, Schachte claimed, the result of an apparent ricochet from an M-79 grenade launcher that Kerry had fired, though this was the least detailed and specific of his memories of that night. Schachte came across as a serious man, wholly convinced of his memory. He claimed no political motive, he was "non-partisan," he said, nor had he joined the SBVT, though he supported their cause. He had decided to speak out only after the publication of the Brinkley book. He was there. Brinkley got it wrong. He never mentioned the *Boston Globe* book or the fact of having been contacted twice by *Globe* reporters, telling one reporter in 2003 that Kerry's wound was "not very serious," and another in 2004 that he had no further comment, passing up the opportunity both times to tell a contrary story that they would have been forced to investigate further. It would later come out that his contributions to the Republican Party far outmatched his contributions to the Democrats.[28]

William Zaladonis and Pat Runyon stuck to their story. And Zaladonis's appearance on NBC was just as persuasive as Schachte's. Oh, he didn't have the detailed precision of Schachte—the dates, the mission orders—but that was in its own way authentic. "I don't know the dates," he said, "I had no reason to pay attention to dates—the only one I was worried about was August 26, 1969," his DEROS (date eligible to return from overseas)—a date burned into the memory of every Vietnam veteran. But he remembered the mission. It was the only such mission he had ever gone on, and he and his friend Runyon had talked about it frequently—"it was one of the scariest nights of my life," he said. He couldn't see how Kerry's wound could have been self-inflicted. He was "absolutely positive" that Schachte was not there that night, and he offered a reasonable explanation for what he believed was Schachte's mistaken memory—that Schachte had gone on several such missions and he'd mixed them up. Zaladonis had only one mission to remember.[29]

How to conclude? They can't both be right, though they both could be wrong. But it comes down to Schachte's word against that of three men. Add in the inescapable "political" meaning of Schachte coming forward in the last weeks of a national election. Add in that if Zaladonis and Runyon were lying, as some right-wingers claimed, why didn't they go the whole hog and say yes, I'm positive we were fired on that night? They didn't, and that adds to their credibility. Their memories deserve to hang more heavily on the scales of justice than Schachte's. But we are still left with an uncomfortable truth, that we have only the word of John Kerry that his sliver of a wound that night was the result of enemy fire.

On February 20 Kerry was wounded a second time. By then, he had become the skipper of his own Swift, PCF-94, and its five-man crew. PCF-94's former skipper, Tedd Peck, had been badly wounded by machine-gun fire, on January 29. Kerry was hit in the leg with a piece of shrapnel from a rocket-propelled grenade. He was treated, X-rayed, and returned to duty immediately. The SBVT never challenged the authenticity of the wound. But Kerry's next three medals were the subject of sweeping and sustained and unprecedented attack. It is likely that these three awards were more widely written about, and more intensively scrutinized, than that of any other medals from any other war.[30]

On February 28 Kerry led a three-boat mission, transporting a platoon of South Vietnamese Popular Force (PF) troops, along with a squad of American explosives experts, to the Dong Cung River. They took small-arms fire from one of the banks. Kerry ordered the Swifts directly into the fire, and they killed one VC. While the PFs searched the area, Kerry took his boat upriver. They took fire again, this time from a B-40 rocket. Again, Kerry ordered the boat into the line of fire, beached it, jumped off the boat—a violation of the navy's blue-water standard operating procedure—and chased and killed a wounded VC soldier who had a B-40 rocket launcher in his hands. A B-40 rocket is a devastating weapon fully capable of sinking a Swift boat and killing or maiming its crew. The after-action report indicates that Kerry's crew returned with the weapon and its attached round, along with other captured weapons, that nine VC had been killed, and that an enemy rest and supply area had been destroyed. For his boldness that day, Kerry earned the Silver Star for "conspicuous gallantry and intrepidity," the nation's third highest award for valor.[31]

The award went unquestioned until 1996 when, in the midst of Kerry's senatorial reelection campaign, David Warsh of the *Boston Globe* strung together two apparent facts, that the VC was wounded and that he sought cover behind a hut, to suggest: "What's the ugliest possibility? That behind the hootch Kerry administered a coup de grace to the Vietnamese soldier—a practice not uncommon in those days but a war crime nevertheless." It was all irresponsible speculation. Kerry reacted angrily. The late ADM Elmo R. Zumwalt Jr., commander of navy forces in the Republic of Vietnam, and who personally awarded Kerry's Silver Star, appeared with Kerry at the Charlestown Navy Yard, along with some of Kerry's crewmates, labeling the article "a terrible insult . . . an absolutely outrageous interpretation of the facts." Kerry's immediate boss at the time was then-LCDR George Elliott. It was Elliott who recommended him for the Silver Star and he traveled from Delaware to speak in his defense that day: "The fact that he chased an armed enemy down is something not to be looked down upon, but it was an act of courage." Interviewed for the *Boston Globe* book, Elliott is quoted as thinking the Silver Star was "well deserved" and that he never questioned Kerry's decision.[32]

The same George Elliott later surfaced in the first Swift Boat ad: "John Kerry has not been honest about what happened in Vietnam." He expanded on his comment in a sworn statement. Kerry did not deserve the Silver Star, Elliott wrote—"I was never informed that he had simply shot a wounded, fleeing VC in the back." But that was precisely David Warsh's claim in 1996, a claim Elliott had publicly denied. Contacted by the *Globe* shortly after, he recanted: "I still don't think he shot the guy in the back. It was a terrible mistake probably for me to sign the affidavit with those words. I'm the one in trouble here." On the same day, the SBVT claimed the *Globe* had misquoted Elliott and released Elliott's second affidavit, reaffirming his first: "Had I known the facts, I would not have recommended Kerry for the Silver Star." The Globe stood by its story. The SBVT stood by theirs. Elliott admitted, not to changing his mind on Kerry's medal three times, but only being a "little naïve" in dealing with the *Globe* reporter. Elliott's bizarre inconsistencies simply underscore the false and fragile case against Kerry's medals.[33]

The SBVT and their allies couldn't let it go. John O'Neill and Jerome Corsi tried to demean Kerry's award; his action of turning his boats into the direction of fire was not spontaneous, but preplanned; Kerry never reported that the fleeing VC was wounded or wearing only a loin cloth; beaching his boat was not an act of courage, but an act of "stupidity"; the citation's reference to Kerry attacking "a numerically superior force in the face of intense fire" was false; and his recommendation of the Silver Star, had it been "reviewed through normal channels," would never have been honored. ADM Roy Hoffman, then a commander and George Elliott's CO, was "shocked" to later find out that "Kerry had beached his boat . . . in a preplanned operation, and that he had killed a single, wounded teenage foe as he fled." Kerry simply didn't deserve the Silver Star. In their zeal to deny Kerry's courage, Elliott and Hoffman, if they were telling the truth, were confessing to their own faults, their own lack of oversight of the navy's award system.[34]

Whether an act of courage was preplanned or spontaneous is irrelevant; the citation simply says that Kerry acted "unhesitatingly." There is no contemporary evidence about the age or dress of the enemy combatant Kerry killed. William Rood, who skippered PCF-23 that day—one of the boats under Kerry's command—would write that he and another witness, Jerry Leeds, had no idea how old the VC was, but that both recalled him as a grown man dressed in standard VC garb, nor could he and Leeds confirm that the VC was wounded. Rood provided a photograph of Kerry with that captured B-40 rocket launcher on his shoulder. And, of course, no bluewater skipper would beach and exit his ship, except at the risk of court-martial, but the brown-water war was different, and finally, Corsi's claim that the citation was false, in its claims of a "numerically" superior enemy force, is itself false. O'Neill would expand on the falsehood. Elliott, Hoffman, Corsi, and other Kerry detractors chose to focus only on Kerry's solitary act. But a cursory reading of Kerry's Silver Star citation makes clear that his award was for the totality of his actions that day: "as Officer in Tactical Command of a three-boat mission . . . as all units came under intense automatic weapons and small-arms fire from an entrenched enemy force less than fifty feet away. . . . KERRY ordered his boat to attack as all units opened fire and beached directly in front of the enemy ambushers." The award went on to indicate correctly that the "PCF gunners captured many enemy weapons," and then noted Kerry's second "charge on the enemy" and his "leading" of a landing party. The award never mentioned his killing of an enemy soldier. "The extraordinary daring and personal courage of Lieutenant (junior grade) KERRY in attacking a numerically superior enemy force in the face of intense fire were responsible for the highly successful mission." The emphasis belongs on "mission," and it is common that the mission's commander, because of the responsibility he bears, will be given a higher award than those whom he commanded. The attack on Kerry's Silver Star may best be understood, in the words of John McCain, as "dishonest and dishonorable."[35]

The attack on Kerry's final medals was no more convincing. On March 13, 1969, Kerry earned his third Purple Heart and his second valor award, a Bronze Star with V device. He had pulled a Green Beret lieutenant, James Rassmann, from the Bay Hap River after an explosion blew him off Kerry's PCF-94. Rassmann had made a surprise appearance at a Kerry rally in Iowa in January 2004. It was the first time they had seen each other since the war. "He pulled me over" [the bow of the boat], Rassmann said. "He [Kerry] could have been shot at any time. . . . I owe him my life." It was a great story and captured the attention of the press and public. A few days later Kerry won the Iowa primary. The SBVT would later claim that Rassmann was mistaken, derisively labeling his memory, in a bizarre reference to Salman Rushdie, the "Rasmannic verses" and asserting that neither Kerry's boat nor Rassmann were under fire that day.[36]

Kerry's mission that day was to deliver a squad of Nung (Chinese Vietnamese) mercenaries to suspected VC villages off the Dong Cung Canal. One of the Nung died after tripping a booby trap. Kerry helped to carry the body back to the boat. While on shore, he and Rassmann decided to blow up a cache of rice, tossing grenades into it. Kerry did not move away quickly enough. "He got some frags and pieces of rice in his rear end," Rassmann recalled, "it was more embarrassing than painful."[37]

Kerry continued the mission, joined by four other Swift boats. Kerry's and Don Droz's boat, PCF-43, were on the right side of the Bay Hap. The other three boats were on the left. As they approached a fishing weir, an explosion lifted PCF-3, Richard Pees' boat, out of the water. Larry Thurlow's PCF-51 went to PCF-3's rescue. Kerry's boat sped away. The Swift boaters would claim cowardice. Kerry, according to Brinkley, recalled that he sought to get his Nungs ashore on the "outskirts of the ambush."

Then Kerry's boat was hit, by either a mine or more likely, according to Kerry's helmsman, Del Sandusky, an RPG. Rassmann fell overboard while Kerry was slammed into a bulkhead, injuring his right forearm. Rassmann, concerned that he would be hit by one of the Swifts, swam to the bottom of the river. Returning to the surface, he recalled that the Swifts were gone; he was "alone taking fire from both banks." He "repeatedly swam under water as long as he could" as he tried to make his way to the river bank, fearful of being shot in the water, or captured on land. But then Kerry rescued him.[38]

Thurlow, Pees, and Jack Chenoweth, skipper of PCF-23, the fifth boat on the river, all members of SBVT, deny that there was any enemy small-arms fire that day or that there was a second explosion. Chenoweth claimed: "There wasn't any fire." Thurlow, who appeared on *Hardball,* would claim that Kerry had a "master plan" to "engineer" his war record, and insisted that they were not under fire. Thurlow was also awarded a Bronze Star for Valor that day, and, undermining his 2004 memory, his citation notes that there was small-arms fire that day. That was also confirmed by a member of Thurlow's crew, Robert Lambert, who was also awarded a Bronze Star for Valor for, in his words, "pulling Lieutenant Thurlow out of the river while we were under fire." Wayne D. Langhofer, the gunner on PCF-43, also confirmed it. He remembered the "clack, clack, clack" of enemy AK-47-fire that day. AK-47s, when fired at you, make a distinctive and unmistakable noise. No veteran is likely to forget it. The onomatopoeic "clack" or "crack" gets it just about right. Kerry's crew also claimed they were under fire, and so too did Rassmann, the Green Beret officer: "No one can tell me that we were not under fire. I saw it. I heard the splashes, and I was scared to death. For them to come back 35 years after the fact to tarnish not only Kerry's record, but my veracity, is unconscionable."[39]

But the Swift boaters continued to insist on their truth. They claimed Kerry wrote the after-action report—that was why Thurlow's citation mentioned small-arms fire. But Kerry had no direct knowledge of what Thurlow was up to—Robert Lambert was the chief witness to Thurlow's bravery that day. In the end, there was no proof that Kerry authored the after-action report, though he may have. It was not signed. Then they seized on Kerry's self-inflicted wound to the buttocks, mentioned in Kerry's medical treatment report. If they could claim that there had been no second explosion, thus no injury to Kerry—also mentioned in the medical report—induced by enemy fire, they could also claim that Kerry's third Purple Heart was fraudulent, and they did. But Kerry's crew and Rassmann attested to the explosion, and Kerry did receive a third Purple Heart, not for the wounds in his buttocks, but for the injury to his arm. Those who are injured as the result of enemy fire are eligible for the Purple Heart, just as those who were wounded are.[40]

After his third Purple Heart, Kerry returned to the United States to a plum job as an admiral's aide in Brooklyn. The circumstances of his departure from Vietnam have been the subject of sharp criticism. Roy Hoffman would later reflect derisively: "He just simply bugged out, and any military man knows what I'm talking about." But navy regulations are clear and explicit. Three wounds are a ticket home. It is the case, however, that Kerry could have requested a waiver, likely quickly granted, and remained in Vietnam. If he was deeply troubled to leave his crew and peers behind, as he later claimed, he moved with great dispatch in requesting reassignment. Only four days separated his wounding from his written request to leave Vietnam.[41]

While Kerry served as an admiral's aide, he took his first steps into the antiwar movement. He had learned to fly at Yale, and volunteered to fly Adam Walinsky, the former speechwriter for Robert Kennedy, around New York state to deliver antiwar talks. He remained in the navy for nine months after returning from Vietnam, and in January 1970 he requested to be discharged early in order to run for Congress against Philip Philbin, a Democrat and a supporter of the war, in Massachusetts. His request was granted. But the then far better known Robert Drinan, a Jesuit priest and former law-school dean and provost at Boston College, became the antiwar challenger to Philbin. In a caucus leading to the primary, Kerry gracefully withdrew and went on to co-chair Drinan's successful campaign.[42]

It was in that role that he first came to the attention of VVAW, a then small and obscure group founded in June 1967 in the Lower East Side New York apartment of Jan Barry Crumb, later known as Jan Barry. Kerry joined VVAW in the summer of 1970. His first appearance on its behalf was on Labor Day of that year at Valley Forge, though an earlier appearance on the *The Dick Cavett Show* gave him his first national audience. Then came the WSI, Dewey Canyon III, *Meet the Press,* testimony before the Senate Foreign Relations Committee, and the powerful scene of scores of veterans, some in anger, some in tears, throwing their medals away.[43]

In a televised interview in the fall of 1971, Kerry explained why the vets had thrown their medals back. They had decided that they would, in protest of the war, "renounce the symbols which this country gives, which supposedly reinforces all the things that they have done, and that was the medals themselves." In response to the question, "How many did you give back, John?" he responded, "I gave back, I can't remember, six, seven, eight, nine." The interviewer mentioned his two valor medals, and his three Purple Hearts. Kerry said: "Well, and above that, I gave back my others." The context clearly suggests that he gave back his medals. But in 1984, while running for the Senate, he showed a reporter a display of his medals in his Back Bay apartment, telling the reporter "he had disagreed with other protest leaders on throwing away medals"—thus contradicting his 1971 account. The medals he had thrown that day were those of a veteran from Lincoln, Massachusetts, at the unnamed veteran's request. Then, during his 1996 reelection campaign, he admitted to throwing his ribbons away, not his medals, and recalled that he also threw away the medals of a New York veteran, in addition to those of the veteran from Lincoln. He could not recall their names. Fair enough. Conservatives would later seize on this story as an example of Kerry's dishonesty—Kerry would claim that there was no distinction between "medals' and "ribbons," and the Kerry campaign website would claim that it was a "right-wing fiction" that he ever threw away his medals, but it seems clear that he had created the confusion himself.[44]

So why does this matter? A word on nomenclature: medals are appended to triangular pieces of cloth and they are worn only rarely and only on occasions of high ceremony. Ribbons are worn on all Class A uniforms, the equivalent of suit and tie business attire. Their color and pattern are identical to the medals they represent. Medals for individual achievement, service, or valor are worn over the heart in specified order, the most important closest to the heart. The military has its own self-deprecating humor about this—an impressive array of ribbons is known as "fruit salad." Most of these ribbons simply represent being there. Men and women who care about this, however, know where to look and know what matters: the small and rare pale-blue ribbon with white stars of the Medal of Honor; the blue and gold of the Navy Cross; the red, white and blue of its army equivalent; the poorly named Distinguished Service Cross; the Silver Star; the red and blue Bronze Star with V clip, signifying valor (without the clip, it is simply a medal for achievement). When Kerry testified before Congress he wore his ribbons— inappropriately—on a navy utility shirt, but in the right order, his Silver Star at the top right.[45]

Medals matter to those who served and to those who respect valor and service. Recall the suicide of the navy's Chief of Naval Operations, Jeremy Michael Boorda, in 1996, after it was revealed that he had worn V clips— signifying personal acts of valor—that he had not earned, on two achievement medals. But Kerry's critics tied themselves in semantics, and missed the larger meaning of the story. Kerry's act in 1971 was a bold and authentic one, utterly compromised by the later display of his medals both in his apartment, and, according to a later report, in his Senate office. I'm reminded of the story of Angelo Liteky, then a Catholic priest, who earned the Congressional

Medal of Honor for his selfless bravery in tending the wounded while under fire in Vietnam. Outraged by the Reagan administration's support for the Contras in Nicaragua, and especially by the murder of nuns, Liteky packed up his Medal of Honor and returned it to the White House—it would never appear on a wall in his home or office.[46]

Kerry's words before the Senate Foreign Relations Committee the day before would earn him even more enmity. Kerry opened his prepared remarks by embracing the findings of the WSI. American war crimes in Vietnam, he said, "were not isolated instances but crimes committed on a day-to-day basis with the full awareness of officers at all levels of command." The Winter Soldier vets, he went on, "told stories that at times they had personally raped, cut off ears, cut off heads, taped wires from portable telephones to human genitals and turned up the power, cut off limbs, blown up bodies, randomly shot at civilians, razed villages in a fashion reminiscent of Genghis Khan, shot cattle and dogs for fun, and generally ravaged the countryside of South Vietnam." Though he had much else to say that morning that no one has questioned ("where are McNamara, Rostow, Bundy . . . now? These are the commanders who have deserted their troops. And there is no more serious crime in the laws of war."), many veterans have chosen to focus on his "slandering" of them and of the vast majority of veterans they believed to have committed no crimes.[47]

In 1971 Kerry admitted that he too had committed atrocities. Crosby Noyes of the *Washington Evening Star* asked the following: "Mr. Kerry you said that . . . you think our policies in Vietnam are tantamount to genocide. . . . Do you consider that you personally . . . committed atrocities in Vietnam or crimes punishable by law in this country?" Kerry answered: "Yes, I committed the same kind of atrocities as thousands of other soldiers in that I took part in shootings in free fire zones. I conducted H&I [Harassment and Interdiction fire]. I used .50-caliber machine guns . . . which were our only weapon against people. I took part in search and destroy missions, in the burning of villages. All this is contrary to the laws of warfare . . . contrary to the Geneva Conventions." Moreover, Kerry went on, all those who designed the policies of free-fire zones and who ordered such missions were "war criminals."[48]

When confronted by these words on *Meet the Press* in 2004 and asked whether he still stood by them, he responded: "I don't stand by the genocide. I think those were the words of an angry young man." Fair enough. Kerry went on: "The words were honest, but on the other hand, they were a little bit over the top." Not wrong, just "over the top." On the question of war criminals, Kerry responded neither to affirm nor deny: "I don't even believe there is a purpose served in the words 'war criminal.' I really don't." This was the sort of evasive performance all too typical of Kerry. Were atrocities pervasive or not? Were there war criminals?[49]

No one either then or now challenged Kerry's 1971 understanding of the laws of war. We may rightly regard some or all of the "atrocities" he enumerated as evil, though none of them violated the Geneva Conventions. Indeed, the claims that the use of .50-caliber machine guns or that H&I fire in themselves violated the laws of war were not simply wrong, but egregiously wrong.[50]

In a later interview on the subject he would sum up by saying, "I think our soldiers served as nobly, on the whole, as in any war." There may not be an actual contradiction between his 2004 belief that Vietnam vets "served as nobly . . . as in any war," and his 1971 testimony that atrocities were not isolated instances, but daily realities, but it is not at all obvious how such statements can be reconciled. Tim Russert further challenged him in 2004 when Russert claimed "that a lot of those stories [told at the WSI] have been discredited"; Kerry responded: "Actually, a lot of them have been documented." Neither was right. And that leads us back to the WSI.[51]

five
The Winter Soldier Investigation

I had the choice between what I knew was morally right and
my loyalty to other soldiers. I couldn't have it both ways.
—Sergeant Joseph M. Darby

The Winter Soldier Investigation (WSI) emerged from the far-left wing of the antiwar movement. Inspired by the International War Crimes Tribunal, organized by Lord Bertrand Russell and his secretary, Ralph Schoenman, and first held in Stockholm in May 1967, the WSI would focus exclusively on American war crimes. The Russell Tribunal, as it came to be known, attracted international attention for its array of left-wing intellectuals—Jean-Paul Sartre and Simone de Beauvoir among them. The tribunal found the United States guilty of the "deliberate, systematic . . . bombardment of civilian targets . . . dwellings, villages . . . medical establishments, leper colonies, schools, churches, pagodas, historical and cultural monuments." It drew its evidence from representatives of the National Liberation Front (NLF), among others, and offered the opportunity for the Chairman of the Cuban Committee for Solidarity with Vietnam, along with others whose politics were equally clear, to sit in judgment of the United States and its allies. Lord Russell extolled "the moving and unparalleled resistance of the people of Vietnam," and utterly dismissed the possibility that the Vietnamese "resisters" could themselves be guilty of war crimes. In a false and ugly assertion, he wrote, "those who would call the rising of the Warsaw Ghetto a crime will consider the resistance in Vietnam in the same light." In his concluding remarks,

119

he drew a clear parallel between the "crimes" of the United States and of Nazi Germany. The second session of the Russell Tribunal, held in Roskilde, Denmark in late 1967, went even further, finding the United States guilty of "genocide." Few today would find the Russell Tribunal's conclusions fair. The then prominent "new left" historian Staughton Lynd had refused to participate at Stockholm. He saw the tribunal as an effort to judge one side by its ends, the other by its means.[1]

Schoenman was interested in staging similar hearings in the United States. Two left-wing activists, Tod Ensign and Jeremy Rifkin, responded by forming the Citizens Commission of Inquiry into U.S. War Crimes in Indochina (CCI) in November 1969. It was a propitious moment. Earlier that month, Americans had first learned of the army's investigation of the massacre at My Lai and of the murder charges brought against 2LT William Calley. In December *Life* published the gruesome pictures of the Vietnamese dead. Convinced that My Lai was the direct outgrowth of U.S. military policy, and not of a few "bad apples" in the army, as Vice President Spiro Agnew put it, Ensign and Rifkin believed, according to Ensign, that the testimony of combat veterans would confirm their beliefs and "advance the larger struggle to end the war."[2]

CCI sponsored thirteen forums over the course of the year. The first, in Toronto, featured American and South Vietnamese deserters. The third, in Springfield, Massachusetts, attracted the attention of the *New York Times* and raised a troubling moral question. Ensign, a lawyer, had determined that veterans separated from the military could not be prosecuted for war crimes. But what of the crimes veterans had witnessed? A helicopter pilot named David Bressem testified in Springfield to what Ensign called a "turkey shoot" in which more than thirty Vietnamese civilians had been killed. Bressem, in a recent phone conversation, confirmed that he overheard the radio traffic and saw the results of the action, but said he would not have likely used the term "turkey shoot." The *Times* story caught the attention of the army. Stung by the publicity over My Lai, the army had no choice but to investigate and "within hours," according to Ensign, army criminal investigators were at Bressem's door. Bressem confirmed this. CCI would take the position that its witnesses "should not cooperate with military investigators." The prosecution of individuals would detract from its focus on the policy-driven nature of Vietnam atrocity. Bressem recalled, however, that this was his decision alone. Years later, Ensign acknowledged that such a policy made CCI appear "indifferent to criminal conduct," and made its leaders appear to be "moral agnostics." It was an important and fateful decision, however determined, that would inevitably qualify if not undermine the truth claims of veteran witnesses. Ensign's retrospective comments aside, there does not seem to be any evidence that such a policy was debated at the time.[3]

By the summer of 1970, CCI had recruited a growing number of veterans—Robert Anderson, a captain and a 1965 West Point graduate, Michael Uhl, an infantry lieutenant, and Ken Campbell among them—and had struck up a partnership with Vietnam Veterans Against the War (VVAW), a then small and obscure group founded in June 1967. Both groups were interested in bringing together a large number of veterans for a single well-publicized meeting. CCI already had plans to hold a National Veterans Inquiry in Washington in December.[4]

VVAW, however, had attracted the support of Jane Fonda and had deeper pockets. CCI's plans would be folded into what was then being called the WSI and, at Fonda's insistence, the meeting would be held not in Washington, where it might have garnered more exposure, but in Detroit, where Fonda, according to Ensign, thought it would more effectively "reach out to blue-collar Americans."[5]

Fonda came to support VVAW publicly on Labor Day 1970. She was the featured speaker at Valley Forge that day, after the conclusion of Operation RAW. Al Hubbard, an energetic African-American veteran and a leader of VVAW, was the creative force behind Operation RAW. He had recruited Fonda, who would be joined by fellow speakers, the conspiracy-theory writer Mark Lane; the civil rights leader James Bevel; the actor Donald Sutherland; and by a then unknown navy veteran, John Kerry.[6]

CCI's alliance with VVAW brought it not only Fonda's baggage—she had recently returned from North Vietnam where she had been photographed gleefully clapping in the gunner's seat of a Russian anti-aircraft weapon that had been fired at American pilots—but also that of Lane and VVAW president Hubbard, who lied on *Meet the Press* about his rank and his service in Vietnam.[7]

Lane brought a different kind of baggage. The author of an extravagant attack on the Warren Commission report on the assassination of JFK linking the CIA and the FBI to the killing, Lane brought the same zealotry to the war in Vietnam. He traveled to Europe during the time of the Russell Tribunal and interviewed a number of deserters, asking them about what they claimed they had seen or done in Vietnam. But his prospective publishers also wanted to hear the voices of soldiers who had not deserted, and Lane complied.[8]

The result was *Conversations with Americans,* published in early December 1970. Lane made his politics clear in the "Introduction," where he explained, pace Mao, that the concept of guerilla warfare required that the insurgents become one with the population. The insurgents could not practice "mass terror"—that would be "self-defeating," indeed suicidal. By definition, therefore, the Viet Cong (VC) and the North Vietnamese Army (NVA) did not engage in systematic atrocity. Americans, however, by measuring success by "body count," conducted a war, according to Lane, "unprecedented in the extent to which its over-all strategy encourages brutality."[9]

Lane had a special interest in atrocity stories, including the most sensational and gruesome accounts of the sexual torture of Vietnamese women. These are hideous, stomach-turning stories whose descriptive details have no clear precedent in past American wars. There is some evidence that such stories circulated as basic-training payback stories for the sexual mutilation said to be practiced by the VC. The worst of the stories had a very short shelf life. Three Winter Soldiers would offer variants of the stories first published by Lane. John Ketwig would offer another in his 1985 memoir, and then the sexual atrocity stories would effectively disappear. Lane was convinced that Americans had been instructed in such techniques—though he believed that it was only a small minority, just as the S.S., he said, was only a "small minority of the German military." The distinguished publishers Simon & Schuster brought the book to market, asserting that it was "one of the most shocking, eye-opening books ever encountered in the annals of wartime reporting." They were right, but not for the reasons they intended.[10]

Lane included an interview with "Richard Dow" who refused to give his real name, or identify the unit with which he served, or the dates that he served. He did, however, claim that he was a sergeant who served in Vietnam for thirty-three months—an extraordinary amount of time—and earned five Purple Hearts for wounds received. He said he personally killed "maybe two hundred fifty" prisoners or wounded, and witnessed the killing of "maybe two, three thousand . . . wounded, and civilians. . . . Men, women, children, everything." "Dow," a suggestive if ham-handed pseudonym, described the torture and killing of a young girl, a VC sympathizer he said. Army of the Republic of Vietnam (ARVN) soldiers "stripped all her clothes, and then they tied her down. Then every man in the battalion had intercourse with her. Then they sewed up her vagina with common wire. They run a brass wire through her head and hung her up. Then the commander of the group, a lieutenant, severed her body from her head with a long saber." Two hundred and fifty prisoners killed personally, two to three thousand killings witnessed, a lieutenant carrying a long saber and commanding a battalion (a lieutenant colonel's billet), an entire battalion, more than one thousand men, all of whom raped a young women. It is a story of utter implausibility, the publishing of which, absent any form of corroboration, was recklessly irresponsible.[11]

"Dow" wasn't finished. He went on to implicate seven Americans in the grotesque killing of another Vietnamese woman. He claimed that she was the daughter of a Vietnamese chief, a "Cong sympathizer." "We stripped her, tied her down and heated a bayonet up with a fire. Run it across her breasts—and into her vaginal area." Lane asked: "Did she die?" "Not right away," he responded. "We had a man with us. Took a leather shoelace from his boot. Wet it down. Tied it around her throat. Left her hanging in the sun. Rawhide shrinks after it gets dry. It just slowly strangled her to death." On the top of my bookcase in my study are two pairs of boots, one from basic training, another from my service in Vietnam, both of which retain their original laces, braided cloth, not leather.[12]

Lane went on. He interviewed Chuck Onan, who claimed he was trained in airborne and undersea warfare and in torture-interrogation training, the latter for five hours a week for more than six months. Lane interjected that this was more intense training than he had experienced in law school—criminal law required only two hours a week for five months. Onan's claims were evil beyond measure. Women prisoners were to be stripped—"pointed sticks or bayonets" driven into their vaginas. "We were also told we could rape the girls all we wanted," and that "phosphorous bombs" could be opened without detonating and placed against eyes and vaginas. Not only were prisoners thrown from helicopters, but at least one was tied between two helicopters and dismembered—a feat of utterly implausible aerial acrobatics. Onan claimed his drill instructor told him he had done this. Onan never had the chance to practice his skills—he deserted after receiving his orders to Vietnam. He was about to study music in Stockholm when Lane found him.[13]

"Harry Plimpton," another pseudonymous deserter, claimed to have been in the army for eleven years (though he had risen only to the rank of sergeant), said he served in Vietnam and witnessed the hideous torture of a young girl—but offered no dates, a unit designation, or a location of the alleged torture incident. The torturers, he said, were Vietnamese rangers. "They took her clothes off. Then they stuck hooks into her legs near the back of her ankles. They spread her apart, hanging her up in a tree like a pig you're going to butcher. . . . Then they took a piece of bamboo about three feet long and about as thick as your wrist and rammed it down into her—into her vagina. Then they put splinters of bamboo through her breasts and into all the soft spots of the body. . . . It took her three days to die." Lane asked: "Did you witness this?" "The Americans were ordered to turn their backs," "Plimpton" said.[14]

Lane solicited these stories, asking Peter Norman Martinson, "Have you ever seen any women tortured?" Martinson, who was not a deserter, described a form of electrical torture: "I saw a girl with electrical wires around her ears . . . tied to a tent post . . . another girl, about eighteen or nineteen, the wires were being touched to her nipples." Martinson, one of only three American soldiers who testified at the Russell Tribunal, was an interrogator with the 541st Military Intelligence Detachment. He testified to beating prisoners with an open hand, so as not to leave marks, witnessing field telephones being used to shock prisoners. But as Lane pressed harder, Martinson either contradicted himself or drew sharper distinctions. "Was there much abuse of women?" Lane asked. Martinson answered: "No, I was involved in an interrogation [of] a Chinese girl, which was rare." Martinson testified to beating her, but when another interrogator demanded she take off her clothes, Martinson said, "No, stop." "There generally was no sexual abuse," he concluded. He had responded in a similar way to leading questions at Roskilde. No, he never practiced or heard of water torture. No, he knew nothing about the execution of any prisoners, and no, he did not torture children.[15]

Billy Conway's account, however, left no room for nuance. Conway said he served with "Second of the Twelfth," 1st Cavalry Division. In October 1968, in the town of Don Tang near the Cambodian border, he claimed to have witnessed the grotesque sexual torture of three NVA nurses. They were raped "many times" by seven of his fellow soldiers; "hand flares" were "shoved" into their vaginas. The flares were activated by striking them, "and they exploded inside the girls." Conway went on: "Their stomachs started bloating up and then they exploded . . . their intestines were just hanging out of their bodies." Maybe Conway misspoke. There is no Don Tang in South Vietnam near the Cambodian border.[16]

James Reston reviewed Lane's *Conversations* for the *Saturday Review*. He wrote that it was a "disreputable book"—a "hodgepodge of hearsay," and that Lane had wholly failed to recognize "soldiers' talents for embellishing." Neil Sheehan, who later authored one of the most widely praised books on the war, went even deeper.[17]

Sheehan, who reviewed *Conversations* for the *New York Times Book Review*, may well have been the first to research the records of those who claimed to serve. He discovered that Chuck Onan was indeed a Marine, that he was trained in aviation mechanics in Memphis, and that he was assigned as a stockroom clerk at Beaufort, South Carolina. Ordered to Vietnam on February 5, 1968, he deserted. There is no record that he went to advanced infantry, airborne or scuba schools, or spent six months learning how to torture.[18]

And then there was Michael Schneider, another deserter, who claimed he was a squad leader and long-range recon leader in the 101st Airborne Division and the 196th Light Infantry Brigade. Schneider reported that he killed three prisoners, witnessed the torture of prisoners, and once tortured a prisoner himself using a field telephone with its electrodes attached to the prisoner's genitals. Schneider's personal story was bizarre. He claimed to have been born Dieter von Kronenberger, the son of a German army captain who served in the "Nazi Army" in World War II, as an aide to Heinz Guderian. His father immigrated to the United States, joined the U.S. Army, and rose to the rank of colonel. The message was obvious. Former Nazis were now in command in Vietnam. At the time of the interview, Schneider claimed that his father was the commanding officer of the 11th Cavalry, having just replaced COL George Patton, the son of the World War II general. Patton was the commanding officer of the 11th Cavalry but, according to Sheehan, there was no record of a Von Kronenberger or a Schneider, or anyone resembling the description. Sheehan went further to discover that Michael Raymond Schneider surrendered to the army in January 1969, subsequently went AWOL, was arrested in July in Denver on a murder warrant from Oklahoma, and was last in residence in the maximum-security ward of the Eastern State Mental Hospital in Vinita, Oklahoma. Sheehan challenged the credibility of two other Lane interviews. Here is another he could have challenged.[19]

"Ed Treratola"—not his real name—offered a story that, at the least, should have provoked skepticism. He said he arrived in Vietnam in February 1968, participated in the full siege at Khe Sanh, and commented second hand on the Marines retaking of Hue in, he said, May 1968. Marines went into Hue, he said, and "killed all the men. . . . They went through every building and they killed everything. . . . They [Marine command, I assume] made it up to be that they were all VC in the infiltrated Hue city, but the Marines just got the order to go in there and destroy everything." And then, after all the VC had been driven out, "they called in the B-52s [and] they leveled it to the ground, and there is no more Hue."[20]

The battle for Hue was over in February 1968, not in May. No one can doubt that Hue was invaded by the NVA and VC and tenaciously held at great cost to American and South Vietnamese soldiers who ultimately prevailed. There are no credible claims that Americans deliberately killed civilians, but we know that the NVA did—3,000 of them, whose mass grave was later found. B-52s were never used at Hue. Indeed, there was limited use of any air support, partly because of weather, partly because of concern for the historic and sacred character of the city, and partly because urban warfare set limits to the utility of such support. Simple fact checking should have prevented publication of this story.[21]

Sheehan challenged Lane. Lane wrote in his introduction that Simon & Schuster wanted documentary support. With lawyerly finesse, he neither affirmed nor denied he was able to provide it. In answer to Sheehan, however, he claimed such fact checking was "not relevant," and that the Department of Defense was the least reliable source on the "verification of atrocities." Simon & Schuster was no better. One editor who preferred anonymity said that searching military records was the equivalent of taking a radical medical theory to the American Medical Association—"They'd just say it was wrong." Sheehan, innocent of post-modern "theory," said, "we were dealing here with facts, not theories." The editor's response: "The motives in publishing this were anti-war motives."[22]

Sheehan was eloquent in his response to Lane: "This kind of reasoning amounts to a new McCarthyism, this time from the left. Any accusation, any innuendo, any rumor, is repeated and published as truth. The accused has no right to reply . . . because whatever the accused said will ipso facto be a lie. Those on the left who cherish their integrity might do well to take a careful look at Mark Lane's methods."[23]

VVAW's association with Fonda, Lane, and Hubbard tarnished its reputation and would provide useful fodder for conservatives for years to come. Indeed, many conservatives made direct links between Lane, Hubbard, and the WSI, conflating the demonstrable falsehoods of Lane and Hubbard with the presumed falsehoods of *Winter Soldier*.

Ensign and others, however, had come to distrust Lane and sought to reduce his role in the investigation. The prominent psychiatrist and author

Robert Jay Lifton had been the first to warn Ensign about Lane. The CCI leadership objected to Lane's inquisitorial manner and his zeal for sensationalism. He was reportedly upset that veterans had too few atrocity stories. At a rancorous meeting in the fall, the CCI leadership demanded Lane's ouster. But Fonda closed ranks behind Lane. CCI withdrew its support from the WSI and went ahead with its own planned meeting in Washington, held at the Dupont Plaza Hotel, December 1–3, 1970. It attracted little attention. A now out-of-print book, James Simon Kunen's *Standard Operating Procedure: Notes of a Draft-Age American* (1971), is the only record of that meeting.[24]

The planning for the WSI continued, but now veterans themselves— including Campbell, Mike McCusker, John Beitzel, and Nathan Hale—took up the fight against Lane and prevailed. Campbell recalls a heated meeting in Detroit after the program had been established without Lane on it, but the vets didn't even want Lane and Fonda in the audience, fearing, as Campbell put it, they would attract too much attention. Lane had no public role in Winter Soldier, none of the men he interviewed for *Conversations* took any part in the proceedings, and neither Lane nor Fonda appeared in the film *Winter Soldier*. But Lane and his book had been visible presences throughout the planning process, and his reported concern that veterans had too few atrocity stories to tell would prove groundless. Indeed, the ugliest stories told at the WSI bore remarkable resemblances to stories of sexual torture in *Conversations*. And the film *Winter Soldier* captured all of the most gruesome testimony.[25]

Winter Soldier: The Film

Winter Soldier was the collaborative effort of a group of radical filmmakers that included Barbara Kopple, who went on to achieve fame with the film *Harlan County*. It aired in 1972 in New York at the Whitney Museum on WNET-TV, at the Cannes Film Festival, and on some college campuses. It never received wider distribution. Though some writers would later claim it was censored because of its challenge to American policy in Vietnam, it would be hard to imagine, even today, that the principal American networks would air stories of American soldiers who claimed to have witnessed the bodies of Vietnamese women skinned, or of having seen entrenching tools, tree branches, or "pop-up flares" inserted into their vaginas.[26]

Fated to remain an ugly period piece known only to scholars and activists, in 2004 *Winter Soldier* became a weapon in the hands of those bent on denying electoral victory to John Kerry. As we've seen, opponents of Kerry did all they could to discredit the film. After the election, however, the film gained a second life. Re-released by Milliarium Zero, a new company dedicated to distributing films of "strong political and social content," *Winter Soldier* was widely seen and widely reviewed in places such as Princeton, Ithaca, Hartford, and Minneapolis.[27]

The reviews were uniformly positive, a few were even euphoric. None questioned the film's authenticity. The *Hartford Advocate* titled its review "The Truth about Vietnam." The *Toronto Star's* reviewer asserted, falsely, that the testimony of the WSI veterans had "all been verified." The *San Francisco Examiner's* reviewer wrote: "Take the most shocking scenes from [the films] *Full Metal Jacket* and *Casualties of War* . . . and they become so much powdered sugar compared to *what really happened* [emphasis added]." Another reviewer wrote that the film was "an unflinchingly clear-eyed extended gaze at military-brand all-American inhumanity." Ann Hornaday of the *Washington Post* exuded: *Winter Soldier* was "pure filmic storytelling," and a "dazzling example of movie-making at its most icongraphically potent." The *Pulse of the Twin Cities'* Jennifer Nemo wrote a review entitled "Winter Soldier: The Horror." If Nemo and her editors knew anything about the Vietnam War, it seems they knew the last words of Marlon Brando in *Apocalypse Now*—"the horror, the horror." Not surprisingly, reviewers focused on the most gruesome testimony—ears cut off live prisoners, bodies disemboweled and skinned, children stoned to death, prisoners thrown from helicopters. One writer cautioned "skepticism" about some of the veterans' accounts, but not as a reason to doubt them, only as a vague and incoherent "reminder of our own responsibilities during wartime."[28]

A few reviewers noted the conservative challenge to the film, but only to dismiss it summarily. Some made the link both backward to the well-known atrocity at My Lai—it "was no aberration," as one reviewer put it—and forward to the prison at Abu Ghraib, making Vietnam the military's training ground for torture. More surprising than the reviewers' politics was the absence of any skepticism about the "realism" of documentary film, despite a generation of film-studies scholarship arguing that the purported "realism" of such work is merely a special case of the framed and fictive quality of all perception.[29]

Some reviewers also claimed to know what the WSI meant to those who testified. "No fiction film about Vietnam has ever come close to this movie's portrayal of American guilt and trauma," wrote Michael Atkinson for *In These Times*. "More than just a case against the war . . . this film is about men shattered by shame and guilt, driven to confess their complicity in barbarous acts committed in the name of their country," wrote a reviewer for a Seattle website. The veterans of *Winter Soldier*, wrote the reviewer for Rochester's alternative paper, were "not making excuses . . . instead bravely owning up to cowardly actions that seemed justifiable in the heat of combat."[30]

Men "shattered by shame and guilt, driven to confess their complicity in barbarous acts," "owning up to cowardly actions"? Such comments are a highly selective reading of the veterans' testimony. Yes, there were veterans at the WSI stricken by shame and guilt, though none confessed to "cowardly actions." The entire investigation, however, was intended to explain away whatever shame and guilt resided in the hearts of those testifying and place it squarely on those who sent them there. War crimes, as William Crandell—a first lieutenant in the 199th Infantry Brigade, Americal Division, who introduced the first morning's testimony—put it, were the "inexorable result of national policy." Robert Jay Lifton, the prominent writer and psychiatrist who spoke at the WSI, offered what would become the most pervasive and effective apologia for soldiers who committed war crimes. The war itself, he said in a subsequent publication, was an "atrocity producing situation." Young men were "forced" by that "situation to act in a way that could have led . . . anyone to act in the same way." Jane Fonda, whose money supported both the investigation and the film, summed it up more than thirty years later, invoking Lifton's phrase as common coin: "It's critical to understand that the soldiers are not to blame," she said in an interview. It was the way they were trained. It was the absence of leadership. "When you put people into an atrocity-producing situation," she continued, "where enemy and civilian are commingled, where the other side is dehumanized, we cannot be surprised by what the men report in the film."[31]

The "star" of *Winter Soldier* was Scott Camil, whose camera presence improved from his deer-in the-headlights look in that opening scene with Ken Campbell. The filmmakers loved him. The camera caught him in close focus. His extraordinary directness and apparent calm, his boyish smile, whispery voice, and unkempt hair, led some writers to compare him to Jesus. What he had to say, however, was horrific. If Camil spoke the truth, young Americans of the 1st Battalion, 1st Marines, had committed hideous atrocities, some of a grotesquely evil sexual nature, worse than any atrocities that have ever been confirmed, none of which have ever been adjudicated. Camil himself claimed that, in a fit of anger over the death of a buddy, he had knifed to death an innocent Vietnamese villager. "It didn't bother me at all," the Jesus-like Camil said. Camil and others were not there to offer individual confessions, however, but to place the blame squarely on the U.S. government at its highest levels.[32]

A few reviewers seemed to recognize that evil was not the inexorable result of combat service in Vietnam. It was the "Christ-like" Scott Camil who provoked a more complex view of atrocity and responsibility. Lisa Kennedy recognized that Camil, who had spoken of his own troubled youth, had "waged war long before he enlisted," and that his comments were "rife with painful, telling, even damning contradictions." Rob Thomas saw even more deeply. He recognized that some veterans were angry, others ashamed, "but the overarching feeling," he wrote, "seems to be one of complete disbelief, as if their actions still exist beyond the limits of their own imaginations." Thomas, too, focused on the "disturbingly gentle and serene" Camil. "His amiable, half-smiling face fills the screen," Thomas wrote, "as he talks frankly about how *he* [emphasis added] burned every ounce of compassion out of his soul in order to function as a soldier."[33]

Such comments aside, the recent reviews of *Winter Soldier* offer little more than well-intentioned liberal bromides. The right-wing critique of the film's authenticity might as well have come from another planet. No reviewers doubted that the men were who they said they were. Few doubted that they spoke the truth. No one doubted that theirs was a fair indictment of the behavior of American soldiers in Vietnam.

So here we are with a chasm so wide it appears unbridgeable. *Winter Soldier* was a lie, or it was the blunt and searing truth. It is somewhat easier to understand the political motives of those conservatives and veterans who wanted so desperately to beat Kerry in 2004 than it is to understand why liberal film reviewers—most of whom were too young to have any stake in the internal wars over Vietnam—would, in full throat, embrace a simplistic view of documentary realism. But it is a measure of how deeply divided the country is and how difficult it is to find public common ground.

Winter Soldier, and the investigation on which it was based, was neither a "lie," nor was it the "truth." The war in Vietnam was, for many Americans, a Manichean moment and the moment lingers. Much of the scholarship and commentary on the war remains locked in positions formed long ago.

Atrocities are the litmus test that continues to divide us—how pervasive were they?—whose fault were they?—and *Winter Soldier* is both a harrowing and illuminating look at those questions.

The WSI: The First Morning, Rusty Sachs, and the "VC Air Force"

Rusty Sachs's stylized image, right hand in the air, about to throw a barely detectable medal onto the grounds of Congress, was used widely in publicity for the re-release of *Winter Soldier*, with the caption "They Risked Everything to Tell the Truth." Sachs was a helicopter pilot, the only Marine officer to testify that morning. His shock of curly blond hair led one reviewer to call him "angelic." He was an impressive and self-critical witness, recalling how he had once pushed a long-haired young man, whom he thought was walking too close to him, off a sidewalk in Cambridge, Massachusetts, after the war; and how, after his wife's remonstrations, he came to regret it.[34]

But he appeared caught off guard in the film's first scene. Joseph Bangert, a former Marine who would offer his own testimony, was interviewing him, taking down the basics—name, rank, unit. Then Bangert appeared to read from a list of questions. He first asked Sachs a leading question, whether he had ever seen a prisoner shot. Sachs paused, and answered clumsily and strangely: "I don't know whether I have or not, off hand." Sachs never testified to witnessing prisoners being killed, so it's fair to assume that he never did. So why didn't he just say so? How plausible is it that any one of us wouldn't know whether we witnessed such an act? By not simply saying no or that he didn't remember, Sachs communicated a desire to be accommodating. He seemed to know what was expected. The WSI organizers were not there to hear forthright denial of atrocities witnessed.[35]

Bangert went on to more fruitful ground: Had he ever witnessed prisoners thrown from helicopters? Sachs responded yes, and subsequent commentators would leap on his comments and utterly misinterpret them. Rusty Sachs said three things. First, that he witnessed bound prisoners thrown from his helicopter while it was on the ground. Enlisted men, watched by officers superior to him, made a cruel and ugly game of it. Second, he said he never witnessed prisoners thrown out while he was flying. He couldn't. The cockpit of his helicopter offered no backward view. Third, he said he was told by an officer senior to him never to count prisoners as they got on, only when they got off.[36]

Was it a probative comment? Perhaps, but it was also a form of black humor, ugly and deeply offensive to many, but especially common to helicopter pilots and crew. Michael Herr reported: "There was a famous story, some reporters asked a door gunner, 'How can you shoot women and children?' and he'd answered, 'It's easy, you just don't lead 'em so much.'" Or, "if a Vietnamese man is running, he's a VC, if he's standing still, he's a smart VC. Shoot him anyway."[37]

Several of the film reviewers who invoked Sachs's comments left their readers to believe that he had told of VC thrown from his helicopter in flight. The *New York Times*'s reviewer described Sachs's "ironic smirk" as he mentioned how he was cautioned not to count prisoners as they were boarding. And then directly following, *Times* readers were told of Sachs's description of contests to see "how far they could throw the bound bodies out of the airplane." The piece made no mention that the helicopter (not an airplane) was on the ground. The *Washington Post*'s reviewer claimed that Sachs "described piloting aircraft from which blindfolded prisoners were routinely thrown," clearly suggesting that he was in the air. You don't pilot aircraft from the ground. Other reviewers told only one part of Sachs's story, mentioning either the counting of prisoners or the throwing of them from his helicopter. I've yet to read a review stating that Sachs said he never witnessed prisoners thrown from the air.[38]

No reviewer who mentioned Sachs's story reported it accurately. At a minimum, these were serious breaches of journalistic ethics, and possibly acts of deliberate dishonesty. More likely, however, the story of prisoners thrown from helicopters—David Bressem's "Viet Cong air force"—had become so pervasive, so naturalized, that it could overwhelm and subvert contrary evidence even when that evidence was offered in the same account. We saw a similar occlusion in some of the reviews of Vietnam nurses' oral histories. Here, some reviewers sought to universalize what they read as the horror, pain, and life-long trauma experienced by nurses when any fair reading of the oral histories under review should have revealed that nurses not only had no common experience of such trauma, but also that many recalled their war experience with intense and positive pride. In this case, the frame of Post Traumatic Stress Disorder (PTSD) seems to have been as powerful as the frame of prisoners thrown from helicopters. Recall David Bressem, who never witnessed it, but as a Veterans Administration (VA) counselor spoke of it as the truth. When Terry Gross interviewed Rusty Sachs on *Fresh Air*, she asked him about the story. Sachs was at pains to quickly make clear what he had witnessed, and what he hadn't.[39]

A recent "Doonesbury" suggests that we may have turned a corner on this story. "B. D.," a veteran of both Vietnam and Iraq, has reluctantly agreed to VA counseling after his return from Iraq. Elias, his counselor, also a veteran, tells his "war story." B. D. responds: "Sure. How about this for a story? Two wars ago, as a grunt in Cu Chi, I shoved a suspected V.C. out of a chopper." Elias: "All right. We can get into that. But I wouldn't tell anyone else. What you're describing's a war crime." B. D.: "I didn't kill anybody. I just made that up." Elias: "I know." The story of prisoners thrown from helicopters is pervasive in oral history and in memoir, but there is no such story that has ever been corroborated.[40]

Three veterans at the WSI told variants of the story. Scott Camil said he witnessed it while on the ground. Specialist Fourth Class Steve Noetzel, a draftee who claimed to have served with the "5th Special Forces Group Augmentation" in the Mekong Delta, 1963–1964, claimed that he flew in an eight-helicopter formation escorting sixteen prisoners from Can Tho to Saigon in November or December 1963. When they landed, there were only four prisoners. An American door gunner said the ARVN guards had pushed them out. Sergeant Murphy Lloyd of the 173rd Airborne Division told the version of the story that would become most familiar. During Operation Junction City, he was flying back with "five or six" prisoners. An unidentified lieutenant decided he would begin the interrogation. So he "asked two or three questions" and not getting any answers he ordered that the middle door of the Chinook be opened, "and without another word, he just pushed one out," then another. Then a third prisoner pointed to one of his fellow prisoners. A search revealed that he was an NVA lieutenant. "On the way in after this," Lloyd went on, "he [the American lieutenant] said if anything was said about this he would make it harder on us." Lloyd then claimed that the lieutenant "wrote himself up for a medal by detaining and getting information from prisoners . . . [and] received a Bronze Star with a V device for valor." Many aspects of these stories strain credulity; for example, draftees serving with Special Forces, officers allowing prisoners to board a helicopter without first searching them, an officer writing his own recommendation for a valor award in the apparent absence of any evidence of valor.[41]

Yet such stories circulated widely. David Halberstam had reported in 1963 a Vietnamese officer had threatened to throw a prisoner from a helicopter, but he was told it was not acted on. In November 1969 a story appeared in both the *Chicago Sun-Times* and the *Washington Post*. A soldier had taken a photograph of what appeared to be a prisoner thrown from a helicopter. Another embroidered upon the story in a letter to his girlfriend that included the photo. Eventually, the picture and the story made their way to the national press. The army's investigation yielded evidence that the body was that of an NVA soldier, already dead, that he had been picked up on February 15, 1969, after a battle in Gia Dinh province. The army issued a reprimand to the helicopter commander, but both soldiers had since been discharged and were no longer subject to army discipline.[42]

Then, in 1974, Peter Davis's emotionally powerful and ideologically manipulative film, *Hearts and Minds,* brought the story to a wider audience. Davis introduced viewers to a stunningly articulate former soldier, Kenneth Barton Osborn. Osborn wore a small-pattern green tie against a light brown shirt. His hair was full, but neatly trimmed; his sideburns were L-shaped as they approached his mouth, a classic '70s look. He appeared to be caught in the middle of his testimony as he said that "they" were instructed to "remove the eyes of the individual and place them in the hole in the middle of the back." "They" were presumably ARVN soldiers, the eyes were those of dead VC, the "hole" in the back was presumably an exit wound. Osborn claimed, in apparent scholarly seriousness, that to the Vietnamese, the eyes were the symbol of "ubiquity," and every VC would understand the meaning—death at the hands of an all-knowing, omnipresent enemy. But such an ugly and desecrating act was apparently too much for American advisers, Osborn asserted, so he claimed that they substituted CBS logo patches, with the eye in the middle, placing them upon VC they had killed. This is a story both unique and fabulous. I've never heard it before or since, though the practice of leaving unit insignia or the ace of spades on dead VC is reasonably well documented, but "every" VC would not have understood the meaning of the all-knowing CBS eye. That was an important symbol only to members of the Cao Dai sect, a tiny minority of fiercely anti-communist South Vietnamese.[43]

Osborn also claimed to have witnessed a VC prisoner thrown from a Marine helicopter. The Marines had brought two VC up that day, he said. Osborn was along for the ride. One of the prisoners had been so badly beaten with a "rubber hose" that he could not talk. The Marines, talking in a "pidgin" Vietnamese the prisoner could not understand, threatened to throw him from the helicopter if he did not tell them what they wanted. And so three to four times, two "hefty EM's," (Enlisted Men) walked the "whimpering" prisoner to the door of the helicopter. All this for the benefit of the second prisoner. Finally they did throw him out—"winged him out," in Osborn's words. The second prisoner immediately began "babbling." Osborn had been telling this story in public since 1970, each time with increasing elaboration. The "rubber hose," the "hefty EM's", the "whimpering," "babbling," and "winging" were all new rhetorical flourishes—a hideous story told by Osborn with a bloodless and obscene relish.[44]

Osborn did not testify at the WSI, but he did at the earlier CCI event and twice more before Congress. He also claimed that he was a part of the Phoenix program, now widely perceived as a U.S.-backed program of assassination, and his various testimonies came to be uncritically embraced by several antiwar writers, including Noam Chomsky and Mark Lane.[45]

We know a great deal about Osborn from his long and frequent testimony, from an extended interview by James Simon Kunen, and from the army's official investigation of his allegations. According to Kunen, Osborn grew up in an upper-middle class family. His father was an engineer at Cape Kennedy; his mother a school psychologist. He attended prep school, then American University. He enlisted in 1966 and was trained as an area intelligence specialist at Fort Holabird, an assignment available only to those who scored high on the army's intelligence tests. While there, he claimed an army colonel told him and his classmates that they were being trained to do work in violation of the Geneva Accords, and that anyone who objected had the opportunity to withdraw from the program. Osborn defined the work he was to do as the "overt, active, aggressive collection of intelligence." No one who heard him, including congressmen and journalists, had the wit to challenge his claim that routine intelligence work violated the Geneva Convention.[46]

Osborn arrived in Vietnam in September 1967 and served for fifteen months. Assigned to the 525th Military Intelligence Group, he claimed to have lived under a cover name as a GS-7 civilian, later "promoted himself" to GS-9, and organized Vietnamese spy nets as a "more or less free agent." It was during this time that he claimed to have joined the Phoenix program, witnessed two VC thrown from Marine helicopters in April 1968, another prisoner killed by a sharpened dowel inserted into his ear, and a Vietnamese women caged, left to starve for ten days, then released back to her village, her jailors getting no information from her. He also claimed that a military intelligence captain killed one of his agents, a Chinese-Vietnamese woman, whom the captain claimed knew too much. It was at this point in his testimony that he claimed that "unilateral" intelligence operations, that is, operations not conducted in collaboration with the Vietnamese, were also violations of the Geneva Accords.[47]

Kunen, a decent and earnest left-winger, the author of the popular *Strawberry Statement,* thought Osborn was the "superstar" of the CCI hearings: "he is a good person and sincere," Kunen wrote, "now sincerely opposed to all that we wreak on Vietnam." Kunen wanted to like him, but he clearly recognized him as "*one of them* [emphasis in the original] suddenly making himself available to the rest of us." Kunen wrote that Osborn knew all the official phrases, "cross-cultural empathy facility," "retrospective plausibility basis," "VC infrastructure detail." "Everybody figured," Kunen went on, "that anybody who knew all these words must know a great deal else as well." Kunen claimed he knew Osborn was CIA because he heard him say "say again" if he didn't immediately understand a comment. "Say again," rather than "what" or something similar, was, according to Kunen, "clandestine short-wave radio talk," marking him as CIA. In reality, "say again" was a common phrase on imperfect military radio nets as soldiers made every effort to get it right. Kunen also knew, from an article in *Playboy,* that the CIA-Phoenix program had targeted two-thirds of the entire population of My Lai, children included, for "systematic elimination." Kunen never had a clue. It never occurred to him that Osborn might be telling false "war stories."[48]

Kunen did recognize Osborn as someone who craved attention, who seemed angrier at the incompetence of American forces than at the immorality of his own actions. Did he try to stop the Marines from throwing those prisoners to their deaths? Kunen asked. "I was there to observe," Osborn responded. Kunen sought confessional guilt; Osborn only offered third-person rationalization. How did he feel when he witnessed those prisoners thrown from a helicopter? "These are unreal things you're doing," Osborn responded, "and you take as realistic an attitude as possible, you might come up with 'this is regrettable and dirty, and so forth, perhaps even immoral, but necessary.' Not only is it the authorized thing to do, but it's very concurrent with the state of mind. You can rationalize an awful lot in that context as self-defense." Osborn's convoluted and morally deadening words clearly evoke Arendt's telling phrase, the "banality of evil." And they do so even if the horrors he so bloodlessly described never happened.[49]

Like many veterans with "war stories" to tell, Osborn added new and more horrific details, embellishing his previous stories while contradicting himself as he retold his tales. In his testimony before Congress he claimed that he had been trained to "terminate" agents at Fort Holabird, that only enlisted men could be agent handlers, that he had never known a VC suspect who had "lived through" an interrogation, and that he had targeted B-52 attacks upon suspected meetings of VC in village hootches. All of these were new claims, at least two of which were demonstrably false. His fellow antiwar witness, Michael Uhl, directly contradicted him. Uhl knew of officers trained as agent handlers. The claim that army PFCs called in B-52 strikes on single hootches is absurdly ridiculous. He elaborated on his story of his female agent killed by a Marine captain. It happened in the "driveway" of his house in Danang. (I was never in downtown Danang, but I was in Saigon and Qui Nhon. I don't recall seeing any "driveways.") The captain himself drove into it, exited his car, and killed the woman as she was returning from lunch. Osborn saw him drive away to his house, just down the street a couple of blocks. He also contradicted himself. There was never any mention of the Geneva Convention in his training, contradicting his earlier testimony, and the Vietnamese woman kept without food and water didn't return to her village, as he originally testified. She died of malnutrition.[50]

His testimony before a committee of Congress yielded an investigation of his charges. When he testified a third time, against the nomination of William Colby, both Colby and Stuart Symington made portions of the investigation public. No female agent had ever been assigned to him. Moreover, the Department of Defense investigation found that he had contradicted himself in his claims about the murder of that female agent, that he refused not only to provide the name of the Marine captain, but also that of the agent he supposedly killed. The investigation found no evidence to support his allegations and "revealed numerous disparities between statements he made while testifying and the factual evidence produced in the course of the investigation." When asked once again to reveal names, he plaintively responded: "Would it reflect seriously upon my credibility if I did not?"[51]

Osborn simply dismissed the investigation as what you would expect from the army, as many others with firm antiwar convictions would, then and now. Until 1995, the army's report on Osborn remained classified, and all that was publicly known came from the brief summary read by Senator Symington and the equally brief response of William Colby. Mark Moyar, then a recent Harvard graduate, gained access to the full and declassified report in 1995 as he was writing *Phoenix and the Birds of Prey: The CIA's Secret Campaign to Destroy the Viet Cong* (1997). Moyar discovered that the army interviewed many of his former colleagues, all of whom indicated that Osborn had made false statements. According to them, Americans were not trained at Ft. Holabird to kill their agents, that Osborn exaggerated the number of agents he controlled, and that he had never been assigned a Chinese interpreter, the latter confirmed by personnel files. Contradicting Osborn's bizarre claim that he worked as a "free agent," his colleagues asserted what anyone with military experience would have expected—that he worked under the close supervision of a superior. One of Osborn's team members stated: "To my knowledge, Osborn never saw anyone pushed out of a helicopter, he never saw anyone shot and he never saw anyone starved to death. I feel very sure that if he had actually observed any of these things that he would have mentioned them to someone on the Team. We lived pretty much as a family and would discuss everything that usually occurred during the day." Many of those interviewed believed that Osborn had heard such stories as they circulated as rumors, and that he had a penchant for making "fantastic statements," and that he "frequently made exaggerated remarks in order to attract attention to himself."[52]

No one can prove the null hypothesis that no prisoner was ever thrown from a helicopter. But again, no such story has ever been corroborated. There is, furthermore, a powerful physical fact that makes a helicopter an improbable place for an interrogation, especially one conducted by infantrymen in the absence of an interpreter. The standard army helicopter used in Vietnam flew with both doors of the passenger bay open. As any soldier who ever flew in a helicopter could tell you, the sound of the main rotor overhead and the rush of wind made it virtually impossible to conduct a conversation, never mind an interrogation.[53]

"Oh! Camil (The Winter Soldier)" Graham Nash

Sachs was followed by Scott Camil, the Marine sergeant who had forgotten about that massacre in Quang Tri, but after prompting, had immediately remembered his participation in it. Camil, however, had not forgotten about "the burning of villages with civilians in them, the cutting off of ears, cutting off of heads, torturing of prisoners . . . corpsmen killing wounded prisoners . . . women being raped, women and children being massacred," as he offered a synopsis of the testimony he was about to give.[54]

By comparison, Ken Campbell's introduction offered less red meat. He would testify to "calling in of artillery on undefended villages, mutilation of bodies, killing of civilians . . . and indiscriminate use of artillery, harassment and interdiction fire." In direct testimony that morning, however, Campbell elaborated only on the blowing up of dead VC on Operation Meade River in November 1968. The next three witnesses—Chris Simpson, Paul Olimpieri, and Fred Nienke—offered little direct evidence. Nienke, a sergeant in Delta Company, 1st Battalion, 5th Marines, offered wildly conflicting testimony. After first stating "we took a lot of prisoners," he later contradicted himself: "We didn't take prisoners." And then directly following: "When we did take prisoners they were always brought back to our local platoon or CO position."[55]

David Bishop caught the audience's attention. He would testify to seeing "four NVA nurses . . . raped, tortured and then . . . their bodies were destroyed." Following Bishop, Joe Bangert went further yet: "My testimony will cover the slaughter of civilians, the skinning of a Vietnamese woman . . . and the crucifixion of Vietnamese either suspects or civilians." It was almost as if the next story had to trump the last. The filmmakers captured the testimony of both Bishop and Bangert, but the "star" of *Winter Soldier* was the "Jesus-like" Scott Camil.[56]

Camil's testimony, as reported in the investigation's transcript, was horrific. He claimed that forward observers had contests to see who could destroy a hootch with the least amount of artillery, that villages were burned and "if people were in the villages yelling and screaming, we didn't help them," that on Operation Stone they had cut heads off and placed them on stakes. A senior officer, later identified by Camil as Colonel Bell, put an end to that, he claimed, but only because of the presence of the press. Camil also claimed that Marines cut off ears and bartered them for beers, that corpsmen killed wounded prisoners, that prisoners were beaten, that one was "staked out on the ground . . . cut open while he was still alive . . . part of his insides were cut out." Camil continued: "When we went through the villages and searched people the women would have all their clothes taken off and the men would use their penises to probe them to make sure they didn't have anything hidden anywhere and this was raping but it was done as searching." In response to a question, he claimed that his company commander was present when this happened.[57]

As long as the press was not in evidence, his company could do whatever it wanted. "I saw one case where a woman was shot by a sniper," Camil claimed. "When we got up to her she was asking for water. And the Lieutenant said to kill her." And then in a scene that ranks with the ugliest of Mark Lane's stories, Camil continued: So [the Lieutenant] ripped off her clothes, they stabbed her in both breasts, they spread-eagled her and shoved an E-tool [a shovel, or "entrenching tool" in the military's jargon] up her vagina. . . . And then they took that out and they used a tree limb and then she was shot." In a phone conversation in 2005 Camil said that he had shot the woman as an act of mercy. He would also many years after his initial testimony identify her as a nurse. In response to a question from the press at the WSI, did the men he served with "think that it was all right to do anything to the Vietnamese?" Camil claimed that he and all the men in his unit were "conditioned" to this, "brainwashed"—"It wasn't like they were humans . . . anything you did to them was okay."[58]

All of this testimony was captured by the filmmakers and reprinted in Beacon Press's heavily edited *The Winter Soldier Investigation: An Inquiry into American War Crimes* (1972). The filmmakers gave Camil even more attention. In his introductory scene with Ken Campbell, he went on to talk about that ville wiped out in Quang Tri. He claimed his unit, 1/1, killed precisely "291 . . . men, women, children, everything"—if true an atrocity exceeded in sheer numbers only by the one at My Lai. We'll examine the truth of that claim in a later chapter. In a subsequent off-stage interview, Camil told of being overrun in his third week in Vietnam. Five Marines died. He resolved: "I would kill anyone I could. . . . If I have to go into a village and kill 150 people just to make sure there was no one there to kill me when we walked out, that's what I did." He was clever in his phrasing—"it was ears for beers," referring again to the barter of body parts for beer. None of his peers contradicted him. In rear areas you could buy a can of beer for the price of a soda. In the field, if delivered, beer was free. Being in Vietnam, he said, was like "hunting every day for free." The camera held him in close focus, his boyish smile and whispery voice filling the screen. He was articulate and captivating in that early '70s way. He drew his off-camera interviewers in, one woman tried to probe his thoughts on masculinity: "Can the concept of what a man is change?" she plaintively asked. This was not the only time that a low-key feminism influenced these interviews. Camil was thoughtful, but in the end he didn't think he wanted to change. Interviewers also elicited tales of his growing up, a story of how he was once put on the spot by a woman in North Carolina who wanted to know if he was ashamed of what he did. He didn't like it, and attempted to shift blame to her, calling her a "crummy voter." In one brief aside, he talked about a friend having been killed, and subsequently asking a Vietnamese for his ID. When it wasn't immediately forthcoming, he said "it just pissed me off." And so, he said; "I just pulled out my knife and killed him. . . . It didn't bother me at all."[59]

Camil was born in Brooklyn, but raised in Florida by a stepfather who he said was a deeply committed anti-communist and who beat him. In an interview in 2002, he offered a balancing perspective on his family background. His Jewish grandmother told him of the horrors of the Holocaust. He claimed a strong social conscience, formed early, as a result—it's "wrong to sit by when you see other people suffering." He couldn't understand why women and children "would be rounded up and killed."[60]

By his own account in *Winter Soldier*, he had been a poor student in Florida, with a criminal record—seven counts of assault and battery. He and his buddies liked to "rumble the Cubans" on the weekend. Facing a prison term, he said, he joined the Marines. Camil served twenty-two months in Vietnam, re-uping after his first tour ended, and rose to the rank of sergeant. He appears to have been an outstanding Marine, decorated and rewarded— his self-proclaimed savagery, to the extent it was true, either overlooked or condoned.[61]

In his extended monologue in *Winter Soldier*, he talked dismissively of medals as "just a bunch of shit." But he also wanted it known that he'd been awarded the Vietnamese Cross of Gallantry with Silver Star and had been put up for three Bronze Stars. He then described three separate instances of valor, though with a self-deprecating and dismissive tone. In one, he picked up a live enemy grenade and threw it back; in another he chased and killed five VC; and in the third, on a night ambush, he killed a VC in hand-to-hand combat. If these were the actions that led to three recommendations for a Bronze Star, the Marines' fourth highest award for valor, there would be little dispute that Camil earned the awards. But Camil's DD-214 contains no mention of any valor awards. Camil's record indicated that he was authorized to wear the Vietnam Service Medal with two service stars, the National Defense Service Medal, the Vietnam Campaign Medal, the Good Conduct Medal, the Purple Heart with one service star (indicating he'd been wounded twice), the Combat Action Ribbon (an award special to any Marine), and the Vietnamese Cross of Gallantry with star device. Despite its extraordinarily impressive name, the Vietnamese Cross of Gallantry with star device was not an award for individual valor, but an award granted to the soldiers or Marines of an entire division. Camil's awards will always stand on their own. They are sufficient honor for any Marine. He had no need to embellish his record by suggesting that he had been "put up" for three Bronze Stars for valor, but embellish it he did.[62]

When he returned to the United States, he still had time to serve in the Marines. Assigned to Camp Lejeune, he and his men were trained in riot control in anticipation of demonstrations against the war, and he recalled frequent weekends of stand-by duty. He said he was appointed riot-control non-commissioned officer (NCO) for the 10th Marines, but he apparently failed to learn the Marines' riot-control lessons that entailed the use of minimum force. In a 2002 film, he claimed that he told his men that if any demonstrator were to throw one rock, indeed, if they threw anything, every man in his unit was to "empty one full magazine into the crowd." At the time, he said, he regarded demonstrators as no better than VC, and he believed that such an action would put an end to demonstrations and that he and his men would have their weekends free once again. Marine superiors, upon hearing of his orders, he said, relieved him.[63]

Within a matter of months, the criminal zealotry he claimed as a Marine would be put at the service of the antiwar movement. He mentioned a speech by Jane Fonda at the University of Florida, where he had enrolled, as a turning point. Fonda called upon veterans to tell the truth about the war to the American people and mentioned a gathering of antiwar veterans soon to assemble in Detroit. In a phone conversation with me, he said it was Joan Baez who inspired him to go to Detroit. Camil went to Detroit, but with a different agenda than the organizers. He told me he went to tell them what "bad things" had happened to him and other Americans in Vietnam. He was not yet against the war. He was, he said, against what was happening to William Calley. The WSI changed him, focused him on what the war was doing to the Vietnamese, and those three days in Detroit, he said, led him to realize that "the Vietnamese people were human beings," and that what Calley had done was "wrong," but that he understood how he could be "conditioned" to it. Camil said of himself: "I was very susceptible to cold war conditioning," comparing his early education to "indoctrination." Like so many other veterans returning to college, Camil was exposed to a whole new narrative about the war. He learned that Ho Chi Minh was once our ally, that he was a nationalist, that the United States had betrayed the Geneva Accords, that the North Vietnamese freely elected Ho, and that Catholics had moved south only because of U.S. propaganda claiming that the "Virgin Mary" was moving south. He bought it all with the same unquestioning zeal he had once brought to his anti-communist "indoctrination."[64]

Camil's mental world contained no gray shadings. He became a deeply emotional leader of VVAW advocating the assassination of American politicians, and recalling years later that he was deadly serious about it. It was a comment that would come to taint John Kerry's association with VVAW. In Gainesville, Camil joined forces with other veterans and students demonstrating against the war. As an attempt to answer the aggressive and often illegal use of police force, Camil devised ammonia-filled balloons to be thrown at the face shields of policemen to be followed by the use of slingshots. These were tactics he would refine further as he and other vets planned to disrupt the Republican National Convention (RNC) in 1972. Camil, by his own account, assumed command responsibility for the VVAW's planned protest at the RNC. With some justification, given the killings at Kent State, he sought to prepare a plan for "collective self defense." That plan soon devolved into outright and bizarre criminal behavior. He bought M-1 rifles, crossbows that he claimed "could fire arrows through a police helmet," wrist-rocket slingshots that could fire ball bearings and glass marbles, fried and glazed so as to fragment and cause more injury, cherry bombs dipped in fiberglass, and balloons filled with ammonia and bleach. Camil, again by his own account, had planned diversionary attacks on police stations, fire stations, and other government buildings with fire and smoke bombs, and had established "fire teams" ready to sabotage Miami's bridges.[65]

He and his fellow "conspirators," who would become known as the Gainesville Eight, were indicted in July 1972. The government's case was compromised by the testimony of a known FBI informant, who had been among the most militant of the group, and by the government's extraordinary and illegal efforts to seek conviction. The case badly divided the VVAW leadership, many of whom believed that Camil was guilty or, at the least, grossly irresponsible. But, in the end, VVAW supported the Gainesville Eight, and a Florida jury refused to convict. The case is remembered now, as it should be, as an example of the Nixon White House's fear and paranoia and of the abuse of police power. But Camil was no innocent in all of this. Even a liberal and law abiding government has an interest in paying close attention to advocates of bombing and assassination. Camil was widely seen by fellow VVAW members as unreliable. Barry Romo, a veteran and VVAW leader, laid the indictments squarely at Camil's feet: "The reason they were able to do it [indict the eight veterans] was because people like Scott Camil were loudmouth, macho, violence-spouting assholes."[66]

It was a measure of Camil's credulity that he regarded one of the FBI informers as a good friend. A few years later, providing no evidence of having learned anything, he took as a lover a female Drug Enforcement Administration (DEA) agent who set him up for a bust that went bad. Camil had for some years been involved in drugs, though how deeply is unclear. The night of the bust, an agent shot him in the back, an ugly act that brought

Camil both sympathy and acquittal. Bitter, he withdrew from any political activity for a decade, but the Reagan-supported insurgencies in Central America reengaged him. In recent years he has devoted himself to local causes in Florida. Now a grandfather with a long gray ponytail and a gray Fu Manchu moustache, he remains articulate, even compelling. It is hard to dislike him. He remains a remarkably open and trusting person confiding to a stranger in a phone conversation about his recent therapy for PTSD and his subsequent award of a 100 percent disability rating from the VA.[67]

Camil may have been the only Vietnam vet other than William Calley who merited his own song. Graham Nash, the rock singer, wrote, "Oh! Camil (the Winter Soldier)," "Tell me what did your mother say," Nash sang, "when you left those people out in the fields/ rotting along with the hay?/ Did you show her your medals?/ Did you show her your guns?/ Did you show her the ears that you wore?" Nash went on to sing that Camil "had stood up for justice."[68]

So who is Scott Camil? A brave Marine? A sociopath? A murderer? And which of his many and conflicting stories can be believed? In the last scene of a film about him, *Seasoned Veteran: The Journey of a Winter Soldier* (2002), an activist friend recalled watching *Winter Soldier* with Camil. He too had been filmed as a younger man, and watching a younger version of himself he had tried to recall what was filtering through his mind at that time. He asked Camil what he had been thinking at the time of *Winter Soldier*. Camil, he said, answered: "Sometimes I don't know who I am."[69]

Joe Bangert and "The Ballad of Ho Chi Minh"

Returning to that first morning of testimony, Camil was a hard act to follow. But David Bishop and Joe Bangert went even further. Bishop identified himself as a lance corporal attached to Hotel Company, 2nd Battalion, 5th Marines, 1st Marine Division. On Operation Meade River, conducted with army, ARVN, and Republic of Korea (ROK) units, Bishop recalled that 1,300 enemy were killed at a cost of 700–800 allies. His unit had come across a large hospital bunker complex and four "NVA nurses." The ROK Marines wanted the nurses. And so they were turned over. Bishop testified, "we were still in the area when the ROK Marines started tying them down to the ground . . . they spread-eagled them; then raped all four . . . they sliced off their breasts, they used machetes and cut off parts of their fingers . . . they took pop-up flares . . . they stuck them up their vaginas . . . and they blew the tops of their heads off." It is a story that is both hideously evil and anatomically implausible. It also bears a remarkable resemblance to the story Billy Conway told Mark Lane.[70]

A questioner from the audience: "A couple of people on the panel mentioned brutalities to women. Is [sic] rape and other sexual brutalities to women—brutalities involving the vagina in particular—is that a usual feature of people on tour in Vietnam?" Chris Simpson, who had said nothing after his introductory comments, responded: "Me, myself. I think it's pretty usual over there. Cause you're out in the bush and you'll meet women out on the trails." Simpson, a corporal in Echo Company, 2nd Battallion, 5th Marines, in the end offered no direct evidence of such brutality, and his claim that running into women on trails was common is nonsense.[71]

Joe Bangert, who identified himself as a sergeant in the 1st Marine Air Wing, also had stories to tell. In his introductory remarks at the WSI he said he would testify to the "slaughter of civilians, the skinning of a Vietnamese woman, and the crucifixion of a Vietnamese man." He claimed that on the first day he arrived in Vietnam, he flew from Danang to Dong Ha, and then had to "hitchhike" on Highway 1 to his unit. He said he was picked up by a truck full of "grunt Marines" and two 1st lieutenants. After traveling about five miles, some Vietnamese children appeared at the "gateway" of a village, and "they gave the old finger gesture at us." Bangert went on: "They stopped the truck—they didn't stop the truck, they slowed down a little bit, and it was just like response—the guys got up, including the lieutenants, and just blew the kids away . . . five or six." "That," said Bangert, "was my first day in Vietnam."[72]

Bangert then addressed the crucifixion stories. "As far as the crucified bodies, they weren't actually crucified with nails, but they would find VCs or something (I never got the story on them) but, anyway, they were human beings, obviously dead, and they would take them and string them out on fences, on barbed wire fences, stripped, and sometimes they would take flesh wounds, take a knife and cut the body all over the place to make it bleed and look gory as a reminder to the people in the village."[73]

Bangert went on. He said he had a friend who worked with the U.S. Agency for International Development (USAID) and the CIA. The friend was a former major. They used to get drunk together, and the former major, who was an adviser to the ARVNs, invited him to come along to a village. ARVNs had found a woman with bandages, and they questioned her: "And the way they questioned her . . . they shot her . . . about 20 times." She was dead. His friend went over to her, "ripped her clothes off, and took a knife and cut from her vagina almost all the way up . . . pulled her organs out . . . and knelt over and commenced to peel every bit of skin off her body and left her there as a sign for something or other."[74]

Bangert's next story was an interpretive and bathetic tour de force. On his last day of staging battalion at Camp Pendleton, prior to going to Vietnam, a staff NCO brought out a live rabbit: "And then in a couple of seconds after just about everybody falls in love with it—not falls in love with it, but you know, they're humane there—he cracks it in the neck, skins it, disembowels it, just like I testified that this happened to a woman . . . and then they throw the guts out into the audience. You can get anything you want out of that you want, but that's the last lesson you catch in the United States before you leave for Vietnam."[75]

Bangert was clear about what the lesson was, and so was the moderator in response to a question from the audience—this was an example of "how it's done in Vietnam." The questioner wanted to know if officers were present at the death of the rabbit, and if this was still part of "Basic Training." The question followed an account of a human atrocity far uglier, but it was the rabbit's death that provoked the questioner.[76]

Several Marines on the morning panel affirmed that they too witnessed the same thing. So did I. This is the only testimony from the WSI that I can personally affirm. I witnessed the death, skinning, and disembowelment of a rabbit, not as the last exercise prior to going to Vietnam, but as one of the last exercises of basic training in the Texas foothills. It was a hard and useful lesson in survival, not a license for how to treat the Vietnamese.

It's hard to take Bangert seriously. Military authority surrounded junior enlisted men arriving in Vietnam on the first day, and yet there he is hitchhiking to his first unit. The common, if not universal, experience was that the new unit would have sent a truck or jeep to pick up new men. And then we have a USAID officer, a former major, unnamed, befriending a junior enlisted man, getting drunk with him, taking him on a helicopter ride to witness the horrible death and mutilation of a Vietnamese woman. Officers rarely drank with enlisted men, or befriended them, and Officers' Clubs, where a USAID officer could drink, were not open to enlisted men. Both stories share something else in common—they take place wholly outside the unit to which Bangert was assigned, and so, unlike the stories told by Scott Camil and others, they cannot be crosschecked.

So who is Bangert? Philadelphian Joseph V. Bangert signed up for a four-year hitch in the Marines in 1967. Born in December 1948, he was nineteen.

He arrived in Vietnam in 1968. According to his brief bio, which he wrote for the military.com website under the name Joe Bangert, he served with VMO-6 at the Ai Tu airbase, just north of Quang Tri City. VMO-6 was a Marine Observation Squadron. Its helicopters flew recon, air support, and medevac missions. Bangert noted that he "worked out of S-4 primarily," that is, he was a supply clerk. But he also claimed that he had been trained in Vietnamese and also worked with "S-5 Psyops in Trieu hong hamlet and gunned on Hueys with VMO as well as Phrogs from HMN 161 and HMN 262"; the latter claims attempt to establish his combat bona fides. According to military records Joseph V. Bangert had a Military Occupational Specialty (MOS) of 3071, aviation supply, and left the Marines with the rank of corporal. Bangert had been honest about his MOS, but not about his rank. In a recent news article he admitted that he had been reduced in rank, but only because he had refused to kill.[77]

Bangert came to the WSI with a reputation among other antiwar veterans as an unreliable blowhard. Though he attended the CCI investigation of war crimes held in Washington the previous fall, CCI leadership did not let him testify. According to one antiwar veteran, they did not trust his stories. The WSI leaders were not as discriminating.[78]

Bangert was one of the very few antiwar veterans to go over to the other side. A letter of his appears on the website of singer/activist Peggy Seeger. Attending a banquet in France at the "World Assembly for the Peace and Independence of the Indochinese Peoples," sometime in 1969 or 1970, he wore a shirt "which had emblazoned on the front of it—the flag of the National Liberation Front." He joined the singer Barbara Dane on stage and sang "Giai Phong Mien Nam"—"We Will Liberate the South"—the anthem of the NLF. Then he said he closed by singing the treacly "Ballad of Ho Chi Minh," written by Seeger's late husband, Ewan MacColl.[79]

MacColl's lyrics tell us that Ho was the "father of the Indochinese people," and that he "went to the mountains where he formed a determined band, heroes sworn to liberate the Indochinese people." He went on: "The army of Uncle Ho" was "sowing freedom with victory seeds." "Sowing freedom"? No one outside the ranks of what remains of the sectarian left can possibly believe this. "Uncle Ho" lived his adult life in the embrace of the Communist Party. He and the "wily" Vo Nguyen Giap, his general, used "Indochinese" nationalism as Stalin had used Russian nationalism, and there seems to have been no limit to the numbers of North Vietnamese young men and women they would have sacrificed for the cause. Bangert reprised this moment at Joe's Pub in New York in February 2003.[80]

Bangert returned to Vietnam to live and work for a number of years, eventually settling in Brewster, Massachusetts, where he appears to have worked as a teacher. He worked in John Kerry's campaigns and was photographed in 1984 endorsing Kerry on behalf of a group of fellow Vietnam vets—the *Boston Globe* identified him as a "Marine Sergeant and helicopter gunner"—and was photographed again standing in back of Kerry and his wife as Kerry celebrated his victory in the New Hampshire primary in 2004. The right used these photographs with great relish. Bangert, in his own words, had supplied all the evidence they needed to call into question, at the very least, Kerry's judgment.[81]

In the last few years, Bangert has become a ubiquitous presence on the Web, joining fellow veterans of VMO-6, and another group called Veterans Against Torture, where he identified himself as a "Warrior of the Independent Ogalala Nation." He also claimed to have been on the security detail at Wounded Knee and wrote an impassioned, if less than coherent, political diatribe on another website.[82]

Bangert's national visibility dramatically increased in 2004, as he became the brunt of right-wing attacks. He apparently never shrank away from them, and if his new-found visibility in *Winter Soldier* was not enough, he took a leading role in *Sir! No Sir!* a 2006 film that attempted to retrieve the history of the antiwar movement among soldiers themselves, but did so in a simplistic and politically tendentious way. Bangert's testimony at *Winter Soldier*—the skinning of the Vietnamese woman, the rabbit story—was excerpted as the "truth." Bangert, interviewed for the film, made for a compelling witness, insisting on the primacy of the truth: "The truth has to be told, you can't duck away from the truth, you can't lie." The context was the atrocity at My Lai. Bangert said he wasn't defending William Calley, but he went on to ask: "Why are they going after Calley? Calley was doing precisely what we were all told to do when we were in Vietnam." And then, a brief qualifier—he modified "precisely," by "essentially, OK," but then concluded with, what "we were all told to do . . . is to kill them all and sort it out later."[83]

Bangert also involved himself in the debate over *Stolen Honor*, claiming to a reporter for the *Cape Cod Times* that the use of scenes from *Winter Soldier* violated copyright. In the same story Bangert said he served as a door gunner for six months and saw "every temple, pagoda, church, and school in Quang Tri riddled with bullets or otherwise destroyed." Bangert's visibility on the issue as well as his questionable credibility, led defense attorneys for *Stolen Honor*'s producer and production company to call for his deposition in the suit brought by Ken Campbell. They wanted him to produce evidence of the atrocities he witnessed.[84]

Shortly after receiving the subpoena, he got drunk, had a run-in with police, and was found in violation of his probation, the result of an earlier arrest for drunken driving. He was remanded to Bridgewater State Hospital for thirty days. On July 7, 2006, he received a token fine of $500 for violating his probation. His probation officer noted that he was a "likeable man" and a veteran trying to recover from a long addiction to alcohol. In commenting on the night of his run-in, Bangert said, "I did kind of lose it. I have character defects . . . and a lot of it is my own [fault]." After his hearing, he noted plaintively: "My war never stopped." He was traveling to Hawaii with a friend, also a veteran, and his AA sponsor. After a month or so, they would fly to Vietnam. "I've always wanted to go to Vietnam sober," Bangert said.[85]

A Summary

The "war stories" offered by Camil, Bangert, Bishop, and others on that first morning were so horrific, and so unbelievable, that subsequent Winter Soldiers seemed to back away—you've heard enough of that, in effect: "I wouldn't like to go too far into the horror stories you've been hearing about for the last few days," Bill Perry said. Indeed, no subsequent testimony came close to the grotesquery of the first morning. Years later, a thoughtful former Winter Soldier recalled that some of the Marines that morning seemed determined to trump each other, as if they were in competition to tell the most shocking story.[86]

The "investigation" ground on. The 1st and 3rd Marine Divisions had their own panels, as did the army's American Division and its 1st Air Cavalry Division. Soldiers from other army units were combined on panels. The focus of the investigation was to be on eyewitness accounts of American atrocity, but the WSI had a broader left-wing agenda. Of the fifteen panels, four were dominated by civilians such as Lifton and focused on the impact of the war on veterans, on Vietnam itself, on POWs, and on the use of weapons—such as chemical defoliants (Agent Orange), CS gas, anti-personnel bombs—the use of which were claimed to be violations of the laws of war.

The civilian-led panels at the WSI provided important and relatively early evidence of the ecological damage done by chemical defoliants, used to deny both forest cover and food to the VC and the NVA. Little was known at this point of the possible dangers to humans, and Bert Pfeiffer, a biologist from the University of Montana, acknowledged that in a reasoned and thoughtful manner. Jim Clark, who worked both for USAID and the Catholic Relief Service, offered a tough but fair-minded analysis of the extraordinary numbers of rural peasants displaced from their villages to deplorable and overcrowded refugee camps. Clark reported that surveys suggested that the United States and its allies were directly responsible for less than half (47.2 percent) of this movement. Clark, who was one of the few voices at the WSI to hold the VC and NVA, as well as the United States, culpable, suggested that local surveys found that up to 30 percent of refugees were driven out by the VC or the NVA, with about 10 percent of refugee movement unaccounted for.[87]

Some of the testimony in these panels, however, was marked by a political tendentiousness extraordinary even at the time. George Smith, a POW who had been released by the VC, testified that he had been treated well and never tortured. His interrogation sessions were lessons in the justice of the VC cause and, in response to a question, no different than the opposite arguments he heard at Fort Bragg. His mild treatment was compared unfavorably not just to the treatment of VC and NVA captives, but also to American soldiers convicted of criminal acts and held in military prisons. One former member of the State Department went to great lengths to defend the North Vietnamese treatment of prisoners—captured American pilots, he said, had only to suffer the same inconveniences as the North Vietnamese. Arguments to the contrary, regardless of the mounting evidence, were, he claimed, simply cynical ploys of the Nixon administration to justify expansion of the war. The historian Howard Zinn made the false and ugly assertion that the American government "has never cared for the fate of the American POWs."[88]

There were other panels on racism, the "Third World," on medical practice and on military journalism, all dominated by veterans. Despite the depth of corrosive racial tension that characterized the military's last years in Vietnam, the racism panel offered little in the way of concrete evidence. The discussion remained at a general level, touching on the sexual roots of racism, relations between blacks and Vietnamese women, and "liberation struggles" around the world. The "Third World" panel offered more specifics—one panelist spent time in the stockade at Long Binh, others talked about infantry companies that were "ninety percent" minority, and others the discrimination faced by minorities in the rear. Discrimination there certainly was, but the claim that blacks and other minorities were disproportionately at risk on the front lines was not true. This panel, too, was marked by more generalized rhetoric about American racism and third-world solidarity. Several of the panelists were clearly familiar with the language of the anti-imperialist left and seemed to embrace the belief that third-world liberation movements were the great hope of the future.[89]

The panels on medical practice and military journalism conveyed the unsurprising truths that Americans received better medical care than the Vietnamese—we would have to live in a world of saints for this to be otherwise—and that military reporters were constrained in what they could write. More surprising, however, were claims that medics, not doctors, operated on prisoners, that Vietnamese civilians were not allowed on American medevacs, that MEDCAP missions—bringing American doctors and medics to Vietnamese villages—were done solely for propaganda purposes, and that military reporters could not report on the extent of American casualties, American weaponry, or the accuracy and range of enemy 122mm rockets—as if this were censorship rather than sound and defensible military practice.[90]

There can be no question that some, perhaps many, veterans spoke the truth at the WSI about what they personally witnessed in Vietnam. Americans did commit war crimes in Vietnam, and even now, no one of good conscience can claim that all of those war crimes have come to light. But as of today, only one war crime testified to at the WSI has been confirmed. James (Jamie) D. Henry, a medic in Bravo Company, 1st Battalion, 35th Infantry, 4th Infantry Division, claimed that on February 9, 1968, in Quang Nam Province, members of Bravo's 3rd Platoon killed nineteen women and children who had been rounded up as VC suspects—"five men," he said, "opened up on full automatic." One of the women had been apparently raped prior to her death. According to Henry, the order came over the radio from the company commander to Henry's platoon leader. The former repeated the battalion commander's comment at the morning briefing: "kill anything that moves"— Henry's words. Henry also testified to witnessing the killing of a Vietnamese boy—"who wants to kill him?" a lieutenant asked. Henry also witnessed a Vietnamese man killed—for target practice—and a suspected VC run over by an Armored Personnel Carrier (APC), all in separate incidents.[91]

Henry had begun telling his story prior to the WSI, at a CCI press conference in Los Angeles on January 11, 1970, and again in a March 1970 issue of the now defunct magazine, *Scanlan's*. When investigators from the army's Criminal Investigation Command (CID) came to him on February 28 and again on March 1, he cooperated fully, unlike the vast majority of those who testified at the WSI, providing names, dates, and locations. It would take years for his stories to be confirmed. Jamie Henry was a beacon of honesty in a troubled, finger-pointing time.[92]

The army's investigation stretched out over three years. There were witnesses who confirmed the killing of the boy, and the soliciting of volunteers to do it by the lieutenant who led Bravo's 2nd Platoon, the shooting of the man by a sergeant and another soldier who had been granted permission "to test fire their weapons," and the death of the man crushed by the APC. Witnesses also confirmed the killing of those nineteen villagers by 1LT Johnny M. Carter and PFC Frank Bonilla, but investigators heard conflicting stories about the order given by CPT Donald C. Reh, the company commander. Carter and Bonilla had left the military. Though there was a legal opinion justifying the trial of former members of the military accused of war crimes, the military did not pursue them. Reh, a 1964 graduate of West Point, refused to make a statement to the CID. The final report concluded that he was "derelict in his duty . . . for failing to investigate the shooting." There was also conflicting evidence of the words used by the battalion commander, LTC William W. Taylor Jr., and his name did not appear in the "summary fact sheet."[93]

Henry deserves praise for his pursuit of justice and for his righteous anger about what he witnessed in Vietnam. Would that we could say the same about so many others who testified at the WSI. Recall the studied refusal of those who testified to hold individuals responsible. But that praise must be tempered. Henry, unlike others, never reported the war crimes he witnessed while he served in Vietnam. He never publically revealed what he knew until two years after the massacre, greatly limiting the army's ability to seek justice.[94]

The army's CID conducted an investigation into every one of the charges of war crimes made both at the WSI and at the earlier CCI hearings. Surprisingly, twenty-five witnesses made no specific allegations of war crimes, and the CID conducted no further investigation. Of the forty-nine witnesses the CID interviewed, thirty-two either refused to make any statement at all or refused to offer any specifics—names, locations, dates. Several of those who gave statements could not recall names or other specifics, or the names they gave could not be located. 1LT Sam Bunge, Bravo Company, 3rd Battalion, 187th Infantry, 101st Airborne Division, presented himself as a responsible officer, disobeying an order he believed illegal, preventing his men from burning a village, but he was willing only to offer names of possible witnesses to the desecration of a grave or to the firing on of an unnamed villager, but not of the officers who ordered or permitted such acts.[95]

Others appeared to back away from their WSI claims. David Stark, who served with the 524th Military Intelligence Detachment, testified to the killing of up to 1,400 residents of Cholon in the aftermath of Tet 1968, the result of a bombing run. Stark also testified to having witnessed what he described as "minor beatings" of VC prisoners by Americans. But in his CID interview, he said he saw no dead bodies, could not identify the planes or the units, and admitted that he had only witnessed one instance of maltreatment—a prisoner pushed by two ARVN soldiers. SGT Robert S. McConnachie, 2nd Battalion, 28th Infantry, 1st Infantry Division, told the WSI audience that he witnessed the killing of "two or three" Vietnamese children, hit by C-ration cans thrown full-force by unidentified soldiers near Quan Loi on Highway 13, and knew of an artillery strike at a leper hospital near Ben Son killing some civilians. "They knew where it was," he said, suggesting a deliberate act. When the CID interviewed him, he admitted that he was not aware of the extent of the children's injuries, that MPs remained with the children after reprimanding his fellow soldiers, that his account of the artillery strike was based on an "assumption," and that, "in retrospect," the strike was "unintentional and accidental." Douglas Craig, who served with the 1st Air Cavalry, testified to nightly mortar rounds fired into a dump knowing that Vietnamese civilians would be there scavenging—two per week were killed. At his CID interview, Craig said he had no direct knowledge of such killings and that he had misgivings about going to the WSI in the first place because he knew that he could not substantiate his allegations.[96]

Did the CID intimidate these men? We can't rule it out. But just as likely, once removed from the emotionally overheated atmosphere of the WSI and the extraordinary tales of that first morning—they were there, after all, to testify to war crimes they witnessed—the CID interviews made clear the full legal consequences of their "war stories." So they backed away, revised their memories, admitted they couldn't substantiate their claims. All but Jamie Henry. But at least they testified, unlike the majority of their peers.

Make no mistake. Americans committed war crimes in Vietnam, and some of those who refused to testify before the CID may well have been able to establish those crimes. But they didn't. Those who would look to the WSI to establish the cold, hard facts of American conduct in Vietnam—names, dates, locations—won't find them. They will have to look elsewhere. So much for *Winter Soldier* as the "truth" about Vietnam.

The "war stories" of the WSI were largely uncorroborated. Some were formulaic—women "spread-eagled," their vaginas subject to hideous abuse, villages wiped out, "men, women, children, everything" killed. The worst of the sexual torture stories, Camil's excepted, implicated Americans as witnesses; the perpetrators were South Koreans or ARVNs. They reprise the ugliest of Mark Lane's false or improbable stories, and they contain their own improbabilities—all those NVA "nurses" serving on the front lines.

Such stories were also forms of "boot-camp propaganda." Ken Campbell spoke of hearing such grotesque stories—sticks implanted in vaginas—from Marine veterans while he was in training. Chuck Onan, was told of "driving "pointed sticks or bayonets" into vaginas. Mark Worrell was told by his DIs: "We could do anything we wanted to them," and "Every effort was made to glorify the extermination and torture of these lowly Vietnamese." Such ugly and improbable stories were the mirror image of those stories—similarly improbable when they weren't simply false—of the risks faced by Americans at the hands of the VC. Let Christopher Ronnau, a veteran of the 2nd Battalion, 28th Infantry (Black Lions), 1st Infantry Division, carry the tale. In bars where the blood alcohol level "was somewhere in the mid-200s," Black Lion veterans regaled the FNGs (Fucking New Guys) with remarkable tales: "Lots of guys died from rectal bleeding in Saigon after VC prostitutes put ground glass in their drinks. One famous whore put razor blades in her cunt and sliced up somebody's dick. It was incredible. Our bar was the epicenter of jungle legend heaven." Ronnau combined these stories of the VC's fabled perfidy, with their moral and equally fabled equivalents—explosive devices placed under pictures of Ho, enticing the stomping feet of soldiers, and, of course, the VC singing "like a canary" in a helicopter after witnessing his fellow VC thrown out.[97]

There were men who spoke the truth at the WSI. Americans did commit war crimes in Vietnam. That chapter awaits. But those who spoke the truth will always be linked to the Camils and the Bangerts, and all the others who succumbed to the power of rumor, second- and third-hand evidence, "boot camp propaganda," and imputed motive. To serve in the military in these years was to live in a world of rumor. In basic training it's the rumored brute of a drill sergeant; in advanced training, it's we're all going to Vietnam, or to Germany, or there will be no pay for those with mustaches; in Vietnam, it's we're all going home, or to Danang, or to LZ English, or to patrol in

"Happy Valley." Junior enlisted men, and at times, junior officers, felt like marionettes—with strings being pulled by senior officers no one knew, but many confidently knew the reasons why. *They* were punishing Bravo Company, or *they* wanted blacks and whites to fight with each other, or tonight on guard duty, *they* were not going to issue ammunition, or *they* have sent the new guy in as an agent of the CID to bust us for marijuana use. I had to live with that story for my first months in Headquarters and A Company, 4th Medical Battalion. And then there were the boot-camp stories: the bamboo viper whose bite would kill you in a matter of seconds, the poisoned Coke or the popsicle sold by a Vietnamese child with glass in it, the VC prostitute with those unbelievable razor blades somehow embedded in her vagina, the spread-eagled VC woman, properly paid back, with a tree branch or an entrenching tool in her vagina. And there were always more stories: It didn't happen to me, but my buddy saw it or knew of it—the prisoner thrown from a helicopter, the five-year-old with a grenade, the "white" Cong, or that island in the Pacific where they sent everyone with incurable VD.

To read or listen to the testimony from the WSI without an awareness of the power of rumor, story, and imputed motive is to surrender to credulousness. Sunny Keyes told of fifty trucks filled with American dead, though he never looked into the trucks. Allan Akers was convinced that they brought whites, with their country music, and blacks, with their soul music, back into garrison duty. "So consequently they get to fighting amongst each other, and the higher brass knows, well, it's about time to cut these guys loose on some villages somewhere." Charles N. Stephens knew that Bravo Company, "boo-boo company," was "always understrength," "always getting ambushed." He never served in the company, but he knew it was "all black." Mike McCusker had been told that "booby-trapped babies are going to be sent against you and old grandmothers are coming to throw bombs at you, which can be very, very true and in many cases is true." Whether it was "can be very, very true" or "is true," McCusker never witnessed it. David Bressem, a helicopter pilot who testified in an earlier hearing and is now a VA counselor in Massachusetts, never witnessed a VC prisoner thrown from his helicopter in flight, but he told me: "I talk about it as the truth." He told me, invoking the deeply black humor of helicopter crews, that such victims were known as the "VC Air Force." He also told me a story, new to me, that he had heard of one American soldier who had suffered the same fate. Another veteran was bluntly honest: "A lot of things I never witnessed myself. However, I heard many, many things."[98]

James Duffy, the only white to appear on the racism panel, also heard many, many things. Duffy, who claimed that non-white people were "the most humane people on this planet Earth," told the gathering of "Sin City" in An Khe. A previous witness, Michael Hunter, had called it "the world's biggest whore house." Army medics, Duffy told the audience, had once kept the women "clean," but the "American public" believed it immoral. So, after imputing motive, he went on: "Some of the worst cases of venereal disease . . . cases that can never be cured" were the result. Duffy claimed that the "American government" had an island in the "South Pacific" where it sent the incurables, an island that could be approached only by plane "because ships don't come in and out." "How do you know about it?" an audience member asked. Duffy said one of his "head medics . . . hipped me on it," showed him on a map where it was, and a "couple of the doctors" confirmed it. "So what do they tell the families?" the questioner continued. Hunter said they were "usually" listed "as missing in action." "Do you have any information on how many men have been sent to this island?" was the next question. Duffy, who seemed intent on moving on, said he had "no idea." It is of course a false and absurd story, but Duffy had heard it from one of his "head medics." In my experience some young soldiers thought that their repeated cases of gonorrhea were marks of virility, rather than symptoms of long-term unpleasantness. I can easily imagine medics, who were usually older and better educated, using such a fantasy for its invigilating effects.[99]

six

This Was "What the War Had Done to Us"

My God what have we done? . . .
Please God, forgive us. What have we done?
They had taught us to kill . . .
and now they were going to court-martial us for killing.
The thing we had done was the result of what the war had done to us.
—Philip Caputo

The purpose of the Winter Soldier Investigation (WSI) was not to indict individuals for war crimes, but rather the U.S. government. Those who testified at the WSI would not be judged. William Crandell, a lieutenant in the American Division—William Calley's division—introduced the first morning's panel. War crimes in Vietnam were, he said, the "inexorable result of national policy." He went on: "We intend to demonstrate that My Lai was no unusual occurrence. . . . We intend to show that the policies of [the] Americal Division which inevitably resulted in My Lai were the policies of other Army and Marine Divisions. We intend to show that war crimes in Vietnam did not start in March 1968, or in the village of Son My or with one Lt. William Calley. We intend to indict those really responsible for My Lai, for Vietnam, for attempted genocide. . . . We are here to bear witness not against America but for those policy makers who are perverting America."[1]

It's important to recall what actually happened at My Lai. William Calley, a platoon leader in Charlie Company, 1st Battalion, 20th Infantry, Americal Division, was then, and continues to be, labeled a "scapegoat." He wasn't. He

157

wasn't a victim taking the blame for someone else's actions—the definition of a scapegoat. He committed murder. One of his acts that day was to order and participate in the killing of women and children who had been herded into a confined area near a culvert. There they sat awaiting their fate.[2]

It has been a settled principle of American military law since the nineteenth century that the killing of prisoners who have submitted to and are under effective military control is murder. An order to commit murder is an illegal order that soldiers are not only permitted to disobey, but one that they have a duty to disobey. In truth, these were principles never widely taught by the Vietnam-era military. But should you have to teach soldiers that the deliberate killing of infants, children, and women at point blank range, who pose no threat, is wrong? This was not a case of soldiers killing civilians in the heat of combat, under fire and afraid. The single most important truth of what happened at My Lai was that no one was shooting back. The murders at My Lai were not the impetuous acts of nervous soldiers—but systematic massacre. By one report, the killings at the culvert took one hour, and required one soldier to reload his M-16 several times. An M-16 clip holds eighteen to twenty rounds. There were other atrocities in Vietnam, but nothing like My Lai, nothing on such a scale, nothing comparable to the deliberate daylight killing at close range of women, children, and old men. It was then and remains one of the most disgraceful days in the history of the U.S. Army. Calley was not the only one who should have been held accountable that day, but the army's failure to effectively prosecute those others does not mitigate his guilt or the guilt of those who followed his orders.[3]

Charlie Company had suffered badly in the weeks leading up to My Lai from snipers and mines. The company was at half-strength. Many were angry, frustrated. The helicopter assault on My Lai on March 16, 1968, would be "pay-back." They were told that the landing zone (LZ) would be "hot," defended by the 48th Viet Cong (VC) Local Force Battalion. The operational commander was LTC Frank Barker. Although a later investigation would find no evidence that Barker's orders, either explicitly or implicitly, called for the killing of civilians, he had made no provision for handling prisoners and there was evidence—from a chaplain—that Barker said that if they came under fire they were to level the village. CPT Ernest Medina, Charlie's commanding officer (CO), attended Barker's briefing. Medina, who would also be charged with murder, testified that Barker had given them wide latitude to kill livestock and burn hootches. Medina's own orders to his men remain the subject of dispute. Though he was tried and found not guilty of murder, some of his men recalled his expansive orders to destroy the ville and its inhabitants.[4]

And so they did. As the command helicopters circled in the air, Charlie Company encountered a "cold" LZ. No one was shooting back. But Charlie Company continued to shoot, to kill—to murder. What would it have taken to stop it? There is a simple answer—a morally competent and honest officer willing to tell his superiors that army intelligence was wrong again, there are no armed VC here, and order "cease fire!"

The tragedy and dishonor of My Lai, contrary to the moral certainties of the WSI's organizers, rests principally on company grade officers—lieutenants and captains. Yes, there is blame that reaches higher—ambiguous orders, cover-ups. I can already hear the dissent. It was an "atrocity producing" war, that's the "way we fought the war," body counts, the "mere gook" rule, every dead Vietnamese is a dead VC. There is an ugly underlying truth here, but it is not the whole truth, and even if it were, it would not be exculpatory. To repudiate individual responsibility flies in the face of long-held values, ones reaffirmed at Nuremberg: "while collective guilt, like the notion of original sin, may have a place in theology, it is not part of Anglo-American jurisprudence," one scholar wrote. "Here guilt is always personal."[5]

The most sweeping case for collective guilt was the widespread assertion that American conduct in Vietnam purposely and consistently violated the Geneva Convention. The Geneva Convention is actually a series of conventions, the first of which grew from the founding of the Red Cross in Geneva in 1863. One year later, twelve nations ratified the "Geneva Convention for the Amelioration of the Condition of the Wounded in Armies in the Field," intended chiefly to protect aid stations, hospitals, and medical staff. The United States signed on in 1882. The second convention, in 1906, extended the principles to war at sea. The third, in 1929, established protection for prisoners of war, and the fourth, in 1949, reaffirmed the earlier conventions while extending protection to civilians, the principal victims of WWII. It is this convention, with its lengthy text and more than 100 articles, which is best known and most frequently cited.[6]

The Geneva Conventions, however noble their intent, have never had the force of law and have consequently remained unenforceable. But no American official argued in the time of Vietnam, as the chief counsel of the White House did in the wake of the 9/11 terrorist attacks, that the Conventions were outdated, even "quaint," and would likely get in the way of the country's prosecution of war. The United States remained formally committed to the Conventions during the war in Vietnam even as the National Liberation Front (NLF) and the North Vietnamese refused to be so bound.[7]

I saved my own Geneva Convention card, identifying me as a medic—a red cross in outline superimposed on the card's text. It was intended to protect me as a noncombatant under the terms of the first Geneva Convention. No medics had any illusion that it would. Unlike the case in previous wars, no army medics or navy corpsmen in Vietnam wore red-cross armbands or red crosses on their helmets. The risk was too great. We were told that the VC or North Vietnamese Army (NVA) expected Americans to attempt to assist fellow soldiers wounded in the open, and so left them alive in order to kill those who were attempting to save them. The only red crosses I ever saw in Vietnam were those painted on ambulances, used exclusively in the rear, and on medevac helicopters. There is no evidence that the VC or NVA respected such missions. The Conventions remain a moral ideal, but it will not do to indict only the United States for violations of that ideal.

Despite the assertions of the WSI organizers, there is nothing in the Geneva Conventions that prohibits the use of .50-caliber machine guns against enemy troops. They are fearsome weapons, capable of tearing apart human bodies, but little different in their effect than artillery rounds. The VC and the NVA also used them effectively. Nor is there any prohibition against the use of unobserved artillery fire on pre-planned coordinates—Harassment and Interdiction (H&I) fire. Nor is there any specific prohibition against the use of white phosphorus, known to troops as Willy Peter or WP. White phosphorus rounds are incendiary weapons used as marking and illumination rounds, but they were also used against enemy troops and against villages. When WP hits a human body it continues to burn. It cannot be extinguished unless it is literally cut out. Though not explicitly prohibited by the Geneva Conventions, it may well fall under the prohibition of the fourth Hague Convention, which attempted to forbid weapons "calculated to cause unnecessary suffering." Oddly, the organizers of the WSI made no effort to claim that the American use of napalm, another incendiary weapon whose effects were as horrific as WP though usually more conclusive, was a violation of the Conventions, despite the extraordinary efforts of antiwar activists to indict Dow Chemical's production of napalm as a principal war crime. Incendiary weapons have never been direct violations of the Conventions, though a humane world would do well to outlaw them.[8]

The American use of the defoliant Agent Orange has provoked extra-ordinary outrage and unquestioned human tragedy. There is no question that the dioxin found in Agent Orange is a powerful carcinogen and that Americans used Agent Orange both to clear fields of fire and to destroy crops with the intent of denying the VC food. At the time Agent Orange was employed in Vietnam, it was similarly employed as a defoliant in the United States. What was known at the time was that exposure to dioxin had caused cases of chloracne, both mild and serious, in chemical plant workers, but little was known about its effects on those who either applied it or encountered it in the environment. As the potential dangers became known, the military curtailed defoliant operations, and suspended the use of Agent Orange on April 15, 1970. Assessing the long-term effects of Agent Orange, both for the Vietnamese and for American veterans, is a difficult and deeply political issue. The Vietnamese, with some outside scientific support, continue to maintain that Agent Orange was responsible not only for environmental damage but for widespread birth defects. Both may be true, though in fairness no epidemiological studies have confirmed the connections. Some American veterans exposed to Agent Orange contracted soft tissue cancers as a result. The most recent studies have clearly shown causal associations between exposure to dioxin and chloracne, Hodgkins disease, non-Hodgkins lymphoma, soft-tissue sarcoma, and chronic lymphocytic leukemia, but causal associations with other diseases are either weak, i.e., respiratory and prostate cancers; unsubstantiated, i.e., bone, skin, renal, testicular cancers, and birth defects (other than spina bifida) and childhood cancers in offspring; or can likely be ruled out for gastrointestinal and brain tumors. All these associations, however, are the result of studies of those who were occupationally exposed. According to studies done by the National Academies of Science, there is no "adequate exposure data on Vietnam veterans," and thus no way to quantify veterans' risk—with one exception. Extensive studies of the air force pilots and crewmembers who sprayed Agent Orange in Operation Ranch Hand have revealed no significant increases in death rates or in cancer between them and their flightcrew peers who did not serve in Vietnam.[9]

Ninety percent of Operation Ranch Hand missions were defoliation missions. Denying cover to the enemy is a legitimate act of war, however tragic the unintended consequences. Ten percent of the missions, however, were intended to destroy crops. Altogether, a total of almost 500,000 acres of cropland were sprayed—3 percent to 4 percent of South Vietnam's cultivated land. The intent was to deny food to the VC in VC-controlled areas in I, II, and III Corps, again a legitimate war objective. But the crops destroyed were civilian crops, and it was civilians who suffered more. Civilian crop destruction flowed logically from Westmoreland's strategy to deny the countryside to the VC, to create ever more refugees, and though it may not have violated the Geneva protocols, it was a deplorable act and one the United States later renounced. In 1975 President Gerald Ford signed Executive Order No. 11850, stating that the United States would not make first use of herbicides in future wars.[10]

Americans made extensive use of tear gas, or more precisely, CS, in Vietnam. The name derived from the last initials of the American chemists, B. B. Corson and R. W. Stoughton, who developed the compound in 1928. CS is now widely used in the United States and abroad as a riot-control agent (RCA). As anyone who has been exposed to it can testify, CS causes immediate irritation to eyes and noses, induces chest pains, and can lead to choking and vomiting. Exposure to CS was a staple of basic training. Recruits had to enter a confined space full of CS, and while there remove their gas mask from its pouch and put it on. Few soldiers will have forgotten the experience.[11]

The Army of the Republic of Vietnam (ARVN) used CS, provided by the United States, beginning in 1964–1965. The North Vietnamese claimed that such gases were poisonous, and criticism of their use surfaced on the floor of the U.S. Senate. Upon instruction from Washington, General Westmoreland suspended the use of CS, though in 1965 it would be authorized for defensive purposes only, including efforts to rescue American prisoners. The policy was broadened in 1966 to authorize use in clearing tunnels and bunkers. Westmoreland had requested the use of CS on behalf of the 173rd Airborne Brigade as it was about to move into the Iron Triangle. Secretary of Defense Robert McNamara approved it with the understanding that Westmoreland would stress the "humane aspects" of its use. Two months later, the Joint Chiefs of Staff gave Westmoreland "unrestricted authority" to use CS at his discretion and that of his subordinate commanders. In a matter of months, U.S. policy on the use of CS had changed dramatically. Initially authorized only for defensive purposes, then for "humanitarian" purposes, CS became a standard weapon in the arsenal of American troops, to be used to flush out the VC and NVA in order to kill them. The American military in Korea had been denied similar authorization. The use of CS dramatically increased between 1965 and 1969 from 367 pounds to over 6,000 pounds.[12]

Following the horror of poison gas attacks in WWI, the Geneva protocol of 1928 banned the use of "asphyxiating, poisonous or other gases, and of all analogous liquids, materials or devices." The United States signed the protocol, but the Senate never ratified it, and during the time of Vietnam, the United States remained one of the few major nations that had not, even though during WWII President Franklin Roosevelt made clear that the United States would make no first use of poison gas.[13]

No one outside the ranks of the ideologically blinkered would claim that CS is a lethal gas comparable in any way to the mustard gas of WWI. Yet the ambiguity in the phrase "other gases" in the 1928 protocol and the United States's use of CS for offensive purposes cannot merely be waved away. As criticism of U.S. involvement in Vietnam mounted, Richard Nixon affirmed in 1969 that the United States would not make first use of lethal gases and resubmitted the Geneva protocol to the Senate. The use of CS and other riot-control agents, however, were explicitly excluded. It wasn't until 1975 that the United States formally ratified the Geneva protocol and by executive order renounced the first use of CS and other RCAs except in defensive circumstances. That remains national policy. The war in Vietnam thus stands as the singular exception, the only time the United States made expansive battlefield use of CS for offensive purposes.[14]

The North Vietnamese insisted that the United States made use of "poison gas," and such claims were brought to the Russell Tribunal and affirmed by the American Committee of Concerned Asian Scholars. Years later, CNN would air a grossly irresponsible story, which it later repudiated, that the United States used sarin gas in an abortive mission to rescue POWs. There is no evidence whatsoever that the United States used anything other than CS or similar RCAs. The Russell Tribunal acknowledged as much when it offered no evidence that the United States used anything more potent than the then standard RCAs—CS, CN, and DM. By referring to these as "poison gases," and claiming that they "are most often lethal in their effect," the experts at the Russell Tribunal had substituted demagoguery for science. The North Vietnamese made extravagant claims of hundreds of villagers killed by "poison" and "toxic" gases, many of which were reported in a 1966 document, "U.S. Imperialist Crimes in South Vietnam." The claims were never subject to corroboration. The United States claimed that it had no evidence of the lethal effects of CS. One Winter Soldier claimed he witnessed such a death. Although the vast weight of scientific knowledge continues to suggest that CS is not a lethal substance, it would be wise not to assert the null hypothesis. In certain circumstances and conditions it is reasonable to believe that infants, the elderly, and those trapped in tunnels might well have succumbed. American forces used too much CS, and used it in a way that may well have fallen under the proscriptions of the Geneva Conventions, and the country's later embrace of a more restrictive policy was wise and humane.[15]

"Free-fire zones" have been widely misunderstood. Despite claims at the WSI and the arguments of antiwar activists, the existence of "free-fire zones," or "specified strike zones" (SSZs), in the army's official terminology, never offered license for the deliberate and indiscriminate killing of civilians. They were not, as many have claimed, a license to kill anything that moved. They were areas, established by Vietnamese province chiefs, where artillery fire and air strikes were permitted without the need for prior approval by South Vietnamese authorities. The creation of such zones was frequently the direct result of the forced removal of civilian populations. The assumption was that there were no civilians in such zones. The reality, however, was frequently different. Some villagers refused to leave. Others chose to return. U.S. tactics, however, ignored the reality. We may rightly deplore such forced relocations, and the subsequent creation of SSZs, as tactically mistaken, inhumane, or immoral, but neither the relocations nor the SSZs were violations of the Conventions.[16]

However, many veterans expressed the belief that any Vietnamese found in a "free-fire" zone was fair game. Did they really mean it? Any Vietnamese? An infant, for example? We may see such assertions as some combination of black humor and ugly bravado. Recall Camil's comment that service in Vietnam was like "hunting every day for free." But we cannot leave it there. If soldiers and Marines sincerely believed they had a license to kill in such zones, then that points to possible failures of command responsibility and underlines the cruel ambiguities of a war frequently fought among villagers who resembled the enemy. But for those who chose to see only the "license" afforded by "free-fire" zones, fairness and honesty requires that they also attend to the evidence of command restraint, of restrictions on retaliatory fire, of the bold line that many veterans drew between the killing of armed enemy and the murder of peasants.[17]

H&I artillery fire was mostly pre-planned fire based on intelligence reports, that is, it was not called in by forward observers in visual contact with the enemy. It was intended to target known or suspected VC or NVA camps, supply centers, or infiltration routes. Forward observers also called it in as a form of precautionary fire to protect night perimeter positions. It was such a mission that resulted in the accidental death of Michael Mullen, whose mother became the principal in the book and TV movie *Friendly Fire*. W. D. Ehrhart, a Marine corporal who plotted H&I fire for the 1st Battalion, 1st Marines, provided an account suggesting just how random the fire selection could be and how poor the intelligence was. There is no way of knowing the numbers of civilians killed or wounded by such fire, but such concerns were put in writing by U.S. Agency for International Development (USAID) advisers and Rand Corporation consultants. Nor is there a way of assessing its effectiveness in killing the enemy. Some senior officers thought it wholly ineffective, a waste of ammunition. However ineffective, ill advised, or poorly justified, H&I fire was not a violation of the Geneva Conventions.[18]

To argue in this way risks surrendering to mere legalism. Did it really matter whether the American military's extraordinary reliance on firepower, especially under Westmoreland's command, fit the Geneva Conventions' definition of a war crime? Those deeply opposed to the war then and now know one answer. No, it didn't. America fought a dirty and immoral war. Those who supported the war then and now have, of course, another answer. Such firepower was necessary to support the troops in the field. It seems to me there is a middle position that will likely suit no one whose mind is already made up.

Bombs and artillery rounds are not the most discriminate of weapons, though they were used far more discriminately than those opposed to the war assumed at the time. For every claim of fire abuse, there are equal and opposite claims of fire restraint imposed by strict rules of engagement. But Americans did make extensive and extraordinary use of air and artillery support. It was not at all uncommon for a fire mission to be called because of a single sniper, rather than employing the traditional infantry tactic of fire and maneuver. Because such support was available, it was used and welcomed by troops on the ground. But senior officers recognized at the time such a heavy reliance on air and artillery support was neither always necessary nor effective. Few people outside of the military analyst community know that General Abrams, upon assuming command in Vietnam in June 1968, dramatically restricted the use of air and artillery support near populated areas while also curtailing unobserved H&I fire.[19]

It had been General Westmoreland's decision in 1965 to take the war to the VC and the NVA in the countryside. It was a decision that would lead to the displacement and death of civilians. There were alternatives. The Marines argued forcefully for a strategy of protecting the coastal villages in partnership with South Vietnamese forces. I have no belief that such a strategy would have worked, but had this strategy been adopted many fewer civilians would have died, atrocities such as My Lai would have been far less likely, and many fewer Vietnamese would have been converted to North Vietnam's cause. Westmoreland, however, was committed to the tactics of World War II, enhanced by air mobility. His was to be a big battalion war in the countryside fought largely by Americans.[20]

It is just and fair to deplore the consequences of Westmoreland's decision for innocent civilians. Westmoreland had given the peasants of Vietnam only three choices: join the VC, leave their ancestral villages to become refugees, or stay and risk death from allied firepower. And it won't do to blandly observe that civilians suffer and tragically die in all wars. Nor will it do to justify American tactics as an appropriate response to the tactics of the VC, who were taught to hold close to civilians and who routinely fired from Vietnamese villages, acts that were violations of the Geneva Conventions. But this is not a brief for moral equivalency. It is a hard truth that American strategy and tactics from 1965 until 1968 sharply increased the risk of death for Vietnamese villagers.[21]

However wrong or ill-advised, such tactics were not intentional efforts to kill civilians. Intent matters. The sophomore's argument is that it doesn't matter to those who died. No. It matters to the living. That's why we care about justice and accountability. The larger evil of the war cannot negate the smaller evils done by men in that war. There is a bright line between the excessive use of H&I fire and the deliberate killing of a prisoner. If we elide the distinction, we effectively wash away individual accountability. If we're all guilty, no one is guilty. In the end, opponents of the war have been too quick to assume that practices that were ill-advised and wrong were wanton crimes of war. Failing to maintain such a boundary risks trivializing legitimate war crimes.

There is no doubt that American soldiers committed atrocities in Vietnam, some of which are known, many of which likely remain unknown. The massacre at My Lai is the best documented and the best known, and the worst and largest yet known. But there were others. Daniel Lang brought one of the ugliest to light in a *New Yorker* article that would become a book and movie, *Casualties of War.*[22]

This was the story of the abduction, abuse, rape, and murder of a teenage girl, Phan Thi Mao, in the fall of 1966 by four soldiers of the 1st Air Cavalry assigned to a recon mission, led by a sergeant in the Central Highlands. The fifth member of the team, a young man from rural Minnesota, "Sven Eriksson"—Lang's pseudonym—who had refused to participate in the rape and murder carried the tale to his platoon leader and to his company commander. Neither, with the likely complicity of the battalion commander, were willing to pursue the matter legally, though the recon team was deliberately split up, the four were each busted one grade for sleeping without a mosquito net, and "Eriksson" was sent back to Camp Radcliff on a carpentry detail—though not before he lived through a suspicious friendly fire incident. One of the four, "Manuel," was a member of a squad that opened up on Eriksson's.[23]

But "Eriksson" didn't give up. He brought his story to a chaplain, "Gerald Kirk," a Mormon who had once worked as a policeman in Ogden City, Utah. "Kirk's" real name was Claude D. Newby. Newby ensured that the story went higher, and higher command took it seriously. With "Eriksson" along, the army Criminal Investigation Command (CID) found Mao's body. The army's pathologists and ballistics experts were able to determine that she had been shot at close range by an M-16.[24]

All four were charged and their court-martials were held at Camp Radcliff in March 1967. The defense counsels made Eriksson the target, trying to portray him as odd, a liar, even a coward. But the four were all convicted, of differing charges, and received differing sentences, ranging from eight years to life, all of which would be reduced on appeal, and reduced further with parole. Newby reports that the company commander, "Otto Vorst," and the battalion commander, whom he knew but chose not to name, both rose to flag rank, their failure to properly pursue a hideous war crime overlooked.[25]

One hundred twenty-two soldiers and Marines were convicted of the murder or manslaughter of Vietnamese while 278 soldiers and Marines were convicted of serious offenses against civilians during the course of the war. None of these cases remotely rose to the numbers murdered at My Lai, and no documented case ever has. Of the twenty-seven Marines who were convicted of the murder of Vietnamese nationals, twenty-five of those Marines convicted were given dishonorable discharges, fifteen received life sentences—only in seven of the cases were sentences less than ten years. On appeal, all of these sentences were reduced, only two Marines were confined for more than ten years. We may legitimately question the justice of such reductions in sentence, but such reductions were not uncommon in civilian courts. Sixteen Marines were tried for murder and found not guilty, an acquittal rate, according to the principal expert on Marine courts-martial in Vietnam, comparable to civilian courts in 1969. Among those sixteen was a then obscure Marine lieutenant, Philip Caputo, who would artfully construct a narrative of his Vietnam experience, his murder trial, and his apologia into *A Rumor of War*, the best-selling memoir of the war, and a Marine captain and lance corporal, all of whom we will meet shortly.[26]

Another writer, former Marine lieutenant William Broyles, recalled the successful prosecution of a Marine for murder; this happened not in combat but in the rear. Broyles wrote, "in war the line between killing and murder is not always easy to define," but he argued, "any soldier knows the difference." He went on: "Murder is different from killing. I saw many people killed, but I saw one man murdered, and I will never forget it. My Lai was like that—not killing, not warfare, but murder."[27]

The Marines also successfully prosecuted LCpl Marian McGhee for the egregious murder of a Vietnamese man in 1965. Seven Marines were charged with the point-blank killing of four Vietnamese men in two separate instances, and a fifth, whose throat was cut after an unsuccessful attempt to hang him, in May 1968 outside of Hue. Four pleaded guilty, another was convicted, a third was found lacking "mental responsibility" and judged not guilty. The squad leader, who was not present at the killings, received non-judicial punishment for "dereliction of duty" and failure to report the crimes. In 1969 two Marines were convicted of the murder of three Vietnamese girls, thirteen, seventeen, and nineteen, and one boy, eleven. There were extenuating circumstances. The four had discovered the Marines in ambush position and shouted a warning to their elders. The Marine court had no choice but to impose the maximum sentence, but all eight members signed a petition for clemency and believed that one of the guilty should be returned to duty. The prosecuting officer, after adjournment, told the court, that included at least two officers senior to him, that they "had just prostituted 190-odd years of Marine Corps history."[28]

The worst atrocity tried by the Marines happened at Son Thang on February 19, 1970, in southern Quang Nam Province. 1Lt Louis R. Ambort, the CO of Bravo Company, 1st Battalion, 7th Marines, sent out a five-man "killer team," led by LCpl Randell D. Herrod, soon to be awarded a Silver Star for "gallantry under fire," and demoted to private for a separate unauthorized absence as determined by a recent special court-martial. Ambort testified that he told his men "to shoot first and ask questions later." He reminded them of a fellow soldier, Whitmore, who had died that day. "I said, 'Don't let them get us anymore. I want you to pay these little bastards back!'" Herrod's team approached three hootches in sequence, killing five Vietnamese women, one of whom was blind; five boys, aged thirteen, ten, and eight, two who were six; and six girls, two who were thirteen, two who were eight, one who was six, and another who was two. Ambort planted a previously captured enemy rifle at the site and filed a false report. Marine command investigated and did not believe the story. One of the patrol members confessed and was found guilty, another was found guilty at trial, but Herrod, with the help of civilian lawyers and his former platoon leader, Oliver North, walked. Ambort, on the advice of the investigating officer, received only non-judicial punishment, a letter of reprimand, and the loss of pay. Justice weeps. The junior enlisted men were guilty, but to convict them and to effectively exonerate their platoon and patrol leader seems grievously wrong. But the trials and the circumstances were sufficiently different to complicate moral judgment. But Ambort and Herrod, the latter the "author" of an unpersuasive assertion of innocence, will have to live with their consciences.[29]

So were these merely show trials, senior Marines paying lip service to the laws of war? However cynical, it's not an argument that can simply be waved away. I've seen no evidence that anyone above the rank of captain was ever charged. Senior Marines may well have been protecting themselves. So what should we think when the Commandant of the Marine Corps, Gen Wallace Greene, wrote in a bulletin to all Commanding Officers: "I am extremely concerned in regard to recent incidents of wanton disregard for the personal lives and property of the civilian populace of the Republic of Vietnam. . . . I charge all CO's with the responsibility to ensure that all personnel receive instruction in regard to the standards of conduct expected of the U.S. Marines." Or when General Krulak wrote: "The nature of the conflict in Vietnam has placed an unusual requirement on low ranking leaders to carry out sensitive combat operations, often in an environment where large numbers of civilians are present." Krulak understood the need to make quick determinations of "right or wrong" sometimes in the heat of battle, by young, inexperienced leaders. "Nevertheless [they] must be fully aware of their responsibilities for their conduct, and the conduct of their subordinates. . . . Moreover, every Marine must be made to understand that deviation from these standards is a grave offense and not to be tolerated." CYA memos? Perhaps. But they are also clear, eloquent statements offering guidance to those who were prepared to hear them that there were Marine standards to be upheld and moral lines not to be crossed.[30]

Those who would argue the pervasive and inevitable nature of atrocity in Vietnam have to address such comments in good conscience. They must also address all of the evidence from memoir and oral history of soldiers who prevented atrocities. Gen Peter Pace, in a commencement address at The Citadel in 2006, described his "rage" as a young lieutenant at the loss of a young Marine—his first loss—from a sniper firing from a village. He called in an artillery strike on the village. His platoon sergeant "didn't say a word, he just looked at me." The look was sufficient. "I realized we were doing the wrong thing," Pace said. He called off the strike and ordered a sweep through the village finding only "women and children." "I do not know how I could live with myself," he said, "if I had carried that first instinct forward." William Van Zanten, a Marine officer who served with the 3rd Battalion, 7th Marines in 1965, wrote of his CO intervening to prevent a Vietnamese interrogator from cutting off the ear of a Vietnamese woman, and contrary to some of the voices at the WSI, also wrote of his unit's strict rules of engagement. They could not return fire from a village unless they were under heavy fire. Jeff Kelly, an enlisted forward observer with 3rd Battalion, 3rd Marines in 1968, wrote of taking aim at a Vietnamese child who had stolen his money, only to have a buddy knock his rifle higher: "Are you fuckin crazy? You waste one of these kids you're in a world of deep shit." Kelly was grateful. John Culbertson, who served with 2nd Battalion, 5th Marines in 1967, recalls his CO demanding that a Marine put down his knife poised threateningly before a civilian: "We are not here to kill women and children." The poet and writer W. D. Ehrhart, who served with 1st Battalion, 1st Marines in 1968, wrote of Sergeant Wilson, a squad leader, demanding that his CO reassign a member of his squad: "He's a headhunter. He tried to take ears last night. . . . I can't help what goes on in other outfits, but I won't have it in my scouts. This whole fuckin' thing's bad enough without butchery." These are stories told in four Marine memoirs, chosen at random. Similar stories could be multiplied several times over. They do not, of course, refute the better-known stories of atrocity, nor do they necessarily even balance America's moral account books. They are, however, evidence of command restraint, of men serving with honor, of doing justice in the face of a greater injustice. The organizers of the WSI and the producers of *Winter Soldier,* like many others who would follow them, were not interested in such stories and did not solicit them. Yet they are important to any balanced view of the behavior of American soldiers in Vietnam and a counter to simple-minded arguments about the inevitability of atrocity.[31]

But those who believed, or maybe just hoped, as I did, that My Lai was an aberration, had to face the painful truth of the 2003 revelations of war crimes committed by the 101st Airborne Division's Tiger Force in a seven-month period in 1967. In a well-sourced expose, the *Toledo Blade* determined that Tiger Force, a recon platoon of the 1st Battalion, 327th Infantry, killed at least eighty-one Vietnamese villagers in Quang Ngai Province. The army conducted a long investigation, stretching from 1971 to 1975, and found probable cause to try eighteen soldiers for murder or assault. The army never brought those charges and allowed six soldiers, including an officer, to resign while the investigation was ongoing. Again, the numbers do not compare to My Lai, but given the length of time Tiger Force was allowed to kill and given the army's failure to seek justice, the result was as disgraceful as the massacre at My Lai.[32]

Deborah Nelson's 2008 book, *The War Behind Me,* based on recently discovered army investigative records, raises the stakes. She found, she said, more than three hundred allegations of war crimes substantiated by the army, and an additional five hundred that were not substantiated. Although her language is measured, she has no doubt that war crimes in Vietnam were pervasive and quotes approvingly John Kerry's summary of what he heard at the WSI. But a closer look at her evidence raises doubts. Her three hundred allegations were made in a total of seventy-seven cases, thirty-six of which resulted in court martial, evidence that army command took the cases seriously, evidence that Nelson slights. Of the remaining forty-one cases, twelve involved the abuse of corpses, seven the abuse of prisoners. There was one case of robbery, another involving a medevac helicopter improperly carrying ammunition. There were a total of fourteen cases of the killing of Vietnamese, including the previously reported Tiger Force case—fourteen too many. Again make no mistake. American soldiers and Marines committed war crimes, officers covered them up. But consider that more than two million men and women served in Vietnam and somewhere between one million and 1.6 million served in combat.[33]

We have likely not heard the end of Vietnam's war crime "war stories," nor of facile arguments about moral responsibility. The effort to push responsibility for war crimes—all of it—up the chain of command was remarkably successful. The WSI and *Winter Soldier,* however, had no real impact on that success. No other work made such a "moral" argument more artfully or more successfully than Philip Caputo's *A Rumor of War.*

Murder and individual accountability were at the center of *A Rumor of War.* Published in 1977 to extravagant critical praise, it became a best seller, and in 1980, a TV-movie of the same name. Widely used in college classes, *Rumor* has sold more than three million copies and was republished by Henry Holt in 1996 with a twentieth anniversary postscript by Caputo. It is likely the most widely read memoir of the war.[34]

Caputo grew up on the outskirts of Chicago, and joined the Marines while a student at Loyola University. Commissioned a second lieutenant in 1964, he landed at Danang in March 1965 with the 9th Marine Expeditionary Brigade, the first ground combat unit sent to Vietnam. After his Marine service, he became a journalist with the *Chicago Tribune,* returning to Vietnam in 1975 when Saigon fell. *Rumor* was his first book, but he went on to several more, novels about the war and a memoir of his work as a war correspondent in Vietnam, Afghanistan, and the Middle East.[35]

Rumor is a self-consciously literary book, from its invocation of the Gospel of Matthew in its title to its use of chapter framing quotes from Shakespeare's *Henry IV,* to Ernest Hemingway, and the WWI writers Siegfried Sassoon and Wilfred Owen, though in an odd lapse of high seriousness, in slipped Howard Fast. It is also a thoroughly conventional war story, leading us from childhood yearning for heroism and manly respect, to the harsh and nasty intensity of basic training, to the pride of commissioning, and then to war. Caputo bought it all. "Fearless" and "aggressive," according to his early fitness reports prior to deployment, he was also said to be impulsive and "too quick on the trigger." "Napoleon once said that he could make men die for little pieces of ribbon," Caputo wrote, "I was ready to die . . . for a few favorable comments in a fitness report."[36]

With his company initially assigned to provide security for the airfield at Danang, Caputo was restless and longed for the "soldier's sacrament"—his "baptism of fire." As he waited, his mind drifted back to other clichés. The view from the Officers Club in Okinawa was "straight out of *South Pacific.*" The watchtowers on the perimeter of the Danang airfield evoked for him *Beau Geste.* He took great pleasure in evenings spent at the Grand Hotel Tourane, under the ceiling fans, watching sampans on the river as the sun went down. He noted with pride that he was part of something called an "expeditionary" force. "It was a peculiar period in Vietnam," he wrote, "with something of the romantic flavor of Kipling's colonial wars." His men were "happy warriors," "Kennedy's knights." Vietnam was "our crusade," our "splendid little war."[37]

In a helicopter on his way to his first combat assault, his nervousness gone, he was happy—"I felt happier than I ever had," under the circumstances, an emotion so unusual that it may well be unique in the annals of war memoir.

"I had read all the serious books to come out of the World Wars, and Wilfred Owen's poetry about the Western front," he tells us. "And yet, I had learned nothing."[38]

We are, of course, being set up. Such romantic innocence must give way to disillusion. With such expectations, war becomes, as Paul Fussell has written, the purest form of irony. The "splendid little war" will turn out to be just its opposite. But "All the poet can do today is warn," as Owen wrote and Caputo duly noted. The war story that Caputo will tell is a thoroughly familiar one, rooted in the experience of WWI—of innocence lost and betrayed.[39]

Caputo leads us, with artful deliberateness, to the ultimate moment of his book and his tour. His platoon sergeant, "Pappy" Crowe, all of twenty-three, reports to him while his platoon is standing down. He has evidence that two young men from the village of Giao Tri are VC. They, along with a younger man, had been questioned two weeks earlier and released—their forged credentials deemed evidence by an ARVN sergeant and a Marine officer that they were draft-dodgers, not VC. Crowe had just come from the village. The younger man, named Le Dung, he thought, had told him that the others were VC. They had been making mines and booby traps. Crowe saw fear in the young man's eyes as one of the others approached. He believed him.[40]

Caputo was angry with Crowe. Their company had lost thirty-five men in the last month, 30 percent of its strength, all to mines and booby traps. Why hadn't he taken them in? They'd been cleared, Crowe responded—by a Marine officer. Caputo's anger turned to dread at the thought of another harsh lecture from his company commander on the importance of aggressiveness. His platoon, on a night mission, had recently broken contact with two VC who had fired on them. Caputo thought it the prudent decision, but his CO did not —"Mr. Caputo, when we make contact with the enemy, we maintain it, not break it." Subsequently, his CO would establish a new policy—any Marine with a confirmed VC kill would get an extra beer ration and the time to drink it. All of this weighed on him as he called in Crowe's report to S-2, battalion intelligence.[41]

Weeks earlier, Caputo had lost control of his men. In the aftermath of a firefight, they had become, in his words, an "incendiary mob," needlessly burning the homes of more than 200 Vietnamese in Ha Na. He felt guilty and sick, "sick of war, sick of what the war was doing to us, sick of myself." His CO, he said, was "rightfully furious at me," and threatened to summarily remove him from command should it happen again. This was the same man who had upbraided Caputo for insufficient aggressiveness in pursuing VC and subsequently offered that extra beer ration. It is all to Caputo's credit that he allows us to see this. To be relieved of command in combat is an unambiguous disgrace. His CO's offer to reward a VC kill with another beer may seem symptomatic of the war's evil for many of Caputo's readers, but the core meaning of this can't be parsed so simply. Caputo's CO expected his men to kill VC without mercy, but he did not expect his platoon leaders to lose control of their men as they wantonly burned whole villages.[42]

By Caputo's account, all of this hung heavy over him. He was afflicted with dreams of death and killing. A year into his tour, "months of accumulated pressures" were now making him agitated, fearful, edgy. And so he resolved to act. He would capture or kill those two VC. He had no authority to do so. His mission was only to set up a night ambush. But his CO wanted bodies—"I would give him bodies, and then my platoon would be rewarded instead of reproved."[43]

He took five of his men aside, Crowe and a Marine named Allen among them. They were to "snatch" the two VC, to bring them back. If they resisted, kill them. "Yes, sir," Allen said, "with a look of distilled hatred and anger, and when he grinned his skull-like grin," Caputo wrote that he "knew that he was going to kill those men on the slightest pretext."

Caputo went on directly:

And, knowing that, I still did not repeat my order that the VC were to be captured if at all possible. It was my secret and savage desire that the two men die. In my heart, I hoped Allen would find some excuse for killing them, and Allen had read my heart.

In that moment of memory, Caputo acknowledged responsibility for what was to happen. Officers are responsible not only for orders that are direct and clear but for those that are suggestively implicit.[44]

His Marines did what Caputo had desired. They killed one man in the village; the second when they said he tried to escape on the way back to the platoon's night position. They captured no weapons, nor were they fired upon. They brought the body of the second man back. Elation and profane humor soon yielded to Caputo's realization that the body was that of the young informer, Le Dung. Crowe insisted he had the right man, though he would not look Caputo in the eyes; Allen confirmed Crowe's story of attempted escape. None of it was believable to Caputo. But he would make it worse. Their story would be that the first man died in an ambush, the second had been captured and tried to escape—"You don't tell anybody that you snatched him out of the village."[45]

Caputo's narrative continued. The—not his—Marines had made a mistake, out of confusion, fear, exhaustion, and "the brutal instincts acquired in the war"—"They had killed the wrong man." And then: "No, not they, *we* . . . that boy's innocent blood was on my hands." "My God what have we done? . . . Please God, forgive us. What have we done?" We, not I. Caputo did not acknowledge that it was his order that led to murder.[46]

It would take five months for Caputo and all five members of his patrol to face a military court-martial. Crowe and Caputo were charged with two counts of premeditated murder. Caputo faced an additional charge based on what he described as his "panicked attempt to deny that I had tried to cover up the killings." His "panicked attempt" was a lie under oath.[47]

He picked up his account the day he was called to testify against Crowe—June 30, 1966. His trial would begin the next morning. Guilt and forgiveness were no longer on his mind—though only one page of *Rumor* would separate his account of the murders from his account of the trial. He now believed the charge to be absurd: "They had taught us to kill, and now they were going to court-martial us for killing."[48]

Caputo had used the second stanza of Wilfred Owen's *Apologia Pro Poemate Meo* as epigram for this, his last chapter. It is a troubling and atypical stanza for Owen, one of the greatest of war poets. More than that, the stanza seems to contradict the principal meaning of the poem that the brotherhood of soldiers was redemptive. But the first couplet served Caputo's purposes well:

> Merry it was to laugh there—
> Where death becomes absurd and life absurder.

The second couplet is far more disturbing, compromising Caputo's prayer for forgiveness:

> For power was on us as we slashed bones bare
> Not to feel sickness or remorse of murder.

Given Caputo's skills as an accomplished and professional writer, his efforts to explain and justify that night are contorted. He understood that the blood of innocents was on his hands and that "something evil had been in [him] that night." Yet in the end, he could not accept any personal responsibility. "The deaths of Le Dung and Le Du [the other villager killed] were an inevitable product of the war." Inevitable. A Greek tragedy. Caputo saw himself as a noble man brought low by circumstance. "America could not intervene in a people's war," Caputo asserted, "without killing some of the people."[49]

A "people's war," in Robert Jay Lifton's formulation, was a war "undertaken by an advanced industrial society against a revolutionary movement of an underdeveloped country, in which the revolutionary guerrillas are inseparable from the rest of the population." Such a war was "inevitably genocidal." The concept owes much to Jean-Paul Sartre. It became an article of faith for that faction of the left who saw such movements as the great revolutionary hope of the future, but it gained a wider audience through the work of writers like Lifton, who drew upon Sartre to define the war in Vietnam as "an atrocity-producing situation." Not men "producing" atrocities, but "situations." Yes, the official language of the war was numbing—"free-fire zones," "search and destroy" missions, and the "mere gook rule." Such context matters and might in certain "situations" be exculpatory. But like the idea of the Vietnam War as a people's war, the war as "atrocity-producing situation" is an obfuscating half-truth. Just as thousands of American soldiers spent their tours fighting the uniformed army of North Vietnam, so thousands of others did not engage in the deliberate killing of the unarmed, however "inevitable" it may have been.[50]

Marine command proposed to try all six men for murder, according to Caputo, just as if it happened on the streets of Los Angeles. He was partly right. In the trial of William Calley, for his actions in ordering the deaths of villagers in My Lai, the army's Judge Advocate General argued that because the "victims were citizens of an allied nation, not enemies protected under the Geneva Convention . . . the My Lai murders were not legally distinguishable from other homicides." But the murder of civilians or prisoners also fell within the customary laws of war. Technically, Caputo and his men would be tried for both murder and a "grave breach"—the most serious violation—of the laws of war as defined by the Geneva Conventions of 1949.[51]

Each man would be tried separately. Caputo's men, by necessity, had to argue that they had simply obeyed a direct order. Caputo, again by legal necessity, but in utter betrayal of his men, had to argue that he had given a clear, lawful order "flagrantly disobeyed"—an excruciating argument for an honorable Marine officer to make. In the end, Caputo asserted that neither the charge, nor his defense, nor his men's defense was false or true. Caputo's truth, once again, was that the war and U.S. military policy were ultimately to blame for the deaths of those two Vietnamese. The entire trial, Caputo claimed, was designed to obscure that: "The thing we had done was the result of what the war had done to us."[52]

So why did the Marine command bring these charges? Caputo did not reflect on it, but we may. At one level, it was a response to the complaint of several villagers, one that made its way to Marine command in Danang. Caputo indirectly suggests that the Marines had nothing to lose whatever the verdict and the trial would not permit a wider discussion of the war's morality. So was this a cynical effort to appease the Vietnamese and make the Marines look like upholders of high moral standards? We're not likely to know. But, as we've seen, such trials were not unusual. In writing to a mother distraught over similar charges brought against her son—this in a far more egregious incident—the Commandant of the Marine Corps wrote: "The Marine Corps is fighting in Vietnam in the name of a nation which requires certain standards of civilized conduct." "Certain standards of civilized conduct"? Cynical rationalization? Possibly. But are we prepared to live with no such standards—even unevenly applied, even knowing the "inevitability" of atrocity?[53]

Caputo took the stand in Crowe's court-martial to testify as a witness for the prosecution; his was scheduled for the next day. He wrote that he recalled nothing of what he had said, but he recalled being well prepared by his lawyer. The court found Crowe not guilty on all charges. Caputo tells us nothing more, but it is reasonable to speculate that the ambiguity surrounding Caputo's order was more than sufficient to raise reasonable doubt among the court-martial board. Caputo's military lawyer informed him the next day that the commanding general (CG) was thinking, as a result of the acquittal, of dropping all charges against the others. He also reported that the CG was prepared to drop the murder charges against Caputo. Caputo, however, would have to plead guilty to lying under oath and accept a letter of reprimand. There would be no time served in the brig. It was an easy decision. It would cost Caputo promotion to captain and an end to a Marine career he no longer sought. But for many hundreds of Marine officers, accepting such an outcome would have been far harder.[54]

Within a matter of days, Caputo flew home. Whatever faith he had once invested in the Marine Corps was now dead and his painful breaking of faith with his men had not been truly tested. In returning to the "rumor of war" passage in Matthew (24:6-13), Caputo's "We had done nothing more than endure" echoed the promise of Matthew's Jesus: "the one who endures to the end will be saved." Caputo had endured. But the test of endurance in Matthew was not the test of war—but the test of faith.[55]

The reviews were timely and well placed, and the praise was effusive. Peter Prescott, in *Newsweek,* regarded it as the "long overdue" work by a combat veteran. C. D. B. Bryan, who would write his own powerful book on Vietnam, *Friendly Fire,* ranked it alongside Erich Maria Remarque and Norman Mailer for its ability to do what all great war books do—convey an atmosphere. Bryan thought it the first book to offer the feeling of what it was like to fight in Vietnam. Theodore Solotaroff, writing in the *New York Times Book Review,* saw the "relentless immediacy" of Caputo's work as "quite equal to the Vietnam reportage of Michael Herr." Herr's *Dispatches* was for many the first great piece of personal journalism to emerge from the war. Solotaroff concluded by asserting that Caputo's voice was nothing less than the voice of America—the "troubled conscience of America speaking passionately, truthfully, finally."[56]

Offering more than praise, Caputo's reviewers also took him at his word, embracing his personal moral reckoning, accepting him as victim. *Library Journal's* reviewer summed up *Rumor* by claiming that the war's "most forgotten victims" were the Americans who fought it. *Newsweek's* Prescott went much further. Caputo had convinced him that the war "was much worse than many of us imagined." It was, he went on, "an unspeakable waste of men . . . [reducing] all combatants to a state of savage frenzy in which atrocities became not only possible but desirable—as seemingly rational extensions of the general horror and futility." *Rumor* led Prescott to claim that the war, "with its peculiar combination of stress and fatigue, of futility and lunatic violence, batters the average American boy loose from his reason—as well as whatever moral and spiritual resources he has."[57]

This was language wholly unmeasured, but Prescott was articulating what many had come to believe. There was something uniquely horrific about the war in Vietnam "with its peculiar combination of stress and fatigue, of futility and lunatic violence." It is impossible to imagine any thoughtful Marine or army combat veteran of WWII concurring. Stress, fatigue, futility, lunatic violence *are* the conditions of war. The war in Vietnam, Prescott tells us, "consumed all . . . and reduced all . . . to a state of savage frenzy" where atrocities were made rational and desirable. Not some. *All.* Recovering a bare minimum of measure, Prescott saw the "average American boy" battered and defenseless in a world where reason, morality, spirituality had no purchase. William Styron, writing in the *New York Review of Books,* took it further. The war in Vietnam, he said, "defiled even its most harmless and well-meaning participants." Prescott and Styron understood Caputo exactly—this was "what the war had done to us."[58]

For C. D. B. Bryan, *Rumor* offered him an explanation for the atrocities of My Lai. Caputo had taken his readers to a place where "heat was so oppressive, backs so heavy, nerves so frayed, muscles so tired, men so weary, numbed, frustrated, that an outsider can understand the inevitable savagery of My Lai." Inevitable—that word once again. The equation of My Lai with that night in Giao Tri displays a blindness to the facts and an inability to make moral distinctions. Whatever Caputo's crimes that night, he did not order the daylight murder of unresisting women and children.[59]

For Solotaroff, Caputo's action that night was "a crime of which he was ambiguously, understandably, and . . . almost inevitably guilty." "Inevitably," once again. Solotaroff saw Caputo as "the articulate and troubled spokesman" for all those who fought in Vietnam. With extraordinary condescension, he wrote of Caputo as a type:

> If you've had much contact with the upper reaches of blue-collar America, you'll know Caputo right away . . . the earthy, hot-blooded adventurous kid . . . the temperamental quarterback who makes some inspired winning play . . . the English major from a working-class family who now and then asks a forthright question that cuts through the literary cant.

There is no basis in *Rumor* for seeing Caputo as a child of the working class. He grew up in the suburbs of Chicago, graduated from Loyola, and never mentioned his parents' work.[60]

Solotaroff would go on. It was Kennedy-era altruism and his desire to test himself that led Caputo to the Marines, where his career was "no less representative and expressive." So how did one of the "best and the brightest" of those who fought the war become, in Solotaroff's words, "a vindictive, desperate, and chronically schizoid killer"? Solotoroff writes of the "fabled sadism" of Marine boot camp, the "mental abuse," the "brainwashing." In fairness, Caputo does write harshly of his experience in Officer Candidate School (OCS). What is missing in Solatoroff's review, however, is Caputo's express sense of pride in his graduation from OCS. And then there was the war itself—"miserable, terrifying, and absurd." Of course it was—but then Solatoroff conflates the killing of VC, with all of its Hobbesian horror, with the killing of non-combatants. "One wants to see Caputo exonerated, as he was."[61]

But he wasn't exonerated. He pled guilty to one charge, while the others were dropped. Other reviewers also reported Caputo's trial inaccurately. William Shawcross, writing in the *New Statesman,* claimed he was acquitted. The *Christian Century*'s reviewer wrote that he was "cleared" of charges. Styron wrote that he was "ultimately exonerated." *Newsweek*'s Prescott understood that the charges had been dropped, but then suggested, without any evidence, that it was because the Marines were embarrassed. Why would five writers get it wrong, four of them wholly so? Did they so identify with Caputo's narrative—that the "horror" of the war in Vietnam overrode individual responsibility—that all they could see was exoneration?[62]

Only one reviewer challenged Caputo. A relatively obscure research-center administrator, writing in *Commentary,* offered a fair summary of *Rumor,* a critique of Caputo's too "neat, consecutive recall of consciousness raising"—comparing it unfavorably to one of the great and little known works of war writing, J. Glenn Gray's *The Warriors*—and a wholly different judgment on Caputo's balancing of the scales. This was William J. Bennett. Where others saw a victim, Bennett saw a rash and impetuous officer, under warning for having lost control of his men, who had violated the Marines' norms of conduct. Bennett understood that one form of war's brutalization was the denial of personal responsibility—"Among the many corruptions of the Vietnam era, the corruption of the meaning of moral responsibility is not the least insidious."[63]

Bennett's moral certainties, then as now, are pompous and grating. Yet he unmasked a truth that eluded Caputo's liberal reviewers who have been much too ready to allow blame to flow upward, leaving only victims on the ground—victims who were responsible for murder.[64]

seven
False Atrocities

At first Krebs, who had been at Belleau Wood, Soissons, the Champagne,
St. Mihiel and in the Argonne did not want to talk about the war at all.
Later he felt the need to talk but no one wanted to hear about it. His town
had heard too many atrocity stories to be thrilled by actualities. Krebs
found that to be listened to at all he had to lie.
—Ernest Hemingway, "Soldier's Home" (1925)

Dennis Apple, known as the Turk, claimed he was a tunnel rat in Vietnam. We meet him in Rod Kane's *Veteran's Day*, a stream of consciousness memoir by a troubled former medic, at a demonstration against the war in Washington, D.C., Kane and the Turk are smoking dope. The Turk tells a war story. While serving with the 1st Infantry in the Iron Triangle, north of Saigon, the Turk is called forward to investigate a tunnel. The story begins well—that's where the 1st was; that's where the tunnels were. His commanding officer (CO) asks: "You know what you're doing son?'" "Yes sir,' he says." "Find out what's in that hole." "Yes sir. I say, saluting him." Kane asks his readers: "Why did he salute?"[1]

The Turk goes on. He enters the hole, it opens out, there is a rope ladder leading deeper. He hears a voice—it echoes. The space below must be larger. The Turk thinks he's onto something big—"Man, I'm gonna get me a medal!" The Turk had entered the hole with grenades: "I pull the grenade pins out with my teeth, wait a second, then let them fly, one after another." Kane's narrative continues. The Turk is crying and tells Kane he needs to

181

leave before the cops can smell his reefer. Kane wants to hear the end. "So, did you get your medal? [The Turk] straightens, shakes his head: 'I blew up a teacher and a classroom full of kids.'"[2]

Samuel Hynes reports this story in his *The Soldiers' Tale*, using it to frame an argument that "dead children are everywhere in Vietnam narratives." "The dead children are what Vietnam *meant* to the men who tell its story." All this may be true, but the Turk's story is false. Kane tells us three pages later that the Turk never served in Vietnam. The Turk wasn't just a wannabe Vietnam vet, but a wannabe killer of children.[3]

Hynes was a Marine fighter pilot in WWII, a professor of English at Princeton, the author of a distinguished memoir of his wartime experience, and an important book on the writings of war veterans, yet he appears to have been taken in by the Turk's story, missing both Kane's conclusion and his clues.[4]

No one salutes in the field, it puts officers at risk; and no one, outside of Hollywood and Marvel Comics, pulls grenade pins out with their teeth. If Hynes missed all this, what hope is there for other readers? Hynes's reading suggests how ready we are to believe the worst of Vietnam veterans, and how difficult it is to understand that some veterans lied about the atrocities they committed and the atrocities they saw.

If some readers were gullible, others were more than willing to see those soldiers who committed real atrocities as victims, aggressively pushing responsibility all the way up the chain of command. (Hey, Hey, LBJ, How many kids did you kill today?) Let's grant, for argument's sake, the moral truth of that simple and ugly question. How does that exonerate the Lieutenant Calleys of My Lai infamy, or others, who deliberately killed unarmed noncombatants in the full glare of Vietnam's sun? No other war in American history produced so many soldiers who lied, not about being heroes, but about being victims. And no other war in American history produced so many apologists for those "victims" who committed real atrocities.

Popular belief in widespread American atrocity persists, and the credulous acceptance of atrocity stories continued long after Neil Sheehan's exposure of Mark Lane should have prompted skepticism. Wallace Terry's *Bloods: An Oral History of the Vietnam War by Black Veterans* was a best seller in 1984, widely and effusively praised. *Time* thought all twenty soldiers whose accounts were collected "uniformly eloquent," the *Washington Post* wrote that it captured "the very essence of war"—"the nastiest . . . in our history," AP that it was "literature with the ring of truth." Michiko Kakutani of the *New York Times* wrote a positive review, echoing Philip Caputo's reviewers that the war was "devoid of rules and moral imperatives," and for black soldiers the war was even worse. The success of the book had much to do with its timing. Americans in general had become more attentive to the service and travail of Vietnam vets, and many had a genuine interest in the underreported experience of black vets. Many Americans also believed falsely that blacks had suffered casualties disproportionate to their percentage of the American population. *Bloods* became the most widely read account of black veterans for both the general public and for college students. Its influence was reinforced by a 1986 *Frontline* feature "The Bloods of 'Nam."[5]

Terry had sought a broad cross-section of blacks who served, officers, senior enlisted men, grunts, and a cross-section of experiences, from Col Fred Cherry, a POW who refused to renounce the war and was tortured for it, to Capt Joseph B. Anderson Jr., a platoon leader whose war would be captured in the French film, *The Anderson Platoon*, to one young man who came home to join the Black Panthers and to another who came home to unemployment. But Terry offered no evidence of his methods—what were his questions? Are the transcripts verbatim?—and no evidence that he sought any form of corroboration.[6]

Not surprisingly, those who told atrocity stories captured substantial attention. And that leads us to the account of Arthur E. Woodley Jr., known as Gene and also, by his own claim, as "Cyclops" and "Montagnard." Woodley is introduced to the readers of *Bloods* as a Specialist 4th Class, a "Combat Paratrooper, 5th Special Forces Group, 75th Ranger Group, 173rd Airborne Division," stationed in An Khe from November 1968 to December 1969. He tells us he returned with five Bronze Stars for valor. By his own account, he was an excellent soldier, walking point in a "dark green-loin cloth, a dark green bandanna . . . and "Ho Chi Minh sandals," and nothing else, hence the nickname "Montagnard." He spent three days on a "POW snatch" with a punji stake in his foot, the point actually protruding through his boot. He believed he killed forty of the enemy, one with an axe: "I jumped out the woods and chopped a fellow's head off with it." He came back, in his own words, as an "animal." Even his mother, he said, "was afraid of me." His unusual choice of "uniform," his ability to walk three days with a punji stake in his foot, his use of an axe as a weapon are stories bizarrely imaginative and uniquely absurd.[7]

He claimed he collected "about 14 ears and fingers," and wore them around his neck. His status as a killer yielded free drugs, sex, and alcohol in

An Khe. His team threw eight Viet Cong (VC) prisoners out of helicopters. He "only remembered" pushing two himself. He participated in the gang rape and murder of two Vietnamese women. He witnessed the grotesque torture of other women, participated in the killing of "20 some people, mostly women and children." "I was some gross animal," he wrote. He fired an M-79 round into his own officers' barracks in a grievance over a promotion. He returned home in his jungle fatigues after having not bathed for six months. He had a full beard, matted hair, and claimed, in a strange but striking metaphor, that he smelled "like a cockroach on Christmas." Somehow he missed the showers at Cam Ranh Bay, or Bien Hoa, as well as the requirement to don khaki Class A's prior to boarding. For some time, and in the wake of My Lai, he feared count martial, for "a lot of us wiped out whole villages."[8]

He said he killed his first VC by emptying an entire clip in his face: "And his face disappeared. . . . And his body stood there for proximately somewhere around ten, fifteen seconds. And it shivers. And it scared me beyond anyone's imagination," violating all the laws of physics. And then his worst story. His team found a soldier, "a white guy," staked to the ground, beaten, mutilated, his upper body skinned, his belly open, flesh holes where animals had eaten, maggots in his throat and stomach. He had been staked out for three days, Woodley claimed, but he was alive. So what did Woodley do? Cut him loose and call in a medevac? No, he was afraid, because the maggots had eaten so much and it would have put him in even more pain. The man pleaded to die. Woodley called headquarters for advice. They couldn't bring him back, he said, they couldn't get there quickly enough, and they had another mission. They said it was up to him. He was in charge—a Specialist 4th Class. So, after agonizing for twenty minutes, he killed him. And for this act of mercy killing, he claimed he was threatened with court-martial.[9]

It is not a believable story. No one should have any illusions about what the VC or North Vietnamese Army (NVA) were capable of, but this takes us to a wholly new level of preposterous evil. No one could survive three days in such a condition, medevac crews did not refuse missions of such urgency, and no command would knowingly allow the body of a dead American to remain in the field.

It is a litany of horror, but it gets worse. Woodley, according to an investigation of his service record by B. G. Burkett, never served in the 5th Special Forces, nor was he awarded any medals for valor, nor did he receive a Purple Heart for that punji stake in his foot. But even without that knowledge, Terry had ample grounds for skepticism. And so did others.[10]

What happened to the filters skeptical editors and producers are supposed to bring to stories like this? Why were otherwise intelligent people prepared to believe wildly improbable accounts without any apparent effort to corroborate them? Whitney Balliett, writing a long review of *Bloods* in the *New Yorker*, singled out Woodley and his stories of the staked out and skinned American and the headless VC body that just stood there, uncritically offering it up as the truth to his upscale readers while writing with breathtaking condescension of the "poetic exuberance" of blacks. Kakutani of the *New York Times* noted Woodley's nightmares at having to kill a fellow soldier, and the *Post's* reviewer, Lieutenant General Julius W. Becton Jr., uncritically evoked Woodley twice And the reviewer for the scholarly journal *Military Affairs* wrote that the "accounts shake our senses and sensitize us to the reality of war."[11]

And in 1986, there was Woodley again in the PBS *Frontline* special, "The Bloods of 'Nam," in which he would repeat his animal theme: "We became animals a lot of us, a lot of us stayed animals, a lot of us are still animals." To illustrate, he mentioned his collection of ears, now grown to "twenty-five, twenty-six." To his credit, the *New York Times's* Walter Goodman cautioned skepticism about Woodley's story, though only because of his "tendency toward self-dramatization." And it goes on. In an article published by Indiana University Press in 2004 in a collection, *Soldier Talk: The Vietnam War in Oral Narrative*, William M. King tells the mercy killing story as the truth and accepts uncritically all of Woodley's account.[12]

Woodley wasn't the only one in *Bloods* to offer bizarre stories of atrocity. A hospital corpsman claimed he witnessed the death of a Vietnamese woman, the result of a white phosphorus flare inserted into her vagina by a Republic of Korea (ROK) Marine. Specialist Richard J. Ford III identified as a 25th Infantry Division LURP (Long-Range Recon Patrol), told a grotesque story of an NVA sergeant stripped and tied to a tree, the victim of a "game called Guts." "Everyone in the unit got in line. At least 200 guys." One "plucked his eye out" with a bayonet. Ford's reaction? "I was amazed how large your eyeball was." Others "sliced his ear off," pulled his teeth out, sliced his tongue, "cut him all over," tortured him to death. Then directly following, in mitigation, Ford mentioned finding the bodies of three soldiers from the 101st hanging from a tree, butchered by the enemy. "We had to bury 'em," Ford said, in violation of deeply held military tradition. Soldiers died attempting to recover the bodies of their comrades so those bodies could be returned to their kin. These are wildly improbable stories, made worse in Ford's case by Burkett's investigation of his service record. There is no record of Ford's service as a LURP, nor of the three Purple Hearts nor the two Bronze Stars for Valor that he claimed. At least three other of Terry's interviewees offered tales of combat and heroism that could not be verified, including one air force staff sergeant who claimed that he and his unit killed the VC who had infiltrated the U.S. embassy during the Tet Offensive. Despite early and false reports that VC had entered the embassy, later reports made clear they never did, and there is no evidence that air force units were engaged on the embassy grounds during Tet.[13]

Terry's collection of oral histories was not the only such collection that should have evoked doubt. Mark Baker's *NAM: The Vietnam War in the Words of the Men and Women who Fought There*, appeared in 1981 published by William Morrow and Company. It was prominently and well reviewed and sold even better. Baker was, by his own account, opposed to the war, but he joined demonstrations only when "convenient," when it would not interfere, in his words, "with my nice, privileged draft deferment." Morrow and Company chose not to heed the lessons that Simon & Schuster should have learned from publishing Mark Lane, and allowed Baker to use wholly anonymous interviewees. "It must be assumed that included here," Baker wrote, "are generalizations, exaggerations, braggadocio and—very likely—outright lies." Baker went on in justification: "But if these stories were told within a religious framework, the telling would be called bearing witness. The human imperfections simply authenticate the sincerity of the whole," a phrase quoted approvingly by the *New York Times* reviewer. George Orwell was fortunate that he did not live long enough to read such cant.[14]

And so Baker's readers learned that one soldier took no prisoners. "We didn't go through that nonsense. I used to shoot them . . . stand them up against the wall . . . pull the trigger. Taking a life was nothing. It was customary." They also learned from this same soldier that "it was encouraged to cut ears off, to cut the nose off, to cut the guy's penis off. A female, you cut her breast off. It was encouraged to do these things. The officers expected you to do it or something was wrong with you." And what happened to the mutilated bodies? "We threw those 100 bodies in the Saigon River," so many that the navy complained that they could no longer properly navigate the river. It is a preposterous story. And so too our informant's claim that American wounded were too quickly placed in body bags: "I believe a lot of guys died in that green bag." One reviewer tried his hand at Orwellian language: the interviewees' "anonymity shades *NAM*'s historicity, but the 'unknown soldier' quality also redoubles the visceral force of Baker's stories." And depending on how we define "visceral force," it may well be true.[15]

John Ketwig's . . . *and a Hard Rain Fell* appeared in 1985, published by Macmillan. Though not as well known as the works of Caputo, Terry, and Baker, it was favorably reviewed, appears on many college bibliographies, and was reprinted in 2002. Ketwig writes he grew up on a farm in upstate New York, his father a bus driver. Graduating from high school in 1965, he says he was accepted at Cornell but went to work instead at a Chevy dealership. It didn't work out—he was fired, making him draft eligible—and so he enlisted for three years, with the army's promise of specialized training. The army kept its promise and Ketwig became a "Wheel and Track Vehicle Repair" specialist. It did not keep him from Vietnam.[16]

Ketwig tells this story. Just before Christmas 1967, stationed near Pleiku and assigned to a maintenance unit he never identifies, he and "Jerry" drive to a Green Beret firebase near the Cambodian border to trade truck parts for steaks. The Green Berets, we are told, "were issued nothing," in order to make them more resourceful. He and his partner undertook the three-hour trip alone and without a radio. Told it was safe, they found three small holes behind the passenger's door after arriving, apparently from small-arms fire they never heard. The Green Berets are framed harshly. They are "wild, uncontrolled men whose sole purpose in life seemed to be violence." "They marauded, they destroyed, they killed with a fury so intense it was sometimes unleashed upon their countrymen." The firebase was simply a clearing—"no hootches, no outhouses, no mess hall," but there was, incongruously, an olive-drab fire truck. Ketwig notes the absurdity, a fire truck in the absence of any clear need.[17]

The fire truck's role would become gruesomely clear. Three "whores," their arms bound, were being interrogated by an Army of the Republic of Vietnam (ARVN) officer. A Green Beret lieutenant named Frost explains that one of his men had visited "these ladies" recently. All that was left was his head "with his cock in his mouth." The Green Berets, having found NVA documents on the women, were now intent on revenge. A "burly black" stood over one of the women. "Where Timmy? Where da resta Timmy? Cunt! Whore! You gonna die, oh, you gonna die bad, Mama-san!" So she would, according to Ketwig as the "giant black" forced the nozzle of the fire hose between her legs—"A scream started from her throat, a sound unlike any other!" Ketwig had been given a joint and a cold Coke. "I was sick. The sweetness of the Coke seemed to seep up my throat. . . . I heaved until my insides ached." He and Jerry, he said, had seen "the real war."[18]

Ketwig had witnessed a war crime, if true, a war crime of extraordinary cruelty. Reflecting on what he calls "the firebase incident," he rambles. He knows it was wrong. How could he have let it happen? Was this routine? What had he become? What "future stress" would lead him back to "inhuman behavior"? The Green Berets were "professional killers." They were "men under stress." It wouldn't have been wise to try to stop them. And then suddenly in the midst of this ramble, he confesses "there was a fascination to the whole affair," not unlike a movie rape or the aftermath of a traffic accident. And from this he leaps to attach blame. The army taught him to kill, to disrespect women and "gooks." But then maybe it wasn't just the army. Maybe it was our parents "who gave us too much" or American society "too infatuated with material goods to remember the ideals America was based upon." Everyone was guilty except him.[19]

He and Jerry made a pact to keep the secret. They would not talk of it again. He never reported it or talked with a chaplain, nor reflected on why he didn't. A year or so later, while serving in Thailand, Ketwig would unburden himself with a friend, summing up all the painful things he had seen; the "torn, battered bodies" of Americans, some being towed behind a personnel carrier, dead NVA with pictures of their families. He did not mention the women at the firebase.[20]

Did it happen? So many elements of the story ring false; two men sent alone into hostile territory without a radio, the AK rounds that they did not hear, three prostitutes in close proximity to a remote firebase in one of the most sparsely populated areas of Vietnam, Green Berets forced by the army to scavenge for all their needs, and then, the fire truck.

His improbable and morally bankrupt torture account is not his only questionable story. He tells one of the ugliest basic-training abuse stories I've ever read. A recruit he calls "Fatso" is unable to complete a two-mile run. His drill instructor (DI) slaps him, hits him with his belt, orders him to strip, "smashed his fist into his face then drove a fist into his stomach," ordered him to defecate on a cigarette butt and to carry the results back, hit him several more times. This happened on a parade field at Ft. Dix, an open post, with traffic streaming by only "a few yards away," according to Ketwig. I don't believe it likely that a DI would do this, but if one ever succumbed to such evil, he would not do it so publicly. Ketwig, nor any of his fellow recruits, nor any of those driving by ever reported the abuse of "Fatso." Ketwig tells us that Fatso deliberately hid himself behind a night-fire target, in an extraordinary lapse of fire-range discipline on the part of his trainers, and died, a suicide.[21]

That's not all. Ketwig tells us that at Aberdeen Proving Ground, the site of his specialized training, "getting sick was a punishable offense." You could go to jail for growing a mustache or peeing without permission, to "lie down from exhaustion was AWOL," and getting a tattoo or VD was "destruction of government property," a court-martial offense. Once in Vietnam, Ketwig learned one of the signature Vietnam "legends" that bamboo vipers could kill with one bite and that "you had about forty-five seconds to blow your own head off before the agony began." I can attest to the legend having treated a frenetic Ranger lieutenant convinced he was going to die, and successfully getting him the necessary antidote well after he was bitten. And then there was the night when Ketwig and his buddies shared a whorehouse with four NVA soldiers, drinking beer, smoking a joint, sharing pictures of home and loved ones, sharing antiwar beliefs.[22]

Toronto's *Globe and Mail* thought Ketwig's book "among the more eloquent and powerful statements about the war," *Kirkus Reviews* stated that "it was a searing gift to his country," and the *Baltimore Sun* wrote that Ketwig's story was "vivid and harsh and incredibly realistic." *Library Journal* recommended it, and *Publishers' Weekly*, acknowledging the suicide, the torture, and the late-night encounter with the NVA, honored Ketwig's experiences "as painful and various . . . as any grunt." The *Washington Post*'s reviewer, a Vietnam vet, compared Ketwig's writings to Céline. The historian, George Herring—to his credit—wrote that Ketwig was "one of the least convincing of the Vietnam memoirs in print," though he provided no detail.[23]

And so we return to the questions with which we started. Why were such outrageous atrocity stories believed? Why were they told? Such stories came to be believed because reviewers, readers, and teachers wanted to believe them. Their desire to believe sprang from several sources, an understandable opposition to the war but also and more importantly a willingness to believe that there was something uniquely evil about the war. Feeding those beliefs was a genuine revulsion at the burning of villages, the intensive bombing of the North, and the bloody images of My Lai. Forgotten or discounted were the terrible lessons of twentieth-century warfare. Civilians had no safe haven. By some estimates one-quarter of the civilian population of Okinawa died during the battle for the island. But the belief that American intervention was wrong and needless made it far easier to discount those lessons. We had to defeat the Japanese on Okinawa, but there was no such moral clarity to the war in Vietnam. Indeed, many on the left believed fervently that the unique evil of the war rested heavily if not exclusively on the United States.[24]

But opposition to the war could have led reviewers and readers in different directions. They could have been as harshly judgmental as Mark Lane had been at Stockholm, holding individual soldiers accountable, a stance requiring a knowledge of specifics—who did what, when, and where?—that might have led to skepticism about questionable atrocity stories. That's not where our reviewers went. Suspension of judgment is often a virtue, but in this case it only added to credulousness. No doubt it would have been better if more reviewers had been veterans of the war, or had at least served in the military, but even that was no assurance of reading with an honest eye. Some conservatives have suggested that liberal reviewers of a certain age "needed" to believe the worst, needed to believe that the war was uniquely horrific, in order to justify their own refusal to serve. So are we looking at just another case of liberal guilt? Over the years, I've seen some evidence of that both publicly and privately. Even the most pacific of post-'60s men may harbor some regret at never having their physical courage truly tested, but most men I know of the right age seem utterly guiltless.[25]

A better place to look is the growing sense that Vietnam veterans were to be pitied rather than judged. As *Library Journal*'s reviewer of Caputo's *A Rumor of War* put it, Vietnam veterans were America's "forgotten victims." By the time the Vietnam Veterans Memorial went up, and Vietnam memoirs turned from disillusion to stark anger as the specters of Agent Orange and Post Traumatic Stress Disorder (PTSD) became widely publicized, the "victimhood" of Vietnam veterans had become widely endorsed. Liberal reviewers had been well schooled. "Blaming the victim" had become a secular sin, a transgression against sensitivity and empathy. And so "victims" would not be blamed, their stories of atrocity would not be challenged. Those who committed atrocities were "scapegoats," even Marine battalion commanders, as one vet at the Citizens' Commission of Inquiry hearings in Washington claimed, were "victims." Reviewers and many others surrendered whatever moral authority they might have summoned to hold men accountable for both atrocities they committed and the lies they told. It was far better to blame higher ups, even America as a whole, and to accept as truth the most outrageous stories.[26]

Lurking behind such thinking was the troubled and angry response of American intellectuals to Hannah Arendt's bold and brilliant argument about the "banality of evil," by which she simply meant the capacity of ordinary men, the Adolph Eichmanns of Nazi Germany, to commit extraordinary evil. The debate over Arendt suggested that Americans were far more comfortable with other explanations—that some men are "monsters," irredeemably evil, or "there, but for the grace of God," I too would have succumbed. The latter argument was especially appealing to liberals committed to environmental explanations of behavior, and was precisely what lay behind Robert Jay Lifton's claim of the Vietnam War as an "atrocity producing situation." Some men may well be monsters, but are there enough such men to explain the world's evil? And there are too many examples of men doing "justice in the face of the great injustice," as Robert Penn Warren put it, to blithely accept that evil is merely circumstantial. Only Arendt's formulation allows us to understand why ordinary men commit evil—or lie about committing it.[27]

So why did they lie? Some may well have thought that's what interviewers and editors wanted to hear. Lane and perhaps others clearly sought such stories. For deserters, it was a way of vindicating themselves. Others no doubt had political motives. Others, struggling with unemployment and other stresses, may well have seen their "victimhood" as a way out. Think of the temptation with a microphone or a camera placed in front of them. Some craved the attention. Pete Andrews confessed to a psychiatrist at St. Alban's Navy Hospital that he and his recon unit in the 1st Infantry Division had "committed atrocities that made My Lai pale in comparison." A fellow recon member, upon hearing the claim, confronted Andrews: "Pete, you're hurting us with all this bullshit." Andrews "broke down" and admitted the lie. "I wanted the [unit] to be famous," he admitted, "we should be." "Not like this," his buddy responded. We'll never be sure why men embellished, exaggerated, and lied about such matters. But we know that they did, and that's enough.[28]

Camil Redux

And so we return to *Winter Soldier* and that moment of recognition between Ken Campbell and Scott Camil. Ken Campbell had joined Bravo Company, 1st Battalion, 1st Marines as an artillery forward observer in February 1968. He recalled hearing of an "incident," involving Bravo, in Quang Tri, that had happened some time in the summer or fall of 1967. The story circulated in the company: "all the guys who were there before me talked about it," Campbell said at the Winter Soldier Investigation (WSI). He recalled hearing of an "investigation." He testified that there was a "big stink about it," and that "we had a black mark against us for the incident."[29]

This was the incident that Campbell asked Camil about in the opening scenes of *Winter Soldier*. Camil said he was there: "We went into the area and it was to set the example to show that we weren't fucking around so the first thing we do is burn down the village and kill everybody." Camil said he had forgotten all about it. He said he had forgotten it twice. In response to Campbell's incredulous question: "How could you forget? I remember it and I wasn't even in on it." Camil said it was one of the last things he did. It was a strange statement, since most of us are more likely to remember the "last" things we did, rather than the earlier ones. Camil said he would need to be prompted on it while on stage. He was never prompted, and never testified to it.[30]

With the camera still trained on Campbell, we hear Camil's voice apparently elaborating on that massacre in Quang Tri. "On Operation Stone," he said, "we were sitting up on a railroad trestle and there was a river on each side and there was another company behind each river and the people were like just running around inside and we were shooting them and the newspaper said 'Operation Stone just like a World-War II movie.'" Camil went on: "we just set up there and wiped them out, men, women, children, everything"—then a pause, "291 of them."[31]

It is not clear whether Camil's memory failed him once again, or the filmmakers spliced in an unrelated comment. (Campbell reports that Camil said that the latter happened.) But the common sense meaning of the scene was clear: the massacre in Quang Tri happened on Operation Stone. Operation Stone, however, took place not in Quang Tri but in the vicinity of Danang, and not in the summer or fall of 1967, but in February of the same year. Second, the reference to a newspaper is telling. The number of killed—291— is the exact number of VC deaths officially reported for all of Operation Stone. A coincidence? Perhaps. In his formal testimony at the WSI Camil made no mention of the "incident" in Quang Tri or of the 291 villagers massacred on Operation Stone.[32]

It wasn't that Camil shied away from telling grotesque atrocity stories. In his public testimony at the WSI, and in his filmed comments in *Winter Soldier*, Camil claimed to have witnessed or participated in the rape of women, the killing of women and children, hideous acts of sexual torture, the burning of villages with civilians in them, and the knifing to death of an innocent villager, all this in addition to the 291 villagers he claimed were killed on Operation Stone. If Camil spoke the truth, then 1st Battalion, 1st Marines committed war crimes every bit the equal of those known at trial to have been committed by the Americal Division's Task Force Barker at My Lai.[33]

Camil was one of the few Winter Soldiers to provide any form of evidence to military authorities. He filed an affidavit with the navy on June 16, 1971, in an attempt to back up his testimony at the WSI, but he would not offer the names of those involved in possible war crimes, nor provide photographs that would, he said, "incriminate other Americans." Repeating his claim that there was an atrocity during Operation Stone, Camil stated that artillery and mortars first rained down upon the village, something he had not mentioned in *Winter Soldier,* that Marines then chased the villagers, including women and children, to "an area where they were boxed in and all killed." There is no river or railroad trestle in this account, no sitting up on that trestle shooting villagers. This time Marines chased them, he said. He saw the bodies of "at least" fifty women and children who had been killed by artillery and automatic weapons fire, not 291. This happened, he said, between February 22 and 27, 1967. He offered the coordinates from what he said was the Dai Loc map sheet as 5840 S 5440, 0200 W 9770, and located the unnamed village as bordered by Rt. 4 on the north and by the Song [River] Ky Lam on the south.[34]

Camil's affidavit did offer evidence of a second incident. But again this was not the one about which Campbell asked. The timing was right, though Camil could be no more precise than that it happened sometime between May and September 1967. But the location was wrong. It happened not in Quang Tri, but in the southern part of I Corps, in the mud flats known to Marines as "Dodge City," seven miles northwest of Hoi An at 5650-0140 on the Dai Loc map sheet, Camil said. Bravo Company had set up at dawn at 5480-0070. Farmers came out to work their fields at 0045-5400. Bravo opened up on them with tanks, mortars, artillery, and "lows" [*sic*], for five minutes, and killed at least fifty. This was the same place and time when Camil said he witnessed the sexual torture of a wounded Vietnamese woman. He said she was a nurse, something he had not mentioned in Detroit, and that his lieutenant ordered her shot as "a humanitarian gesture," another addition to his earlier testimony. In a 2006 phone conversation, he said to me he shot her, and defended his action as putting her out of her misery.[35]

So was this wounded Vietnamese woman a nurse, and was she killed by Camil or by his lieutenant? Does it matter? Was it a lapse of memory, a simple mistake? Perhaps, but only if we believe Camil to be a reliable informant. Neither in his formal testimony at the WSI nor in his later affidavit did Camil elaborate on that massacre in Quang Tri, about which he had forgotten, but had immediately recalled after Ken Campbell's prompting. Nor did he mention that he had knifed an innocent villager to death. Camil's testimony was contradictory and inconsistent, and his story has changed dramatically over time. Camil told me the navy never followed up on his affidavit. He hadn't made it easy.[36]

So what can we know? Operation Stone I and II, under the command of LtCol Van D. Bell—"Ding-dong Bell"—began on February 12, 1967, and ended on February 22, not on the 27th as Camil wrote—a minor error. It involved Bravo, Charlie, and Delta Companies of the 1st Battalion, 1st Marines, joined sequentially by Foxtrot Company, 2nd Battalion, 26th Marines and Echo Company, 2nd Battalion, 1st Marines. Camil was assigned to Alpha Battery, 1st Battalion, 11th Marines and served as part of an artillery forward-observer team for Bravo and Charlie Companies, 1st Battalion, 1st Marines (1/1). He took part in Operation Stone and was wounded, he said, on February 18, 1967. His separation papers, DD-214, note the award of the Purple Heart.[37]

The Command Chronology of 1/1 for February 1967 offers no evidence of anything remotely resembling Camil's claims. During Operation Stone, Bravo and Charlie Companies reported numerous encounters with VC and NVA troops, but the daily tally of confirmed enemy dead rarely rose above the single digits. On the 18th and 19th, however, the war became more intense. Bravo encountered two VC in khaki uniforms at 0815, killing one; at 0845, a member of Bravo stepped on a Chicom grenade mine; at 1410, another Bravo Marine tripped a 105mm round rigged as a mine; and early in the evening another Bravo member stepped on a punji stake. A platoon leader from Charlie Company also tripped a mine that day. It is likely that Camil was wounded in one of these mine explosions. Bravo also killed another VC on the 18th and detained a forty-four-year-old male who was sent back to the regiment collection point. On the 19th, Bravo tripped three additional mines, killed three VC in separate incidents, and, at 1630, engaged in the only large encounter for either Bravo or Charlie Companies on Operation Stone. Elements of Bravo observed forty-five to fifty VC across a river at coordinates

AT 978594 carrying automatic weapons and three machine guns. Marines opened fire with small arms and reported fifteen confirmed KIAs and thirteen probable. But this happened a day after Camil said he had been wounded.[38]

The Command Chronology was a monthly operational report, prepared under the direction of the battalion's executive officer, the second in command. It contained a journal of every incident, message, or order received by the Battalion's Command, Operations, and Communications Center for the month—nothing was too trivial to report. In addition, the S-2 (Intelligence) daily summary—the Isum—reported on any and all contact in the field, any engagement with the enemy, any mine or booby trap found or exploded, any prisoners captured or any civilian detainees taken for questioning. The Isum was prepared under the direction of the S-2, a junior lieutenant often just recently back from a field assignment, assisted by a gunnery sergeant who served as Intelligence Chief. The report itself was actually prepared by junior enlisted men, intelligence assistants who were usually among the brightest and most capable young Marines. The antiwar writer and poet, W. D. Ehrhart, was an intelligence assistant and later assistant intelligence chief for the 1st Batallion, 1st Marines from February 1967 to February 1968, a year he recounted in *Vietnam-Perkasie: A Combat Marine's Memoir* (1983). Ehrhart signed a number of the Isums in this period in his own name.[39]

The Isums were only as good as the information that came in from the field. But their purpose was not merely as a record. It mattered deeply where, and when, American Marines encountered the enemy—how many there were, what weapons they had, what the results of the encounter were. That was the duty of the S-2 shop, to plot where the enemy was, to help focus and protect fellow Marines.

Could the killing of 291 Vietnamese civilians, committed by and witnessed by most of an entire Marine company, go unreported? It's possible, but not likely. Somebody would have talked, and after all, given the emphasis on body count, it would have been far more likely that the civilian KIAs would have been reported as VC or NVA, as was the case in the Americal Division's report on the "battle" at My Lai. Moreover, as the veterans of the WSI accurately testified, body count was the measure of military success, and thus subject to exaggeration. And, Camil, Sachs, and others at the WSI gave voice to one of the war's uglier pieces of black humor—any dead Vietnamese was a dead VC. Moreover, there is a significant silence in Ehrhart's memoir of his service in 1/1's S-2 shop. He appears to have arrived in Vietnam about the time of Operation Stone, and claimed it as one of the operations in which he served. He makes no mention of it. A deeply committed anti-Vietnam war writer and poet, Ehrhart wrote of his shock over the Marine's harsh treatment of civilians, clearly expressing empathy. As an intelligence staffer, he would have been in an ideal position to learn of Camil's "massacre" on Operation Stone—if it had happened.[40]

The absence of evidence of course cannot disprove Camil's claims, but the Command Chronologies offer no support for his claims. Far better evidence comes from men who served with him. Michael S. Frazier, who served with Bravo, 1/1 from September 1966 to May 1967 and participated in Operation Stone, told me in an email exchange: "Civilians were not burned up in their homes and the charge that 291 men women and children were killed is *absolutely false*" (emphasis added). Rick Bazaco served in Charlie Company, arriving in Vietnam at the end of 1966. He, too, participated in Operation Stone, and remained with Charlie Company until July 1967 when he was badly wounded, leaving substantial portions of his two legs in the "mud flats" near Hoi An. Bazaco, who now runs his own computer company in Charleston, South Carolina, told me that he and others "lost some humanity" in Vietnam, but they did not mistreat women and children. Camil's story of a woman staked out and stabbed was, he said, "a boldface lie." If something like that had happened, everyone in Charlie Company, he said, would have been talking about it. There was "no massacre" in the mud flats, he went on, and no village wiped out on Operation Stone. Ronald D. Kincade, who was platoon leader, 2nd Platoon, Bravo Company on Operation Stone, used earthier language, calling Camil's claims "pure, unadulterated bull-shit." He recalled seeing no villagers while on Stone, dismissed Camil's tale of prisoners thrown from helicopters, and ridiculed his claim of contests to see who could destroy hootches with a minimum of artillery. All fire missions required layers of approval through 1/1 as well as through Alpha Battery 1/11, the unit to which Camil was actually assigned. Kincade, who left the Marines as a major, was one of the Marines chosen to debrief after Operation Stone in a taped interview for Marine historians. Camil's claims, which have never been corroborated and remain to this day without foundation, have now been contradicted.[41]

Enter Terry Whitmore

There was, however, another story of an atrocity in Quang Tri. This was the story about which Campbell asked. Mark Lane's *Conversations with Americans* included an interview with a deserter named Terry Whitmore who claimed participation in a grotesque atrocity in Quang Tri as a member of Bravo Company, 1st Battalion, 1st Marines. Whitmore was a young black man from Memphis who joined the Marines out of high school and was assigned to Bravo in July 1967. He was wounded at Con Thien in December 1967 and eventually medevaced to Japan. He found a Japanese girlfriend, Taki, and a network of her antiwar friends who did not want him to return to Vietnam.[42]

He recounts in his later published memoir, however, that he decided to return. He reported for his flight back to Vietnam on two consecutive days. On the first day, there were no available seats. On the second day, flights were cancelled. On the third day, he remained in bed with Taki. She had connections with a Japanese organization, Beheiren, which assisted American soldiers seeking to desert. And so, Terry Whitmore, an accidental deserter, was spirited out of Japan, feted in Moscow, and settled in Sweden, where Mark Lane found him.[43]

Lane interviewed Whitmore for his discredited *Conversations*. Whitmore said he was on patrol with Bravo Company, 1/1 near Quang Tri, just after Operation Medina that had concluded on October 18. His buddy, "Kam," a Polish kid named Kominski, was walking point. Another soldier, Jessup, was with them. They were fired on: "a hail of fucking bullets came right across [Jessup's] head," Whitmore recalled. They returned fire. Whitmore remembered placing "about" four M-79 rounds, "dead-eye hits," onto a hootch to which some people, women, but no children, were running. "I annihilated that mother-fucker," he said, "so, if they stopped in that hootch, they were dead." An old woman then emerged from a bunker and "Kam," according to Whitmore, emptied "half of his magazine" into her. Whitmore claimed it scared him: "God damn, man, you shoot that old lady?" Lane asked, why did he do it? Whitmore had no better explanation than: "he says he just wanted to do something." And then, Whitmore said, "we" started to burn the hootches: "There were people in them. When they tried to come out *we* shot them" (emphasis added). "We stayed around that place for a long time," Whitmore continued, "and we smelled burned-up bodies. That's a goddam horrible smell."[44]

According to his account, his platoon had been assigned a blocking position—the "anvil" in infantry tactical language—to cut off the escape of any villagers and, he said, to "kill any that came our way." He continued directly: "We got them." Another platoon, serving as the infantry's "hammer," was, according to Whitmore, "killing them, massacring the whole village." And then there were the cows. He fired his M-79 into them, and they ran, he said, "right into a machine-gun team." They were "cut to pieces. It was a big kick . . . looking at these cows get slaughtered."[45]

Whitmore recalled thirteen hamlets, each, he said, with a population of about thirty: "We just went through that mother-fucker and left nothing that I saw." If Whitmore spoke the truth, the killing of almost 400 villagers would have been the equivalent of the massacre at My Lai. But that wasn't the worst.[46]

"Later that night," Whitmore claimed, "I heard an officer give the order to kill the children." A soldier had stepped on a "booby trap," he said, and as a medevac came in, Whitmore "just happened to be standing alongside the officer when the radioman said: 'Look sir, we got children rounded up. What do you want us to do with them?'" The officer said: "Goddam it, Marine, you know what to do with them. Kill the bastards. If you don't have the goddam balls to kill them Marine, I'll come down there and kill the mother-fuckers myself." The unnamed Marine said "Yes, sir." Some two to three minutes later, Whitmore recalled hearing "a lot of automatic fire—and a lot of children screaming . . . babies crying . . . children screaming their fucking lungs out. I heard them. And that got next to me. I heard a machine gun go off. . . . There were a lot of children. It lasted only twenty or thirty seconds. We didn't, they didn't get all the children though." So was it they or we?[47]

The next day, he and Jessup were on patrol in the same area. Whitmore saw a young girl, five or six, with an infant brother, standing under a tree. He knew her parents were dead: "It really bugged me," he said. After Jessup decided to toss grenades at two nearby water buffaloes and watch them die— "flipping over this. Laughing," Whitmore said—they left. The infant was crying, the young girl was "just looking at us." "I think [Marines] killed that kid," Whitmore said, "I left. I didn't want to see it. . . . I'm sure some guy killed her." And then directly following, Whitmore continued: "It was one of my plans to adopt one of those kids. They were so groovy to me. I really dug those kids." It is a story of hideous evil, told by Whitmore in an ugly and utterly contradictory moral register.[48]

When Neil Sheehan reviewed Lane's book, he followed up on Whitmore's story. He wrote that he contacted Whitmore's former battalion commander and a former platoon leader, then a teaching assistant at Appalachian State, both unnamed. The former was LtCol Alfred Belbusti, and the latter was likely Lt John C. Bailey. Both denied, according to Sheehan, that such an atrocity took place. They were operating at the time in an "unpopulated area near the DMZ," Sheehan reported. But Whitmore's "war story" resembled an earlier incident in which four Vietnamese—a man, two women, and a child—had been killed in a hostile area at night. Sheehan learned that a company commander and an enlisted man had been court-martialed for murder, but both had been "acquitted on the ground that the company had just been fired on, and it had been impossible to distinguish the moving figures as civilian." Sheehan asked: "Is Whitmore transmogrifying this incident into a massacre of several hundred? The conflicting accounts certainly raise the question."[49]

Sheehan had only a part of the story, and his suggestion that Whitmore was guilty only of "transmogrifying" one incident into another was a kindness Whitmore did not deserve. Two Marines were court-martialed, but their trials were not resolved in the manner Sheehan reported. Nor was the incident in question an earlier one. It was the same incident, as we shall see.

Neither Sheehan's review nor the denials of a battalion commander and a platoon leader had any influence on Doubleday and Company that went on to publish Whitmore's own account, *Memphis-Nam-Sweden: The Story of a Black Deserter*, in 1971. Whitmore's book, written with the assistance of Richard Weber, a lawyer and film writer in Stockholm, was based on a long, filmed interview done by Swedish television. We should then hear Whitmore's own voice across the two versions. In 2000 the University of Mississippi Press reprinted the book with a fawning afterword by Jeff Loeb, a Marine veteran of Vietnam and an English teacher at Pembroke Hall School in Kansas City. The University of Mississippi Press, in an extravagant and poorly considered blurb, claimed that Whitmore's book was "one of the finest memoirs of the Vietnam experience."[50]

Whitmore's chapter, "Bravo Company," opened with more detail than that of his interview with Lane. 1st Battalion, 1st Marines was just back from a previous operation in which it had taken, according to Whitmore, "50% casualties." Bravo Company had taken only "25%," so when the Command Post came under mortar fire, Bravo was chosen to go out to suppress it.

The company captain was a popular leader, according to Whitmore, protective of his men, and had only recently been promoted from platoon leader, a lieutenant's billet. He told them if they took one sniper round from a nearby village, they were to "level it." They were fired upon by a sniper, who never fired again—no "hail of fucking bullets" in this account.[51]

The captain gave the order three times to "level it." Whitmore said: "this was hard for some of the guys to believe." The company began killing, but not Whitmore, contradicting his interview with Lane. He retold, in largely the same form, the story of killing the cows, though without any expression of glee: "We had to do something to keep busy. We weren't up for killing unarmed people." But he was a witness to a "complete slaughter"—"he could see the whole scene."[52]

The killing of the children was precipitated by the need to evacuate a Marine wounded by a booby trap. "Where should we bring [the children], sir," a Marine asked. "Bring them?" the captain responded, "What the hell you talkin' about? You know goddam well what to do with them. Now." "Sir?" the Marine replied. "You kill them Marine. You hear me? You kill them." Whitmore interjected: "Goddam! This man ain't bullshiting. This man ain't human! . . . Now Marines are usually freaks around kids. Try to be good to them, avoid hurting them . . . he must be crazy. Nobody kills kids intentionally." The captain again: "Marine, if you ain't got the balls, bring them up here," not "I'll come down there," as the first version had it—"Bring them to me. And I'll do it."[53]

Do the inconsistencies matter? They certainly would in a court-martial. Indeed, the failure to identify the "officer" who ordered the killing of the children in the first version would likely doom the successful prosecution of the captain. The second version, in addition to its cleaned-up language, seemed to offer a more consistent, though utterly self-serving, moral tone. All Whitmore did was kill the cows. He expressed no guilt, he also offered no names—no "Kam," no "Jessup"—nor did he provide specific dates. That makes it harder to understand why he identified his company commander, whom he had respected and praised, as the perpetrator of a hideous atrocity. But he did it, making it possible for anyone with sufficient curiosity to identify him.

Whitmore also offered a coda to the second version. He wrote: "typical gung-ho Marines, they started to shoot their mouths off. Man, you should have seen us level that ville. . . . We were a proud company." Then, Whitmore went on: "After a day or so, one kid started to get soft. All this shit got next to him"—"got next to him"—Whitmore's initial phrase describing to Lane his reaction to the killing of children. "He was going crazy inside," Whitmore continued, "tearing him up." So this "soft" soldier, according to Whitmore, went to the chaplain who went to the Battalion CO. His company commander, according to Whitmore, was relieved of command, 1st Platoon was "confined to the compound," the remainder "of the company was placed under a temporary command, and sent out." When they returned, Whitmore continued, "civilian investigators in fatigues . . . had swooped down on the CP [Command Post] and done a job on the first platoon."[54]

Then another stark contradiction: "We were just as guilty," Whitmore said, "the rest of us had killed and burned as much as the first platoon." That platoon, he said, was "transferred to another company." The company closed ranks. The investigators, "assholes," Whitmore called them, heard nothing but denials, that is, lies: "I don't know nuthin'. When I get shot at, I shoot back. That's all I know." That was the young Marines' answer: "Some lifer sergeant must have clued them in on what to say," Whitmore claimed. There were consequences, Whitmore recalled: "rumor had it that the Captain was thrown out of the military." A new, black CO led them to Con Thien, Whitmore wrote, where Whitmore would be wounded a few weeks later.[55]

And so Terry Whitmore, who so "grooved" on the young children of Vietnam, participated in the lies and cover-up of the purported murder of some of those children. He believed the investigation was "a big joke," once again displaying a stunning lack of moral consistency.[56]

Two hundred ninety-one killed on Operation Stone, or possibly only fifty; 400 killed in Quang Tri. If Camil and Whitmore are to be believed 1st Battalion, 1st Marines, in less than a year, committed more atrocities than any other battalion in Vietnam. It would be especially easy to dismiss Whitmore's claims, as inconsistent and contradictory as they are, as a deserter's efforts to justify his act. But as copies of *Winter Soldier* become more widely available in college libraries and classrooms, who will be there to contest Camil's stories? And as some American academics, and one university press, continue to regard Whitmore as a reliable memoirist, who will be there to challenge Whitmore? Does it matter? I've been told by two antiwar veterans it doesn't. What if half the atrocity stories prove to be false, one veteran asked, would that justify the war? The answer is of course no, but that's not the point.

The reason to expose false atrocity stories is so we can retain our outrage at true atrocity stories. Otherwise it's all noise, feeding into the widespread belief that atrocities defined American conduct in Vietnam. The credulous belief in such stories dishonors the service of those soldiers who acted with honor, who did not kill Vietnamese villagers, and who were not party to covering up the killing of children.

eight
What Happened in Quang Tri?

*It is important to find out if this [atrocity at Hurriyah] really happened
in order to separate the hyperbole from the merely horrible in Iraq, so that
the horrible will still have meaning. Otherwise it will all become din.*
—Tom Zeller Jr.

Terry Whitmore's morally deadening and conflicting accounts of his behavior
that morning in Quang Tri have now been published twice and republished
once. They remain the only account to date of a horrendous "massacre."
Whitmore lived most of his adult life in Sweden, marrying and fathering two
children. He appeared in an antiwar documentary, *Gladiatorerna (The Peace
Game)* (1969), as an actor, then in the documentary, *Terry Whitmore, for
Example* (1969), that would become the basis for his book. He also acted in
the Swedish film *Georgia, Georgia* (1972), written by Maya Angelou, the story
of a love affair between a black singer and an American deserter. Whitmore
played the role of the deserter, Bobo. He also appeared in a television drama,
Fallan (The Trap) (1975). However, he principally earned his living as a bus
driver.[1]

After the 1977 amnesty proposed by President Jimmy Carter, Whitmore
returned to the United States. Required to report back to the military, as all
deserters were, he processed out of the Marines at Quantico, Virginia. In
an interview with Jeff Loeb, Whitmore claimed: "I was treated like a hero .
. . and asked to stay" (in the Corps). Loeb never challenged his claims. The
Marine motto—"Semper Fidelis" (always faithful)—can't easily be stretched

to embrace a deserter. It's another of Whitmore's "war stories" that is not believable. Whitmore returned to Sweden, but sometime in 2000 he came home to Memphis, reconciling both with his mother, who had turned against him after his desertion, and his daughter, Tonia, whom he saw for the first time in 1977 and whom his mother raised. An aging and unhealthy-looking Whitmore made a brief, angry, and only marginally coherent appearance in *Sir! No Sir!* a 2005 film about the antiwar movement in the military ("And then you think about this shit, man, and then you say 'God damn!' Did I do that? Did I actually live in that shit? Did the government push me into that shit?") He also authored a note, "Why I'm Still Alive" for the film's website. He had nothing further to say, however, either in the note or the film, about that "massacre" in Quang Tri. Terry Whitmore died July 11, 2007, in the Memphis Veterans' Medical Center. The obituary mentioned no cause of death. He was sixty.[2]

We now know that the incident reported by Neil Sheehan and the "massacre" claimed by Whitmore were the same event, because Whitmore had some of the story right. The company commander, whom Whitmore said had been recently promoted from platoon leader, was 1stLt R. W. Maynard. Robert Maynard was a "mustang," enlisting as a private in 1960, commissioned an officer in 1965. He arrived in Vietnam in 1967 as a first lieutenant and joined Bravo Company as a platoon leader. On September 9, 1967, he assumed command of Bravo. Whitmore had claimed a "soft soldier" had gone to the battalion chaplain to report the "massacre." A "soft soldier"? It's another of Whitmore's stunning moral inconsistencies. A deeply troubled young Marine had gone to the chaplain, and Maynard was relieved of command in the aftermath of the incident—just as Whitmore said. And Bravo's new commanding officer (CO) was an African American. The company did close ranks as investigators descended upon the company, but they were not civilians, as Whitmore claimed, rather they were navy or Marine criminal investigators wearing utilities without visible rank. Marine command was acting swiftly to determine what had happened on the morning of October 22.[3]

Four days earlier, Bravo had returned from Operation Medina, an eight-day search and destroy mission into the Hai Lang forest. The company, along with other elements of 1/1 had encountered well-equipped North Vietnamese Army (NVA) soldiers. Charlie Company had taken the brunt of casualties, attacked on two sides by approximately 150 NVA at 1515 on October 12. The battle continued at close range into the hours of darkness.

Reinforcements from Delta Company prevented the NVA from encircling what remained of Charlie Company. Charlie suffered 11 killed in action, 75 wounded in action, 60 to 65 of whom had to be medevaced, out of a total strength of 187—the company had been badly shot up.[4]

Whitmore's casualty claims, however—50 percent for the entire battalion, 25 percent for Bravo—were wild exaggerations. Even after Operation Medina, 1/1 suffered an overall casualty rate of 14 percent for the entire month of October. But Whitmore had remembered correctly that his company was "relatively" unscathed. The company stood down for one day only. Battalion command ordered Bravo and Alpha Companies out again at 0900, October 20, on Operation Liberty II, a mission coordinated with the South Vietnamese and designed to provide security for Vietnamese elections scheduled for October 22. Among the "coordinating instructions" in Operations Order 3-67 was the following: "suspects captured by U.S. forces will be brought to reference points 'A' or 'B' where they will be turned over to ARVN [Army of the Republic of Vietnam]." The battalion CO, LtCol A. F. Belbusti, signed the order. Bravo patrolled all day on the 20th. On the 21st, the company woke at 0430, patrolled all day and dug in for the night at 1800. Sometime between 2145 and 2200, the company received orders to move out to locate a Viet Cong (VC) or a NVA mortar position.[5]

Rudy Diener, a nineteen-year-old lance corporal who grew up on the Jersey shore, recalled being jostled awake—he thought by mistake—when he still had time to sleep before his next watch. He learned it was no mistake. Bravo was to move out to intercept an enemy rocket or mortar team. He had been with Bravo since December 1966 when he first reported to 1/1's S-1 section. In back of the reporting desk was a mylar chart with the names of Marines and their assignments. Several Bravo names had been recently erased. Diener got it. He was replacing men who had been killed or seriously wounded. That night, tired and frustrated, he gave voice to a harsh prediction of a sort that his mother had once warned him about—"don't say it," she told him, "it might happen." "Somebody's going to get killed tonight," he recalled saying—"it was dangerous enough patrolling during the day." "What happened that night," he told me, "would forever change my life."[6]

First platoon—Diener's—took point. Diener recalls the platoon's point man stopping. On one side was a tree line, on another a hill. The tree line spooked the point man, according to Diener, and so he chose the hill. Years later, Diener would say that had they chosen the route to the tree line, they might have all been wiped out. Tired and frustrated, they climbed that hill toward a decimated ville in the vicinity of Thon Nai Cuu at coordinates YD 280520 on the Ba Long map sheet. As they did so, LCpl Ronald B. Pearson, the 1st Platoon's radioman, triggered a booby trap. Pearson, twenty-one years old, from Port Angeles, Washington, died that morning. He was popular with other Marines. He had taught Diener how to use the radio, and he shared a shelter half with his platoon leader, 2ndLt John C. Bailey. Two other Marines, Corporal Dennis and PFC Klang, were wounded and required medical evacuation. Dennis was a squad leader. Diener would replace him. The logs of 1/1, according to later testimony, indicated that Bravo called for a medevac at 0200 on the 22nd. Bailey was also wounded by shrapnel, but remained. The company set up a perimeter. There were reports of VC or NVA seen crawling through the grass, of fire directed at the rear perimeter. Years later, Maynard would recall an enemy effort to divert the medevac—two white flashlights illuminating the night. Bailey, according to Maynard, was directing the medevac in with a white and a green light.[7]

Maynard's company had dug in below the crest of a hill. He recalled a battalion order to stay in position, but he recognized that he was not in a sound defensive position. He concluded it was too risky to move higher, toward the decimated and unfamiliar ville, where A Company, he said, had taken a casualty the day before. He sent out two patrols instead, each consisting of a "reinforced squad plus gun teams." The patrols returned at 0430 to 0500. He did not debrief them—"I felt it more important that they get some rest."[8]

Lieutenant Bailey led one of the patrols. Bailey had grown up in Davidson, North Carolina, where his father was a dean at Davidson College. He attended Guilford College, a Quaker school about ninety miles to the northeast, and graduated in 1964. He joined the Marine enlisted reserve along with six or seven of his classmates, taught for a time, and then decided to become a Marine officer. He graduated from Marine Officer Candidate School and was the "honor man"—the top graduate—of his platoon (2nd Platoon, Hotel Company) in Marine Basic School Class 4-67. When I mentioned this to him in a phone conversation, he deflected the honor. The top man in his platoon had become the company "honor man," he said. Basic School was a six-month course where young Marine officers learned leadership and infantry tactics prior to deployment. Bailey arrived in Vietnam in June 1967 and was assigned to Bravo 1/1 as a platoon leader.[9]

Bailey recalled moving along "well-worn village trails," but saw no houses. They had all been previously destroyed. He was walking fourth in column when his point man sent word back that he had seen or heard something. He moved up to find a bunker: "we heard no noise," he said. He threw a grenade in, then they heard movement in the bunker, and somebody threw in another. At that point, "several figures began moving in front of us." "We opened fire," he said. He could not tell how many "figures" there were, nor could he tell their age, their sex, whether they had weapons, or even whether they had come from the bunker. When the smoke cleared, Bailey found two adults, a man and a woman, of twenty to thirty years of age, and one child, one to two. He said they appeared to be either "unconscious or dead." He ordered that they be placed back into the bunker. He made no mention of anyone shouting "Lai Dai"— come out.[10]

They continued the patrol, finding several more bunkers. At one, they heard people call to them and saw a light. One man, thirty to forty, and five to six children, age twelve and below, came out of the bunker. "We had orders to clear the ville," he said, so they took them and their belongings toward the river crossing. The man, however, tried "several times to turn off on a different route, but was restrained." The kids were sent across the river. Bailey and his squad leader discussed whether they should take the man back—he was of military age and he had no ID. Then, Bailey said, the man made a sudden move toward him. Bailey hit him, knocking him down the riverbank: "I fired several shots at him as he moved into the bushes. He was hit but we did not pursue." According to several witnesses, Bailey was deeply troubled about what happened that night.[11]

His corpsman, HM3 Richard H. Hamming, said that Bailey had told him: "the sights we saw that night wasn't [sic] a pretty sight, but it was the result of war and he hoped that we wouldn't be bothered by it that much, that we wouldn't dream about it." 2ndLt William L. Steen, who had joined the company just two weeks earlier, accompanied Bailey on the patrol, witnessed the dead bodies at the first bunker, but said he was too far away to witness any of the events at the second bunker. Steen reported that Bailey "wasn't proud of what happened, but wasn't going to order anyone not to say anything about it. Possibly he said something about not being ashamed about it." Sgt Don Allen, his platoon sergeant, reported that Bailey "was sick to his stomach about the whole thing." Why, he was asked? He responded: because "people had been killed . . . women and children."[12]

Allen, who led the second patrol, had a distinguished record. This was his second tour in Vietnam. On his first in 1965–1966, he had been awarded the Silver Star for ambushing an entire NVA company, killing several and chasing the remainder of the company back up the hill where they had first emerged. Shrapnel wounds to his face, fracturing his skull and crushing his nose, truncated his first tour.[13]

In Allen's squad that morning was LCpl Olaf Christian Skibsrud, born in 1946, in Pierre, South Dakota, the son of a Lutheran pastor. Skibsrud was new in country, arriving at the end of August 1967. He joined Bravo about a week later and served on a machine-gun team as an ammunition carrier, though his most intensive training had been in mortars. Soon to turn twenty-two, he was older than most enlisted Marines and had attended college—St. Olaf in Northfield, Minnesota, for one year, where his father, brother, and uncle preceded him. He did not do well, and a second start at the University of Wisconsin, Green Bay, went no better. Moved by an article he had seen— he thought in *National Geographic*—on the brutality of the VC, he enlisted in the Marines at the end of May 1966. His older brother joined the Marines at about the same time and saw service in Vietnam as an officer. Because his brother was in Vietnam, he believed he didn't have to serve there—but he volunteered: "that's why I joined," he told me.[14]

What Skibsrud witnessed on Allen's patrol shocked him. He brooded over it for a few days before visiting the battalion chaplain, LT Richard M. Lyons, USN, to tell him what happened that night. Dick Lyons was then a Catholic priest—he would later leave the priesthood—and was highly respected by members of 1/1. He would earn the Silver Star for his heroism in Hue, and also a Purple Heart. Skibsrud, whose memory of the men with whom he served has faded, recalled Lyon's response to his story with stunning clarity—"this can't happen," Lyons said to him.[15]

Lyons brought Skibsrud's story to his superiors by October 27, five days after the incident. The battalion CO, Belbusti, ordered an investigation that day. Shortly after, Skibsrud was summoned out of the field by the battalion XO (the second in command), Maj C. A. Folsom. When Maynard got word of this, he assumed incorrectly that Skibsrud had jumped the chain of command. But a Marine has the right to see a chaplain at any time, operational conditions permitting, and need not divulge why. According to Skibsrud, Maynard defended his decision to send patrols out after Pearson's death, suggesting that if Skibsrud had been in the field longer and seen his buddies die he would have a better understanding of what happened that night. Maynard continued, quoted by Skibsrud: "If you go to the Major don't color this thing up because a lot of people are going to be hurt by it.

Don't lie, just don't go up there and color anything up." In his account to me, Skibsrud said that Maynard was upset he did not come to him first, that he could have gotten him transferred out of the field, suggesting to Skibsrud that this was what Maynard understood his motivation to be. Other Bravo Marines would come to believe the same thing, but would take it one step further, believing that Skibsrud lied about what he saw in order to get out of the field. Maynard's warning: "don't color this up," would have an even longer life in the stories members of Bravo continued to tell each other more than thirty-five years after the incident. The narrative that seemed to convey the most authority was one in which the Marine who went to the chaplain exaggerated what happened—colored it up.[16]

Skibsrud never returned to Bravo. Folsom heard his story, and transferred him immediately within the battalion to the Headquarters and Supply (H&S) Company, where he was assigned to inventory the sea bags of deceased Marines. When I asked him whether he thought this was deliberate, he responded with his own question: "what do you think?"[17]

Staff from the legal office of the 1st Marine Division completed their preliminary investigation on November 1 and submitted it to Belbusti. On November 9, Belbusti recommended that three Marines be charged with premeditated murder—Maynard, recently promoted to captain, Bailey, and LCpl Rudolph O. Diener—and submitted his recommendations to Col Herbert E. Ing Jr., CO, First Marine Regiment. Charges were pending against a fourth Marine, PFC John E. Heald, who was recovering from wounds received on November 20 and could not be present. Those charges were ultimately dropped for lack of evidence and because he had not been properly warned of his rights prior to giving a statement.[18]

On November 15, 1st Marines ordered an Article 32 Investigation, roughly the military equivalent of a grand jury investigation. On the 17th, Belbusti relieved Maynard of command. On the next day, six Marine lawyers had their case loads rescheduled to allow priority treatment for the investigation, and in an unexpected turn of events, Ing relieved Belbusti of command. Belbusti, in a phone conversation, had only the haziest of memories of the case, and did not recall relieving Maynard, nor of signing off on charges of premeditated murder. He recalled no officers being charged, only enlisted men, and not for murder, but for something like "conduct unbecoming," though he acknowledged that the charge involved a war crime. However, he remembered clearly his own unceremonious relief. Ing offered no explanation, telling him simply: "here's Gravel, the new Battalion

CO, you're my XO." Belbusti had been kicked upstairs. He had held his command for less than three months. Ing was a "mustang," earning his commission in the pre–World War II Marines. He had commanded a company on Iwo Jima. He would tell me that Belbusti had never commanded infantry in battle—he owed his promotion to an unnamed general—and a series of incidents, not just the murder charges, led Ing to relieve him.[19]

On November 21, the Article 32 Investigation convened in Quang Tri under the direction of a single investigating officer, Maj Arthur A. Bergman. Bergman was thirty-five at the time and likely the oldest man in the room. Born in De Soto, Missouri, in 1932, of German descent, he earned his B.A. in physics from William Jewell College, and an M.A. in electronics engineering at the Naval Post Graduate School in Monterey, California. He was not a lawyer, but a career Marine officer who would retire as a colonel. He died in 2001. Bergman conducted the investigation with an even hand, sometimes allowing greater latitude to the lawyers than would normally be the case in an Article 32 Investigation. Rudy Diener, facing charges that could lead to life in prison, remembered him as fair and professional. Over the course of the next few days, Bergman would become increasingly frustrated and increasingly outspoken about what he believed was a lack of honesty on the part of young Marine witnesses.[20]

Maynard, Bailey, and Diener were each represented by Marine counsel; Maynard by Capt Jay D. Reynolds, Bailey by Capt B. Acton Allen, and Diener by 2ndLt James G. Ehlers. Diener noted that his lawyer was not a captain. "Is there something I should know," he recalled asking Ehlers. Ehlers explained that the difference in rank had nothing to do with legal qualification, but the manner in which each had entered the Marines. Representing the government were captains Ross T. Roberts and Don E. Whittig. The investigation opened exactly thirty days after the incident near Thon Nai Cuu. Marine command had moved with remarkable speed, in a combat environment, to ascertain the truth of what happened that morning. It is a measure of the seriousness with which they took the allegations.[21]

On November 22, Bergman, the five attorneys, the defendants, and several witnesses went to the scene of the incident, as they were duty bound. They observed three uniformed VC or NVA, and received twenty to thirty rounds of automatic weapon fire while members of a heavily armed security force protecting them, from Hotel Company, 2nd Battalion, 2nd Marines, took two casualties from a booby trap—one requiring a priority medevac. Ehlers recalled that the CO of the security force told him, with a certain strained humor, that he wished he could have such firepower available on his ordinary missions. It was also clearly established that Bravo had sent patrols to the same area after Operation Liberty II. First Platoon had been ambushed and mortared, the point man shot through the spine. A second patrol to the same area was also ambushed and mortared.[22]

Whitmore was right about his CO being relieved and he was right as well that Bravo began to close ranks. There was talk of not cooperating and of otherwise hindering the investigation. Several witnesses affirmed that they overheard such talk. As far as the men of Bravo initially knew, Skibsrud was the only witness. His immediate transfer was the obvious indication. Skibsrud told me that a gunnery sergeant threatened to kill him and that he lived his final months in Vietnam in "constant dread and fear," sleeping with loaded weapons to protect himself from his fellow Marines.[23]

Skibsrud's Witness

Skibsrud witnessed the death of Lance Corporal Pearson, and then began to hear "whispers," as he put it to me, that his platoon was to destroy the ville and leave no one alive. His memory matched his testimony: "They said we were going to kill everyone in the ville and burn it down." He thought that he had heard that from Lance Corporal Harkins, but he wasn't certain. However, he never heard a direct order to that effect nor had he been present at a briefing. He fell in behind Sergeant Allen's patrol.[24]

In his testimony, Skibsrud said that his patrol had come upon a bunker. He identified the patrol's members and said that Diener had taken over third squad after Dennis had been medevaced. He saw a group of Vietnamese "gathered" inside the bunker, and then he saw them outside. He heard Allen say to Diener "that he couldn't kill any kids." He could not remember, at the time, what had prompted Allen's order. But years later, he told me he could have "hugged" Allen at that moment. Then he testified he heard Diener say there was an order: "I believe that he said that 'Bravo 6' had given the order that all people in the village were to be killed, that the ville was to be burned down." Bravo 6 was Maynard. Allen prevailed. The children were not killed. As he came closer to the bunker, Skibsrud was able to identify eight to nine children, the youngest about three.[25]

Thirty-five years later, Skibsrud recalled that what happened next "horrified" him. He testified that Diener separated the woman, who was perhaps twenty-five to thirty-five years old and whose name the Marine investigators never learned, shoved her in front of him, turned her into a field, and shot her in the back three to six times with his M-16 at point-blank range. Whittig established that Skibsrud was fifteen to twenty meters away from Diener, that he had an unobstructed view and could clearly identify him. Marines then began to burn the bunker and any property they could find. Someone threw something belonging to the children into the fire, and the children began to cry. Skibsrud overheard a Marine say about the kids that "they didn't cry when their mother got killed, but they do when they burn such-and-such. I don't know what the item was, sir."[26]

After the patrol, he recalled talking to the two other members of his machine-gun team, lance corporals Robert L. Labicki and Roger L. Garrett, about what happened that night, and testified that Diener told him he had been tight with Pearson and "if I had seen a lot of my buddies blown away like he had that I would feel the same way about the Vietnamese." He later had a conversation with Lance Corporal Ferguson, who was on Bailey's patrol. Ferguson told him that "a woman with a baby in her arms" had been killed, and that he was glad that he had nothing to do with it. It is a measure of the intense concern that some in Bravo felt, of the countless company conversations that you would expect after such an incident, conversations that continue to this very day, but also of how quickly events became exaggerated. No evidence was ever brought forward of a woman killed with a baby in her arms.[27]

Skibsrud weathered the cross-examinations relatively well as lawyers for the defense tried to suggest his field of vision was obstructed, that he couldn't be sure that Diener killed the woman because he didn't see a muzzle-flash, and that he could not say with certainty who had informed him of the patrol's mission. Reynolds accused Skibsrud of offering only "impressionistic" accounts of the orders he received. At that point Bergman stepped in and said to Reynolds: "I think in the instance you gave, the circumstances are quite clear"—Skibsrud was testifying to the impressions he believed pervaded the patrol, and "were not specific orders received from a platoon or squad leader." Twice, he was asked if he had seen PFC Ronald P. Toon on the patrol, and his responses were: "I can't recollect where he was," and "No, I don't know where he was." The questions had a clear purpose.[28]

A few days after Skibsrud went to the chaplain, a second witness gave a statement to Marine investigators. This was Toon, the point man on Allen's patrol. Toon testified that he was present at a pre-patrol briefing in which he heard Diener say that we were to "burn everything the VC could use for food and shelter, and children were up to our conscience." Diener, according to

Toon, told the patrol he had just come from a briefing by Maynard, attended by several others. There is no other evidence that Diener attended the CO's briefing, and Diener told me that he was not there. Toon was also the only one who recalled a briefing by Diener. It was Sergeant Allen's patrol and the preponderance of evidence suggests that he gave the briefing. Toon, however, had a better memory of who attended the briefing. Harlan (PFC Dennis M.), Manness (LCpl Ronald L.), Beard (PFC Lester A., III), Trantham (PFC Donald R., who would later die from a booby trap), and a Marine named Harkins, in addition to Diener. Toon also testified, as several others did, that the patrol was voluntary. Though no one testified that they knew why it was voluntary, they all made clear that they had no previous experience of being told as a group that any patrol was voluntary.[29]

Toon testified that he intended to remain behind, but when Allen told him to walk point he complied. As they approached the populated bunker, Toon saw an "old" lady, of about fifty. Recall that Skibsrud thought that she was much younger, but it was very difficult for Americans to judge the age of mature Vietnamese women. Toon yelled for her to come out, using the Vietnamese expression, "Lai Dai." Diener, however, was trying to push her back in, he said. He and another Marine, Henderson, pulled pins on their grenades and were about to throw them into the bunker, when Allen arrived and said: "Don't kill the kids." Toon heard Diener argue back that Allen was disobeying "Bravo 6." The live grenades were used to destroy the bunker, but not to kill the kids.[30]

Then Toon testified to the following: Diener "turned the old lady into the rice paddy. She started walking and he just raised his rifle and started firing." Diener fired "six rounds into her back." Toon said he was six to ten feet from Diener when the latter fired. He could not say with certainty that the women died, but he testified he saw no movement and heard no moans. Then Beard took a bundle that looked like clothing from the oldest girl and threw it into a fire: "The kids all started to crying and there was a remark, I don't remember who said it, they didn't cry when they saw their mother get shot," the same comment that Skibsrud heard. As the patrol returned to the landing zone (LZ), Toon overheard Diener "boasting" about his killing of an old lady: "It was like it was just some kind of game."[31]

Toon's testimony differed from his written statement. He apparently did not recall stating that Diener's order included the phrase "kill everything that moved," and said he did not recall two other statements—"this was the most shocking moment of all," and "from 18 and under were considered kids." Defense counsel did their best to underline the discrepancy, to challenge Toon's memory, and to suggest that his original statement was not unambiguously his own. But on the key question, Toon never wavered. He had witnessed Diener shooting a Vietnamese woman in the back, and his account of Sergeant Allen's intervention, Diener's actions, and the ugly comment about the children crying closely paralleled that of Skibsrud, neither of whom knew of the other's testimony. Toon had only a vague idea of who Skibsrud was, and Skibsrud could not remember Toon at all. The government counsels, Skibsrud said, kept him totally in the dark—wholly understandably for legal reasons, but frustrating for him nonetheless.[32]

Toon also offered evidence that Diener was encouraging his fellow platoon members "to stick together and beat this rap." Once it became known that Toon had joined Skibsrud as a witness against Diener, Diener importuned Toon to change his statement: "He said he didn't like the idea of being sent up for murder and that I wouldn't like it either." He promised Toon that he could rejoin the squad. Toon appears to have bowed to Diener's personal pressure, telling him he would change his testimony. Toon had reason to be cautious and wary. He testified that a gunnery sergeant whom he did not know vowed to kill him should he catch him in the field and he had heard of the threats directed against Skibsrud: "there was a lot of talk in the squad that if Skibsrud went out with the platoon there would be an accidental discharge, and I was afraid someone would have an accidental discharge with me."[33]

Toon, who is a retired truck driver now living in a trailer park in Santa Maria, California, had some difficulty in recalling the details of his statement and his testimony in a recent phone conversation. But he remembered with vivid clarity what Diener had done that morning. It was, he said, "outright murder," and he could not condone it. It wasn't the same as killing in combat. He later recalled that Diener had his left hand on the woman, his right on his M-16, and the woman's "smock flying forward with the impact of the rounds." Unlike Skibsrud, Toon did not seek out a chaplain nor Marine investigators. But when the investigators sought him out, he told them the truth of what he had seen.[34]

Some members of first platoon elected to attack Skibsrud's character. Labicki was Skibsrud's tent mate and the leader of his M-60 team. He thought there "was something wrong with him," and that it seemed "like he doesn't gave a damn about anything . . . doesn't care about anyone else," that he was "foggy-minded" and "slow." He also testified that Skibsrud had refused to carry Pearson's body to the medevac. Labicki also claimed that

Skibsrud wanted to get out of the field—"he couldn't hack the field"—that he had extended his enlistment to come to Vietnam and now wanted to get it dropped. He had written to his congressman or senator and Labicki had seen the return letter. Garrett, under questioning by Ehlers, confirmed that Skibsrud wanted out of the field and out of Vietnam—"He said something about his getting a bad deal on one of his extensions," and that he was writing his congressman and his brother, the Marine officer. PFC Lloyd believed that was his motive. Question: "Do you think that Skibsrud fabricated this story to get out of the field?" Answer: "yes, sir, I do." Labicki recalled when Skibsrud went to the chaplain and that the reason he gave was to see about getting his extension dropped. When Skibsrud returned, however, he learned that he had told the chaplain "some story about . . . some woman killed." What was his response? he was asked: "I was amazed and pretty puzzled. I didn't know what to think," Labicki said. What was the likelihood that he was hearing a story of a woman killed for the first time? There were some limits members of 1st Platoon imposed on themselves. When Lloyd was asked, "Have you ever heard that Skibsrud smoked 'pot,' or anything like that?" he said, "No, sir."[35]

Skibsrud, who remembered Labicki only as "Bob," and had no clear memory of Garrett, denied to me that he had refused to carry Pearson's body or that he had ever signed an extension. He told me he served for two years only, enlisting on June 1, 1966, and leaving active duty on May 20, 1968. He did tell me that his father had written to someone in Washington, he thought possibly Robert Kennedy, but not at his request. He also told me that he was so deeply upset about what he had seen that he was in "shock," and that he just couldn't "handle" it. He resisted my praise for him as a truth-teller. That wasn't why he went to the chaplain, he seemed to say, he just couldn't "handle" what he saw and he needed to talk to someone who might understand. He told me that he was so troubled at that moment that he thought about shooting himself in the foot in order to get out of the field, and telling this to Bob. He never did, and Labicki never testified to it.[36]

Robert Labicki left the Marines as a sergeant and came to settle near Lake Geneva in Wisconsin. He had a long career with the telephone company and "never" talked about Vietnam according to his daughter, Melissa, to whom I first talked. He was not home that night, she said, but in Missouri where she owned a condo. A few minutes later, Robert Labicki called me. He remembered the death of Pearson, that his lungs were blown out and that he was "gurgling" in his death throes. He helped to carry him to the LZ. His blood was on him. He also told me that Diener "went crazy" that morning, and that Pearson was Diener's "best friend," a claim that never came out in the Article 32 Investigation, but which was affirmed by Diener's attorney, Ehlers. He told me he witnessed the death of that Vietnamese woman, but that he had no memory of testifying, no memory that Captain Maynard was charged, but volunteered that Maynard was "one of the best people I've ever met." He also had no memory of Olaf Skibsrud or of Don Allen.[37]

He called me back the next morning, saying he been up all night with his memories. He is a soft-spoken and articulate man, and he was deeply troubled by what he told me the previous night, and he was trying to get it right. No, he was no longer sure it was Diener—Marines that night were wearing helmets and flak jackets—he was no longer sure that the woman had died, though he did see a muzzle flash and a woman fall.[38]

The attacks on Toon were milder. Immediately after Whittig's question to Lloyd: "Did you think Skibsrud fabricated his story to get out of the field?" Whittig asked: "What of a PFC Toon?" Answer: "Toon, he's alright." Then a follow-up: "Is he a good man?" Lloyd had a chance to recover: "He's kind of odd." Whittig pressed: "Is he any different from you?" Answer: "No, sir, I don't think," and then: "I'm not a psychiatrist, I couldn't say." Later, Whittig asked: "Would you say Toon is susceptible to influence?" Lloyd answered: "I guess so. I guess you can say that. You can use Toon." But Lloyd would go only so far. Question: "Is Skibsrud the type of person who would use Toon?" Answer: "I couldn't say sir."[39]

Though it may seem odd that the government counsel would open up this line of questioning, it's important to understand that this was not a trial but an investigation. Diener, Bailey, and Maynard may have had defense counsels; the government's counsels, however, were not functioning as prosecutors. They had an affirmative duty to seek the truth, wherever it would lead.

Other members of 1st Platoon sought to place Skibsrud and Toon in patrol locations far from the bunker. Allen testified that he placed his machine-gun team as rear security, and that Skibsrud could not have seen the bunker from that far back. Tetlef M. Kroll, the patrol's corpsman, went much further. He testified that Toon was with him on rear security all that morning. Toon, he said, was ill, had a high temperature, and was sick to his stomach. He should not have even gone out. Out of concern, Kroll said he stayed with Toon. Toon had testified that he was point man that night, and other witnesses confirmed that. Whittig, barely concealing his sarcasm, said: "I think you should be congratulated on your concern for the individual."

Roberts pressed the issue: "Is your testimony then Toon could not have possibly been up at that hootch?" Kroll: "That's right, sir." Somewhat later, Kroll stated that Toon "does walk around in a dream most of the time, he wouldn't make a very good point," and that he had the same look on Operation Lancaster, the operation that followed Liberty II. "I would have never put him on point," Kroll said. Bergman had heard enough. Question: "How long had Toon been point man?" Answer: "As far as I remember, he was point man down South too." Kroll was one of six patrol members whom Bergman believed should be investigated for perjury.[40]

Among the others were LCpl Richard E. Brown, who was on Bailey's patrol and who heard no explosions, no firing, and saw no Vietnamese. It was, in his account, an utterly uneventful patrol. LCpl Luis W. Guzman was a fire-team leader on Allen's patrol. Lloyd, Harkins, and Coleman were on his team that night. Harkins and Coleman had been subsequently wounded. Guzman testified he heard no firing and no explo-sions in the vicinity of the bunker, he saw no woman, and at no time since the incident had he heard from members of 1st Platoon that a woman had been killed that night. Lance Corporal Garrett was on Allen's patrol, along with Labicki and Skibsrud. He testified that he had heard firing, though he could not be sure of its direction, saw some children, saw Diener throw a grenade into a bunker, but he saw no woman and heard nothing about a woman being killed until he heard "scuttle-butt" back in the rear. "It was just another patrol," he said.[41]

Bergman singled out two other members of Allen's patrol for investiga-tion of possible perjury. One was PFC Dennis M. Harlan, who recalled that he was third man in the column. He testified to seeing Diener, Manness, Beard, and Henderson at the bunker, but he said he never saw Allen nor recalled any conversation about what to do with the kids, nor did he hear any subsequent conversation about a woman killed. Harlan's testimony was more detailed than the written statement he had signed as part of the initial investigation, and seemingly contradictory as well. The last Marine Bergman believed to be lying was PFC Lester A. Beard III, the radioman on Allen's patrol. Beard recalled seeing Diener and Henderson at the bunker, overheard Allen's order not to kill the kids, and testified to overhearing a radio conversation between Bailey and Maynard, to which we will return. But his recollection was sufficiently confusing to call down Bergman's wrath: "You do realize you are under oath?" and "From the varied stories you have given us, about the same incident, I really don't know whether you could be believed or not."[42]

Bergman believed that others had committed perjury. The six he singled out were only the "most flagrant in their distortion of truths, alleged lack of memory, and outright prevarications." Whether charges were ever filed against the six is as yet unclear, but of the four whose records I found, three had been promoted, Beard and Harlan by a full three grades. Both left the Marines as E-5s. Skibsrud and Toon were never promoted again after their testimony.[43]

Of the eleven members of Allen's patrol called to testify—excluding Skibsrud, Toon, and Allen himself—five faced further investigation for perjury. The case against Diener appeared strong—Skibsrud and Toon described Diener's killing of the women in remarkably similar terms and whatever questions Bergman might have had about where Skibsrud was that night, there was little doubt that Toon was at the bunker. Six Marines had placed Toon either as point man, at the bunker, or as assigned to 3rd Squad, the squad sent to the bunker. Three Marines, in addition to Toon and Skibsrud, placed Diener at the bunker. The clumsy and unprincipled efforts of six other Marines to either deliberately lie about or deliberately obscure what happened that morning unwittingly strengthened the case against young Rudy Diener. But Marine investigators did not believe that it was likely that Diener acted on his own, and so the question of what orders he and others received that night became the principal focus of the investigation.[44]

Maynard's Orders and Bailey's Patrol

Maynard and Bailey both gave voluntary statements. Maynard said his orders were to "take no chances, in view of the previous history of that village and our previous encounters of the evening, to prep fire treelines, to throw grenades in the many fighting holes in the village, to clear the village of all persons who were cooperative by escorting them to the river crossing site and insuring that they cross, and then to shoot at any moving shadow or bush to insure that no one gets hurt through hesitation." "To the best of my knowledge," Maynard wrote, "these instructions were carried out."[45]

Bailey told his patrol that they were entering a ville that "was definitely VC and that our mission was to clear the ville and burn any houses that still remained," that the rear platoon had received sniper fire, and "that any unusual or suspicious movement encountered would be considered VC." Maynard had made no mention of burning houses in his statement. Bailey repeated what his men already knew—they had taken casualties and the VC knew their current position. Bailey chose to report the orders he gave rather than those he heard from Maynard. It is standard practice for a unit commander to give mission orders in his own voice, but no Marine would have doubted that the orders came from Maynard or that Bailey was following them.[46]

Two witnesses, in addition to Bailey, saw the incident at the first bunker. As the patrol approached the bunker, the point man, PFC Edward Johnson, saw a light flickering on and off and heard "whispering." He called Bailey forward, and passed the word that somebody was in the bunker, or "hootch," as Johnson called it. The other witness, LCpl Wilson B. Dozier III, Bailey's new radioman, was walking fifth in column, behind Bailey. He recalled that a Marine called out "Lai Dai," another repeated the order in English. Dozier heard no response. Johnson had no memory of such, and Bailey had not mentioned it in his statement. Bailey said he threw the first grenade, heard movement, and ordered a second to be thrown. They immediately heard screams of agony. Members of the other patrol could hear the screams. As the occupants of the bunker tried to run or crawl away, Marines opened fire. Bailey reported, "someone yelled that they [the bunker's occupants] were still moving, so I ordered them to fire again." His statement referenced Operation Medina, when he said a wounded VC had crawled to within a few feet of Marines after they had shifted their attention elsewhere. When the firing stopped after less than a minute, Marines approached the bunker.[47]

Bailey had testified that they found the bodies of two adults, a man and a woman, twenty to thirty years old, and a child, one to two years old. Johnson testified he saw three bodies, a woman between thirty and forty, and two children, one about two or three, another younger. Dozier saw the bodies of two adults, a man and a woman, both over forty. He also said he noticed a third body, an adult, behind the bunker. He did not see a dead child, but acknowledged that other Marines did, "which made everyone upset, including myself," he said. Several witnesses testified that Bailey ordered them to place the bodies found in front of the bunker back into the bunker and then cover the bunker up. Johnson and Dozier testified that they saw no movement nor heard any sounds from the inert bodies. One Marine, however, PFC Clifford Bijou, said that as he moved an adult woman of forty or fifty back into the bunker, he heard her "moaning" softly, and she continued to moan as he went about his work. The government asked several witnesses whether there was a corpsman on the patrol, and if so, whether he had been called up to the bunker. Yes, there was a corpsman. No, he had not been called up.[48]

Three, and possibly four, Vietnamese died that morning at the first bunker—one child among them certainly, and possibly two. The discrepancies in the Marines' testimony were not probative. It was dark and it was a dangerous mission. The platoon recovered no weapons. Bailey had testified that the Vietnamese were either unconscious or dead. If the former, why hadn't he called up the corpsman and why did he order the bunker covered up after the bodies where placed back? He hadn't mentioned the covering-up in his statement. Whittig and Roberts, the government's lawyers, pressed on the former point. Bailey had placed his corpsman at the end of the column. Corpsmen and medics typically walk nearer the front, where danger more likely lurks.[49]

Dozier testified that he radioed a report of the incident, including the killing of women and children, back to the company command post. He spoke, he believed, to Corporal Harvard, the company operator. He did not talk to Maynard, nor did he believe Maynard was listening in. He heard no indication that Harvard passed the word on, but for Harvard to do anything other than inform Maynard is hardly conceivable.[50]

The second incident occurred as Bailey's patrol moved back toward the LZ. The patrol found a second populated bunker. This time there was no question about whether the occupants were ordered out. According to the testimony of Corporal Terry L. Spann, eleven or so women and children appeared, and one man, about thirty-five. Spann checked the man—who was wearing "the little white jacket that they wear" and black pants—for an ID card. He had no card, just a "pack of tobacco." The bunkers were blown. The women and children were sent ahead of the patrol and told to cross a nearby river.[51]

According to Spann, he and Bailey followed behind the Vietnamese man, who walked behind the women and children as they approached the river. There were, he said, only three other Marines with them, the radioman (Dozier), a corpsman (Hamming), and the M-79 man Spann identified as Lance Corporal Brown. Spann testified that the Vietnamese man tried to duck off the trail four times. When the women and children were sent across the river, he was retained. Spann said that he and Bailey were in discussion about whether to bring him back to the regiment or let him go when the man made a sudden move. Bailey then hit him with the stock of his shotgun and he fell down the bank to the river's edge.[52]

Spann testified that he fired at the man after he made that sudden move. But his M-16, he said, malfunctioned. There appear to have been numerous problems with Marine weaponry that night. Spann's M-16 had also jammed during the first incident, as did Johnson's. He also testified that Bailey's shotgun jammed as he tried to fire at the Vietnamese man. Bailey reverted to his .45 and fired two rounds, but Spann could not tell whether he hit the man. Spann fired one round, but he said he missed the man. He recalled hearing two rounds hit the water, one of his and one of Bailey's. He heard no screams, no sounds at all from the man. He testified that three to four minutes had elapsed between the time Bailey had laid down his malfunctioning shotgun and fired his .45. "Three to four minutes?" Roberts asked. Lamely, Spann responded that Bailey "had to put a round into his pistol before he had a chance to fire it." During this time, Spann testified he was preoccupied with clearing his weapon. "Did you give any thought to running after him and trying to grab him?" Roberts asked. Answer: "No sir, I didn't." Bergman later asked how far the man had moved in those three to four minutes, and Spann answered twenty to twenty-five feet. Bergmann: "In four minutes, he got only twenty-five feet?" Spann responded: "I guess the time was four minutes, sir, I didn't have a watch, and I couldn't actually tell." Spann testified that he and Bailey went to look for the man, Spann covering forty to forty-five meters, to no avail. Spann had given an earlier statement to Marine investigators that did not include the second incident: "I just forgot about it, sir," he said.[53]

The only other witness to the second incident was Dozier, the radioman. He recalled seeing six to ten villagers emerge from that second bunker. His testimony concurred with Spann's—the women and children were pushed across a river, though he remembered that they crossed it reluctantly. He recalled the Vietnamese man who had been kept behind, who was searched for his ID, and who made a "quick movement," but could not state what caused it. He testified that Spann pointed his rifle in the direction of the Vietnamese man and that it jammed. He saw Bailey fire his shotgun twice, but made no mention of it jamming, or of Bailey's reported use of his .45. "What happened after that?" Roberts asked. "They returned up to my position," Dozier responded.[54]

All three accounts were in accord until the firing started. Bailey stated that he fired "several shots" and hit the man. Dozier saw Bailey fire his shotgun twice. Spann's story of jammed weapons, a three to four minute period when no shots were fired, and a man in fear for his life managing to flee only twenty to twenty-five yards strains credulity. Spann was also the only one to claim that they searched for the man. Bailey explicitly said otherwise, and Dozier noted that after the firing, both returned to his position.

There was one other troubling aspect to the accounts. Both Bailey and Spann testified that they had a discussion about whether to take the man in. Why a discussion? There could only have been three choices—take him in; let him go, as Spann explicitly suggested; or . . . kill him. This was a VC area, he was of military age, and he had no ID. Belbusti's orders had been to bring in suspects. But whatever the content of the discussion, Bailey and Spann were in agreement that the Vietnamese man made a sudden move. He had either escaped—wounded, according to Bailey's testimony—or had been killed. Marine investigators had found no bodies.

What orders had Bailey given? PFC Johnson could not tell a consistent story. When the prosecutors questioned him, he claimed that Bailey said: "We was going to kill anything that we see and anything that moved." When the defense lawyers questioned him, he said he did not hear Bailey give such an order, and he alternated his conflicting responses more than once. Six other witnesses claimed they could recall no such order. LCpl Eddie Kelly Jr., however, said that Bailey had told them they were to "search and destroy everything in the village," if true, an ambiguous order at best, but he also said he heard no order having to do with men, women, or children. Kelly said he heard only part of the briefing; several others testified to the same. Lieutenant Steen testified, to the apparent incredulity of the government, that he had missed Maynard's briefing because it had taken him twenty minutes to remove his rain suit. He had to take off his boots, he said. Brown testified that he heard nothing at all, including any explosions or small-arms fire. He was the only one on Bailey's patrol singled out for possible perjury charges. Spann testified that they were to chase people out of the ville and bring in men of military age. He was the only one who heard such an order. But Dozier offered more. He testified that he heard Bailey say that we were to kill anyone of military age, but that the women and children were simply to be gathered up and pushed out the other side of the ville. He did not hear Bailey say that we were to kill anything that moved. But his testimony was challenged too. On cross-examination, Captain Allen claimed that Dozier had told him "last night" he had "heard no talk of killing people in the ville. I heard we could kill people but I didn't hear it from Lt." Allen's question suggested that Dozier's testimony was rife with contradiction. But Dozier answered, "I don't remember saying that sir. We were told that we would kill men, that women and children be gathered up and swept out of the ville."[55]

There was also something highly unusual about both patrols. Marines were offered the opportunity to remain behind. Johnson, Toon, Anderson, Dozier, Kelly, Brown, and Allen all testified to the fact. Dozier said it had never happened before. Not everybody heard it. When I mentioned the fact to Skibsrud, it was the first time he had heard about it. "Well, that tells you something, doesn't it," he said. Whittig and Roberts also thought it meaningful. But they could not establish a reason. No one knew why. Allen speculated that it was because the men were shook up after Pearson's death. But Bailey never offered a reason, just as he never offered a reason to his corpsman, Hamming, for telling him to walk at the end of the patrol. The government's effort to suggest that Bailey's decisions were evidence that he knew that civilians would be killed, in the end, were no more than suggestions. There was no evidence.[56]

There was talk. Skibsrud testified to a conversation he had with Lieutenant Steen two days after the incident. This was immediately following Skibsrud's exchange with Maynard. Steen seemed solicitous, Skibsrud recalled. Steen "told me to do what I thought was right." Then Skibsrud testified that Steen had said "Lieutenant Bailey was a fine man with a wife back in the states, but the other night he just took a man out and shot him." Steen denied under oath talking to Skibsrud. When informed of this, Skibsrud said: "I'd have to say that that is not the truth, sir."[57]

Steen, however, was not a witness to Bailey's actions, and the case against Bailey was weak. The deaths at the first bunker could not be construed as premeditated murder. The Rules of Engagement (ROE) did require that Marines shout "Lai Dai" before grenading a bunker, and Dozier claimed that happened. Bailey's omission of the fact was, in a certain sense, positive. He could have easily lied. The stories of what happened at the riverbank with the Vietnamese man were troublingly inconsistent, so inconsistent, however, that they actually pointed toward the absence of a clear and compelling "cover-up." Marine investigators would have warned witnesses not to talk among themselves or to compare stories but they could not, and did not, prevent it from happening. In the end, only Bailey and Spann know what happened that morning. And they were consistent on one critical point. The Vietnamese man had tried to escape. The ROE permitted firing at an escaping prisoner. There was no evidence of premeditated murder.[58]

Nor was there compelling evidence that Bailey had issued illegal orders that morning. Johnson's evidence was contradictory, and six witnesses testified that they heard no orders about wholesale killing. Kelly's statement that "we were to search and destroy everything in the ville" could not be construed as an order to commit murder. And Spann and Dozier had testified that their orders were to sweep people from the ville, orders that were followed.

Sergeant Allen's Story

It was PFC Lloyd's testimony that opened a new door. Lloyd was a rifleman who had been in country since September 23. He believed, as we've seen, that Skibsrud was lying, but he also displayed a kind of unguarded honesty. He never heard that Skibsrud smoked pot and didn't know whether Skibsrud could manipulate Toon, though it would have been easy, had he chosen, to answer such questions in the affirmative if his goal had merely been to discredit—after all, the questions weren't posed in a way that could yield perjury charges. He was just being asked what he had heard and what his opinion was. He was also bluntly honest about his feelings about the investigation: "this is a bunch of bullshit," he said, and that's what "everyone thinks."[59]

Allen returned from his briefing with Maynard and Bailey to brief his own squad. Lloyd testified that he was in that briefing and he specifically recalled that Toon, the corpsman (Kroll), and Johnson were there. He testified that Allen said: "we were going to this ville and we would search and destroy and we were suppose [sic] to kill all the men and women and let our conscience be our guide as to the children." "Let our conscience be our guide as to the children." Toon had heard a similar phrase—"children were up to our conscience"—though he thought he heard it from Diener. Lloyd recognized the order as "unusual" and recalled the corpsman telling him "he didn't like it." The corpsman was Kroll, who was so concerned about Toon's fever that he never let him get out of earshot. Lloyd's testimony contradicted his. Kroll had testified that he never received a briefing nor learned what the patrol's mission was. Regardless of Kroll's reported concerns about the order, Lloyd stated, "at the time it seemed the right thing to do." When Ehlers also asked him why he thought Allen's order unusual, he responded, "I've heard things like this could get you in trouble." Captain Allen tried to make it seem like a joke. "Have you ever heard the troops kidding and joking around and saying—I know this because we did it ourselves when we were in basic training—'Kill all the men and rape all the women'—and just a joking thing— or 'there's a church up there, blow the church up,' have you heard anyone joking like this before." "No, sir," Lloyd said.[60]

Lloyd's testimony that Allen's order was to kill the men and women of the village opened a door that could not be closed. Whittig wanted to pry it open further, apparently convinced that Lloyd knew even more, and was covering for Diener. He presented him with the Manual for Courts Martial, opened to the page on perjury. This galvanized the defense counsels. Reynolds immediately wanted the record to reflect that this was an investigation, not an "inquisition." Bergman ignored Reynolds. Whittig went on to ask: "Since twenty-two October . . . have you heard anything whatsoever of any source that would indicate to you that Lance Corporal Diener, that man right over there, shot or shot at a person that evening[?]" Lloyd: "No, sir, I haven't." Allen then rose in protest: "The government counsel is not either interested in prosecuting somebody or letting somebody go. It's their job to find facts and I think this whole proceeding has been orientated towards trying to prosecute these people." Bergman responded: "Both sides have taken the form of a trial at times. The investigating officer has chosen to ignore those aspects where the lawyers have taken liberties that would normally be taken in court but not necessarily be for an investigation."[61]

Several other witnesses were called that afternoon, November 24. The investigation recessed at 1620 for an early dinner. At 1742, Allen was called as a witness. The questions began routinely. When Roberts asked him what his patrol orders were, Allen responded: "At this time, sir, I stand upon article 31," the Uniform Code of Military Justice's (UCMJ) equivalent of the Fifth Amendment.[62]

Roberts responded: "you realize you've been granted immunity," and apologized for not saying that initially. The grant of immunity, clearly advocated by Marine legal, had come from Col Herbert Ing, the regimental commander. Allen wanted to be sure. Nothing he said could be held against him, "Now and in the future, is that true, sir?" Allen asked. "That is correct," Bergman responded.[63]

Allen's heroism on his first tour had been made known previously. He was a feisty witness, not intimidated by Marine lawyers, and clearly unhappy at having to be there. He had nothing but praise for Maynard, whom he said was the best CO in the Marine Corps, and for Bailey, whom he believed deserved at least the Navy Cross for his actions in tending the wounded that night in an area that could well have contained additional booby traps. Whatever his admiration for Maynard and Bailey, it was apparent that he was not going to allow Lloyd to finger him as the sole author of a manifestly illegal order to kill all the men and women in that ville.[64]

Allen testified that he was present at Maynard's briefing. He recalled that Maynard said that 1st Platoon would have "first crack" at the ville. He later elaborated on that point, despite the efforts of Maynard's counsel to establish that perhaps Maynard sent out 1st Platoon simply because the others had all dug in: "it's only right to go on patrol." Allen said, "because we had taken the wounded and the dead." Second Lieutenant Bowman confirmed that 1st Platoon was sent as a "get even type thing."[65]

Allen related the rest of Maynard's order: "there was nothing to be left alive or unburned, as far as the children goes let our conscience be our guide." Once again, the phrase "let our conscience be our guide," the same phrase that Lloyd and Toon heard. A third Marine, Harlan, would also testify that he heard the exact phrase: "I heard we were supposed to search and destroy, kill anything under forty-five years of age and let your conscience be your guide about the children." Labicki had also heard that they were to kill "everything under forty-five," though he also said he didn't believe it. Neither Harlan nor Labicki recalled who said it.[66]

With a clear sense of military pride, Allen recounted how he organized his patrol, set in security in a "small 360," and sent his 3rd Squad, led by Diener, to investigate voices he had heard: "I said there's people [meaning Vietnamese] up there, take your people, you know your orders." As he continued to place his men in position, he heard rifle fire from the direction of the bunker. When he walked up to it he was told that a woman had tried to run from the bunker and had been shot. No one else confirmed his account. He never saw the woman, and could identify no one other than Beard. But he repeated that he sent 3rd Squad up and later identified them as Beard, Harlan, Diener, Henderson, and Toon. At that point, he saw some children. Someone he could not identify "said there was children there and he wanted to shoot them. I said no you aren't going to shoot the kids, they said yes, we're going to shoot them, and I said goddamn it you ain't shooting the damn kids." Allen had reversed the sequence of events reported by Skibsrud and Toon, the woman had been shot first, before the argument over killing the children.[67]

Whether deliberate or not, Allen's reversal of events had the benefit of allowing him to more convincingly say he never saw a woman. Toon had testified that she had come out with the children, and two other witnesses would effectively contradict Allen when they testified that they saw the woman come out from the bunker to stand with the children, that is, they did not see a woman killed as she ran from the bunker, an ugly act that nevertheless would have been permitted under the ROE at night. Moreover, Skibsrud recalled that Allen witnessed Diener kill the woman, though he was never asked to testify to it. Allen knew that under the grant of immunity, he had to testify against his CO, but he apparently wasn't willing to testify against Diener, even though he had little respect for him—"Diener wasn't intelligent enough to make decisions and direct his men." It must have been painful for Diener to hear that, but it may have worked to his benefit.[68]

At this point in his testimony, Allen reported what Beard told him he overheard on the radio: "Bravo One was . . . talking to Bravo Six, or so the radioman says. Bravo One Actual said there was going to be a lot of children killed if they carried this thing out. Bravo Six came back and said, "so, they grow up to be VC." Bravo One was Bailey's radioman, One Actual was Bailey, the Six was Maynard. Allen testified that he heard no claim by Diener or anyone else that he was disobeying Maynard's order, as Toon had recalled.[69]

Allen, like some others, had added more to his testimony than he first related to Marine investigators. He was questioned two or three days after the incident and dictated a statement. It took him more than a week to decide to sign it. His initial report contained no mention of Maynard's phrase "let your conscience be your guide." Captain Allen used his omission to question the accuracy of the sergeant's memory. Repeatedly, the defense counsels had asked Allen, to his growing irritation, to restate Maynard's order that there was nothing to be left alive or unburned and let your conscience be your guide. How could he be so sure those were the exact words, when there was so much else about the patrol he did not remember? It was a clever piece of cross-examination and, in the end, Allen had to admit that it was possible that he had forgotten even more about the order. But that's as far as the defense could go. Allen did not invent the phrase after the fact. Toon testified that he heard it as well, and so did others. Allen's testimony ended as the investigation recessed at 2250. Allen had been questioned for four hours.[70]

As to the children, "let your conscience be your guide." Ehlers told me that the phrase came up so often, it appeared rehearsed. He doubted that it came from Maynard, and was deeply suspicious of Allen. Years later, he recalled a sinister quality in Allen. He believed that Allen had become a mercenary after leaving the Marine Corps. He thought Bailey was a better candidate for immunity. Both Allen and Harlan had failed to note the phrase in their written statements. It appears that Lloyd was never asked to make a written statement. It's entirely possible that Allen made it up, but the evidence is clear that the statement was not made up after the fact. Toon and Sergeant Phillip Battelle had included the phrase in their written statements. Battelle thought he heard it from Bailey, which would suggest that it did come from Maynard. But he reversed himself at the investigation, saying he was no longer sure who said it. Battelle accompanied Allen's patrol that morning. No member of Bailey's patrol reported the phrase, suggesting that either Bailey heard it from Maynard and elected not to repeat it or that Allen made it up, or more charitably, misheard it.[71]

Allen's testimony offered an opening for Bailey's attorney, and for Maynard's as well. If Maynard had ordered men and women to be killed, why hadn't the order been followed? Why had Bailey let women and children exit the village? Reynolds actually tried to get Allen to admit that Bailey had disobeyed orders. "What is your first obligation?" he asked. Answer: "to carry out orders." But Allen offered an instructive if syntactically challenged qualifier: "when somebody is made a unit commander . . . this person who made him a unit leader also believes that this guy, to carry out the orders, uses integrity, his judgment to carry out these orders, the way he sees fit."[72]

The last two to testify were Maj Ernest T. Cook Jr., the Battalion S-3, operations officer, and LtCol Alfred F. Belbusti. Cook established that the area in and around Thon Nai Cuu was considered by ARVN and Government of the Republic of Vietnam officials to be VC controlled. It was a free-fire zone, a term that needs to be properly defined. A free-fire zone was not an area where the American military had a license to kill anything that moved, as many on the antiwar left assumed and continue to assume. A free-fire zone was simply an area where the American military could exercise its own judgment, without the need for prior approval by ARVN, to provide air or artillery support for troops on the ground. Cook also testified that the villagers of Thon Nai Cuu had been ordered to leave the village several times by the Vietnamese district chief.[73]

Cook's presence was the first opportunity for both sides to discuss the ROE. As issued by Belbusti as Battalion Order 3300.1, on September 8, 1967, the ROE required all unit commanders to "apply only that force necessary to accomplish their mission, giving due regard to the safety of their command and the importance of preventing injury to non-combatant populace." Further, the ROE stated that "Civilian dwellings will not be burned, nor will private property, including livestock, be destroyed except as an unavoidable consequence of combat action." Cook was repeatedly asked by defense counsels to respond to hypothetical questions framed around the facts of the case, but he resisted, saying that he would not "interpret" the ROE, but he also resisted Reynolds' statement that were "merely guidelines," answering: "They're pretty clear and pretty strong guidelines." Pressed further, however, he admitted, "the line between a violation of these rules and the mere exercise of judgment or application [on the part of a unit commander] can be a very thin one." That was as much as the defense was going to get from him.[74]

Belbusti's testimony established that there were no entries in the operation journal or the watch officer's log from Bravo after the report on the casualties suffered from the booby trap. Regulations required the filing of a spot report on all enemy contact, and a Serious Incident Report for any incident involving the killing or wounding of civilians. Neither had been done. All Marines received training in these matters, he said. He also established that the procedure for clearing a suspected enemy bunker required that a warning be first issued, and that Bailey's order to burn the ville, as read to him from Bailey's statement, was a violation of the ROE: "We don't have the authority to burn any houses," he said and continued to insist on this in the face of several hypotheticals offered by Captain Allen. He had given a briefing to all officers and battalion staff on October 19, 1967, addressing a directive from III Marine Amphibious Force on atrocities—rape, mutilation, and murder— and their impact on the war effort. He was also given an opportunity by Captain Reynolds to comment on the performance of Maynard as a field commander. Belbusti responded: "By virtue of the fact that he retained his command, his performance was satisfactory." Question: "Would you wish to make any additional remark in his favor?" Answer: "No."[75]

It is noteworthy that 1/1's daily logs for the period covered by Operation Liberty II no longer exist. There is a gap in the logs beginning at 2400, October 21, 1967, and ending at 2400, October 25. Three full days are missing, including the morning hours of October 22, when Bravo's 1st Platoon entered the ville of Thon Nai Cuu.[76]

The investigation adjourned at 1330, November 26. It had produced more than 500 pages of testimony, and had stretched over five days. It would, however, take until December 31 for clerks from the 1st Division's Legal Section to finish typing the transcript. Bergman's written recommendations, addressed to the CO, 1st Marines, were finished on January 5, 1968.[77]

After recommending that there was no point in pursuing charges against PFC Heald, he continued by placing the actions of Bravo in context. The company was "physically tired," he said. They were in an area where "most of the normal living structures had been previously destroyed," and was "hostile to U.S. forces."[78]

But then he got to the heart of the matter. He stated that Maynard's order "if obeyed, would result in the killing of persons not normally considered combatants . . . and that Lance Corporal Diener did, in fact, kill or attempt to kill a grown woman for no apparent reason other than he was ordered to do so in a patrol briefing." He went on: "Some members of B/1/1 considered the people in the village . . . to be responsible for the death of a Marine who was respected by all, and the Vietnamese living in the village site were of little consequence compared to the death of a good Marine."[79]

But none of this was intended, he said, "to absolve the persons being investigated of the charges against them." He concluded that the evidence was sufficient to charge Maynard and Diener with "violations of the Uniform Code of Military Justice." He was recommending that both be subject to court-martial.[80]

Bergman, who was required to fill out a lengthy form, DD457, added several comments under the form's heading "explanatory or extenuating circumstances." "Lance Corporal Diener," wrote Bergman, "is a young Marine . . . who possibly does not know the difference between a legal order and an illegal order . . . he appears to be a Marine of above average intelligence and natural leadership ability, but does not possess the same set of values in regard to human life as that required under all circumstances by the rules of engagement in Vietnam." That was a comment that might well help Diener. But Bergman's next comments were not exculpatory: "It was obvious . . . that Diener was aware of the seriousness of the crime of which he was charged, and that he made a partially successful effort to coerce the witnesses into omitting facts and distorting facts during their testimony."[81]

"In the case of Second Lieutenant Bailey," Bergman concluded, "the evidence reveals that some horrible acts were committed by his group, but [I have] concluded from the evidence that these acts were not premeditated and were the result of actions that would be automatic from military training and experience in a combat environment." He recommended that the charges against Bailey be dropped, as they were.[82]

It's hard to imagine he could have done otherwise. The killings at the first bunker may or may not have been preceded by the command "Lai Dai," but there was no compelling or consistent evidence that they were premeditated.

Clearing a bunker by fire, especially given the awful consequences that we now know, may seem ugly and preemptory to those who have never known war, but it was dark and Marines were patrolling in an area known to be hostile in the aftermath of the death of a fellow Marine, killed by a booby trap whose placement was almost certainly known to the Vietnamese remaining in the ville.

John Bailey now lives in Thomasville, North Carolina. He left the Corps as a first lieutenant in 1968. He is recently retired after a career as a teacher, principal, and coach. His memory of what happened at the two bunkers was not fully consistent with the investigative record. He was sure, he said, that he had shouted "Lai Dai." He did not recall the name of his radioman who had died, nor the number of dead at the first bunker. He remembered that the Vietnamese man was of "military-age" and he was sure that the man thought "we were going to execute him." "We weren't," he said. The man moved "aggressively," and Bailey recalled hitting him. He fired, but missed him. Why had he stated that he "hit" him? "I was just being a Marine," he said, "but I really didn't know." "That might have led to the charge," he thought, "but it's not likely. It says something powerful about Marine culture, however, that he didn't want to admit that he missed, or simply didn't know whether his shotgun discharge found his target.[83]

Bailey was charged because Marine investigators believed they had evidence of an illegal order issued by Maynard, and there was enough killing on Bailey's patrol to implicate him. Bailey could not recall what orders Maynard gave that morning, but he was sure that Maynard had never ordered everyone to be killed. He wasn't that kind of man. He was a good CO. He would never issue such an order, Bailey believed. After all, he had sent those children across the river. He recalled being "astounded" when he first learned that he was to be charged with premeditated murder.[84]

The Courts-Martial

On January 7, 1968, Bergman's recommendation arrived in the Headquarters of the 1st Marine Division. There was a delay resulting from the move of the 1st Marine Regiment to Camp Evans. The paperwork was returned to regimental headquarters for revision on January 21. On that day the charge of "premeditated murder" was dismissed, and replaced by a charge of "attempted premeditated murder." The woman's body had never been found. Diener recalls Ehlers telling him he had "good news and bad news."

The "good" news was that he faced a thirty-year sentence rather than a life sentence. The paperwork was resubmitted on that day. Staff at the Division's Legal Office reviewed the case and in a memorandum dated February 8, the head of the office, Col Clyde R. Mann, recommended that Diener be tried by general court-martial.[85]

Mann's recommendation shed light on the Legal Office's conclusions about Diener and Maynard. Accepting the testimony of Sergeant Allen, Mann concluded that "the accused's company commander and patrol leader ordered the killing of all adult Vietnamese men and women in the village." The order, Mann went on, "was unquestionably illegal."[86]

In returning to Diener, Mann wrote: "Ordinarily, a subordinate's acts, carried out in good faith in compliance with the orders of a superior, are legally justifiable. Under our system of law, however, compliance with orders will not constitute legal justification for a homicide or other crime if the order is in fact illegal and of such nature that a man of ordinary sense and understanding would know it to be illegal. . . . Every person of ordinary sense understands that certain basic humanitarian limitations are called for, even in war."[87]

Mann directly addressed the fairness of holding a young lance corporal to legal and moral account. "One might ordinarily have some misgiving in recommending trial by general court-martial of a [whited out] year old Lance Corporal for a crime which he may, however indirectly, have been ordered to commit by his company commander and platoon sergeant." However, the evidence made clear to Mann

> that the accused's demeanor and attitude, suggest rather than a reluctant youth forced by circumstance and command to do a moral wrong, an individual bent on revenge for the death of his deceased friend. The accused's abortive attempt to grenade a bunker with an unarmed woman and children inside, the same children that were "up to his own conscience," is an example in point. An exhaustive study of the evidence, and an evaluation of the total circumstances of this case, lead me to believe that any possible degradation of the officer-enlisted command relationship which may be engendered by holding this accused responsible for his actions is far outweighed by the affront to basic morality, law and order, and human dignity which such actions represent.

It was a noble and powerful moral statement, in a time of war, by an honorable Marine, who rose to the rank of brigadier general.[88]

The case of *United States v. Lance Corporal Rudolph O. Diener* was ordered to trial by the CG First Marine Divison (Rein) on February 11, 1968. On the following day, Diener requested the participation of civilian counsel, and on March 15 requested, as was his right, that enlisted men be added to the jury that would decide whether or not he serve twenty years of confinement at "hard labor," reduction to pay grade E-1, and a dishonorable discharge. The trial was set for March 18.[89]

Diener was never placed in the brig. After the Article 32 Investigation, he was assigned to Headquarters Company, 1st Marine Regiment. He recalls being treated harshly by the sergeant to whom he reported and by a medical officer; both knew who he was. As he left Company Headquarters after being told he would stand guard that evening, he noticed a chaplain's tent. He went in and began talking to CDR Carl Auel, USN, a tall imposing Lutheran who was the regimental chaplain. If he was seeking religious solace—he had been raised a Methodist—it wasn't something he wanted to talk about with me. "We talked," is all he said to me. Auel needed a driver. "Are you a good shot?" Auel asked. The question surprised Diener. "Probably too good," Diener recalled responding with some irony. Auel asked Colonel Ing, the regimental commander and his nightly cribbage partner, to assign Diener to him. He took me "under his wing," Diener recalled, "no one could mess with me again." Diener didn't stand guard that night.[90]

The members of the court were the law officer, LtCol Donald E. Holben, the President of the Court, Col Russell E. Corey, and its members, LtCol Logan Cassidy, LtCol Charles S. Webster, Maj James V. Sullivan, 1stSgt Billie W. Reed, 1stSgt Russell A. Van Horn, 1stSgt Richard J. Maughan, and MSgt John D. Sattler. Captains Roberts and Whittig continued to represent the government. James G. Ehlers, now a first lieutenant, was joined by Robert A. McKinley, a lieutenant colonel in the Marine Corps Reserve, for the defense.[91]

Only three witnesses were called for the prosecution: Toon, Cpl S. R. Henderson, who had been at the bunker with Diener, and PFC Harold Coleman. Called for the defense were patrol members Beard, Harlan, Battelle, Trantham, Labicki, and Garrett, all of whom had testified at the Article 32 Investigation, three of whom Bergman had thought guilty of flagrant perjury. Also testifying was Bailey, now a first lieutenant, and Don W. Allen, now a civilian. Ehlers thought Diener was a "good kid," "personable," though also young and impressionable. He and McKinley took the risk of putting him on the stand and Ehlers thought he made a good impression. Diener has a distinct memory of McKinley placing his hand on his shoulder and telling him not to worry and then hearing for the first time that McKinley would not contest the facts of the case. Diener was "shocked." His legal defense would rest exclusively on his following of orders.[92]

His attorneys had one other advantage. They called several character witnesses; two sergeants; two navy doctors, including the one that had originally treated him dismissively; and two chaplains, Auel and LTCD Elden H. Luffman, USN, a Baptist who had replaced Auel as regimental chaplain and had retained Diener as his driver/body guard. Auel was the critical witness. He had moved on to serve as chaplain to Task Force X-Ray. According to Ehlers, Auel's testimony was of great consequence. Auel had a commanding presence. With a silver cross on one of his collars, a silver oak leaf on the other, only Colonel Corey outranked him in the courtroom. He didn't look like a chaplain, Ehlers told me; he looked like a Marine. And he was well known and highly respected. Luffman called him "a natural leader," and Colonel Ing thought him "the finest person I've ever known."[93]

At the conclusion of the trial, Holben, the legal officer, gave instructions to the court. His instructions reversed the thrust of Mann's recommendation for trial. Making the same distinction between legal and illegal orders, he placed the burden of responsibility, however, squarely on the commander giving the order. The subordinate must assume that the orders he receives are legal except in rare instances when they are, he said, of "palpable illegality." Anything else would erode military discipline. Subordinates cannot be expected "in conditions of war discipline, to weigh scrupulously the legal merits of the orders received."[94]

"The defense has introduced evidence," Holben continued, "to show that . . . the accused was under the mistaken belief the order of Sergeant Allen was a lawful one." In such a case, Holben advised the court, "if the accuser was laboring under such a mistake and if the mistake was honest he cannot be found guilty of attempted murder." Diener was not required to "establish the honesty of his mistake." The defense couldn't have hoped for instructions more favorable.[95]

Diener recalled being offered a plea bargain—plead guilty, serve two to three years in prison, be demoted to private, and accept a dishonorable discharge. He refused. He believed then, as he continues to believe, that he had done nothing wrong. "My belief was in the Corps," he told me, "I did what I was asked to do." Allen's orders were that "everything was to be killed," there were to be "no prisoners." Diener couldn't be sure if he had heard the phrase "children are up to your own conscience."[96]

The court retired to deliberate and came back with a verdict of not guilty. The president of the court, Colonel Corey, eighty-nine at the time I called him, had a strikingly clear memory that the court was unanimous. Corey, like Ing, was a "mustang," a Marine who rose from the enlisted ranks to become an officer. He had first enlisted in 1937, and, also like Ing, served as a company commander on Iwo Jima. There was no question in his mind, a full thirty-five years after the trial, that a twenty-year-old lance corporal should not bear the brunt of a responsibility that rested, he believed, with his company commander. The trial had taken portions of three days, ending on March 20, 1968.[97]

Ehlers told me he had heard that the court was divided, the officers voting for conviction; the sergeants voting not guilty. A tie goes to the defense. Corey was emphatic that the vote was unanimous, but then he told me he remembered Diener's parents sitting in the courtroom. Diener told me they were not there.[98]

Capt Robert Maynard went to trial as well, but no record of his court-martial survives in the Judge Advocate General archives at Suitland, Maryland, only the jacket. By his own account, he was acquitted of the most serious charges, but found guilty of a failure to report, ending the possibility of a Marine career he had once sought. He told me that he had made an oral report to the battalion's S-3, Maj Walter Murphy. Murphy could not testify to it. He died in Hue, in the same attack that wounded Chaplain Lyons. Those who knew Maynard regarded him as a fine officer—even Terry Whitmore had praised him—making it harder to understand why Belbusti was so damningly curt. One of his platoon leaders that night, Edward B. Stollenwerck, a lieutenant, recalled him as a "no-nonsense" tough guy. Toon had nothing but praise for him. Ehlers and Bailey, in particular, believed that he was not the kind of man to ever give an order to wipe out an entire ville.[99]

To my knowledge he has broken his silence publicly only once, this on a website guest book for 2nd Battalion, 1st Marines. The copy of his entry that I have is undated, but would have appeared sometime after February 2002. Maynard had changed his name to Menard, he said, in 1974 "to be true to the family name in Quebec." "I was the CO of B 1/1," he wrote during the "serious incident" to which Robert Black, a fellow Marine officer, had referred. Black would take command of Bravo and lead the company into Hue. Menard said that what had happened was "worthy of a book/movie" and was "what we commonly refer to as 'WAR' and the end result of the Judicial process was that Myself and LCpl Deiner [*sic*] were acquitted at Courts-Martial and sent back to duty . . . but there are scars . . . those who know me and know what happened said I should have received a medal for the action . . . but once the judicial process started the Div cmdr didn't have the guts to reverse it." Menard suggested that he was soon to tell the whole story. The transcript of his trial was more than 1,000 pages, he said, "and that does not tell all the stories . . . surrounding the action itself and the ensuing judicial circus . . . not the least of which is the fact that the Govt had two witnesses and hustled them to a safe assignment in DaNang, while all of the voices on our side stayed in combat and several key witnesses were killed before the trials in March 68 . . . including my good friend Maj Walter Murphy who was killed on the first day of Hue City trying to pull a wounded Marine back to shelter." Menard said he wasn't sure he wanted to revisit it, but he didn't want any misinformation out there either. "If you weren't there," he wrote, "you don't know, no matter what you may have heard."[100]

Maynard—now Menard—currently lives in Marshall, North Carolina, near the Blue Ridge Mountains and works in a land-surveying firm. He is currently separated from his third wife. He was born in Rutherford, New Jersey, in 1943, attended Fairleigh Dickinson College for a semester, and joined the Marines as a private in 1960. He was encouraged to pursue a commission through the NROTC Fleet Candidate School. He enrolled at the University of South Carolina, and did the officer basic course over two summers. He was commissioned in 1965, stationed first as a platoon leader at Camp Lejeune in 2nd Batallion, 8th Marines. He arrived in Vietnam in 1967, first serving as a platoon leader in Bravo Company, and later taking command as a first lieutenant. He completed his tour in Vietnam and resigned from the Marines in 1969, writing an angry letter denouncing the war and Marine leadership. He was given the option of leaving the Corps sooner if he retracted the letter, which he did.[101]

When I contacted him, he wasn't at all defensive, though occasionally combative and sarcastic. He initially told me the case doesn't matter, nobody cares, and "who even knows about Whitmore"—this in sharp contrast to his comments on the 2/1 website. He confirmed what Ehlers had told me, that he was convicted on a lesser charge, but not on three others, and not on the most serious one of attempted murder. He said he took the stand in his own defense and recalled that he told the court that if he faced the same situation, he would do nothing differently. He confirmed the radio conversation he had with Bailey. He told me he could not recall if he said anything about children being up to your own conscience, but that young enlisted men could be brutal. He believed that Allen had given the order to "waste her." What order did he give? I asked. "I don't want a living thing alive," he said. But he later followed that up with the language of his sworn statement of 1967, "take the women and children across the river." He recalled that Allen missed the first part of the briefing. Could he have misinterpreted your orders? I asked. Yes, he could have, was the answer.[102]

At a minimum, Maynard's order was ambiguous—not at all unlike Caputo's order in *A Rumor of War.* But if his memory is accurate, then, like Caputo, he bears some responsibility for what happened. Orders that can be misinterpreted will be. Maybe he didn't really mean "I don't want a living alive." Maybe, he meant something closer to the orders he acknowledged in his voluntary statement—"shoot at any movement, so that no one gets hurt through hesitation." Bailey heard and acted on the less ambiguous part—the legal part—and either did not hear, or chose to disregard the "I don't want a living thing alive." To this day, he believes that Maynard was not the type of man who would give such an order. Allen heard and acted on the illegal part, but even he drew the line at the killing of children. But a young lance corporal, who had been taught to follow orders, did not have—the what?— the experience, the wisdom, the moral sense?—to distinguish between a legal and an illegal order. And so a Vietnamese woman died that morning—shot in the back in front of her children. Mourn for her. She did not deserve to die in that way.

For those seeking justice and moral closure, particularly for those who believe that Americans acted with consistent dishonor in Vietnam, this will not be a satisfying conclusion. Diener murdered a woman, and Maynard's orders led to it. But in all honesty, I would not feel better about any of this had they been convicted. It is an overused cliché, but even overused clichés can convey a moral truth. They both paid a price—Diener in the memory he must live with, Maynard in the loss of a career he sought. I'll let others judge the sufficiency of the price. I prefer to recall the courageous witness of Skibsrud and Toon and the actions of Allen in preventing the death of eight to nine children, even as he apparently turned his back on the murder of the woman who was likely their mother.

And so we return to Whitmore, to where we started. Whitmore lied. He didn't exaggerate. He lied. An exaggeration is when you claim that fifty Vietnamese were killed, when ten were, or twenty. He claimed that an entire village was wiped out—300 or so Vietnamese. He offered graphic depictions of those killings—killings that never happened. He claimed his company commander ordered the deaths of children after they had been rounded up, having somehow escaped the general carnage. There wasn't another incident. The incident he lied about was the incident I just unraveled. It happened after a big operation—Medina. It was precipitated by a Marine dying from a booby trap. There was radio traffic about children. There was an investigation that some enlisted Marines tried to thwart. Bravo's CO was relieved. The investigating team witnessed an NVA or VC attack when they ventured to the area. Whitmore got all that right, even as he surrounded it with his big and ugly lie.

Coda

ROBERT MENARD

It took me more than a year to track down Robert Menard. It didn't help that I spent most of that time looking for Robert Maynard. I am grateful to former Marine Robert Black for offering the clue that unlocked Menard's identity. Black, like so many who knew Maynard in the Marines, thought him an outstanding officer. "I would follow him," Black told me. Among Marines, there can be no higher praise.[103]

Menard has led an unusual life. After leaving the Marines, he and his first wife and two children moved to Boston. He told me he worked for the Service Bureau Corporation, a company that did computer processing for other companies. He also worked as a substitute teacher and turned against the war. He was quite sure he had been targeted by COINTELPRO, Nixon's counterintelligence program.[104]

He and his wife then decided to move to Canada. They bought a farm in New Brunswick and made plans to create a school based on A. S. Neill's Rousseauian dream of Summerhill, the school Neill founded in England, a school with no rules. Let the children do what they wanted. Let them find their own way to truth and knowledge. Of all the educational reformers of the 1960s, Neill was the most radical, the most hopeful. It didn't work out for the Menards and they returned to South Carolina. Menard sought entry into the law school at the university, but he was waitlisted—that didn't work out either. Then there were ten years working for a land survey company, a brief stint with drumming up investors for an insurance company, and then a decision to move to Ashland, Wisconsin, on the shores of Lake Superior, to teach outdoor education at Northland College. There wasn't enough money in it, and so he joined the police force in Ashland, working as an "under sheriff." The position of sheriff was an elected position, and in 1994 he ran for the office, losing to Mike Hanson, a fellow policeman.[105]

He and his second wife were active in community theater. In 2000 he played the part of a "famous Italian tenor, Tito Morelli, incapacitated by tranquilizers and wine just before the opera," in a performance of "Lend Me a Tenor," written by Ken Ludwig, at the Rinehart Theatre. A year later, Menard starred in a film, *The Last Stage Coach Robber*, written by Ray Maurin, the curator of the Ironwood Historical Museum and directed by Bill Rebane. Menard played the part of "Reimund Holzhay," a German immigrant who had robbed trains on the Upper Peninsula. Finally caught, convicted, and incarcerated in the Michigan State Penitentiary in Marquette, he suffered from terrible headaches. Agreeing to surgery in 1890, he afterward became a model prisoner, pardoned in 1913, and went on to a career as a nature photographer in the southwest. Rick Olivo, a writer for the Ashland *Daily Press*, asked what the film asked: was Holzhay a "ruthless . . . murderer . . . or a man crazed by an undiagnosed medical condition that drove him to sudden violence?" The film included a trial scene. Rebane praised Menard's efforts to make the film a success: "He went from being an actor wannabe to an actor."[106]

Sometime in 1997 he resigned from the police force. He was involved with a very young woman who would eventually become his third wife. Menard moved on and founded Woodland Productions, a video production studio. Woodland Productions offered the video filming of weddings, anniversary parties, and graduations. In 2003 it had finished a documentary, *The Zen of Canoe Poling*. Menard told Claudia Curren of the *Daily Press* that he was working on a full-length feature drama starring Lauren Bacall and Jack Palance. "We have a goldmine," he said.[107]

In early December 2004 the *Daily Press* of Ashland, Wisconsin, covered a forty-person protest of the Iraq War. Some protesters chanted: "George Bush, you can't hide. We judge you in genocide." It appeared a standard left-liberal protest, if a little over-heated. But the story then seemed to turn uglier. "Robert Menard," identified incorrectly as a "soldier" in the Marine Corps (all Marines are simply and proudly Marines), but located correctly along the demilitarized zone where he served in 1967–1968, "recommended fighting fascism," according to the reporter, "by forming small cells of no more than five or six people." Menard, speaking through a megaphone in front of Ashland's Post Office, was quoted as saying: "You don't go around with a button that says I'm a member of cell No. 13 in Ashland, Wisconsin. Here's my phone number." Instead you work only with a small number of people you can trust, he continued. "I'm not talking paranoia," he said. The FBI and the CIA were infiltrating "mundane organizations." And then a stunningly ugly twist. "Several protestors cheered," the reporter wrote, "as Menard described the U.S. as an extension of Adolf Hitler's Third Reich." "People don't want to talk about that," Menard said, "Oh, you can't compare this administration to Hitler. Well, yes you can. Read *Mein Kampf*. And if you don't see it, go back and do it again." The similarity, he argued, was in how "a very small handful of people [are working] to control the lives of the rest of the people on Earth, and to control it in a very negative way."[108]

After moving to North Carolina, he did security work for a time, and then moved back into land survey work. Recently divorced from his third wife, he established an Internet presence, calling attention to his "Impeach Bush" anti-imperialist politics and to his "ardent" opposition to "violent conflict resolution," but also his "ardent" realism: "there are some times when force becomes the only option in defense of self and others, such as children, elders, and the otherwise helpless." But he has not repeated his United States/Third Reich comparisons on any of the sites I've seen.[109]

In June 2007 he joined the Gaia Community site, a kind of Gnostic self-actualizing Internet "community" whose mission statement is sprinkled with such language as "realizing our highest selves," and discovering "that which we're truly meant to become." Menard's page, marked by an American flag in the upside-down "distress" position and his "title," "Prince of the People," communicates a bizarre sort of left-wing survivalism informed by Eastern mysticism. He tells us he is a "New Kadampa Tradition Tibetan Buddhist," a martial arts devotee, a proponent of "peaceful conflict resolution," an "Outdoor educator," teaching "low tech skills to be able to stay in the forest for a long time, generations." Among the "Things Prince Robert Loves" are such books as: *Chronicles of Tao, The Education of Little Tree*, and Philip Caputo's *A Rumor of War*. Among his "Heroes" and "Teachers" are Gandhi, Martin Luther King Jr., the legendary Marine "Chesty" Puller, and, incongruously, Che Guevara.[110]

My intent is not to mock. Menard's stark and embarrassing inconsistencies, his blustery and ugly politics, seem to conceal a sad yearning, a searching for something now long lost, a searching that I expect will be inexplicable to those who once knew him as a Marine officer—a company commander, highly respected by his men. Perhaps this is the price he's paid.

RUDY DIENER

I don't think Rudy wanted to meet me. I know he made several calls to John Bailey and others to try to find out who I was. His phone number was unlisted. And I don't think he would have met me but for a remarkable and unexpected set of friendships he had helped to foster over the last few years.

I found my way to Rudy through Colonel Ing. I called the colonel one morning at his home in Virginia, expecting little. He commanded several thousand Marines in Vietnam, but maybe he would remember the court-martial. "Oh, that was the case involving Rudy," he responded. I was speechless for a moment. Skibsrud knew him only as Diener; I knew him from the records only as Rudolph. "Excuse me, sir," barely recovering my speech, "how is [it] that you, a regimental commander, can recall a young lance corporal by his nickname? He seemed briefly hurt. "I made it a point of knowing my men," he said. "Yes sir, I don't doubt that, but I must say it still seems unusual: can you tell me more?" I asked.[111]

For many years, Herbie and his wife had welcomed Rudy and his wife to their home in Quantico around Mother's Day. The Rev. Elden Huffman, since retired from the navy, drove up from Florida and joined them. They were drawn together by their love and respect for Carl Auel, who had died August 15, 1997.

The Rev. Carl Auel ran off the road in rural Virginia. He had been drinking. He was in a coma for two weeks before he died at the age of sixty-seven. He had retired from the navy as a captain, and continued to serve as an interim pastor in the 1990s at Christ the King Lutheran Church in Great Falls, Virginia, as well as at a Methodist church in his hometown of Purcellville, Virginia. He had a serious drinking problem, and he suffered from Post Traumatic Stress Disorder (PTSD). Ing recalled listening to an Auel sermon in Great Falls that was simply "incoherent." According to his daughter, he never recovered from Vietnam. "He helped so many people," Juliana Auel said, but "he didn't have anything left for himself." Ing did his best to help, bringing Auel to hospitals at Andrews AFB and to the Veterans Administration (VA) in Martinsburg, West Virginia, and pleading with the Methodist pastor, whom Auel had stood-in for, to intervene, to help Auel.

The pastor refused, and Ing recalled that he and his son were furious. That pastor was John Plummer, the man who falsely claimed responsibility for napalming "the girl in the picture."[112]

Auel was buried in Quantico National Cemetery. When the Dieners and the Ings, joined by Pastor Luffman, get together yearly, they visit the grave. Luffman offers a prayer, and they lay a wreath. Then they drive the short distance to the Globe and Laurel Restaurant, a well-known gathering place for Marines and FBI agents, to eat lunch. In 2007 they graciously allowed me to join them.

Colonel Ing remains the leader—a fit and friendly man in his eighties wearing an Iwo Jima veteran's baseball cap. Pastor Luffman, a few years younger, is slight and gray with a quiet but discerning demeanor. He had brought me a copy of his recently published memoir, *Bringing God To War.* Rudy Diener is in his sixties, a short, balding man, a bit overweight. He and I were both nervous. I told all three the story of my quest to disprove Whitmore's story, a quest that led me to uncovering what had happened that morning. I told Rudy I was not out to get him and that I would not press if he didn't want to talk. He was defensive, and remained relatively closed, but he gradually loosened up. I saw no trace of guilt. He was following orders, he said. There were questions I wasn't prepared to ask in the presence of Ing and Luffman. Luffman later told me he had never known what Diener had done. But Rudy went on, talking so much about Vietnam that his plate was still full as the three of us finished. Ing teased. He had never heard Rudy talk so much. By the end of lunch, he had become affable, and displayed both an excellent memory and a better sense of humor. When lunch was over, he gave me a brief tour of the restaurant, its walls full of Marine, FBI, and police insignia, medals, flags, and photographs.[113]

Sometime later, we had dinner together in Carteret, New Jersey, near his home. He arrived in a coat and tie, and a Globe and Anchor tie tack. He looked dapper. He was relaxed and quick to smile. But his first question was: "How am I going to look in your book?" I repeated that I wasn't out to get him, that my purpose was to refute Whitmore. I'm not sure that was the answer he sought. We went over the incident in more detail. Allen's orders to the patrol were to kill "everything" in the ville, children were "up to your conscience." Did he think about that day often? I asked. "Every day," he said. Perhaps it's true, but I again saw no trace of guilt, nor any willingness to enlarge on his relationship to Reverend Auel. Was he even in search of religious solace or forgiveness:? If he was, he never said so to me, but he was under no obligation to, nor was he obliged to communicate to me his sense of guilt. But what he did say was chilling enough. Auel was his protector, not his counselor—"no one could mess with me again," and "my belief was in the Corps, I did what I was asked to do."[114]

I'm glad that Rudy received the help he did from both Auel and Luffman, and I continue to marvel at this unusual friendship and good-humored camaraderie between a colonel, a chaplain, and a former lance corporal, though Rudy left the Marine Corps as a sergeant. But I could not help thinking of Olaf Skibsrud. No chaplain ever embraced him. Father Lyons deserves credit for passing his story up the chain of command. Not every chaplain did that. But when I asked what further relationship he had with Father Lyons, Skibsrud had a vivid memory of Lyons passing him once and asking sarcastically: "Are you having fun, Skibsrud?"[115]

OLAF SKIBSRUD

When I first called Olaf Skibsrud in Fargo, North Dakota, he was initially hostile. He had just received a disability rating from his local VA, and he initially thought my call was in some way related to that and likely in a negative way. But he eventually told me his story. He never fully recovered from that morning in Quang Tri. His remaining months in the Marines were hell. He was full of self-pity. He had been a "stupid kid," joining the Marines out of a "misdirected sense of adventure."[116]

His life after the Marines was deeply troubled. He drank. He used drugs. He was married and divorced. He worked sporadically, on the railroad, in the Montana woods. His father, the Lutheran pastor, tried to help and sent him to Norway to learn wooden-boat building skills. He met his wife, an American, there. They had two children. He worked in England for a time, and then settled in Nova Scotia, working at a boat yard for four years. He and Maynard must have been in the Maritime Provinces at the same time. Then he did residential carpentry in Kingston, Ontario. He never spoke about being a Marine. Those who worked with him in Canada thought he had been a draft dodger. He never corrected them. Then a second relationship, a third child, a second split-up. He moved west to British Columbia. His father stepped in again, hiring him to fix up the family vacation home in South Dakota. In the last few years, his life had improved. He joined AA, received a full disability from the VA. He lived in a home next door to his family's home in Fargo. He spoke with pride of one of his daughters who is in a creative writing program at Concordia in Montreal.

Why had he taken his story to the chaplain? He resisted any notion that he had been morally courageous, or even acted as an "honest man." His act did not spring from religious faith. He had stopped going to church after he had been confirmed. He went to the chaplain, as he put it, because "I can't handle this." He couldn't believe it happened. He "wanted to die." Yet whatever his self-described motives, he acted honorably and he told the truth, and if he had not so acted, there would never have been a Marine investigation and Whitmore's "massacre" could continue to circulate unchallenged. No Marine who survived that patrol that morning paid a higher price than Olaf Skibsrud.[117]

Conclusion

War is the activity of man about which more lies are told
than about any other.
—Nigel Nicholson

So here I stand, on a narrowing moral ledge—angry at the politicians and generals who sent us fecklessly to war, angry at my highly literate fellow countrymen for framing us as pathetic and guilty victims, angry at those veterans who chose to embroider and lie about war crimes, or who failed to report those who committed real war crimes, angry at the Swift Boaters who distorted John Kerry's war service beyond rational recognition, and who continued to insist on the flimsiest of evidence that those who testified at the Winter Soldier Investigation (WSI) were frauds. These are angers that do not readily cohere and will seem strange and improbable to many—but they are mine.

But perhaps they are more than just mine. We will not understand the war in Vietnam unless we come to understand the bizarre and ubiquitous "war stories" that seem to so characterize that war. Let me close with three. They all have a different tenor than the false atrocity stories I've examined, but all three shed light on the war's strangeness—its capacity to produce false stories credulously believed.

The first is well known, though poorly understood. In the spring of 2001, the *Boston Globe* revealed that Joseph Ellis, a Pulitzer Prize-winning historian who taught a popular course on the Vietnam War at Mount Holyoke College, had lied about his service in Vietnam. By all accounts he was an excellent teacher. He had a gift for making the subject come alive. He had been there, he said, and he taught with great emotion. Some students recalled his tearing up in class. Others recalled a story he told of a young infantry lieutenant crying as he read the poetry of Emily Dickinson. He told his students he had served as an infantry platoon leader in one of the most storied divisions in the history of the U.S. Army, the 101st Airborne Division. Indeed, he told a reporter in 1994 that he had parachuted into Vietnam—a ridiculous and foolish lie that proved to be the beginning of his undoing. He claimed also to have served on the staff of William Westmoreland, commanding general of American forces in Vietnam. One student recalled him saying, with some emotion, that he had led a patrol in the area of My Lai sometime prior to the atrocity that will always be linked to that name, though the import of Ellis's lie was not clear. Mount Holyoke students weren't likely to know that My Lai was not in the 101st's Area of Operations.[1]

None of this was true, as he later admitted. He never served in Vietnam. His first apology was Nixonian in its passive-voice grudgingness. "Even in the best of lives, mistakes are made," offered only to family, friends, colleagues, and students. Two months later, his Boston lawyers issued his apology to veterans, but he did not apologize to the army, which had treated him with extraordinary consideration. An ROTC graduate of the College of William & Mary in 1965, Ellis was able to delay his active duty while he completed his Ph.D. at Yale, after which he was assigned to teach history at West Point. None of the stories mentioned how coveted and honored such an assignment was among army officers. He left the army in 1972 with the rank of captain.[2]

Ellis had his defenders. Some thought the *Globe* had no business writing the story. Mount Holyoke's PR office, desperate to kill the story, argued that Ellis was a private individual and that it was wrong legally and journalistically to publish his classroom comments. The *Globe* properly ignored the assertion. Mount Holyoke's president, Joanne Creighton, first called into question the *Globe*'s motives in writing the story; only later did she call for a full investigation that led to Ellis's surrender of his endowed chair and his suspension without pay for one year. It was a slap on the wrist, and it hardly mattered to Ellis's wealth. His work on the generation of the founding fathers had found a wide popular audience.[3]

Several students and professors rose to his defense. One student wrote clumsily that "being caught in an embellishment" could not detract from his ability to turn "history into the timelessness of humanity." The historian

Richard Jensen believed Ellis's misdeeds to be morally "trivial," claiming that Ellis's fictive claims were irrelevant to the larger disputes over the war. He found the dispute "curiously postmodern." Other scholars, embracing postmodern explanations, would elaborate on the "invented" character of all our lives. Mount Holyoke's dean of students explained that "great teaching" is often a form of theater. And then there was Edmund Morris, the author of *Dutch,* a much-derided biography of Ronald Reagan that had included wholly fictive elements. "Well of course he's woven the fabric of his life partly out of whole cloth and partly out of the shot silk of fantasy," he wrote. "Don't we all." It was a remarkably generous defense, given Ellis's full-throated attack on what he considered Morris's "outrageous blending of fact and fiction" in a review of *Dutch.*[4]

For many academics, the central issue was whether Ellis's historical writing, all of it centered on the early republic, could be trusted. The general verdict seemed to be yes. Peter Hoffer would actually claim that his historical writing improved after he created his fictive self. No one has yet come forward with evidence that Ellis fabricated anything in his writing, and Ellis has returned from his year's leave with his standing as an historian of the founding fathers as high as ever. Some historians, David Garrow in particular, were far more troubled. Garrow saw no difference between lying in print and lying in the classroom. Michael Burlingame and Larry Tise thought he should be fired. Others were more charitable. Elliot Gorn, in the *Chronicle of Higher Education,* found that many of his colleagues felt sympathy. Gorn was perplexed by the lack of outrage. David Oshinsky tried to place it a larger context, not the war alone, but the '60s generally, a decade that offered so many and conflicting avenues of sacrifice that "the greatest sin . . . was to pass through the decade with an empty slate." So Ellis then was just another Woodstock wannabe "chasing the magic of a very special time."[5]

In general, liberal columnists and academics were perplexed and puzzled. None offered anything close to a convincing, or even coherent, argument about the meaning of his lies. Geoffrey Wheatcroft came the closest. He imputed it to liberal guilt. War protestors "saw no reason to fight in a war they didn't support . . . [b]ut they are haunted by the knowledge" that their places were unfairly taken by the poor. Perhaps. There is some evidence for the argument, but I suspect there is even more for the absence of guilt. Clancy Sigal tried to explain. Ellis had simply found himself "caught up in the infectious phantasmagoria" of a war characterized by lies. So Ellis, the professional historian, bore no moral responsibility. He had simply contracted a disease spread by Lyndon B. Johnson and others. Ellen Goodman of the *Boston Globe*, more modestly, threw up her hands. "We may never know why Joseph Ellis fabricated a heroic past." But Goodman didn't get it. There is no evidence that Ellis claimed he was a hero. He apparently never lied about medals received. None of the student comments on the one website devoted to Ellis mentioned that he had ever talked about direct combat. Even the *Globe* reporter who broke the story, Walter Robinson, a Vietnam veteran, missed a key element of its meaning. He acknowledged the anger of veterans, but for him it was "wonderful that Vietnam service has come full circle so that people who didn't go now claimed they went."[6]

Many veterans and conservatives found nothing "wonderful" in the story and had no doubt about the meaning of Ellis's lies. They were outraged, for they understood the politics of his lies with a sharp clarity. For that you needed to understand the full trajectory of Ellis's story, for he told his students he had returned from Vietnam to join the antiwar movement. This wasn't true either. Ellis offered his students a version of the best-known war narrative of the twentieth century—innocence lost and betrayed. Ellis's story thus lent extraordinary authenticity to a customary, but by no means universal, antiwar view. Indeed, it's fair to say that most liberal academics have come to naturalize such an antiwar view. Imagine the outrage if an antifeminist professor, teaching a course on feminism, buttressed the authenticity of her arguments by falsely claiming participation in the first wave of radical feminist action and then service on the staff of Gloria Steinem. Wheatcroft was gentle in his view that Ellis had invented "a doubly admirable past for himself, as a man who first fought for the home of the brave and then didn't study war no more." Wheatcroft captured the core meaning. Some veterans came to the same conclusions quickly and harshly. One veteran got it exactly. "The path of Ellis and this modern attack on the Vietnam War is that of service, disillusionment, and then protest . . . this way phony veterans . . . can have it both ways. They can gain honor and victimhood simultaneously."[7]

A second story. The writer Laura Palmer discovered a poem left at the Vietnam Memorial written in green magic marker. It was signed "Dusty." Somehow Palmer found "Dusty" and included her story and some of her poems in *Shrapnel in the Heart* (1988), Palmer's widely praised book of letters home from soldiers who did not return home. Never offering her last name, nor the hospital in which she served, "Dusty" told Palmer a heart-wrenching story of two tours as a nurse in Vietnam, of cutting through soldiers' uniforms and having legs fall out, of staying on her feet for seventy-two hours during

Tet, her feet swelling so badly she could not take her boots off for two days, of standing by the beds of dying soldiers—"I don't think that any of them died alone," she said. She returned to fail at marriage, to suffer a miscarriage, and then bear a stillborn child, to discover she had dioxin in her body fat from Agent Orange, to contemplate suicide, and to experience a trauma so deep that: "I changed my name, my profession, my residence, my past." Coming in the wake of Lynda Van Devanter's gothic tale of the horrors of Vietnam and the pain of homecoming, "Dusty's" war story seemed to Palmer wholly believable.[8]

Palmer published two of her poems, including the treacly and sentimental "Hello, David—my name is Dusty," an account of her vigil beside the bed of a dying soldier. The poem closes with "Goodbye, David—my name is Dusty/I'm the last person you will see./I'm the last person you will touch./ I'm the last person who will love you." And then the final stanza: "So long, David—my name is Dusty./ David—who will give me something/for my pain?" "Dusty" would soon be discovered.[9]

"Hello, David" and two other of "Dusty's" poems were included in the first anthology of women's Vietnam War poetry in *Visions of War, Dreams of Peace* (1991), edited by Lynda Van Devanter and Joan A. Furey. "Dusty" was identified only as a critical-care nurse in the "Iron Triangle area in Vietnam." There were several other poems by a woman named Dana Shuster who identified herself as a nurse who served two tours in Vietnam and worked in the OR, ER, and ICU. Shuster and "Dusty" were the only nurses in the anthology who did not identify the hospital where they worked. Shuster and "Dusty" were the same person. If the editors knew that, they gave no indication that they did. Vice President Albert Gore would read "Hello, David" at the dedication of the Vietnam Women's Memorial in 1993. Other poems of Shuster's were included in the anthology *Between the Heartbeats* (1995) and in several issues of *Incoming!* from 1995 to 1998. She went on to publish her own book of poetry, *Battle Dressing: Poems About the Journey of a Nurse in Vietnam* (2000), reprinted in 2003.[10]

In the fall of 2006, Laura Palmer learned that Dana Shuster had never served in Vietnam, had never served in the military, and had never been a nurse. She had been prompted to ask Dana directly by a skeptical veteran. Palmer regarded her as a friend and had even traveled to Vietnam with her. She had never suspected. Yet, at the very beginning of the story, there was ample room for skepticism—"Dusty's" desire for anonymity, her failure to identify the hospital where she served, her claim that she changed her name.

She also told Palmer that she never told her second husband that she served in Vietnam. And if you could find trace elements of dioxin in the body fat of Vietnam veterans, there never would have been a controversy about the extent of Agent Orange's damage.[11]

And then there were her stories—seventy-two hours on her feet, legs falling out of uniforms, and the stunning and wholly false assertion that soldiers in Vietnam did not die alone. When I first read Palmer, I underlined that claim, knowing how false it was. Men in war die alone almost all of the time. Only in Hollywood do men die with their bodies intact and in the arms of a buddy or a nurse, whispering a last word. Of the more than 97,000 wounded soldiers who entered military hospitals in Vietnam, 97.4 percent survived. The figure would have been even higher except for the rapid evacuation of badly wounded men who would have died on the battlefield in previous wars. Those who were badly wounded and often unconscious were placed alone behind a screen so as not to trouble the other wounded. I have no doubt that some small number of nurses, medics, and chaplains did remain by the bedside of dying soldiers, and for that we should be grateful. But the invocation of that deeply false and sentimental image by a woman who never served was a lie, and gave false comfort to those who desperately wanted to believe that their sons, their husbands, their fathers did not die alone.[12]

Shuster offered a deeply emotional and deeply strange apology that was published on a number of Vietnam War listserves. She claimed to have suffered "a dissociative disorder, as well as PTSD [Post Traumatic Stress Disorder]," from early childhood. With a poetic flair, she wrote that her "psyche" was an example of what might happen "if a sponge and a mirror were to marry." She claimed to have had no memory of the years from 1966 to 1968, but she had "daily flashbacks" of Vietnam, and so for "some years" she "truly thought I had served as a nurse in Vietnam." And then Palmer discovered her, but this after she realized that she hadn't served—that her dreams of Vietnam were "not mirrors of my direct experience, but, rather, metaphors for other sinister events in my life." But she found that her poems had helped veterans "to heal." She says she could not betray their hope—"What if a suicidal veteran who had written to me now made good on his previous impulse?" So she remained silent, except whenever she "was pressured to appear as Dusty." "I sometimes relented," she said, failing to explain how she continued to write and publish through the '90s and into a new century.[13]

Her poems so effectively captured the language of the war, the United States as the "big PX," "FNGs [Fucking New Guys]" "one shift and a "wake-up," "didi mau and dinky dau," that few would have realized just how good a student of the war she was. She made it all up, including the story of college students protesting her homecoming—though not with archetypal spit, but with beer cans, a novel touch: "one splashing my skirt, another dinging my shin," as she wobbled "down the jetway" in pumps and her "Class A skirt." She even assumed the anger some nurses felt toward male veterans who were slow to understand the depth of their service. Her poem "Boys' Club" closes with: "I am boocoo tired and have titi patience/with your REMFing No Girls Allowed/You will let me in because you well know/I've lived in your jungle/I've climbed your tree/We both know you can't bullshit me." But she could. And she did.[14]

A third story—equally false—reveals the credulousness of some of those who defended the war and the veterans who fought it, and who came to exercise their deepest ire—not on the North Vietnamese Army (NVA) or the Viet Cong (VC), nor on LBJ and his advisers, nor on Westmoreland and his staff, but on the chameleonesque Jane Fonda. Fonda was no innocent in this, as we shall see, but the ugliest story that circulated about her is utterly false.

That story was that Fonda, on her visit to North Vietnam in 1972, had met with American prisoners of war (POWs) who surreptitiously had given her notes with their social security numbers on them. "Aren't you sorry you bombed babies?" Fonda supposedly asked. Fonda then turned the notes over to her hosts. "Three men died from the subsequent beatings," according to the story, while another, Larry Carrigan, a colonel in the air force, barely survived the beatings to tell the tale. Another pilot, Jerry Driscoll, was badly beaten after he reportedly spat at Fonda when his captors demanded he describe the "lenient and humane treatment" he was receiving. And a civilian economic adviser held as a POW claimed that he told his captors that he wanted to meet with Fonda to tell her the truth about POW treatment and was subsequently punished and beaten. The adviser was identified as Michael Benge in some of the posts, though in others he was quoted anonymously. To invest in such a story took substantial credulousness. By 1972, as a result of the prior release of some POWs, the Department of Defense had a substantial list of those held in captivity, and mail between POWs and their families had become more frequent.[15]

The stories may have derived from the claims of LCDR David Wesley Hoffman, a POW who told television reporters in 1972 that he initially had refused to meet with Fonda, but had done so only after being tortured. Hoffman's story has been disputed by antiwar activists, and has never been corroborated by fellow POWs, and Hoffman apparently no longer chooses to talk about it. Hoffman was one of seven POWs who met with Fonda in July 1972, all of whom had been carefully chosen by the North Vietnamese and two of whom, LtCol Edison Miller and CDR Walter Wilbur, were later charged with collaboration and mutiny by James Stockdale, one of the POWs' senior officers. The navy elected not to pursue the charges, substituting letters of censure. Hoffman's story may have been intended to justify his having met with Fonda and may not have been true, but the North Vietnamese, according to Col Robinson Risner's memoir, tortured Jeremiah Denton, who had refused to meet with visiting delegations, and Risner reported that they also tortured him.[16]

The ugly story of Fonda's complicity in the death of American POWs apparently began circulating on the Internet in the wake of a Barbara Walters' 1999 special, "A Celebration: 100 Years of Great Women," in which Fonda was included. That story can still be found, with its summary of Fonda's crimes: a woman who "chose to be a traitor, and went to Hanoi, wore their uniform, propagandized for the communists, and urged American soldiers to desert. As we were being tortured, and some of the POWs murdered, she called us liars."[17]

Larry Carrigan, who had been shot down in 1967 and who somehow survived the "beatings," denied the story. "It's a figment of someone's imagination," he said, "I never met Jane Fonda." Jerry Driscoll, the "spitter," also claimed the story false. "Totally false," he said, "It did not happen." Benge reconfirmed the truth of his story, though he was unaware of how his story became attached to those of Carrigan and Driscoll.[18]

The false stories are testament to the deep and ugly hatred many veterans felt and continue to feel toward Fonda, a hatred so deep that it led some to embrace falsehood, others to create and actually use "Hanoi Jane's Urinal Stickers" featuring Fonda legs' spread in a workout pose—a hideously vulgar form of misogyny. Defenders of Fonda have been quick to note the gendered nature of the hatred. One folklorist wrote that Fonda had been singled out for hate because of her "dramatic transformation from the ever available" *Barbarella*, the 1968 film in which she played "a kind of sexual Alice in Wonderland of the future," to Hanoi Jane. Other women visited North Vietnam, we're told, but never provoked similar levels of hatred. But, Cora Weiss, Denise Levertov, and Mary McCarthy were barely known outside the highly literate neighborhoods of New York City. The attacks on Fonda unquestionably had an ugly misogynistic dimension, but that is not the whole story.[19]

In truth, there was a great deal that Fonda did and said that was more than sufficient to provoke contempt, and her own retrospective explanations and "apologies" seemed designed to obscure that. While in Hanoi, Fonda made ten propaganda broadcasts for the North Vietnamese. In one, directed to Americans serving on aircraft carriers in the Gulf of Tonkin, she said: "I don't know what your officers tell you, those of you who load the bombs on the planes, but one thing that you should know is that these weapons are illegal and the use of these bombs, makes one a war criminal." She went on to claim that the naval officers giving such orders were comparable to the German and Japanese officers who were "tried and executed" after WWII. In another broadcast, this to U.S. pilots, she asserted that if "they [your officers] told you the truth, you wouldn't fight, you wouldn't kill." Technically, she wasn't directly urging sailors and pilots to mutiny, but she did cross the line in an address to Army of the Republic of Vietnam (ARVN) soldiers when she praised the men of the "56th Regiment of the Third Division" whom she had been told defected to the National Liberation Front (NLF), "including officers, who may retain their rank." Years later she would claim that she went to Hanoi to "help end the killing, end the war," but her words make clear that the end she sought was on North Vietnamese terms. Former POW Eugene "Red" McDaniel recalled: "I felt betrayed and hurt. . . . I don't think the right to dissent extends to the capital city of the enemy in time of war." Many others would share his view, though the U.S. government wisely chose not to prosecute her. "I thought the interests in favor of free speech in an election year," Attorney General Richard Kleindienst stated, "far outweighed any specific advantage of prosecuting a young girl like that who was in Vietnam acting rather foolish." It was a patronizing comment, however correct the decision, but Fonda was not a "young girl." She was thirty-four.[20]

Fonda's comments on American POWs were equally inflammatory. In a response to the claim that the POWs she met had been tortured, she said: "I think they're lying." Had she confined her remarks to the claims of David Wesley Hoffman, she may well have been right. And it is likely the case that those who met with her, Miller, Wilbur, and the others, had of their own volition turned against the war, and had neither been tortured nor "brainwashed." But she went on recklessly. American pilots were "carrying out acts of murder," she said. They would have to live with that as well as their lies about torture for the rest of their lives: "it was not a policy of the North Vietnamese to torture prisoners."[21]

She couldn't seem to let it go. She told an audience at UCLA that skepticism about torture was warranted: "We have no reason to believe that U.S. Air Force officers tell the truth," she said, "They are professional killers." She conceded some ground: "Guys who misbehaved and treated their guards in a racist fashion or tried to escape were tortured. Some pilots were beaten to death by the people they had bombed when they parachuted from their planes." Claims that torture was systematic and driven by policy were lies. The POWs should not be acclaimed as heroes. They were "hypocrites and liars" and "war criminals according to law." Is it any wonder that the POWs and other veterans held her in contempt? Her ugly and hyperbolic claims clearly crossed a line. She was no longer simply protesting a war she claimed she wanted to end, but recklessly impugning the character and the veracity of Americans who had suffered terribly.[22]

To her credit she now acknowledges that POWs were tortured, though not after 1969. For reasons that remain unclear, the treatment of POWs improved after the death of Ho Chi Minh, though not necessarily because of that. However, POWs were still not accorded their Geneva Convention rights. Fonda's acknowledgment of torture is a vast improvement on the ugly insinuations of Mary Hershberger, one of Fonda's most ardent defenders, who claimed that the "hard-line officers . . . place all their torture stories during the time they were in solitary—and unobserved by other POWs." So, Denton and Risner and others were lying? Apparently so. She quotes approvingly Seymour Hersh, who "concluded in 1971 that there was no evidence of systematic abuse of American POWs in Hanoi."[23]

It was, of course, the film footage that captured her clapping and smiling in the gunner's seat of a Russian anti-aircraft piece that had the longest shelf life. It was, she said, her "only regret" about her trip to Hanoi. But she tells us in her autobiography that it was all inadvertent. Yes, she had been given a North Vietnamese helmet to wear, but the North Vietnamese always required Americans to wear such helmets during air raids; yes, she is clapping, but it was because the young soldiers were singing her a song whose lines evoked Ho Chi Minh's use of our Declaration of Independence; and yes, she did sit in the gunner's seat, but her visible emotions had, she wrote, "nothing to do with *where*" (emphasis in the original) she was sitting. It may well be true. She also writes that she immediately recognized the problem—"*Oh my*

God. It's going to look like I was trying to shoot down U.S. planes" (emphasis in the original). In her 1988 interview with Barbara Walters, her response to Walters' question: "Did you realize the effect it [the picture of her sitting on the gunseat] would have." Fonda answered "No." Consistency has never been her hallmark.[24]

Fonda today remains proud of her trip to Hanoi, and the "evidence" she brought back was that American bombers were deliberately targeting the elaborate system of dikes in the Red River basin. In her recent autobiography she backed away from claims she made at the time: "While the United States may not have been waging an all-out bombing campaign to obliterate the dikes, they *were* targeting the dikes during the spring of 1972. The evidence that I and many others saw was incontrovertible." But how could it be? How could you distinguish between deliberate and accidental damage? On the facing page she ends the chapter with: "The bombing of the dikes stopped that August," leading gullible readers to think that her visit, and her "evidence" had led to that.[25]

The preponderance of evidence suggests that the United States never targeted the dikes. Had we done so, and done so systematically, the resulting flooding might have killed thousands, and such an act would have been a war crime.

Yes, Fonda and others have cited President Nixon's blustery bravado: "I still think we got to take the dikes out now. Will that drown people?" Henry Kissinger's response: "About two hundred thousand people." Nixon: "No, no, no . . . I'd rather use the nuclear bomb . . . does that bother you? . . . I just want to think big, Henry, for chrissakes." Whatever one's position on Nixon's revival of the bombing campaign against the North in 1972—part of the ugly denouement of American involvement in Vietnam—the truth matters. His Oval Office screed is not evidence of a decision to attack the dikes.[26]

As a the result of a renewed offensive by the NVA in the spring of 1972, Nixon greatly increased the tactical flexibility of American air power and increased the numbers of potential targets throughout the country while maintaining the no-strike zone near the Chinese border and limiting attacks near the centers of Hanoi and Haiphong. He also authorized the mining of Haiphong harbor and a coastal blockade. The targets of the air war were MIG bases, power plants, and POL (Petroleum, Oil, Lubricants) facilities, the latter within the ten-mile radius. There is no question that dikes which were often close to roads and rail lines and were used as anti-aircraft artillery sites were damaged during these assaults, but there appears never to have been serious flooding, and even critics of the war concluded at the time that there was no evidence of deliberate attacks on the dikes. And the air campaign ended when the North Vietnamese returned to the bargaining table.[27]

But if Jane Fonda often let her emotions and her politics obscure her search for truth, those who reviled her did the same. It's time to let to go. Fonda, like others on the far left in the 1960s, embraced a naïve hope in the Vietnamese communists. Unlike others who shared her views, her words and images linger. And also unlike some of those on the far left, she attempted, however quixotically, to embrace those GIs who were opposed to the war. She doesn't deserve the continued iteration of false stories.

So what's the harm? Both Ellis and "Dusty" had their defenders. POWs have ample reason to hold Fonda in contempt. So what if a single false story intrudes? False war stories have taken many forms, some like those false stories of German atrocities in Belgium during the first years of the Great War appeared to have been effectively used to summon an Allied citizenry to anger and outrage, leading them inexorably to the horror of the trenches. Those were "war stories" far worse than the classroom lies of a tweedy Walter Mitty or the bathetic lies of a deeply disturbed woman. Perhaps. But my subject is not the state politics of war. The "war stories" that concern me are closer to the bone. They are about choice and accountability, and, in the end, the elusiveness of truth—men and women who chose to deceive, other men and women all too ready to believe those deceptions because of both the way in which the war in Vietnam had been framed and because their politics and beliefs overrode evidence easily gathered.

The lies of Joseph Ellis and of "Dusty" are as equally dishonorable as the lies of a Terry Whitmore. In some ways they are worse, because both indirectly fed the sentimental myths of war. "Hello, David" was the hoped-for lie, the false comfort for which every mother might have prayed—a scene out of a Victorian novel transposed to Hollywood, John Wayne on the beach at Iwo Jima, Tom Hanks at that bridge in France. Not even Steven Spielberg, who promised D-Day authenticity in *Saving Private Ryan*, could resist the trope. Ellis reprised WWI's grand narrative of innocence lost and betrayed. He never lied about being a hero. He lied about being a noble victim—a man who went to war, saw the "truth," and returned to oppose it. He was an "honorable" man, imparting to his students a thoroughly clichéd and sentimental idea of what it means to act with honor in wartime. His students were too young and inexperienced to be faulted for their credulity, but what of his colleagues? Ellis was believed because he told a story all too believable to university faculty, and so too, "Dusty" was believed, because all too many of her readers, including veterans, were thoroughly prepared to accept her agitated gothic tale.

Ellis knowingly lied. "Dusty" tried to explain that she really believed she was there. The veterans who repeat the lies about Fonda no doubt believe them. Each in his or her own way has kept the war alive in a culture made mad by that war. The falsehoods—the exaggerations—the score-settling keep us from a deeper and more honest understanding of what the war did to us all. As I come to the end of this book, I have a better understanding of what Michael Herr meant when he wrote, "Vietnam Vietnam Vietnam, we've all been there."[28]

A final story. I learned in February 2009 that Olaf Skibsrud, the young Marine who spoke the truth about what he witnessed in Quang Tri and who suffered for it, had died a year earlier. I had first talked to him on a Saturday afternoon in December 2006—his initial suspicion giving way slowly as he gave voice to memory. I was in that peculiar place as a historian who, in some ways, knew more than he did about what had happened, and especially its aftermath. But his memory of what he experienced was so vivid and so emotional that it was clear that he was still living in the nightmare of that moment. I recall that he was coughing and not feeling well. He suffered from emphysema. I said I'd call him again in the new year. A few days later, I sent him a copy of his testimony in the Article 32 Investigation and offered to put him in touch with Ronald Toon, the other young Marine who told the truth. I wasn't sure then about the persistence of his religious belief. He was the son of a Lutheran pastor. So I approached him in my letter a bit obliquely, offering what I hoped were words of comfort. The day after I spoke with him, we sang in church the beautiful Advent hymn "Comfort, Comfort, O My People." I quoted to him the line, "Tell them that their war is over." I will never hear that hymn again without thinking of him, and I will never hear that line again without believing that it's time—time for all of us.

Notes

Introduction

1. Cardinal Joseph Bernardin, *The Seamless Garment: Writings on the Consistent Ethic of Life* (Maryknoll, NY: Orbis Books, 2008), is the most recent edited version.

2. Vance Packard, *The Status Seekers* (New York: D. McKay Co.), 1959; David Riesman, *The Lonely Crowd* (New Haven, CT: Yale University Press, 1950); William Whyte, *The Organization Man* (New York: Doubleday, 1956); Erich Fromm, *The Art of Loving* (New York: Harper & Row, 1956); Walter Kaufmann, ed., *Existentialism from Dostoevsky to Sartre* (Cleveland: World Publishing, 1956); Dietrich Bonhoeffer, *Letters and Papers from Prison* (New York: Macmillan, 1962). A thoughtful article on "Christian existentialism" and the quest for authenticity is Doug Rossinow's, "The Break-through to New Life: Christianity and the Emergence of the New Left in Austin, Texas: 1956–1964," *American Quarterly* 46/3 (September 1994).

3. There was an exhibition on the Elizabeth City Tutorial Project at St. Michael's in 2006—see *Saint Michael's College Magazine* 6/3, Summer 2006, 25.

4. William J. Duiker, *Ho Chi Minh: A Life* (New York: Hyperion, 2000), 323.

5. Lawrence M. Baskir and William A. Strauss, *Chance and Circumstance: The Draft, The War, The Vietnam Generation* (New York: Alfred A. Knopf, 1978), 51.

6. *The Confessions of Felix Krull* (1957).

7. www.operant.com/seminary/main_page.html.

8. Director, Historical Unit to Chief, Military Personnel Branch, Walter Reed Army Medical Center (WRAMC), "Deletion of Enlisted Man, PFC Gary B. Kulik . . . from Oversea Levy, 13 March 1970. Cover sheet endorsement, CG, WRAMC to TSG, DA, ATTN: MEDPT-TA, 18 March 1970."

9. Michael D. Doubler, *Closing with the Enemy: How GIs Fought the War in Europe, 1944–1945* (Lawrence: University Press of Kansas, 1994), 236; John M. Shaw, *The Cambodian Campaign: The 1970 Offensive and America's Vietnam War* (Lawrence: University Press of Kansas), 2005, 146–147.

10. http://www.history.army.mil/moh.html; Bonni McKeown, *Peaceful Patriot: The Story of Tom Bennett* (Capon Springs, WV: Peaceful Patriot Press, 1987). The second CO was Joseph G. LaPointe Jr. See Dale Huffman, "Flag Ceremony

Recalls Medic's Sacrifice 40 Years Ago," *Dayton News*, June 2, 2009. See also Jean Anne Mansavage, "'Sincere and Meaningful Belief': Legal Conscientious Objection During the Vietnam War," Ph.D. Diss., Texas A&M, 2000, 209.

11. Lewis Sorley, *Thunderbolt: General Creighton Abrams and the Army of His Times* (New York: Simon & Schuster, 1992).

12. http://www.tioh.hqda.pentagon.mil/MedVet/61st%20Medical%20Battalion.htm.

13. Peter G. Dorland and James S. Nanney, *Dust-Off: Aeromedical Evacuation in Vietnam* (Washington, DC: Center of Military History, U.S. Army, 1982), 110–112; Keith William Nolan, *Into Laos: The Story of Dewey Canyon II/Lam Son 719* (Novato, CA: Presidio, 1986), 128–130, 134–137, 369; Lieutenant Colonel William R. Bentley, "After Action Report—Lam Son 719," April 19, 1971, in author's possession.

14. James Webb, *Fields of Fire* (New York: Bantam, 1978); John M. Del Vecchio, *The 13th Valley* (New York: Bantam, 1982); Michael Herr, *Dispatches* (New York: Alfred A. Knopf, 1977); C. D. B. Bryan, *Friendly Fire* (New York: Bantam, 1982); Neil Sheehan, *A Bright Shining Lie: John Paul Vann and America in Vietnam* (New York: Random House, 1988); S. L. A. Marshall, *The Fields of Bamboo* (New York: Dial, 1971); Richard Gabriel and Paul Savage, *Crisis in Command: Mismanagement in the Army* (New York: Hill and Wang, 1978); Guenter Lewy, *America in Vietnam* (New York: Oxford University Press, 1978); Robert Jay Lifton, *Home From the War* (New York: Simon & Schuster, 1973); Lewis Puller, *Fortunate Son* (New York: Grove Weidenfeld, 1991); John Wheeler, *Touched with Fire* (New York: Franklin Watts, 1984).

15. Samuel Hynes, *The Soldiers' Tale: Bearing Witness to Modern War* (New York: Allen Lane, 1997); Samuel Hynes, *Flights of Passage* (New York: Penguin, 1988).

16. Hynes, *The Soldiers' Tale*, 203, 180, 219.

17. Ibid., 222, 190, 217; Ron Kovic, *Born on the Fourth of July* (New York: Pocket Books, 1976); Philip Caputo, *A Rumor of War* (New York: Ballantine, 1977); Tim O'Brien, *If I Die in a Combat Zone* (New York: Dell, 1973); Robert Mason, *Chickenhawk* (New York: Viking, 1983); John Ketwig, *. . . and a Hard Rain Fell: A GI's True Story of the War in Vietnam* (New York: Macmillan, 1985); Rod Kane, *Veteran's Day: A Vietnam Memoir* (New York: Orion, 1990).

18. Ron Steinman, ed., *Women in Vietnam* (New York: TV Books, 2000), 77, 110, 217; Donna M. Dean, "Lest They Be Forgotten," H-Minerva, April 2003, www.h-net.org/reviews/showrev.php?id=7487.

19. Lynda Van Devanter, *Home Before Morning* (New York: Beaufort Books, 1983).

20. Bob Greene, *Homecoming* (New York: G. P. Putnam's Sons, 1989).

21. Michal R. Belknap, *The Vietnam War on Trial: The My Lai Massacre and the Court-Martial of Lieutenant Calley* (Lawrence: University Press of Kansas, 2002), 211–212; Alexander Cockburn, "Shocked Over Kerrey? It's How We Fought the War," *Los Angeles Times*, May 3, 2001; Susan Faludi, *Stiffed: The Betrayal of the American Man* (New York: William Morrow & Co., 1999), 358.

22. Caputo, *A Rumor of War*, 305. On the convergence of hawk and dove beliefs regarding war-crime accountability, see Belknap, *The Vietnam War on Trial*, 130; Lifton, *Home From the War*, 41.

23. On the background of the WSI, see Gerald Nicosia, *Home to War: A History of the Vietnam Veterans' Movement* (New York: Crown, 2001), 73–97; *Winter Soldier* (1972); *Stolen Honor* (2004).

24. Andrew Lam, "US Silence Muzzles Vietnam's Dissidents," *Nation*, April 13, 2007.

Chapter 1: Framing the War

Epigraph. Charles A. Krohn, *The Lost Battalion: Controversy and Casualties in the Battle for Hue* (New York: Praeger Publishers, 1993).

1. Gregory Vistica, "One Awful Night in Thanh Phong," *New York Times Magazine,* April 25, 2001, expanded in Vistica, *The Education of Lieutenant Kerrey* (New York: St. Martin's Press, 2003).

2. Bob Kerrey, *When I Was a Young Man: A Memoir* (New York: Harcourt, 2002), 183–185; Vistica, *Education,* 167–181.

3. Vistica, *Education,* 255–256, 115.

4. *U.S. Army Field Manual 27-10: The Law of Land Warfare* (Washington, DC: Department of the Army, 1956), Chapter 2, Section III, Paragraph 85.

5. Hentoff makes the point about Klann in an article on Hugh Thompson, the helicopter pilot who, along with his crew, attempted to stop the massacre at My Lai, "The Americans Who Stopped My Lai," *Village Voice,* May 29, 2001. See also Hentoff, "Who Made Bob Kerrey Do It?" *Village Voice,* May 22, 2001.

6. On "Confirmation Bias," see R. S. Nickerson, "Confirmation Bias: A Ubiquitous Phenomenon in Many Guises," *Review of General Psychology* 2, 1998, 175–220; Alexander Cockburn, "This is How We Fought the War," *Los Angeles Times,* May 3, 2001; Robert Mann, "The Guilt of Political Leaders," *New York Times,* Op-Ed, April 30, 2001; Tobias Wolff, "War and Memory," *New York Times,* Op-Ed, April 28, 2001; Mackubin T. Owens, "Bob Kerrey's Vietnam War," *Weekly Standard,* May 14, 2002; Vistica, *Education,* 266.

7. "The War Within Bob Kerrey," *New York Times,* April 26, 2001, editorial page; Bowman, *TLS,* July 20, 2001, 14.

8. Buzzanco, "How I Learned to Quit Worrying and Love Vietnam and Iraq," *Counterpunch,* 16/17 (April 2005), 2, hww.counterpunch.org/buzzanco 04162005.htm. See also Susan Jeffords, *The Remasculinization of America: Gender and the Vietnam War* (Bloomington: Indiana University Press, 1989); Kali Tal, *Worlds of Hurt: Reading the Literatures of Trauma* (New York: Cambridge, 1996); Fred Turner, *Echoes of Combat: The Vietnam War in American Memory* (New York: Anchor, 1996); Patrick Hagopian, *The Vietnam War in American Memory: Veterans, Memorials and the Politics of Healing* (Amherst: University of Massachusetts Press, 2009). See also the related work of Jerry Lembcke, *The Spitting Image: Myth, Memory, and the Legacy of Vietnam* (New York: NYU, 1998) and *CNN's Tailwind Tale: Inside Vietnam's Last Great Myth* (New York: Rowman and Littlefield, 2003).

9. Adam Garfinkle, *Telltale Hearts: The Origins and Impact of the Vietnam Anti-War Movement* (New York: St. Martins Griffin, 1997), 15, 158, 174.

10. Michael Herr, *Dispatches* (New York: Alfred A. Knopf, 1977). The Leonard, Just, and le Carré quotes can be found on the front and back covers of the paperback edition (New York: Avon, 1978). Page numbers for all citations are from the Avon paperback.

11. Paul Lauter, gen. ed., *The Heath Anthology of American Literature,* vol. 2 (Lexington, MA: D. C. Heath, 1990); Joseph Heller, *Catch-22* (New York: Delacorte, 1973). Scholarly writing on Herr can be found on "Google Scholar."

12. Paul Ciotti, "Michael Herr, A Man of Few Words: What is a Great American Writer Doing Holed Up in London, and Why Has He Been So Quiet All These Years?" *Los Angeles Times Magazine,* April 15, 1990, 22.

13. Ciotti, "Michael Herr."

14. Ibid.

15. O'Brien, *The Things They Carried* (Boston: Houghton Mifflen, 1990), 89.

16. O'Brien's cleverness dishonors men who continue to act with such extraordinary self-sacrifice. See the stories on Ross A. McGinnis, a private in the First Infantry Division, and Michael A. Monsoor, a Navy SEAL, both of whom fell on grenades to save their comrades. See "Bush Awards Medal of Honor Posthumously," www.upi.com/Top_News/2008/06/02/Bush_Awards_Medal_of_Honor_Posthumously/UPI-79861212435221/, and "Tearful Bush Awards Medal of Honor to SEAL," www.cbsnews.com/stories/2008/04/08/national/main 4002523.shtml.

17. Herr, *Dispatches*, 215; Samuel Hynes, *The Soldiers' Tale* (New York: Allen Lane, 1997), 201–206.

18. Herr, *Dispatches*, 61, 66.

19. Norman Mailer, *The Naked and the Dead* (New York: Holt, Rinehart & Winston, 1948).

20. Herr, *Dispatches*, 185, 87, 252, 138.

21. Ibid., 132–133, 122.

22. Ibid., 101, 145, 159, 203–204.

23. Ibid., 122.

24. William Broyles Jr., *Brothers in Arms: A Journey from War to Peace* (New York: Alfred A. Knopf, 1986), 138.

25. Herr, *Dispatches*, 6; O'Brien, *The Things They Carried*, 82–83; Broyles, *Brothers in Arms*, 195–196. Broyles's reference is Ernest Hemingway, ed., *Men at War* (New York: Crown, 1942).

26. Herr, *Dispatches*, 209.

27. See Hynes, *The Soldiers' Tale*, 215.

28. Paul Fussell, *The Great War and Modern Memory* (New York: Oxford, 1975), 7.

29. Paul Fussell, *Wartime: Understanding and Behavior in the Second World War* (New York: Oxford University Press, 1989), 132.

30. Denise Chung, *The Girl in the Picture: The Story of Kim Phuc, the Photograph, and the Vietnam War* (New York: Viking, 1999).

31. Ibid., 185, 94, 146, 205, 276, 217, 353.

32. Tom Bowman, "Veteran's Admission to Napalm Victim a Lie," *Baltimore Sun*, December 14, 1997, 1A.

33. Chung, *The Girl in the Picture*, 361.

34. Bowman, "Veteran's Admission"; *Nightline*, "John Plummer's Burden," June 6, 1977; "A Picture of Forgiveness," *Christian Century*, February 19, 1997, is characteristic of the way churches and church publications picked up the story uncritically.

35. Bowman, "Veteran's Admission."

36. Ibid.

37. Ronald N. Timberlake, "The Fraud Behind the Girl in the Photo," January 1999, http://www.ndqsa.com/myth.html.

38. Robert Jay Lifton, *Home From the War* (New York: Simon & Schuster, 1973), 75–76.

39. Chaim F. Shatan, "Post-Vietnam Syndrome," *New York Times*, May 6, 1972, 35; J. Nordheimer, "From Dak To to Detroit: Death of a Troubled Hero," *New York Times*, May 26, 1971.

40. Shatan, "Post-Vietnam Syndrome."

41. Sandra L. Bloom, "Our Hearts and Our Hopes are Turned to Peace: Origins of the International Society for Traumatic Stress Studies," in the *International Handbook of Human Response to Trauma*, edited by Arieh Y. Shalev et al. (New York: Kluwer/Plenum, 2000). See also Sandra L. Bloom, "The Lost is Found: Post-traumatic Stress Disorder," in Shalev et al., *International Handbook*.

42. Lifton, *Home From the War,* 19, 101.
43. Richard Homan, "Guilt Feelings Seen for Returning GI's," *Washington Post,* May 3, 1969, A6.
44. Stuart Auerbach, "Vietnam Veterans Most Frustrated, Senate Told," *Washington Post,* January 28, 1970, A3.
45. Charles Figley, ed., *Stress Disorders Among Vietnam Veterans: Theory, Research and Treatment* (New York: Brunner/Mazel, 1978); John P. Wilson, *Identity, Ideology, and Crises: The Vietnam Veteran in Transition* (Cincinnati: Disabled American Veterans, 1977); William P. Mahedy, *Out of the Night: The Spiritual Journey of Vietnam Vets* (New York: Ballantine, 1986).
46. Shad Meshad, *Captain for Dark Mornings: A True Story* (Winter Park, FL: GR Press, 1994). Meshad is quoted in Wilbur J. Scott, *Vietnam Veterans Since the War: The Politics of PTSD, Agent Orange, and the National Memorial* (Norman: University of Oklahoma Press, 2004), 37; Lynda Van Devanter, *Home Before Morning* (New York: Beaufort Books, 1983), 296. There has been, in recent years, a rethinking of the efficacy of such intensive and intrusive therapy. See Jerome Groopman, "The Grief Industry: How Much Does Crisis Counseling Help or Hurt," *New Yorker,* January 20, 2004; Malcolm Gladwell, "Getting Over It: The Man in the Grey Flannel Suit put the war behind him. What's changed?" *New Yorker,* November 8, 2004, 75–79; Lauren Slater, "Repress Yourself," *New York Times Magazine,* February 23, 2003; Sharon Begley, "Is Trauma Debriefing Worse Than Letting Victims Heal Naturally? *Wall Street Journal,* September 12, 2003.
47. Meshad, *Captain for Dark Mornings,* 117–141, 147–150. The Meshad quote is in Myra MacPherson, *Long Time Passing: Vietnam and the Haunted Generation* (Garden City, NY: Doubleday & Co., 1984), 232; B. G. Burkett and Glenna Whitley, *Stolen Valor: How the Vietnam Generation was Robbed of its Heroes and its History* (Dallas: Verity Press, 1998), 152–153.
48. Wilbur Scott interviewed Haley for his *Vietnam Veterans Since the War,* 4–6.
49. Sarah A. Haley, "When the Patient Reports Atrocities," *Archives of General Psychiatry* 30, 1974, 191–196.
50. Ibid.
51. Ibid.
52. Ibid.
53. Scott, *Vietnam Veterans Since the War,* Chapter 2 and 238–239. Scott's book was first published as *The Politics of Readjustment: Vietnam Veterans since the War* (New York: Aldine de Gruyter, 1993).
54. Scott, *Vietnam Veterans Since the War,* 28–32, 238. See also Ben Shepherd, *A War of Nerves: Soldiers and Psychiatrists, 1914–1994* (Cambridge: Harvard University Press, 2001), and Eric T. Dean Jr., *Shook Over Hell: Post-Traumatic Stress, Vietnam, and the Civil War* (Cambridge: Harvard University Press, 1997).
55. Richard J. McNally, *Remembering Trauma* (Cambridge: Harvard University Press, 2003), 8; Shatan, "Post-Vietnam Syndrome."
56. Allan Young, *The Harmony of Illusions: Inventing Post-Traumatic Stress Disorder* (Princeton: Princeton University Press, 1995), 5. The work of Young and McNally undergird the growing sense that PTSD has been over-diagnosed. See Sally Satel, "The Trauma Society," *The New Republic,* May 19, 2003, http://www.aei.org/article/17181; Ellie Lee, "The Invention of PTSD," http://www.spiked-online.com/Articles/0000000054B0.htm; Ellie Lee, "Treating Soldiers as Victims, http://www.spiked-online.com/Printable/00000006DDAB.htm; Simon Wessely, "War Stories: Invited Commentary on . . . Documented Combat

Exposure of U.S. Veterans Seeking Treatment for Combat-Related Post-Traumatic Stress Disorder," *British Journal of Psychiatry* 186, 2005, 473–475; Simon Wessely and Edgar Jones, "Psychiatry and the 'Lessons of Vietnam': What Were They, and are They Still Relevant?" *War and Society* 22, 2004, 89–103.

57. Lifton, *Home From the War,* 65; Lifton, "Testimony before Subcommittee on Veterans Affairs, U.S. Senate, January 27, 1970, cited in Gerald Nicosia, *Home to War: A History of the Vietnam Veterans' Movement* (New York: Crown, 2001), 159.

58. Michael E. Doubler, *Closing with the Enemy: How GIs Fought the War in Europe* (Lawrence: University of Kansas Press, 1994), 236–240.

59. Shepherd, *A War of Nerves,* 123–132.

60. Ibid., 348, 369–376; Edward M. Colbach and Matthew D. Parrish, "Army Mental Health Activities in Vietnam, 1965–1970," *Bulletin of the Menninger Clinic* 34/6, November 1970, 333–342. I owe the reference to Eric T. Dean Jr.'s compelling *Shook Over Hell,* 41.

61. Haley, "When the Patient Reports Atrocities"; Lifton, *Home From the War,* 421; Dean, *Shook Over Hell,* 41.

62. Richard A. Kulka et al., *Trauma and the Vietnam War Generation: Report of Findings from the National Vietnam Veterans Readjustment Study* (New York: Brunner/Mazel, 1990), 130, 223ff.

63. Centers for Disease Control, "Vietnam Experience Study: Health Status of Vietnam Veterans," *Journal of the American Medical Association* 259/18, May 13, 1988, 2701–2719; Robert E. Hoffman, "Which Soldiers Break Down: A Survey of 610 Psychiatric Patients in Vietnam," *Bulletin of the Menninger Clinic* 34/6, November 1970, 343–351.

64. Centers for Disease Control, "Vietnam Experience Study."

65. J. F. Borus, "Reentry 1: Adjustment Issues Facing the Vietnam Veteran," *Archives of General Psychiatry,* vol. 28, 1973, 501–506.

66. Bruce P. Dohrenwend et al., "The Psychological Risks of Vietnam for U.S. Veterans: A Revisit with New Data and Methods," *Science* 313, August 18, 2006, 979–982; Richard J. McNally, "Revisiting Dohrenwend et al.'s Revisit of the National Vietnam Veterans Readjustment Study," *Journal of Traumatic Stress* 20/4, August 2007, 481–486.

67. Dohrenwend et al., "The Psychological Risks of Vietnam."

68. B. Christopher Frueh et al., "Documented Combat Exposure of U.S. Veterans Seeking Treatment for Combat-Related Post-Traumatic Stress," *British Journal of Psychiatry* 186, June 2005, 467–472.

69. Dohrenwend et al., "The Psychological Risks of Vietnam."

70. Ibid.

71. Stephen D. Nice et al., "Long-term Health Outcomes and Medical Effects of Torture Among U.S. Navy Prisoners of War in Vietnam," *Journal of the American Medical Association* 276, August 7, 1996, 375–381, cited in McNally, *Remembering Trauma,* 98. Other studies correlating education and IQ with PTSD include, R. K. Pitman et al., "Pre-Vietnam Contents of Posttraumatic Stress Disorder Veteran's Service Medical and Personality Records," *Comprehensive Psychiatry* 32, September–October 1991, 416–422, and M. L. Macklin et al., "Lower Pre-Combat Intelligence is a Risk Factor for Posttraumatic Stress Disorder," *Journal of Counseling and Clinical Psychiatry* 66, April 1998, 323–326, both studies cited in McNally, 91–92.

72. Tom Wicker, "The Vietnam Disease," *New York Times,* May 27, 1975, 29; the correction ran August 1, 1975, 27. CBS/Dan Rather, "The Wall Within," 1988; Kristin A. Hass, *Carried to the Wall: American Memory and the Vietnam Veterans Memorial* (Berkeley: University of California Press, 1998), 88–89, 149n4.

73. Burkett and Whitley, *Stolen Valor,* 296-300.
74. Centers for Disease Control, "Postservice Mortality among Vietnam Veterans," *Journal of the American Medical Association* 257/6, February 13, 1987, 790–795; P. Breslin et al., "Proportionate Mortality Study of U.S. Army and U.S. Marine Corps Veterans of the Vietnam War," *Journal of Occupational Medicine* 30/5, May 1988, 412–419; D. A. Pollock, et al., "Estimating the Number of Suicides among Vietnam Veterans," *American Journal of Psychiatry* 147/6, June 1990, 772–776; N. L. Farberow et al., "Combat Experience and Postservice Psychosocial Status as Predictors of Suicide in Vietnam Veterans," *Journal of Nervous and Mental Disease* 178, January 1990, 32–37.
75. Deborah Sontag and Lizette Alvarez, "Across America, Deadly Echoes of Foreign Battles," *New York Times,* January 13, 2008, A1; Sontag and Alvarez, "Combat Trauma Takes the Witness Stand," *New York Times,* January 27, 2008, A1; Erik Eckholm, "Surge in Number of Homeless Veterans is Anticipated," *New York Times,* November 8, 2007, A20; "The Suffering of Soldiers," *New York Times,* May 11, 2008, editorial; Scott Shane, "A Flood of Troubled Soldiers is in the Offing, Experts Predict," *New York Times,* December 16, 2004, A1; Jonathan Shay, *Achilles in Vietnam: Combat Trauma and the Undoing of Character* (New York: Simon & Schuster, 1994). A representative challenge to the *New York Times* homicide story is Ralph Peters, "Smearing Soldiers," *New York Post,* January 15, 2008, Op-Ed. See also David Botti, "More Fallout from New York Times Murder Story," January 17, 2008, http://blog.newsweek.com/blogs/soldiershome/archive/2008/01/17/more-fallout-from-new-york-times-murder-story.aspx. For the follow-up story, see Kyle Burchett et al., "Post-Deployment Homicide," *Newsletter of Section VII of the American Psychological Association,* Spring/Summer 2008, 13–14.
76. Emily Buzzell and Samuel H. Preston, "Mortality of American Troops in the Iraq War," *Population and Development Review* 33/3, September 2007, 555–566; Atul Gawande, "Casualties of War—Military Care for the Wounded of Iraq and Afghanistan," *New England Journal of Medicine* 351/24, December 9, 2004, 2471–2475. See also Sean Flynn, "How to Save a Soldier," *New York Times Magazine,* March 16, 2003.

Chapter 2: A Nurse's Tale

Epigraph. Lynda Van Devanter with Christopher Morgan, *Home Before Morning: The Story of an Army Nurse in Vietnam* (New York: Beaufort Books, 1983).
1. Vera Brittain, *Testament of Youth* (London: Victor Gollancz, 1933).
2. Lynda Van Devanter with Christopher Morgan, *Home Before Morning: The Story of an Army Nurse in Vietnam* (New York: Beaufort, 1983).
3. Graeme Zielinski, "Obituary," *Washington Post,* November 21, 2002, B7. On Agent Orange, see two fair-minded analyses, Michael Gough, *Dioxin, Agent Orange: The Facts* (New York: Plenum, 1986), and Wilbur J. Scott, *Vietnam Veterans Since the War: The Politics of PTSD, Agent Orange, and the National Memorial* (Norman: University of Oklahoma Press, 2004).
4. *China Beach* (1988–1991).
5. Pete Earley, "Effects of War on Female Veterans Are Only Now Emerging," *Washington Post,* March 25, 1981, A1.
6. Myra MacPherson, *Long Time Passing: Vietnam and the Haunted Generation* (Garden City, New York: Doubleday, 1984), 442; e-mails from Steve Streeper, who served with Van Devanter, May 22 and 28, 2003. See also www.streeper.com/71st/, *Home Before Morning,* 171

7. On its widespread use in college classrooms, see Patrick Hagopian, *Report on the 1990–1991 Survey of Courses on the Vietnam War* (Fairfax, VA: George Mason University, 1993).

8. Van Devanter with Morgan, *Home Before Morning*, 21–31.

9. Ibid., 30, 49.

10. Carol Shevis, "Vietnam From a Woman's View," *Herndon Observer*, November 12, 1982, cited in B. G. Burkett and Glenna Whitley, *Stolen Valor* (Dallas: Verity Press, 1998), 472.

11. Van Devanter with Morgan, *Home Before Morning*, 76–78.

12. See the map and photos in http://www.rjsmith.com/pleiku-ne-nf.html.

13. Van Devanter with Morgan, *Home Before Morning*, 82, 85, 144, 97.

14. Ibid., 156; e-mails from Steve Streeper.

15. Van Devanter with Morgan, *Home Before Morning*, 206; Christine Kane, "Inside the Death Factory," *Boston Review*, June 1981; "Deaths, April and May 1970, 71st Evacuation Hospital," photocopy of typescript provided by Steve Streeper, in author's possession.

16. Van Devanter with Morgan, *Home Before Morning*, 163.

17. Lt. Col. D. E. Lounsbury, MC, Director of the Borden Institute, Editor-in Chief, Textbooks of Military Medicine, WRAMC, to author September 10, 2003.

18. Van Devanter with Morgan, *Home Before Morning*, 108, 118, 124; Suzy Kalter, *The Complete Book of MASH* (New York: Harry N. Abrams, 1984).

19. Van Devanter with Morgan, *Home Before Morning*, 121–124; H. R. (Helen Rogan), "Review," *Harper's* 266, May 1983, 91–92.

20. *MASH* (1970).

21. Van Devanter with Morgan, *Home Before Morning*, 173.

22. Ibid., 176, 179–180.

23. Ibid., 132.

24. Ibid., 135.

25. Eugene B. Sledge, *With the Old Breed At Peleliu and Okinawa* (New York: Oxford, 1990), 148.

26. Christine Kane, "Inside the Death Factory," *Boston Review*, June 1981.

27. Van Devanter with Morgan, *Home Before Morning*, 208–209.

28. Ibid., 210–212.

29. Ibid., 239–263.

30. Ibid., 263–277.

31. Ibid., 278–279.

32. Ibid., 288.

33. Ibid., 290.

34. Ibid., 296. See Note 46 in Chapter 1.

35. Van Devanter with Morgan, *Home Before Morning*, 297, 303.

36. The *Ms. Magazine* quote appears on the back cover of the reprint published by the University of Massachusetts Press in 2001. Carol Van Strum, "Healing and Hurting in Vietnam," *Washington Post*, April 11,1983, B6; *Voice of Youth* 6, August 1983, 155; *Library Journal* 108/5, March 1, 1983, 488; *Harper's* 266, May 1983, 91–92; *Atlantic* 251, May 1983, 103.

37. Sandra G. Boodman, "War Story," *Washington Post*, May 23, 1983, C1.

38. Webb, "Another Vietnam Story That Isn't True," *Washington Times*, June 15, 1983, cited in Burkett and Whitley, *Stolen Valor*, 473–474.

39. Patricia L. Walsh, *Forever Sad The Hearts* (New York: Avon, 1982); Pat H. Broeske, "Nurses at War!" *Los Angeles Times*, December 6, 1987.

40. Broeske, "Nurses at War!"; http://www.patriciawalsh.com.

41. Van Devanter with Morgan, *Home Before Morning,* 195; Burkett and Whitley, *Stolen Valor,* 473.
42. Barry M. Kroll, *Teaching Hearts and Minds: College Students Reflect on the Vietnam War in Literature* (Carbondale: Southern Illinois University Press, 1992).
43. Patrick Hagopian, *Report on the 1990–1991 Survey of Courses on the Vietnam War;* http://www.westridge.org/academics/upper/SummerReading/hist220-221.html; http://www.university.k12.nj.us/curr/languagearts.
44. On Agent Orange, see Wilber Scott, *Vietnam Veterans Since the War,* 75–122 and Michael Gough, *Dioxin, Agent Orange: The Facts.* See the spray map on http://www.lewispublishing.com/orange.html.
45. Keith Walker, ed., *A Piece of My Heart: The Stories of Twenty-Six American Women Who Served in Vietnam* (Novato: CA, Presidio, 1985).
46. Ibid., 1, 6.
47. Ibid., 168–169, 146, 271, 42, 14, 300.
48. Kathryn Marshall, ed., *In the Combat Zone: An Oral History of American Women in Vietnam* (Boston: Little, Brown, 1987), 3, 15–16, 262.
49. *In the Combat Zone,* 228, 31, 33, 122; Mel D. Lane, "Review of Marshall," *Library Journal* 112/1, January 1987, 86.
50. Winnie Smith, *American Daughter Gone to War: On the Front Lines with an Army Nurse in Vietnam* (New York: Pocket Books, 1992), 7, 297.
51. Ibid., 44–45, 120.
52. Ibid., 52.
53. Ibid., 205–206.
54. Ibid., 322–327.
55. Ibid., 319, 314.
56. Lynn Hampton, *The Fighting Strength: Memoirs of a Combat Nurse in Vietnam* (New York: Warner, 1990); Bobbi Hovis; *Station Hospital Saigon: A Navy Nurse in Vietnam, 1963–1964* (Annapolis: Naval Institute Press, 1992); Mary Reynolds Powell, *A World of Hurt: Between Innocence and Arrogance in Vietnam* (Chesterland, OH: Greenleaf, 2000); Ron Steinman, ed., *Women in Vietnam: The Oral History* (New York: TV Books, 2000); Olga Gruhzit-Hoyt, *A Time Remembered: American Women in the Vietnam War* (Novato, CA: Presidio, 1999). A review of the latter by Pat Jernigan suggests its unreliability, http://www.h-net.org/reviews/showrev.cgi?path=147421019150431; Dan Freedman and Jacqueline Rhoads, eds., *Nurses in Vietnam: The Forgotten Veterans* (Austin: Texas Monthly Press, 1987); Elizabeth M. Norman, *Women at War: The Story of Fifty Nurses Who Served in Vietnam* (Philadelphia: University of Pennsylvania Press, 1990).
57. Mel D. Lane, review of *American Daughter Gone to War, Library Journal* (August 1992), 116–117; Francke, "The Things She Carried," *New York Times Book Review* (December 27, 1992), 8; Coburn, Review of *A Piece of My Heart, New York Times Book Review* (May 25, 1986), 15; Mel D. Lane, review of *A Piece of My Heart, Library Journal* (February 1, 1986), 72; Carol Lynn Mithers, "The Other Veterans," *Nation* 245/1 (July 11, 1987), 27–28.
58. Laura Palmer, "How to Bandage a War," *New York Times Magazine,* November 7, 1993, 36ff; Laura Palmer, ed., *Shrapnel in the Heart: Letters and Remembrances from the Vietnam Veterans Memorial* (New York: Vintage, 1988).
59. Palmer, "How to Bandage a War."
60. Donna M. Dean, "Lest They Be Forgotten," h-net.msu.edu...h-minerva, July 16, 2003; Steinman, *Women in Vietnam,* 77, 110, 217.

61. Robert H. Stretch et al., "Posttraumatic Stress Disorder Among Army Nurse Corps Vietnam Veterans," *Journal of Consulting and Clinical Psychology* 53/5, October 1985, 704–708; Richard J. McNally, "Revisiting Dohrenwend et al.'s Revisit," *Journal of Traumatic Stress* 20/4, August 2007, 481–486.

62. Norman, *Women at War,* 145, 149.

63. Hampton, *The Fighting Strength,* 217; Walker, ed., *A Piece of My Heart,* 169.

64. Powell's comments are quoted in a pamphlet on the dedication of the Vietnam Women's Memorial, November 10–12, 1993, in the Vietnam War Special Collection, Connelly Library, LaSalle University. The "Prayer of an Army Nurse" can be found on http://www.history.amedd.army.mil/ANCWebsite/miscinfo.htm.

Chapter 3: Spit-Upon Veterans

1. See Richard A. Gabriel and Paul L. Savage, *Crisis in Command: Mismanagement in the Army* (New York: Hill & Wang, 1979).

2. See John E. Mueller, "Reflections on the Vietnam Antiwar Movement: The Curious Calm at War's End," in Peter Braestrup, ed., *Vietnam as History: Ten Years After the Paris Peace Accords* (Washington, DC: Woodrow Wilson Center and University Press of America, 1984).

3. Robert Jay Lifton, *Home From the War* (New York: Simon & Schuster, 1973), 99; Tim O'Brien, *If I Die in a Combat Zone: Box Me Up and Ship Me Home* (New York: Delacorte Press, 1973); Ron Kovic, *Born on the Fourth of July* (New York: Simon & Schuster, 1977); Robert Mason, *Chickenhawk* (New York: Viking, 1983); John Sack, *M* (New York: Avon, 1985); Michael Herr, *Dispatches* (New York: Knopf, 1977); Al Santoli, ed., *Everything We Had: An Oral History of the Vietnam War by Thirty-Three American Soldiers Who Fought It* (New York: Random House, 1981); Wallace Terry, ed., *Bloods: An Oral History of the Vietnam War by Black Veterans* (New York: Random House, 1984); Mark Baker, ed., *Nam: The Vietnam War in the Words of the Men and Women Who Fought There* (New York: William Morrow and Co., 1981), 269, 273.

4. Jerry Lembcke, *The Spitting Image: Myth, Memory, and the Legacy of Vietnam* (New York: New York University Press, 1998); Lindgren posted five comments on February 3, 8, 21 (two comments on that date), and 24, 2007, http://www.volokh.com/posts/1170928927.shtml.

5. Lindgren, as above.

6. Jack Shafer, "Drooling on the Vietnam Vets," *Slate,* May 2, 2000, http://www.slate.com/id/1005224; Jack Shafer, "Pickett's Charge," *Slate,* March 6, 2007, http://www.slate.com/id/2161038/; Jack Shafer, "Delmar Pickett Jr. Stands by his Spit Story," *Slate,* March 7, 2007, http://www.slate.com/id/2161383/.

7. For coverage of the Minarik story, see Jack Shafer, "More Spit Takes," *Slate,* February 12, 2007, http://www.slate.com/id/2159470

8. *First Blood* (1982).

9. *Coming Home* (1978), *China Beach,* "The World, Part 1," April 26, 1989. Thanks to John Baky, Vietnam War Special Collection, Connelly Library, LaSalle University.

10. Lifton, *Home from the War,* 208–209; Keith Walker, ed., *A Piece of My Heart: The Stories of Twenty-Six American Women Who Served in Vietnam* (Novato, CA: Presidio Press, 1985), 270–271; W. D. Ehrhart, *Vietnam-Perkasie: A Combat Marine's Memoir* (Jefferson, NC: McFarland, 1983), 275; Joseph Klein, *Payback,* 5; Peter Goldman and Tony Fuller, *Charlie Company: What Vietnam Did to Us* (New York: Newsweek and Ballantine Books, 1983), 232.

11. Greene, "Yes, Veterans Say, They Were Spit Upon," *Chicago Tribune,* July 23, 1987.
12. Ibid., The next articles ran on August 24, 25, and 26, 1987.
13. Ibid.
14. Greene, "Not Spat Upon, but Hounded and Hurt," *Chicago Tribune,* August 26, 1987.
15. Bob Greene, *Homecoming: When the Soldiers Returned from Vietnam* (New York: G. P. Putnam's Sons, 1989).
16. Ibid., 9–13, 16.
17. *Homecoming,* passim.
18. *Homecoming,* 62, 77, 19, 30.
19. Ibid., 63.
20. Ibid., 44
21. Ibid., 24.
22. Ibid., 195; Green, "Not Spat Upon, but Hounded and Hurt," *Chicago Tribune,* August 26, 1987; Frederick Downs, *The Killing Zone: My Life in the Vietnam War* (New York: W. W. Norton & Company, 1978) preface
23. Greene, *Homecoming,* 37–38, 63, 177, 21, 75, 202–203.
24. Ibid., 37–38.
25. Ibid., 38.
26. Ibid., 79–80. I've read only one claim of a spitting incident witnessed. Thirty-one years after the fact, the late Stephen Ambrose wrote that, in New Orleans in the fall of 1971, he saw a woman student with long hair, wearing a T-shirt with no bra, go up to a discharged veteran, spit in his face, and ask, "How many children did you kill over there?" The veteran was apparently not in uniform, his short hair was the giveaway, Ambrose claimed in his *To America: Personal Reflections of an Historian* (New York: Simon & Schuster, 2002), 141.
27. Shirley Dicks, *From Vietnam to Hell: Interviews with Victims of Post-Traumatic Stress Disorder* (Jefferson, NC: McFarland, 1990), 7, 27.
28. Ibid., 9–12, 18–23, 24–28.
29. Ibid., 93, 37. Coulbourn H. Godfrey Jr., the "Outstanding Man" of Platoon 1005, Marine basic training, Camp Lejeune, whose return home was troubled with drugs and alcohol and police records, recalled coming through Norton AFB, greeted at the front gate by protesters: "Oh they cussed us out . . . threw cans at us. Called us baby killers." W. D. Ehrhart, *Ordinary Lives: Platoon 1005 and the Vietnam War* (Philadelphia: Temple University Press, 1999), 112–113.
30. Dicks, *From Vietnam to Hell,* 4–8.
31. H. W. Chalsma, *The Chambers of Memory: PTSD in the Life Stories of U.S. Vietnam Veterans* (Northvale, NJ: Jason Aronson, 1998).
32. Greene, *Homecoming.* 43–44.
33. Kovic, *Born on the Fourth of July,* 184.
34. Lembcke, *The Spitting Image,* 6.
35. Ibid., 4.
36. Ibid., 8, 4, 6, 9.
37. Greene, *Homecoming,* 70; Lembcke, *The Spitting Image,* photo adjacent to p. 93; Santoli, *Everything We Had,* 103.
38. *Winter Soldier,* 1971; *Stolen Honor,* 2004.
39. Affidavit, Steven J. Pitkin, September 2004, http://ice.he.net?~freepnet/kerry/staticges/indexphp?pagePitkinAff. The earlier affidavit is dated August 31, 2004. For a transcript of Pitkin's speech at the "Kerry Lied Rally," September 12, 2004, see http://ice.he.net/~freepnet/kerry/staticpages/index.php?page=PitkinKLR.

40. Pitkin's testimony was reprinted in Vietnam Veterans Against the War, *The Winter Soldier Investigation: An Inquiry into American War Crimes* (Boston: Beacon Press, 1972), 159–160.

41. Ibid.

42. See note 39, Affidavit, Steven J. Pitkin, August 31, 2004.

Chapter 4: The Swift Boat Veterans and the "Truth"

1. *Congressional Record*, 92nd Congress, 1st Session, April 22, 1971; Vietnam Veterans Against the War, *The Winter Soldier Investigation: An Inquiry into American War Crimes* (Boston: Beacon Press, 1972); *Winter Soldier* (1972). The Thomas Paine quote can be found in Phillip S. Foner, ed., *The Complete Writings of Thomas Paine*, vol. 2 (New York: Citadel, 1945), 48. Transcripts and audio tapes of a second inquiry, "The 'We Accuse' Investigation," held in Philadelphia, March 26–27, 1971, can be found in the Jon Bjornson Collection at The Vietnam Center and Archive, Texas Tech University. Although many of the participants also testified at the WSI, others chose not to. The Philadelphia sessions deserve further study.

2. Sherwood's bio can be found on www.stolen.honor.com/about-producer.asp. *Inquisition: The Persecution and Prosecution of the Reverend Sun Myung Moon* (Washington: Regnery, 1991).

3. *Winter Soldier* (1971).

4. *Winter Soldier;* interview with Scott Camil, September 16, 2005.

5. *Stolen Honor* (2004); Owens, "Vetting the Vet Record," http://www. national review.com/owens/owens200401270825.asp; http://wizbangblog.com/archives/007766.php. The claim that many of the veterans at the WSI were "imposters," came to be treated as common knowledge on the right. See Daniel Clark, "Liberals and Hoaxes—Perfect Together, *The Jewish Press,* (January 25, 2006), http://www.free republic.com/focus/f-news/1565776/posts.

6. *Campbell v. Sherwood, et al.*, filed October 18, 2004, in the Court of Common Pleas, Philadelphia, followed by *Campbell v. Vietnam Veterans Legacy Foundation*, August 25, 2005. Jon Bjornson, who also testified at the WSI, brought a similar suit though it was withdrawn prior to discovery. The suits were withdrawn July 7, 2006. One version of the conclusion of the suits can be found in Shannon P. Duffy, *The Legal Intelligencer Online*, July 13, 2006, posted on www.vvlf.org/default.php?page_id=52. Interview, Kenneth Campbell, December 18, 2006.

7. Gerald Nicosia, *Home to War: A History of the Vietnam Veterans' Movement* (New York: Crown, 2001), 50–51, 56–73, the Lincoln-Kennedy quote, 72.

8. Ibid., 98–157.

9. Ibid., 128; William Overend, "Who is Al Hubbard," *National Review*, June 1, 1971.

10. Nicosia, *Home to War*, 217, 224–225; Vietnam Veterans Against the War, *The Winter Soldier Investigation: An Inquiry into American War Crimes* (Boston: Beacon Press, 1972), xiii–xiv, dedication.

11. Guenter Lewy, *America in Vietnam* (New York: Oxford University Press, 1978), 317, 500n.

12. Interview, Paul O'Donnell, NCIS, October 13, 2005; Tom Bowman, "Kerry Went from Soldier to Anti-War Protestor," *Baltimore Sun*, February 14, 2004, A1; interview, Guenter Lewy, October 14, 2005.

13. Kenneth J. Campbell, "The International War Crimes Conference, Oslo, June 1971: Excerpts from the Diary of One of the Witnesses," in *Nobody Gets Off the Bus: The Vietnam Generation Big Book*, vol. 5, No. 1-4, March, 1994, http://www2.iath.virginia.edu/sixties/HTML_docs/VNG_News_5&1_4.html;

Frank Browning and Dorothy Forman, eds., *The Wasted Nation: Report of the International Commission of Enquiry into United States Crimes in Indochina, June 20–25, 1971* (New York: Harper & Row, 1972); Ad Hoc Hearings on Command Responsibility for War Atrocities in Vietnam, U.S. House of Representatives, April 26–29, 1971, published as *The Dellums Committee Hearing on War Crimes in Vietnam: An Inquiry into Command Responsibility in Southeast Asia* (New York: Vintage Books, 1972); e-mail from Kenneth Campbell, December 1, 2005; *Hearts and Minds* (1974).

14. Interviews, Paul Olimpieri, November 16, 2005, and Fred Neinke, October 26, 2005.

15. Interview, Thomas Heidtman, February 4, 2006.

16. Interview, Olimpieri, Nov. 16, 2005; Interview, Ken Campbell, Aug. 23, 2005; Interview, David Bressem, November 14, 2005.

17. Michael S. Foley, *Confronting the War Machine: Draft Resistance During the Vietnam War* (Chapel Hill: University of North Carolina Press, 2003), 310–319.

18. Ibid.

19. Olimpieri e-mail, December 29, 2005.

20. Nicosia, *Home to War*, 215, 490.

21. Scott Swett and Tim Ziegler, *To Set The Record Straight: How Swift Boat Veterans, POWs and the New Media Defeated John Kerry* (New American Media Publishing, LLC, 2008), 81.

22. Michael Kranish et al., *John F. Kerry: The Complete Biography by the Boston Globe Reporters Who Know Him Best* (New York: Public Affairs, 2004), 1–5, 18–34, 35–57, "an excess of interventionism," 54.

23. Kranish, *Kerry*, 58–70, "I didn't really want to get involved," 77; Douglas Brinkley, *Tour of Duty: John Kerry and the Vietnam War* (New York: William Morrow, 2004), 92.

24. Admiral Elmo Zumwalt Jr. and Lieutenant Elmo Zumwalt III, *My Father, My Son* (New York: Macmillan, 1986), 47.

25. Brinkley, *Tour of Duty*, 138, 147.

26. Ibid., 146–148; Kranish et al., *Kerry*, 70–76.

27. Kranish et al., *Kerry*, 74; Dave Eberhart, "Swift Boat Veterans Condemn Kerry as Unfit for Command," http://archive.newsmax.com/archives/articles/2004/5/4/132751.shtml; http://swiftvets.com/videos/anyquestions.mpeg; Wesley K. Clark, "Medals of Honor," *New York Times*, Op-Ed, April 28, 2004.

28. NBC News, "Adm. William Schachte: 'No enemy fire,'" August 27, 2004, http://www.msnbc.msn.com/id/5840657/.

29. NBC News, "Zaladonis: Schachte Wasn't in the Boat," August 27, 2004, http://www.msnbc.msn.com/id/5843180/.

30. Brinkley, *Tour of Duty*, 261–266, 287–289.

31. Ibid., 289–295.

32. David Warsh, "Behind the Hootch," *Boston Globe*, October 27, 1996; Brian MacQuarrie, "Senator Hits Column Hard, Defends His War Record," *Boston Globe*, October 28, 1996; Kranish et al., *Kerry*, 103–104, 322.

33. Michael Kranish, "Veteran Retracts Criticism of Kerry," *Boston Globe*, August 6, 2004; "Affidavit of George Elliott," State of Delaware, County of Sussex, August 6, 2004, copy in author's possession; Swett and Ziegler, *To Set the Record Straight*, 138.

34. John E. O'Neill and Jerome R. Corsi, *Unfit for Command: Swift Boat Veterans Speak Out Against John Kerry* (Washington, DC: Regnery, 2004), 80–86, quotes, 84, 84, 80, 84.

35. Kerry's Silver Star citation is quoted in O'Neill and Corsi, *Unfit for Command*, 81–82; William B. Rood, "Anti-Kerry vets not there that day," *Chicago Tribune*, August 21, 2004; McCain's quote is cited in Sean O'Sullivan, "Two Delaware Residents in Ad Attacking Kerry," *News Journal*, August 10, 2004.
36. Kranish et al., *Kerry*, 376–377; Jim Rassmann, "Shame on the Swift Boat Veterans for Bush," *Wall Street Journal*, Op-Ed, August 10, 2004; Swett and Ziegler, *To Set the Record Straight*, 176.
37. Brinkley, *Tour of Duty*, 300–318. Rassmann is quoted in Michael Dobbs, "Swift Boat Accounts Incomplete," *Washington Post*, August 22, 2004, A1.
38. Brinkley, *Tour of Duty*, 314; Dobbs, "Swift Boat Accounts Incomplete"; Rassmann, "Shame on the Swift Boat Veterans."
39. Dobbs, "Swift Boat Accounts Incomplete"; Dobbs, "Records Counter a Critic of Kerry," *Washington Post*, August 19, 2004. The Lambert quote is in Paul Fattig, "Swift Boat Memories," *Mail Tribune*, August 26, 2004, http://archive.mailtribune.com/archive/2004/0826/local/stories/01local.htm; *Hardball*, August 19, 2004, http://www.msnbc.msn.com/id/5765243/print/1/display mode/1098/; Swett and Ziegler, *To Set the Record Straight*, 184; Rassmann, "Shame on the Swift Boat Veterans."
40. O'Neill and Corsi, *Unfit for Command*, 87–93; Dobbs, "Swift Boat Accounts Incomplete"; copy of after-action report SL358 can be found at http://home page.mac.com/chinesemac/kerry_medals/PDFs/PCF-94_spot_reports.pdf.
41. Michael Kranish, "Kerry Faces Questions Over Purple Hearts," *Boston Globe*, April 14, 2004; Kranish et al., *Kerry*, 108; Brinkley, *Tour of Duty*, 461.
42. Kranish et al., *Kerry*, 112–113; Brinkley, *Tour of Duty*, 340.
43. Brinkley, *Tour of Duty*, 342, 346–377.
44. "Kerry blasts phony controversy' over medals," April 27, 2004, http://www.cnn.com/2004/ALLPOLITICS/04/26/kerry.medals; Jeff Jacoby, "The Kerry medals mystery," *Boston Globe*, Op-Ed, April 29, 2004.
45. The protocol for the wearing of Navy medals and ribbons can be found on www.navy.mil/navydata/infoIndex.asp, under Awards and Medals.
46. Liteky's Medal of Honor citation can be found on www.homeofheros.com/moh/citations_living/vn_a_liteky.html. Now using Charlie as his first name, his website is www.peacehost.net/Charlie/index.html. The Boorda story can be found in Colonel David H. Hackworth, *Hazardous Duty* (New York: William Morrow, 1996), 285–297.
47. John Kerry, "How Do You Ask a Man to Be the Last Man to Die in Vietnam? testimony before the Senate Foreign Relations Committee, April 23, 1971, in http://hnn.us/articles/3631.html.
48. "Vietnam 30 Years Later: What John Kerry said on Meet the Press," http://hnn.us/articles/3552.html, February 20, 2004.
49. Ibid.
50. See Chapter 6.
51. "Vietnam 30 Years Later." See also Jodi Wilgoren, "Kerry Backs Off Statements on Vietnam War," *New York Times*, April 19, 2004, A15.

Chapter 5: The Winter Soldier Investigation

Epigraph. Sergeant Joseph M. Darby, the MP at Abu Ghraib, Iraq, who first revealed the abuse of prisoners. Darby, as told to Will S. Hyton, "Prisoner of Conscience," *GQ* (Sept. 2006), http://men.style/gq/features/landing?id=content_4785.
1. Jean-Paul Sartre, "Verdict of the Stockholm Session," in John Duffett, ed., *Against the Crime of Silence: Proceedings of the Russell International War Tribunal* (New York: O'Hare Books, 1968), 309. Lord Bertrand Russell, "Opening

Statement to the First Tribunal Session," in Duffett, ed., *Against the Crime of Silence*, 50; and "Closing Address to the Stockholm Session," 311. The verdict of "genocide" is in "Summary and Verdict of the Second Session," Duffett, ed., *Against the Crime of Silence*, 650. The Lynd reference is in Guenter Lewy, *America in Vietnam* (New York: Oxford University Press, 1978), 312.

2. Gerald Nicosia, *Home to War* (New York: Crown, 2001), 75–76. On My Lai, I've relied on Michal R. Belknap, *The Vietnam War on Trial: The My Lai Massacre and the Court-Martial of Lieutenant Calley* (Lawrence: University Press of Kansas, 2002), 117. The *Life* story appeared on December 5, 1969. The Agnew and Ensign quotes appear in Tod Ensign, "Organizing Veterans Through War Crimes Documentation," *Nobody Gets Off the Bus: The Vietnam Generation Big Book*, vol. 5/1-4, 1994, www2.iath.Virginia.edu/sixties/HTML_docs/Texts/Narrative/Ensign_War_Crimes.html.

3. Nicosia, *Home to War*, 77–78; Ensign, "Organizing Veterans"; interview, David Bressem, November 14, 2005.

4. Nicosia, *Home To War*, 16–17, 76.

5. Ibid., 69; Ensign, "Organizing Veterans."

6. Nicosia, *Home To War*, 56–73

7. Ibid., 81

8. Ibid., 108–109, 128; Mark Lane, *Conversations with Americans* (New York: Simon & Schuster, 1970), 10–11. Lane's other work includes *Rush to Judgment* (New York: Holt, Rinehart, and Winston, 1966) and *The Strongest Poison* (New York: Elsevier-Dutton, 1980).

9. Lane, *Conversations*, 10–11.

10. Ibid., 12 and book jacket.

11. Ibid., 49–55.

12. Ibid., 54.

13. Ibid., 25–30, quotes on 30 and 28.

14. Ibid., 105–109, quote, 107–108.

15. Ibid., 157, 162–163; Duffett, ed., *Against the Crime of Silence*, 447, 455–457; Martinson also testified at the CCI hearings in Washington, see James Simon Kunen, *Standard Operating Procedure: Notes of a Draft-Age American* (New York: Avon Books, 1971), 177–189. He did not testify at the WSI.

16. Lane, *Conversations*, 182–183.

17. Reston, *Saturday Review*, January 9, 1971, 26, quoted in Lewy, *America in Vietnam*, 316.

18. Lane, *Conversations*, 13; Neil Sheehan, "Review of Mark Lane, *Conversations with Americans*," *New York Times Book Review*, December 27, 1970, 5.

19. Lane, *Conversations*, 110–116; Sheehan, "Review."

20. Lane, *Conversations*, 87–101, quote, 90–91.

21. On artillery and air support at the battle of Hue, see Eric Hammel, *Fire in the Street: The Battle for Hue, Tet 1968* (Chicago: Contemporary Books, 1991), 274–275; Nicholas Warr, *Phase Line Green: The Battle for Hue, 1968* (Annapolis: Naval Institute Press, 1997), 91–92. On the destruction of Hue, see Peter Braestrup, *Big Story: How the American Press and Television Reported and Interpreted the Crises of Tet in Vietnam in Washington, 1968* (Boulder, CO: Westview Press, 1973), 265–278. On the VC-NVA killings at Hue, see Braestrup, *Big Story*, 279–286. See also Keith William Nolan, *Battle of Hue: Tet 1968* (Novato, CA: Presidio Press, 1983), and LTC Marcus J. Gravel, USMC, 17 July 1973, "Tactical Considerations Relating to the Battle of Hue, 1968," Marine Corps Oral History Program, typescript, Archives, Alfred M. Gray Marine Corps

Research Center, Marine Corps Base, Quantico, VA. Gravel was the CO of 1st Battalion, 1st Marines, during the battle of Hue.

22. Sheehan, "Review."

23. Ibid.

24. Nicosia, *Home To War*, 83; Kunen, *Standard Operating Procedure.*

25. Interview, Kenneth Campbell, November 29, 2005; Nicosia, *Home To War*, 83–84.

26. *Winter Soldier*, press kit from Milliarium Zero, distributors for the re-release in 2005. On its unsuitability for prime time, see Wesley Morris, "A Searing Look Through Veterans' Eyes," *Boston Globe*, November 3, 2005, http://www.boston.com/news/globe/living/articles/2005/11/03/a_searing_look_through_veterans_eyes.

27. http://www.wintersoldierfilm.com.

28. Alistair Highet, "The Truth About Vietnam," *Hartford Advocate*, September 22, 2005; Geoff Pevere, "Winter's Chill Felt Again," *Toronto Star*, December 21, 2006, www.thestar.com/article/163116; Jeffrey M. Anderson, "Something 'Winter' This Way Comes," *San Francisco Examiner*, September 1, 2005; Ann Hornaday, "'Winter Soldier': Cold Days in Hell," *Washington Post*, December 9, 2005, C5; Jennifer Nemo, "Winter Soldier: The Horror," *Pulse of the Twin Cities*, January 13, 2006, www.tcdailyplanet.net/node/433; Lisa Kennedy, "The Grief of Vietnam Veterans Feels Disturbingly Fresh," *Denver Post*, October 17, 2005.

29. Michael Atkinson, "When We Were Psychos," *In These Times*, September 27, 2005; Colin Covert, "Winter Soldier," *Minneapolis Star Tribune*, September 16, 2005. The Geneva Convention, however compromised, remained in force for American soldiers in Vietnam, though the NLF and the PRV refused to acknowledge it as applicable to them. No one argued as Alberto Gonzales, then White House counsel, did in 2002, that it was "obsolete" in an age of terrorism. The abuses at Abu Ghraib were rooted not in Vietnam but in the White House of George W. Bush. See Jane Mayer, "The Memo," *New Yorker*, February 27, 2006, 32–41, and her *The Dark Side: The Inside Story of How the War on Terror Turned into a War on America Ideals* (New York: Doubleday, 2008).

30. Atkinson, "When We Were Psychos"; Sean Aymaker, review of *Winter Soldier*, http://www.seattlepi.com/movies/247891_limited11; Dayna Papaleo, "Choose your weapons," *City, Rochester's Alternative Weekly*, December 7, 2005, http://www.rochester-citynewspaper.com/archives/2005/12/choose+your+weapons.

31. Crandell's testimony can be found in *The Winter Soldier Investigation: An Inquiry Into American War Crimes* (Boston: Beacon Press, 1972); Robert Jay Lifton, *Home From the War: Vietnam Veterans, Neither Victims Nor Executioners* (New York: Simon & Schuster, 1973), 41. The Fonda interview is reported by Christina Talcott, "Fonda's 'Winter' of Redemption," *Washington Post*, December 9, 2005, WE34.

32. On the "Jesus-like" Camil, see David M. Halbfinger, "Film Echoes the Present in Atrocities of the Past," *New York Times*, August 9, 2005, and Nicosia, *Home To War*, 85.

33. Kennedy, "The Grief of Vietnam Veterans . . . "; Rob Thomas, "'Winter Soldier' Chills with Vietnam Stories, *Wisconsin State Journal* (Nov. 10, 2005), (http://www.madison.com/articles/read.php?ref=wsj/2005/11/10/0511090422.php.

34. *Winter Soldier*, http://www.wintersoldierfilm.com.

35. Ibid.

36. Ibid.
37. Herr, *Dispatches*, 35; *Winter Soldier.*
38. Hornaday, "Winter Soldier"; Halbfinger, "Film Echoes the Present"; Cynthia Fuchs, "Winter Soldier," www.popmatters.com/film/reviews/w/*winter-soldier-1972-dvd*.shtml; Colin Covert, "Winter Soldier," *Minneapolis Star Tribune*, Sep-tember 16, 2005; and Roger Moore, "Film is Stark Document of Vietnam War and the Times," *Orlando Sentinel*, September 29, 2005, are representative. The latter two reviews can be found on www.wintersoldierfilm.com/reviews.htm.
39. Interview, David Bressem, Nov. 14, 2005. On nurses and PTSD, see Chapter 2. See also Terry Gross, *Fresh Air*, "Rusty Sachs Discusses his Participation in the Vietnam War," August 10, 2005.
40. "Doonesbury," *Baltimore Sun*, January 28, 2006.
41. When possible, I will cite the more accessible Beacon Press edited version of the WSI; but when necessary, I will cite the *Congressional Record*. Camil, Noetzal, and Lloyd's testimony can be found in Beacon's *Winter Soldier Investigation*, 101–102, 107–108. Camil's reference is in the *Congressional Record*, April 6,1971, 92nd Congress, 1st Session, 9950.
42. David Halberstam, "Helicopter Assault in the Ca Mau Peninsula: April 1963," in *Reporting Vietnam: American Journalism: 1959–1969*, vol. 1 (New York: Library of America, 1998), 73; "Pictures Studied by Army," *Washington Post*, Nov. 30, 1969, 25; Guenter Lewy, *America In Vietnam* (New York: Oxford University Press, 1978), 321–322.
43. *Hearts and Minds* (1974); Vere Langford Oliver, *Caodai Spiritism: A Study of Religion in Vietnamese Society* (Boston: Brill Academic Publishers, 1997).
44. *Hearts and Minds;* Osborn's testimony can be found at Hearings Before a Subcommittee of the Committee on Government Operations, "U.S. Assistance Programs in Vietnam," U.S. House of Representatives, 92nd Congress, 1st Session, July 15, 19, 21, August 2, 1971, 287–362; Hearing Before the Committee on Armed Services on the Nomination of William E. Colby to be Director of Central Intelligence, U.S. Senate, 93rd Congress, 1st Session, July 2, 20, 25, 1973, 71–118. I owe the references to Mark Moyar, *Phoenix and the Birds of Prey: The CIA's Secret Campaign to Destroy the Viet Cong* (Annapolis: Naval Institute Press, 1977), 93–96.
45. Noam Chomsky and Edward Herman, *The Washington Connection and Third World Fascism* (Boston: South End Press, 1979), 325–327; Mark Lane, *Plausible Denial* (New York: Thunder Mouths Press, 1991), 79–80. See also Douglas Valentine, *The Phoenix Program* (New York: William Morrow, 1990), 307–308, 347, 376, 382; William Blum, *The CIA: A Forgotten History* (London, Zed Books, 1986), 145.
46. James S. Kunen, *Standard Operating Procedure: Notes of a Draft-Age American* (New York: Avon, 1971), 225, 206–207.
47. Ibid., 207–225, quoted 207, 217.
48. Ibid., 228n, 227, 226, and James S. Kunen, *The Strawberry Statement: Notes of a College Revolutionary* (New York: Random House, 1969).
49. Kunen, *Standard Operating Procedure*, 229.
50. Moyar, *Phoenix and the Birds of Prey*, 93–96.
51. Senate "Hearings on the Nomination of William E. Colby," 110.
52. Moyar, *Phoenix and the Birds of Prey*, 95–96.
53. The same was true of Marine helicopters—e-mail from Rusty Sachs, May 8, 2006.

54. *Winter Soldier Investigation*, 12–15.
55. *Congressional Record*, April 6, 1971, 92nd Cong. 1st Sess., 9949.
56. Ibid.; Halbfinger, "Film Echoes."
57. *Congressional Record*, April 6, 1971, 92nd Cong. 1st Sess., 9950.
58. Ibid.; interview, Scott Camil, September 16, 2005.
59. *Winter Soldier.*
60. "Transcript of Scott Camil's Memoir," Nancy Miller Saunders Collection, Virtual Vietnam Archive, The Vietnam Center and Archive, Texas Tech University.
61. *Winter Soldier.*
62. Ibid.; Scott Camil's DD-214, obtained through the Freedom of Information Act.
63. Stuart Landers, "Interview with Scott Camil," October 20, 1992, University of Florida Oral History Program; *Seasoned Veteran: Journey of a Winter Soldier* (2002).
64. Landers, "Interview"; interview, Scott Camil, Sept. 16, 2005.
65. Landers, "Interview."
66. Nicosia, *Home To War*, 258–282. The Romo quote is in Richard Stacewicz, *Winter Soldiers: An Oral History of the Vietnam Veterans Against the War* (New York: Twayne, 1997), 338.
67. Nicosia, *Home To War*, 277, 544; *Seasoned Veteran;* interview, Scott Camil, Sept. 16, 2005.
68. Graham Nash, "Oh! Camil (The Winter Soldier)" (1973). Calley's song was Tony Nelsen, "The Battle Hymn of Lieutenant Calley" (1971).
69. *Seasoned Veteran.*
70. *Congressional Record*, April 6, 1971, 92nd Cong. 1st Sess., 9951, 9954; Lane, *Conversations with Americans,* 182–184.
71. *Congressional Record*, April 6, 1971, 92nd Cong. 1st Sess., 9953.
72. Ibid., April 6, 1971, 92nd Cong. 1st Sess., 9951.
73. Ibid.
74. Ibid.
75. Ibid.
76. *Congressional Record*, April 6, 1971, 92nd Cong. 1st Sess., 9954.
77. Biographical information is from the website www.military.com and from a member profile that Bangert added to the site. Copies in possession of the author. Bangert has since removed his name from the site. See also Kevin Dennehy, "The Odyssey of Joe Bangert," *Cape Cod Times*, August 6, 2006, www.capecodonline.com.
78. Ken Campbell recalled that the leadership of CCI refused to allow Bangert to testify, and he also recalled Bangert haranguing a woman—who had lost her son in Vietnam—on a Philadelphia street corner. He died for nothing, Bangert reportedly said. Interview, Ken Campbell, Augu. 23, 2005.
79. www.pegseeger.com/html/ewancheers.html.
80. Barbara Dane and Irwin Silber, *The Vietnam Song Book* (New York: Monthly Review Press, 1969); Bill Homans, "Songs of Protest," *Veteran*, Spring 2003, 30. See also www.vietnamsongbook.org.
81. The photo of Bangert endorsing Kerry in front of the Massachusetts State House, September 12, 1984, can be found on www.boston.com/globe/nation/packages/kerry/images/day5/04.htm.
82. www.veteransagainsttorture.com/Flag/opinions.htm; www.vietnamsongbook.org.
83. *Sir! No Sir!* (2005).
84. Dennehy, "The Odyssey of Joe Bangert."
85. Ibid.
86. *Congressional Record*, April 6, 1971, 92nd Cong. 1st Sess., 10032.

87. Ibid., 9960–9962; 10016–10021.
88. *Congressional Record,* April 6, 1971, 92nd Cong. 1st Sess., 9990, 9997–9998, 9999.
89. Ibid., 9973–9977, 10009–10013.
90. Ibid., 10027, 10049–10054.
91. *The Winter Soldier Investigation,* 42–45.
92. Nick Turse and Deborah Nelson, "Civilian Killings Went Unpunished," *Los Angeles Times,* August 6, 2006, 1.
93. Ibid.
94. Deborah Nelson, *The War Behind Me: Vietnam Veterans Confront the Truth about U.S. War Crimes* (New York: Basic Books, 2008), 15.
95. Case files of the Army Criminal Investigation Command (CID) investigation are in the National Archives, College Park, Maryland, but are no longer open to the public because personal information had not been redacted as required by the Privacy Act of 1974. During the time they were open, 1994 to 2003, an unnamed historian made copies and made them available to Scott Swett and John Boyle who posted them on the right-wing site, FrontPageMagazine. Com. See www.wintersoldier.com/staticpages/index.php?page=WSI_CID. The copies—with the printed margin note, "Reproduced at the National Archives"—appear authentic. "Bunge Allegation," as of August 4, 1972, www.wintersoldier. com/cid/Bunge.pdf.
96. "Stark Allegation," as of July 29, 1971, www.wintersoldier.com/cid/Stark. pdf; "McConnachie Allegation," as of November 4, 1971, www.wintersoldier. com/cid/McConnachie.pdf; "Craig Allegation," as of August 19, 1971, www. wintersoldier.com/cid/DCraig.pdf.
97. Interview, Ken Campbell, Aug. 23, 2005; Lane, *Conversations with Americans,* 28, 36; Christopher Ronnau, *Blood Trails: The Combat Diary of a Foot Soldier in Vietnam* (New York: Ballantine Books, 2006), 97.
98. *Congressional Record,* April 6, 1971, 92nd Cong. 1st Sess., 10026, 9968, 10010; *The Winter Soldier Investigation,* 6; interview, David Bressem, Nov. 14, 2005.
99. *Congressional Record,* April 6, 1971, 92nd Cong. 1st Sess., 9974, 9977; the "Black Syph" island story can be found in Kregg P. J. Jorgenson, *Acceptable Loss* (New York: Ivy, 1991), 127. See also John Baky, "White Cong and Black Clap," in *Nobody Gets Off the Bus: The Viet Nam Generation Big Book,* Tal and Duffy, eds., vol. 5, no.1-4, March 1994.

Chapter 6: This Was "What the War Had Done to Us"
Epigraph. Philip Caputo, *A Rumor of War* (New York: Holt, Rinehart & Winston, 1977), 304, 305, 309.
  1. The Winter Soldier Investigation: An Inquiry into American War Crimes (Boston: Beacon Press, 1972), 1–4.
  2. Michal Belknap, *The Vietnam War on Trial: The My Lai Massacre and the Court-Martial of Lieutenant Calley* (Lawrence: University Press of Kansas, 2002). See also Michael Bilton and Kevin Sim, *Four Hours in My Lai: A War Crime and its Aftermath* (New York: Viking, 1992); John Sack, *Lieutenant Calley: His Own Story* (New York: Viking, 1971); Richard Hammer, *The Court-Martial of Lieutenant Calley* (New York: Coward, McCann and Geohegan, 1971).
  3. The first instructions on the treatment of prisoners, the "Lieber Code," was issued by President Lincoln to the Armies of the United States in 1863; Francis Lieber, *Instructions for the Government of Armies of the United States in the Field* (Clark NJ: Lawbook Exchange, 2005); Belknap, *The Vietnam War on Trial,* 70.

4. Belknap, *The Vietnam War on Trial*, 61–62.
5. Guenter Lewy, *America in Vietnam* (New York: Oxford University Press, 1978), 315.
6. Gerald I.A.D. Draper, *The Red Cross Conventions* (London: Stevens, 1958).
7. Lewy, *America in Vietnam*, 224–226; Jane Mayer, *The Dark Side: The Inside Story of How the War on Terror Turned Into a War on American Ideals* (New York, Doubleday, 2008).
8. Lewy, *America in Vietnam*, 242. All of the conventions are available through the Avalon Project of the Lillian Goldman Law Library of the Yale Law School, http://avalon.law.yale.edu/subject_menus/lawwar.asp.
9. Michael Gough, *Dioxin, Agent Orange: The Facts* (New York: Plenum, 1986), 13–61, 68–82; Lewy, *America in Vietnam*, 257–266; Wilbur J. Scott, *Vietnam Veterans Since the War: The Politics of PTSD, Agent Orange, and the National Memorial* (Norman: University of Oklahoma Press, 2003), 75–97, 163–227; Committee to Review the Health Effects in Vietnam Veterans of Exposure to Herbicides (Fifth Biennial Update), *Veterans and Agent Orange: Update 2004* (Washington, DC: National Academies Press, 2005), 9–10.
10. Lewy, *America in Vietnam*, 257–266.
11. Ibid., 248.
12. Ibid., 248–251.
13. Ibid., 253–254; "Protocol for the Prohibition of the Use in War of Asphyxiating Gas, and of Bacteriological Methods of Warfare, 8 February 1928," Avalon Project.
14. Lewy, *America in Vietnam*, 252–257.
15. Committee of Concerned Asian Scholars, *The Indochina Story: A Fully Documented Account* (New York: Pantheon, 1970), 105–107; Nguyen Khac Vien, ed., *Chemical Warfare* (Hanoi, Vietnam: Xunhasaba [distributor] 1971), 121; Lewy, *America in Vietnam*, 251: Abraham Behar, "Incendiary Weapons, Poison Gas, Defoliants Used in Vietnam," in John Duffett, ed., *Against the Crime of Silence* (New York: Simon & Schuster, 1970), 327–331; Edgar Lederer et al., "Report of the Sub-Committee on Chemical Warfare in Vietnam," in Duffett, ed., *Against the Crime of Silence*, 338–348; F. T. Fraunfelder, "Is CS Gas Dangerous?: Current Evidence Suggests Not But Unanswered Questions Remain," *British Medical Journal* 320, February 19, 2000, 458–459.
16. Lewy, *America in Vietnam*, 226–230.
17. On expansive definitions of "free-fire zones," see *The Winter Soldier Investigation*, 16–17, 28, 52, 62, 75; for restrictive definitions, see *The Winter Soldier Investigation*, 19. See also William Van Zanten, *Don't Bunch Up: One Marine's Story* (New York: Ballantine, 1993), 151: "we were not allowed to engage . . . Charlie unless we were under heavy fire" [from a village]; Frederick Downs, *The Killing Zone: My Life in the Vietnam War* (New York: W. W. Norton, 1978), 75; William L. Buchanan, *Full Circle: A Marine Rifle Company in Vietnam* (Mill Valley, CA: Baylaurel Press, 2003), 24. For the best-known account of American fire restraint as it pertains to the air war over North Vietnam, see Jack Broughton, *Going Downtown: The War Against Hanoi and Washington* (New York: Orion Books, 1988), and Jack Broughton, *Thud Ridge: F-105 Thunderchief Missions Over Vietnam* (New York: J. B. Lippincott, 1969).
18. Lewy, *America in Vietnam*, 99–101; C. D. B. Bryan, *Friendly Fire* (New York: Putnam, 1976). The movie of the same name was released in 1979. See also Peg Mullen, *Unfriendly Fire: A Mother's Memoir* (Iowa City: University of Iowa Press, 1995); W. D. Ehrhart, *Vietnam-Perkasie: A Combat Marine's Memoir* (Jefferson, NC: McFarland, 1983), 102–105.

19. Lewis Sorley, *A Better War: The Unexamined Victories and Final Tragedy of America's Last Years in Vietnam* (New York: Harcourt Brace & Company, 1999), 219–221, and Lewis Sorley, *Thunderbolt: General Creighton Abrams and the Army of His Times* (New York: Simon & Schuster, 1992), 201–202, 236, 238. For a persuasive critique of Sorley, see Dale Andrade, "Westmoreland Was Right: Learning the Wrong Lessons from the Vietnam War," *Small Wars and Insurgencies* 19/2 (June 2008), 145–81.

20. On the Marine's proposed strategy in Vietnam, see Jack Shulimson and Charles M. Johnson, *U.S. Marines in Vietnam: The Landing and the Buildup, 1965* (Washington, DC: U.S. Marine Corps, 1978); Lewis W. Walt, *Strange War, Strange Strategy: A General's Report on Vietnam* (New York: Funk & Wagnalls, 1970); William R. Corson, *The Betrayal* (New York: W. W. Norton, 1968). The source of the proposed strategy was *Small Wars Manual: U.S. Marine Corps, 1940* (Washington, DC: GPO, 1940). On tactics, see Michael E. Peterson, *The Combined Action Platoons: The U.S. Marines' Other War in Vietnam* (Westport, CT: Greenwood, 1989), and Bing West, *The Village* (New York: Pocket Books, 2003). On Abrams's attitude on Marine leadership, see Sorley, *Thunderbolt*, 208–209. For Westmoreland's response to the Marines and his defense of his strategy, see William Westmoreland, *A Soldier Reports* (Garden City, NY: Doubleday, 1976), 200–203.

21. On VC tactics, see S. L. A. Marshall and David Hackworth, *Military Operations: Vietnam Primer* (Washington, DC: Department of the Army, 1967).

22. Daniel Lang, *Casualties of War* (New York: McGraw Hill, 1969). A film of the same title was released in 1989.

23. Lang, *Casualties,* 25–54, 57–65, 70–71; Claude D. Newby, *It Took Heroes: A Chaplain's Story and Tribute to Combat Veterans and Those Who Waited for Them,* 2d ed. (Bountiful, UT: Tribute Enterprises, 2000), 47, 50.

24. Lang, *Casualties,* 79–81; Newby, *It Took Heroes,* 43–53.

25. Lang, *Casualties,* 88–89; Newby, *It Took Heroes,* 51.

26. Gary D. Solis, *Marines and Military Law in Vietnam: Trial by Fire* (Washington, DC: GPO, 1989), 175–177, 186–190.

27. William Broyles Jr., *Brothers in Arms: A Journey From War to Peace* (New York: Alfred A. Knopf, 1986), 250–251.

28. Solis, *Marines and Military Law in Vietnam,* 175–177, 186–190.

29. Gary D. Solis, *Son Thang: An American War Crime* (Annapolis: Naval Institute Press, 1997), 27; Randell D. Herrod, *Blue's Bastards: A True Story of Valor under Fire* (Washington, DC: Regnery, 1989); Oliver L. North with William Novak, *Under Fire: An American Story* (New York: Harper Collins, 1991).

30. CMC Bulletin 5370, Subj: "Personal Conduct of Marines in the RVN," 28 November 1966 (Parks folder, Marines and Military Law in Vietnam file), Marine Corps History Center; FMFPacO 1610.2, 28 November 1966 Subj. "Individual Responsibility (War Crimes folder, Military and Military Law in Vietnam file), Marine Corps History Center, cited in Solis, *Marines and Military Law in Vietnam,* 59.

31. Pace, "Commencement Address," The Citadel, May 6, 2006, http://external affairs.citadel.edu/grad06_GenPeterPace; Van Zanten, *Don't Bunch Up,* 151; Jeff Kelly, *DMZ Diary: A Combat Marine's Vietnam Memoir* (Jefferson, NC: McFarland, 1992), 194; John J. Culbertson, *Operation Tuscaloosa: 2nd Battalion, 5th Marines, at An Hoa, 1967* (New York: Ivy Books, 1997), 61; Ehrhart, *Vietnam-Perkesie,* 112; Downs, *The Killing Zone,* 175, 225.

32. The *Toledo Blade's* stories were the basis of Michael Sallah and Mitch Weiss, *Tiger Force: A True Story of Men and War* (Boston: Little, Brown, 2006).

33. Deborah Nelson, *The War Behind Me: Vietnam Veterans Confront the Truth about U.S. War Crimes* (Basic Books, 2008), 3, 210–24.
34. Philip Caputo, *A Rumor of War* (New York: Holt, Rinehart and Winston, 1977). Henry Holt and Company published the twentieth anniversary edition in 1996. Book sales are from Simon & Schuster's website, www.simonsays.com.
35. Among Caputo's other books are the novels *DelCorso's Gallery* (New York: Holt, Rinehart and Winston, 1983); *Indian Country* (New York: Bantam, 1987); and the memoir *Means of Escape: A War Correspondent's Memoir of Life and Death in Afghanistan, the Middle East, and Vietnam* (New York: Harper Collins, 1991).
36. *Rumor,* 35 (page numbers from the Ballantine edition, 1978).
37. Ibid., 68, 38, 63, 46, 66.
38. Ibid., 76, 77.
39. Paul Fussell, *The Great War and Modern Memory* (New York: Oxford, 1975), 7.
40. *Rumor,* 292–293.
41. Ibid., 294.
42. Ibid., 288–289.
43. Ibid., 296, 299.
44. Ibid., 300.
45. Ibid., 304.
46. Ibid.
47. *Rumor,* 305.
48. Ibid.
49. *Rumor,* 290, 306; Wilfred Owen, *Collected Poems,* C. Day Lewis, ed. (New York: New Directions, 1963).
50. Robert Jay Lifton, *Home From the War* (New York: Simon & Schuster, 1973), 41.
51. Solis, *Son Thang,* 59, 186, 108.
52. *Rumor,* 309.
53. Letter, Col. Max G. Halliday, Head, Military Law Branch to Mrs. Kenneth D. Coffin, 19 March 1970, cited in Graham A. Cosmas and Terrence P. Murray, *U.S. Marines in Vietnam: Vietnamization and Redeployment, 1970–1971* (Washington, DC: History and Museum Division, U.S. Marine Corps, 1986), 347.
54. *Rumor,* 306–319.
55. *Rumor,* 320. Matthew 24:6 and 9-13, *New Revised Standard Version,* "And you will hear of wars and rumors of wars; see that you are not alarmed; for this must take place. But the end is not yet . . . they will hand you over to be tortured and will put you to death, and you will be hated by all nations because of my name. Then many will fall away, and they will betray one another and hate one another. And many false prophets will arise and lead many astray. And because of the increase in lawlessness, the love of many will grow cold. But the one who endures to the end will be saved."
56. Peter Prescott, "Combat Zone," *Newsweek,* June 6, 1977, 86; C. D. B. Bryan, "Review of *A Rumor of War,*" *Saturday Review* 4/36, June 11, 1977; Erich Maria Remarque, *All Quiet on the Western Front* (Boston: Little Brown, 1929); Norman Mailer, *The Naked and the Dead* (New York: Modern Library, 1948); C. D. B. Bryan, *Friendly Fire* (New York: Putnam, 1976); Theodore Solotaroff, "Memoirs for Memorial Day," *New York Times Book Review,* May 29, 1977, 9.
57. "Review of *A Rumor of War,*" *Library Journal* 102, May 15, 1977, 1175; Prescott, "Combat Zone."
58. William Styron, "A Farewell to Arms," *New York Review of Books* 24/11, June 23, 1977.
59. Bryan, "Review."

60. Solotaroff, "Memoirs for Memorial Day."
61. Ibid.
62. William Shawcross, "Body Count," *New Statesman* 94, September 23, 1977, 406–407; Alfred P. Klausner, "A Marine's Education," *Christian Century* 95, October 1978, 884–885; Styron, "A Farewell to Arms"; Prescott, "Body Count."
63. William J. Bennett, "Review of *A Rumor of War,*" *Commentary* 64, October 1977; J. Glenn Gray, *The Warriors: Reflections on Men in Battle* (New York: Harcourt, Brace and Company, 1959).
64. William J. Bennett, ed., *The Book of Virtues* (New York: Simon & Schuster, 1993).

Chapter 7: False Atrocities
1. Rod Kane, *Veterans' Day: A Vietnam Memoir* (New York: Orion, 1990), 143.
2. Ibid., 145–146.
3. Samuel Hynes, *The Soldiers' Tale: Bearing Witness to Modern War* (New York: Viking, 1997), 190.
4. Samuel Hynes, *Flights of Passage: Recollections of a World War II Aviator* (New York: Penguin, 2003).
5. Wallace Terry, *Bloods: An Oral History of the Vietnam War by Black Veterans* (New York: Random House, 1984); Paul Grey, "Beleaguered Patriotism and Pride," *Time Magazine,* August 20, 1984; Julius W. Becton Jr., "They Were Brothers in Arms," *Washington Post Book World,* September 23, 1984, 4; Michiko Kakutani, "Books of the Times," *New York Times,* August 27, 1984, C14; "The Bloods of 'Nam" aired on PBS, May 20, 1986.
6. "The Anderson Platoon" (1967).
7. Terry, *Bloods,* 236, 244–245, 250–251, 253, 254.
8. Ibid., 244, 248–249, 252–253.
9. Ibid., 237, 241–243.
10. B. G. Burkett and Glenna Whitley, *Stolen Valor: How the Vietnam Generation Was Robbed of its Heroes and its History* (Dallas, TX: Verity Press, 1998), 458–459.
11. Whitney Balliett, "Black Talk," *New Yorker,* November 12, 1984, 189–192; Kakutani, "Books of the Times"; Becton, "They Were Brothers"; Alan M. Osur, "Review of *Bloods,*" *Military Affairs* 51/1, January 1987, 45.
12. "The Bloods of 'Nam"; Walter Goodman, "Black Soldiers in Vietnam," *New York Times,* May 20, 1986, C18; Burkett and Whitley, *Stolen Valor,* 259; William M. King, "Bloods: Teaching the Afroamerican Experience of the Vietnam Conflict," in Paul Budra and Michael Zeitlin, eds., *Soldier Talk: The Vietnam War in Oral Narrative* (Bloomington: Indiana University Press, 2004), 183–196.
13. Terry, *Bloods,* 69–70, 45–46, 161–164; Burkett and Whitley, *Stolen Valor,* 457.
14. Mark Baker, ed., *Nam: The Vietnam War in the Words of the Men and Women Who Fought There* (New York: William Morrow & Company, 1981), 12, 14; Marc Leepson, "Vietnam Voices," *New York Times Book Review,* May 17, 1981.
15. Baker, *Nam,* 84–85, 82; James Kaufmann, "Vietnam War Recalled," *Christian Science Monitor,* July 1, 1981, 21.
16. John Ketwig, *. . . and a Hard Rain Fell: A GI's True Story of the War in Vietnam* (New York: Macmillan, 1985), 8–10, 19–20 (page numbers from the Sourcebooks edition, 2002).
17. Ibid., 84–85.
18. Ibid., 86–88.
19. Ibid., 88–89.
20. Ibid., 269.

21. Ibid., 23–28.
22. Ibid., 30, 84, 148–149, 82.
23. "Review of Ketwig," *Publishers Weekly,* August 12, 2002; Josiah Bunting, "Vietnam: Three Years of Living Dangerously," *Washington Post Book World,* August 4, 1985, 1; George Herring, "Vietnam Remembered," *Journal of American History* 73/1, January 1986, 152–164.
24. "Battle of Okinawa," www.globalsecurity.org/military/facility/okinawa-battle. htm.
25. On "guilt" for not serving in Vietnam, see Mark Helprin, "I Dodged the Draft and I was Wrong," *Wall Street Journal,* October 16, 1992; William F. Buckley Jr., "Rich Man, Poor Man, and the Vietnam War," *Washington Post,* November 1,1992, B4; and James Fallows, "What Did You Do in the Class War, Daddy?" *Washington Monthly,* October 1975.
26. "Review of *A Rumor of War,*" *Library Journal* 102, May 15, 1977, 1175; James Simon Kunen, *Standard Operating Procedure: Notes of a Draft-Age American* (New York: Avon, 1971), 39.
27. Hannah Arendt, *Eichman in Jerusalem: A Report on the Banality of Evil* (New York: Viking, 1963). On the American debate over Arendt, see Mark Greif, "Arendt's Judgment," *Dissent,* Spring 2004.
28. David Christian and William Hoffer, *Victor Six* (New York: McGraw Hill, 1990), 158–159.
29. *Winter Soldier* (1971); *Congressional Record,* April 6, 1971, 92nd Congress, 1st Session, 9949.
30. *Winter Soldier* (1971).
31. Ibid.
32. Ibid.; *Congressional Record,* April 6, 1971, 92nd Congress, 1st Session, 9949–9950. Two hundred ninety-one VC were reported killed in Operation Stone—see Gary L. Telfer, Lane Rogers, and V. Keith Fleming Jr., *U.S. Marines in Vietnam: Fighting the North Vietnamese, 1967* (Washington, DC: History and Museum Division, U.S. Marine Corps, 1984), 52.
33. *Winter Soldier* (1971).
34. Camil's "Affidavit," June 16, 1971, copy in possession of the author. It can also be found on the Milliarium Zero DVD, *Winter Soldier.*
35. Camil's "Affadavit"; interview, Scott Camil, Sept. 26, 2005.
36. *Winter Soldier* (1971); interview, Scott Camil, Sept. 26, 2005.
37. "Command Chronology," 1st Battalion, 1st Marines, February 1967, 10 March 1967, Library of the Marine Corps, Quantico, VA; Scott Camil's DD-214, copy in possession of the author.
38. "Command Chronology."
39. Ibid.; W. D. Ehrhart, *Vietnam-Perkesie: A Combat Marine Memoir* (Jefferson, NC: McFarland, 1983).
40. For representative examples of body count and "any dead Vietnamese was a dead VC," see Vietnam Veterans Against the War, *The Winter Soldier Investigation: An Inquiry into American War Crimes* (Boston: Beacon Press, 1972), 13, 58; Ehrhart, *Vietnam-Perkesie,* 25, 313.
41. Interviews, Rick Bazaco, August 15, 2006, and Ronald Kincade. Kincade and others were interviewed in Danang, February 23, 1967. A CD-ROM, #615, "Operation Stone: Phase Two," is contained in the Van D. Bell Oral History Collection at the U.S. Marine History Division, Quantico, VA; e-mail, Michael S. Frazer, March 1, 2006.
42. Mark Lane, *Conversations with Americans* (New York: Simon & Schuster, 1970),

31–34, 68–83; Terry Whitmore, *Memphis, Nam, Sweden: The Story of a Black Deserter* (Garden City, NY: Doubleday & Company, 1971), 91–167, from the University of Mississippi reprint, 1997).

43. Whitmore, *Memphis, Nam, Sweden*, 113–121.
44. Lane, *Conversations*, 73–74.
45. Ibid., 74.
46. Ibid.
47. Lane, *Conversations*, 75.
48. Ibid., 75-6.
49. Neil Sheehan, "Review of *Conversations with Americans*," *New York Times Book Review*, November 27, 1970.
50. Whitmore, *Memphis, Nam, Sweden*, 191–202.
51. Ibid., 59–60.
52. Ibid., 61.
53. Ibid., 64.
54. Ibid., 65–66.
55. Ibid.
56. Whitmore, *Memphis, Nam, Sweden*, 66.

Chapter 8: What Happened in Quang Tri?

Epigraph. Tom Zeller Jr., "Separating Hyperbole from Horror in Iraq," *New York Times*, December 4, 2006, C4.

1. Jeff Loeb, "Afterword," in Terry Whitmore, *Memphis, Nam, Sweden: The Story of a Black Deserter* (Jackson: University of Mississippi Press, 1997), 193. Whitmore's film credits can be found at http://www.imdb.com/name/nm0926249/.
2. Loeb, "Afterword" in Whitmore, *Memphis, Nam, Sweden*, 193–194; *Sir! No Sir!* (2005). Whitmore's obituary is in the *Memphis Commercial-Appeal*, July 25, 2007, B5.
3. "Command Chronology, 1st Battalion, 1st Marines," September 1967, October 20, 1967, U.S. Marine Corps History Center, Quantico, VA; interview, Robert Maynard (Menard), May 19, 2007.
4. "Command Chronology, 1st Battalion, 1st Marines," October 1967, November 2, 1967, U.S. Marine Corps History Center. See also Doyle D. Glass, *Lions of Medina: An Epic Account of Marine Valor During the Vietnam War* (Coleche Press, 2007).
5. "Command Chronology, 1st Battalion, 1st Marines," October 1967; "U.S. v. Lance Corporal Rudolph O. Diener, Background Stipulation," March 18–20, 1968, U.S. Navy, Judge Advocate General, Washington, DC. The court-martial record contains the full record of the Article 32 Investigation of the charges against Lance Corporal Diener, Lieutenant John C. Bailey, and Captain Robert W. Maynard (*United States v. Lance Corporal Rudolph O. Diener*, hereafter cited as *U.S. v. Diener*).
6. Interview, Rudy Diener, June 18, 2007.
7. Ibid.; "Command Chronology, 1st Battalion, 1st Marines," October 1967; interview, Robert Menard, May 19, 2007; *U.S. v. Diener*, 60. Biographical information on Ronald B. Pearson can be found on http://thewall-usa.com/index.asp#search.
8. *U.S. v. Diener*. Robert Maynard statement.
9. Interview, John C. Bailey, February 15, 2007. Bailey's status as honor man can be found at www.usmc-thebasicschool-april1967.com/reunion_40.htm.
10. *U.S. v. Diener*, John C. Bailey statement.

11. Ibid.
12. *U.S. v. Diener*, 122, 137, 346 (all page numbers are from the Article 32 Investigation unless otherwise noted).
13. *Ibid.*, 371–373.
14. Interview, Olaf C. Skibsrud, December 16, 2006.
15. Interview, Skibsrud, December 16, 2006. Richard Lyons's interview is in Ron Steinman, *The Soldiers' Story: Vietnam in Their Own Words* (New York TV Books, 1999), 163–166. See also Keith William Nolan, *Battle for Hue: Tet, 1968* (Novato, CA: Presidio, 1983), 219.
16. *U.S. v. Diener*, Stipulation of Chronology, Skibsrud testimony, 218; interview, Skibsrud, Dec. 16, 2006. On "coloring it up," see the message of Robert Black about the Marine who "embellished the incident out of proportion" posted to the Bravo 1/1 website, March 6, 2006, copy in the author's possession.
17. Interview, Skibsrud, Dec. 16, 2006.
18. *U.S. v. Diener*, Stipulation of Chronology; Colonel H. E. Ing Jr., to CO, 1st Marine Division, "Pretrial Investigation into the alleged killings of Vietnamese Nationals in Thon Nai Cou Village on 22 October 1967."
19. Interview, Albert Belbusti, February 9, 2006; interview, Herbert Ing, January 27, 2007; interview, Ing, May 15, 2007.
20. *U.S. v. Diener*, Major Arthur A. Bergman to CO, 1st Marines, "Investigation Conducted in accordance with Article 32, UCMJ, 5 January 1968" interview, Diener, June 18, 2007; Bergman's obituary can be found at www.jeffersoncountyonline.org/obit/2001/b.htm.
21. *U.S. v. Diener*, Stipulation of Chronology; interview, Diener; interview, James Ehlers, January 27, 2007.
22. *U.S. v. Diener*, 235–236, 303, 353.
23. Interview, Skibsrud, Dec. 16, 2006; Whitmore, *Memphis, Nam, Sweden*, 65–66.
24. *U.S. v. Diener*, Skibsrud testimony, 207.
25. Ibid., 212.
26. Ibid., 216, 212, 213–214.
27. Ibid., 217–218.
28. Ibid., 234, 221–234, 213–214.
29. *U.S. v. Diener*, Toon testimony, 153, 152.
30. Ibid., 155.
31. Ibid., 157–158, 161.
32. *Diener*, Toon testimony, 194; interview, Skibsrud, Dec. 16, 2006; interview, Toon, February 3, 2007.
33. *U.S. v. Diener*, Toon testimony, 170, 192.
34. Interview, Toon, Feb. 3, 2007.
35. *U.S. v. Diener*, 241–260, 258, 312–313, 241, 280.
36. Interview, Skibsrud, Dec. 16, 2006.
37. Interview, Robert Labicki, February 3, 2007.
38. Ibid.
39. *U.S. v. Diener*, 277, 283.
40. Ibid., 429, 432–433, 436.
41. Ibid., 77–81, 296, 291–303.
42. Ibid., 449–450, 452–454, 396.
43. Brief service records can be found on www.military.com. Interviews, Skibsrud, Dec. 16, 2006; Toon, Feb. 3, 2007.
44. *U.S. v. Diener*, see 270, 308, 351, 427, 442, 449 for Toon; 339, 442, 419 for Diener.

45. *U.S. v. Diener,* Maynard statement.
46. *U.S. v. Diener,* Bailey statement.
47. *U.S. v. Diener,* 7, 8, 39–40, 348; Bailey statement.
48. *U.S. v. Diener,* 40–41, 43, 74, 121.
49. Ibid., 122–123; Bailey statement.
50. *U.S. v. Diener,* 126–127.
51. Ibid., 82–91.
52. Ibid.
53. *U.S. v. Diener,* 94, 95, 105.
54. Ibid., 45–47.
55. Ibid., 6, 32, 39, 49–50, 76–81, 84–85, 107, 130.
56. *U.S. v. Diener,* 6, 60, 49, 108, 78; interview, Skibsrud, Dec. 16, 2006.
57. *U.S. v. Diener,* 219, 222.
58. Ibid., 491.
59. Ibid., 274.
60. Ibid., 269–270, 282, 288.
61. Ibid., 289–290.
62. Ibid., 335.
63. Ibid., 335–336.
64. Ibid., 354, 358.
65. Ibid., 361, 316.
66. Ibid., 336, 448; interview, Labicki, Feb. 3, 2007.
67. *U.S. v. Diener,* 339, 350–351.
68. Ibid., 339.
69. Ibid., 344.
70. Ibid., 375.
71. Ibid., 402, interview, Ehlers, Jan. 27, 2007.
72. *U.S. v. Diener,* 367.
73. Ibid., 474–475.
74. Ibid., 478–480, "Command Chronology," 1/1, October 1967.
75. Ibid., 484, 491–494, 489.
76. "Command Chronology," 1/1, October 1967.
77. *U.S. v. Diener,* Ing to CO, 1st Marine Division; Bergman to CO, 1st Marines.
78. *U.S. v. Diener,* Bergman to CO, 1st Marines.
79. Ibid.
80. Ibid.
81. *U.S. v. Diener,* Bergman, Investigating Officer's Report, January 4, 1968.
82. *U.S. v. Diener,* Bergman to CO, 1st Marines.
83. Interview, Bailey, Jan. 15, 2007.
84. Ibid.
85. *U.S. v. Diener,* Charge Sheet, DD-458, 21 January 1968; interview, Diener, June 18, 2007.
86. *U.S. v. Diener,* Clyde R. Mann to CG, 1st Marine Division, 8 February 1968.
87. Ibid.
88. Ibid. On Mann's promotion to brigadier general, see www.military.com.
89. *U.S. v. Diener,* Diener to CG, 1st Marine Division, 15 March 1968.
90. Interview, Diener, June 18, 2007.
91. *U.S. v. Diener,* Record of Court-Martial, 1a.
92. Ibid., 11; interviews, Ehlers, Jan. 27, 2007, Diener, June 18, 2007.
93. *U.S. v. Diener,* Record of Court-Martial, 11; interviews, Ehlers, Jan. 27, 2007, Ing, Jan. 27, 2007, and Elden H. Luffman, the latter on May 15, 2007.

94. *U.S. v. Diener,* Record of Court-Martial, AE 5-7.
95. Ibid.
96. Interview, Diener, June 18, 2007.
97. *U.S. v. Diener,* Record of Court-Martial, Clyde R. Mann to Distribution List, April 8, 1968; interview, Russell Corey, April 14, 2007.
98. Interviews, Ehlers, Jan. 27, 2007, Corey, April 14, 2007, Diener, June 18, 2007.
99. Interviews, Maynard (Menard), May 19, 2007, Toon, Feb. 3, 2007, Ehlers, Jan. 27, 2007, Bailey, June 15, 2007, and Stollenwork, the latter on August 5, 2007.
100. Menard post on 2nd Battalion, 1st Marines website, http://www.i-mef.usmc .mil/DIV/IMAR/2BN/, copy in author's possession.
101. Interview, Menard, May 19, 2007.
102. Ibid.
103. Interview, Robert Black, June 28, 2006.
104. Interview, Menard, May 19, 2007.
105. Ibid., May 19, 2007; Alexander S. Neill, *Summerhill: A Radical Approach to Child Rearing* (New York: Hart, 1960). Interviews, Mike Hanson, John Kovach, May 17, 2007.
106. Steve Tomasko, "Tenor' Promises Evening of Laughs," *Ashland Daily Press,* August 23, 2002, www.ashlandwi.com/articles/2002/08/23/community/ 20020823-archive57.prt; Rick Olivo, "Area Filmmaker Previews Historic Tale of Robbery and Murder," *Ashland Daily Press,* August 23, 2002, www.ashlandwi. com/articles/2002/08/23/news/20020823-archive1251.txt.
107. Claudia Curran, "Ashland's Woodland Productions Offers Digital Video Options, *Ashland Daily Press,* January 7, 2003, www.ashlandwi.com/articles/2003/01/ 07/business/20030107-archive.txt?
108. Andrew Broman, "Protestors Object to Iraq War, Vietnam Veteran: Take Resistance to the Next Level," *Ashland Daily Press,* December 6, 2004, www .ashland-wi.com/articles/2004/12/06/news/20041206-archive4.prt.
109. http://www.ashvid.net/profile/PrinceRobert; the impeach Bush site is now defunct, http://impeachbush.meetup.com/cities/us/nc/Asheville; last accessed Jan. 31, 2007; photocopy in author's possession.
110. Robert Menard's profile, http://chopwoodcarrywater.gaia.com/; last accessed Oct. 9, 2008; photocopy in author's possesion; the message on the site now reads "The user Prince Robert isn't around any more."
111. Interview, Ing, Jan. 27, 2008.
112. Interview, Ing, Jan. 27, 2008; "List Remembers Vietnam Veterans Not on the Wall, *USA Today,* February 8, 2003, http://www.usatoday.com/news/ nation/2003-02-08-vietnam-memorial_x.htm.
113. Interviews, Ing, Jan. 27, 2008, Luffman, May 15, 2007, Diener, June 18, 2007; Elden H. Luffman, *Bringing God to War* (Williamstown, NJ: Phillips Publications, 2006).
114. Interview, Diener, June 18, 2007.
115. Interview, Skibsrud, Dec. 16, 2006.
116. Ibid.
117. Ibid; e-mail from Johanna Skibsrud to author, Feb. 23, 2009.

Conclusion

Epigraph. Nigel Nicholson, quoted in Paul Fussell, *Doing Battle: The Making of a Skeptic* (Boston: Little Brown, 1996), 160.
  1. Walter Robinson, "Professor's Past in Doubt," *Boston Globe,* June 18, 2001, A1; Jack Thomas, "The Road to the Ellis Story," *Boston Globe,* July 2, 2001, A11.

2. Ben MacIntyre, "Top U.S, Scholar Invented Role in Vietnam War," *Times of London,* June 20, 2001, www.powernetwork.org/phonies/phonies58.htm. Ellis's second apology of August 17, 2001, can be found at www.mtholyoke.edu/offices/comm/news/ellisstatement.html.

3. Thomas, "The Road to the Ellis Story," *Boston Globe,* July 2, 2001, A11; Bonnie Goodman, "Has Scandal Taken Its Toll on Joseph Ellis?" History News Network, November 29, 2004, http://hnn.us/articles/8656.html.

4. Meghan Elizabeth Freed, "Letter," *Boston Globe,* June 22, 2001, A18. For Jensen's comments, see "Poll: Readers Sound Off about Joseph Ellis's Suspension," History News Network, http://hnn.us/articles/205.html; Josh Tyrangiel, "A History of His Own Making," *TIME,* June 24, 2001, http://www.time.com/time/arts/article/0,8599,165175,00.html?lid=fb_share; Edmund Morris, Op-Ed, *New York Times,* June 22, 2001; Joseph Ellis, "Role of a Lifetime," *Washington Post Book World,* October 3, 1999, 1.

5. Peter Hoffer, *Past Imperfect: Facts, Fictions, and Fraud—American History from Bancroft and Parkman to Ambrose, Bellesiles, Ellis, and Goodwin* (New York: Public Affairs, 2004); David Garrow, "Ellis Broke Golden Rule of Teaching," *Boston Globe,* June 20, 2001, A13. The Tise and Burlingame comments are at "Poll: Readers Sound Off"; Elliot Gorn, "Why Are Academics Ducking the Ellis Case?" *Chronicle of Higher Education,* July 20, 2001, B14; David Oshinsky, "The Way We Live Now; You Had to Be There, Man," *New York Times Magazine,* July 1, 2001.

6. Geoffrey Wheatcroft, "Not So Macho: Americans Love the Idea of Glorious War, But It's All Pretend," *Guardian,* June 22, 2001, www.guardian.co.uk/books/2001/jun/22/comment.news; Clancy Sigal, "Caught in a Fantasy Amid Subterfuge," *Los Angeles Times,* June 29, 2001, B17; Ellen Goodman, "Why, Joe Ellis, Why?" *Boston Globe,* June 28, 2001. Walter Robinson is quoted in Thomas, "The Road to the Ellis Story."

7. Jim Griffiths, "Historian's Embellishments a Red Flag for Vietnam Researchers," www.11thcavnam.com/main/historian_embellishments_a_red_f.htm.

8. Laura Palmer, *Shrapnel in the Heart: Letters and Remembrances from the Vietnam Veterans Memorial* (New York: Random House), 1988, 124–131; Lynda Van Devanter with Christopher Morgan, *Home Before Morning: The Story of an Army Nurse in Vietnam* (New York: Beaufort Books, 1983).

9. Palmer, *Shrapnel in the Heart,* 127–128.

10. Lynda Van Devanter and Joan A. Furey, eds., *Visions of War, Dreams of Peace: Writings of Women in the Vietnam War* (New York: Warner Books, 1991); Joanne Banks, Cortney Davis, and Judy Schaefer, eds., *Between the Heartbeats: Poetry and Prose by Nurses* (Ames: University of Iowa Press, 1995); Barbara and Edward Whitmarsh, *Incoming!* (Aurora, MO: Hawks Nest Publishing), vol. I, Issue III, 1996, Issue IV, 1997, Issue V, 1998; Dana Shuster, *Battle Dressing: Poems About the Journey of a Nurse in Vietnam* (Houston: Writers League Press), 2003.

11. Diantha Parker, "Celebrated Military Nurse, Poet Revealed as Fraud," NPR, September 30, 2006, www.npr.org/templates/story/story.php?storyid=6173681.

12. Palmer, *Shrapnel in the Heart,* 127; Major General Spurgeon Neel, *Medical Support of the U.S. Army in Vietnam: 1965–1970* (Washington, DC: GPO, 1973), 50-51.

13. "From Dusty," distributed October 3, 2006, VWAR-L@LISTSERV.BUFFALO.EDU.

14. Dana Shuster, *Battle Dressing* (Houston: Writers League Press, 2000), 6, 9, 10, 17.

15. The best source for the stories is http://www.snopes.com/military/fonda

.asp. On POW lists and mail, see Stuart I. Rochester and Frederick Kiley, *Honor Bound: American Prisoners of War in Southeast Asia, 1961–1973* (Annapolis: Naval Institute Press, 1999), 374, 440–441.

16. Rochester and Kiley, *Honor Bound*, 552–553, 568; Mary Hershberger, *Jane Fonda's War: A Political Biography of an Antiwar Icon* (New York: New Press, 2005), 148–156, 183–184, Robinson Risner, *The Passing of the Night: My Seven Years as a Prisoner of the North Vietnamese* (New York: Random House, 1975), 147–148, 161–175.

17. http://www.snopes.com/military/fonda.asp.

18. Ibid. See also Nathaniel Bates, "What Did Jane Fonda Really Do Over in Hanoi?" History News Network, December 13, 2004.

19. http://www.snopes.com/military/fonda.asp.; Carol Burke, *Camp All-American, Hanoi Jane, and the High-And-Tight* (Boston: Beacon Press, 2004), 157.

20. Christopher Anderson, *Citizen Jane: The Turbulent Life of Jane Fonda* (New York: Henry Holt), 1990, 254–255, 9–10; Jane Fonda, *My Life So Far* (New York: Random House, 2005), 323.

21. Anderson, *Citizen Jane*, 10; Rochester and Kiley, *Honor Bound*, 562.

22. Anderson, *Citizen Jane*, 267–268.

23. Fonda, *My Life So Far*, 327; Hershberger, *Jane Fonda's War*, 147, 141; Seymour Hersh, "The P.O.W. Issue: A National Issue is Born," *Dayton Journal-Herald*, February 13–18, 1971.

24. Fonda, *My Life So Far*, 291, 316; Anderson, *Citizen Jane*, 8.

25. Fonda, *My Life So Far*, 322–323.

26. Ibid., 289. See also Daniel Ellsberg, *Secrets: A Memoir of Vietnam and the Pentagon Papers* (New York: Penguin, 2003), 418.

27. The authoritative article is W. Hays Parks, "Linebacker and the Law of War," *Air University Review* 33/2, January-February 1983, 2–30. See also Seymour Hersh, "War Foes See No Evidence of Deliberate Dike Attacks," *New York Times*, June 24, 1972; "The Battle of the Dikes," *Time*, August 7, 1972; Guenter Lewy, *America in Vietnam* (New York: Oxford University Press, 1980), 410–411.

28. Herr, *Dispatches* (New York: Knopf, 1977), 260.

Selected Bibliography

Atkinson, Rick. *The Long Grey Line: The American Journey of West Point's Class of 1966*. Boston: Houghton Mifflin, 1989.

Baker, Mark, editor. *Nam: The Vietnam War in the Words of the Men and Women Who Fought There*. New York: William Morrow and Company, 1981.

Baskir, Lawrence M. and William A. Strauss. *Chance and Circumstance: The Draft, the War and the Vietnam Generation*. New York: Alfred A. Knopf, 1978.

Belknap, Michal R. *The Vietnam War on Trial: The My Lai Massacre and the Court-Martial of Lieutenant Calley*. Lawrence: University Press of Kansas, 2002.

Bourke, Joanna. *An Intimate History of Killing: Face-to-Face Killing in Twentieth-Century Warfare*. London: Granta Books, 1999.

Braestrup, Peter. *Big Story: How the American Press and Television Reported and Interpreted the Crisis of Tet, 1968*. Boulder, CO: Westview Press, 1977.

Brennan, Matthew. *Brennan's War: Vietnam, 1965–69*. Novato, CA: Presidio Press, 1985.

Brinkley, Douglas. *Tour of Duty: John Kerry and the Vietnam War*. New York: William Morrow, 2004.

Broyles, William Jr. *Brothers in Arms: A Journey from War to Peace*. New York: Alfred A. Knopf, 1986.

Budra, Paul and Michael Zeitlin, eds. *Soldier Talk: The Vietnam War in Oral Narrative*. Bloomington: Indiana University Press, 2004.

Burkett, B. G. and Glenna Whitley. *Stolen Valor: How the Vietnam Generation was Robbed of its Heroes and its History*. Dallas: Verity Press, 1998.

Caputo, Philip. *A Rumor of War*. New York: Holt, Reinhart and Winston, 1977.

Chong, Denise. *The Girl in the Picture: The Story of Kim Phuc, the Photograph, and the Vietnam War*. New York: Viking Press, 1999.

Cutler, Thomas J. *Brown Water, Black Berets: Coastal and Riverine Warfare in Vietnam*. Annapolis: Naval Institute Press, 1988.

Dean, Eric T. Jr. *Shook Over Hell: Post-Traumatic Stress, Vietnam, and the Civil War*. Cambridge: Harvard University Press, 1997.

Downs, Frederick. *Aftermath: A Soldier's Return from Vietnam*. New York: W. W. Norton & Company, 1984.

———. *The Killing Zone: My Life in the Vietnam War*. New York: W. W. Norton & Company, 1978.

Duiker, William J. *Ho Chi Minh.* New York: Hyperion Books, 2000.

Ehrhart, W. D. *Vietnam-Perkesie: A Combat Marine Memoir.* Jefferson, NC: McFarland, 1983.

Estep, James. *Company Commander Vietnam.* Novato, CA: Presidio Press, 1996.

Fussell, Paul. *Doing Battle: The Making of a Skeptic.* Boston: Little, Brown, 1996.

———. *Wartime: Understanding and Behavior in the Second World War.* New York: Oxford University Press, 1989.

Gabriel, Richard A. and Paul L. Savage. *Crisis in Command: Mismanagement in the Army.* New York: Hill & Wang, 1978.

Glass, Doyle D. *Lions of Medina: An Epic Account of Marine Valor During the Vietnam War.* Louisville, KY: Coleche Press, 2007.

Goldman, Peter and Tony Fuller. *Charlie Company: What Vietnam Did to Us.* New York: William Morrow and Company, 1983.

Greene, Bob. *Homecoming: When the Soldiers Returned from Vietnam.* New York: G. P. Putnam's Sons, 1989.

Hampton, Lynn. *The Fighting Strength: Memoirs of a Combat Nurse in Vietnam.* New York: Warner, 1990.

Herr, Michael. *Dispatches.* New York: Avon, 1978.

Hynes, Samuel. *The Soldiers' Tale: Bearing Witness to Modern War.* New York: Penguin, 1997.

Isaacs, Arnold R. *Vietnam Shadows: The War, Its Ghosts, and Its Legacy.* Baltimore: Johns Hopkins University Press, 1997.

Kane, Rod. *Veteran's Day: A Viet Nam Memoir.* New York: Orion, 1990.

Kerrey, Bob. *When I Was a Young Man: A Memoir.* New York: Harcourt, 2002.

Ketwig, John. *. . . and a hard rain fell: A GI's True Story of the War in Vietnam.* New York: MacMillan, 1985.

Kirschke, James J. *Not Going Home Alone: A Marine's Story.* New York: Ballantine, 2001.

Kunen, James Simon. *Standard Operating Procedure: Notes of a Draft-Age American.* New York: Avon, 1971.

Lane, Mark. *Conversations with Americans.* New York: Simon & Schuster, 1970.

Lang, Daniel. *Casualties of War.* New York: McGraw-Hill, 1969.

Lanning, Michael E. *The Only War We Had: A Platoon Leader's Journal of Vietnam.* College Station: Texas A&M, 1987.

Lewy, Guenter. *America in Vietnam.* New York: Oxford University Press, 1978.

Luffman, Elden H. *Bringing God to War: Glimpses of a Chaplain's Ministry With U.S. Marines in Vietnam.* Williamstown, NJ: Phillips Publications, 2006.

Mason, Robert. *Chickenhawk.* New York: Viking, 1983.

———. *Chickenhawk: Back in the World.* New York: Viking, 1993.

McPartin, Greg. *Combat Corpsman: The Vietnam Memoir of a Navy SEALs Medic.* New York: Berkley Trade, 2005.

Moore, Harold G. and Joseph L. Galloway. *We Were Soldiers Once . . . And Young.* New York: Random House, 1992.

Newby, Claude D. *It Took Heroes: A Chaplain's Story and Tribute to Combat Veterans and Those Who Waited for Them.* Vol. I, Springville, UT: Bonneville Books, 1998. Vol. II, Bountiful, UT: Tribute Enterprises, 2000.

Nicosia, Gerald. *Home To War: A History of the Vietnam Veterans' Movement.* New York: Crown, 2001.

Norman, Michael. *These Good Men.* New York: Simon & Schuster, 1991.

Novosel, Michael J. *Dustoff: The Memoir of an Army Aviator.* Novato: CA, Presidio Press, 1999.

O'Brien, Tim. *If I Die in a Combat Zone*. New York: Delacorte, 1973.

———. *The Things They Carried*. New York: Houghton Mifflin, 1990.

Palmer, Laura. *Shrapnel in the Heart: Letters and Remembrances from the Vietnam Vets Memorial*. New York: Random House, 1987.

Powell, Mary Reynolds. *A World of Hurt: Between Innocence and Arrogance in Vietnam*. Cleveland: Greenleaf, 2000.

Puller, Lewis B., Jr. *Fortunate Son: The Autobiography of Lewis B. Puller, Jr*. New York: Grove, 1991.

Ronnau, Christopher. *Blood Trails: The Combat Diary of a Foot Soldier in Vietnam*. New York: Ballantine, 2006.

Sallah, Michael and Mitch Weiss. *Tiger Force: A True Story of Men and War*. Boston: Little, Brown, 2006.

Santoli, Al. *Everything We Had: An Oral History of the Vietnam War*. New York: Random House, 1981.

———. *To Bear Any Burden: The Vietnam War and its Aftermath in the Words of Americans and Southeast Asians*. New York: E. P. Dutton, 1985.

Smith, George E. *P.O.W.: Two Years with the Viet Cong*. Berkeley, CA: Ramparts Press, 1971.

Smith, Winnie. *American Daughter Gone to War: On the Front Lines with an Army Nurse in Vietnam*. New York, William Morrow, 1992.

Solis, Gary D. *Marines and Military Law in Vietnam: Trial by Fire*. Washington: GPO/U.S. Marine Corps, 1989.

———, *Son Thang: An American War Crime*. Annapolis: Naval Institute Press, 1997.

Van Devanter, Lynda. *Home Before Morning: The Story of an Army Nurse in Vietnam*. New York: Beaufort Books, 1983.

Van Toai, Doan and David Chanoff. *The Vietnamese Gulag*. New York: Simon & Schuster, 1986.

Van Zanten, William. *Don't Bunch Up: One Marine's Story*. New York: Ballantine, 1993.

Vietnam Veterans Against the War. *The Winter Soldier Investigation: An Inquiry into American War Crimes*. Boston: Beacon, 1972.

Walker, Keith, editor. *A Piece of My Heart: The Stories of Twenty-Six American Women Who Served in Vietnam*. Novato, CA: Presidio, 1985.

Wheeler, John. *Touched with Fire: The Future of the Vietnam Generation*. New York: Franklin Watts, 1984.

Whitmore, Terry as told to Richard Weber. *Memphis, Nam, Sweden: The Autobiography of a Black American Exile*. Garden City, NY: Doubleday, 1971. Republished as *Memphis, Nam, Sweden: The Story of a Black Deserter*. Jackson: University of Mississippi Press, 1997.

Index

About the Author

Gary Kulik most recently served as a deputy director of the Winterthur Museum, Garden & Library. Previously, he was a department head and an assistant director of the National Museum of American History, Smithsonian Institution, and the editor of *American Quarterly*. A graduate of St. Michael's College, he earned a Ph.D. in American Civilization at Brown University. He is also a decorated veteran of the war in Vietnam, having served as a medic in the Fourth Infantry Division and in the Sixty-first Medical Battalion. He lives in Wilmington, Delaware.